D1609312

Microsoft
.NET SERVER
SOLUTIONS
for the Enterprise

PUBLISHED BY
Microsoft Press
A Division of Microsoft Corporation
One Microsoft Way
Redmond, Washington 98052-6399

Library of Congress Cataloging-in-Publication Data
Microsoft Windows .NET Server Solutions for the Enterprise / Microsoft Corporation.
    p. cm.
    Includes index.
    ISBN 0-7356-1569-1
    1. Microsoft Windows server.   2. Operating systems (Computers).   3. Client/server computing.   I. Microsoft Corporation.

QA76.76.O63 M524132253   2002
005.7'13769--dc21   2001059608

Printed and bound in the United States of America.

1 2 3 4 5 6 7 8 9   QWE   7 6 5 4 3 2

Distributed in Canada by Penguin Books Canada Limited.

A CIP catalogue record for this book is available from the British Library.

Microsoft Press books are available through booksellers and distributors worldwide. For further information about international editions, contact your local Microsoft Corporation office or contact Microsoft Press International directly at fax (425) 936-7329. Visit our Web site at www.microsoft.com/mspress. Send comments to *mspinput@microsoft.com*.

Acquisitions Editor: Juliana Aldous Atkinson
Project Editor: Maureen Williams Zimmerman

Body Part No. X08-68163

Contributors to this book

Managing Editor

James Wilson

Project Manager

William J. Harding

Authors

James Wilson, William J. Harding, Steven Baker,
Jim Christensen, Carl Stephen Smyth, Scot Vidican

Technical Editor

Mary North

Production

Sigrid Elenga

Graphic Designer

Curtis Christman

Lead Software Design Engineer

Tony Green

Indexers

Tony Ross, Lee Ross

Contributors

Erwin Abinion, Ahmed Abou-Taleb, Ahmed Bassiony, Mary Browning,
Doug Carrell, Stephen Cawood, Alex Cobb, Patrick Copeland, Liz Crawford,
David Downing, Bill Duemmel, Nick Duncan, Dan Evers, Diane Forsyth, Keith Hamilton,
Zach Jason, David Kiker, Antero Koskinen, Paul Larsen, Liza Leif, Ritu Manocha,
Rick Mittelstaedt, Michael Nappi, Jim Pauley, Cynthia Redine, Jerry Santos, Paul Schafer,
Margaret Sherman, Tom Uusnakki, Dave Wascha, Anne Weiler, Renee Wesberry,
Jeff Wierer, Jack Wight, Scott Woodgate, Adam Zilinskas

Table of Contents

PART ONE Overview **1**

Chapter 1 Introduction **3**

Purpose 4

Audience 4

   Information Technology and Business Managers 4

   Information Technology Architects 5

   Consultants, Independent Software Vendors, Solution Providers, and Application
   Service Providers 5

   Database Administrators, Application Developers, and System Integrators 5

   Project Managers 5

Scope 6

   Major Focus: E-Business Servers 6

   Minor Focus 7

   Beyond Scope 7

Plan of the Book 8

   Part 1: Overview 8

   Part 2: Enterprise Application Integration 8

   Part 3: Business-to-Business Integration 9

   Part 4: Business-to-Consumer Integration 9

   Part 5: Wireless Integration 9

   Part 6: The Future 10

Summary 10

Chapter 2 .NET in Plain English **11**

   .NET Framework 12

   .NET Server Platforms 19

   .NET My Services 20

   Additional Information 21

Chapter 3 Overview of .NET Enterprise Servers **23**

Application Center 2000 24

   Application Center 2000 Documentation Resources 26

BizTalk Server 2002 26

   BizTalk Server 2002 Documentation Resources 28

Commerce Server 2002 29
   Commerce Server 2002 Documentation Resources 30
Content Management Server 2001 32
   Content Management Server 2001 Documentation Resources 32
Exchange 2000 Server 33
   Exchange 2000 Server Documentation Resources 34
Host Integration Server 2000 35
   Host Integration Server 2000 Documentation Resources 37
Internet Security and Acceleration (ISA) Server 2000 38
   Internet Security and Acceleration Server 2000 Documentation Resources 39
SQL Server 2000 40
   SQL Server 2000 Documentation Resources 42
Mobile Information 2001 Server 43
   Mobile Information 2001 Server Documentation Resources 44
SharePoint Portal Server 2001 45
   SharePoint Portal Server 2001 Documentation Resources 46
Summary 46

PART TWO Enterprise Application Integration **47**

Chapter 4 Integrating Applications into the Enterprise **49**
The Integration Challenge 50
The Business Case for Integration 53
Integration Approaches 54
   Integration Using the User Interface 54
   Integration Using Data Sources 55
   Integration Using Application Programming Interfaces 56
   Integration Using Business Logic 57
Implementing Application Integration 58
The Market for EAI 61

Chapter 5 Integrating SQL Server with DB2 . . . . **63**
Scenario 65
   Understanding the Data 67
   Understanding the Process 68
Solution 69
Tools and Technologies 71
Implementation 73
   Variations on a Model Solution 74
   Windows 2000 Server and SQL Server Editions 77

Installing and Configuring Software 78
    Configuring Host Integration Server 78
    Prepare the DB2 Tables on the AS/400 90
    Installing and Configuring SQL Server 2000 93
    Configuring SQL Server DTS Packages 94
    Working with DTS Packages 102
    Scheduling DTS Packages for Execution 105
    Sample Applications Using DTS 107
    Data Integration Using DTS 111

Chapter 6 Integrating Employee Benefits Self-Service with SAP R/3 . . . . **113**
Scenario 116
    Understanding the Process 119
    Understanding the APIs 120
        Challenges Specific to SAP 123
Solution 126
    SAP Integration Using BAPI 127
    SAP Integration Using IDocs 130
Tools and Technologies 131
Implementation 132
    Web Middleware 132
    MSMQ Message Body Format 133
    SAP Application Connector 134
        Application Integration Using APIs and Interfaces 136

Chapter 7 Integrating Host Data into the Web **137**
Scenario 137
Solution 138
    The Sample Application 140
Tools and Technologies 144
    Hardware and Software Requirements 144
        Microsoft Host Integration Server 2000 144
        Visual Studio .NET 145
        Cedar Bank Files and Folders 145
        Cedar Bank Components and Remote Environments 147
        COBOL Programs 149
Implementation 150
    Running Cedar Bank with a Live Mainframe Connection 150

Chapter 8   Integrating BizTalk with SAP **157**

Scenario 157

Solution 157

Tools and Technologies 159

Hardware and Software Requirements 159

BizTalk Adapter for SAP Components 160

BizTalk Adapter for SAP Manager 160

IDoc Handler 161

Application Integration Component 161

Microsoft Message Queuing 161

Implementation 161

Installing Prerequisite Software 162

Installing BizTalk Adapter for SAP 162

Configuring Components 162

Configure SAP R/3 System 163

Configure DCOM Connector 163

Configure COM for ABAP 164

Configure Microsoft Message Queuing 166

Configure BizTalk Adapter for SAP Manager 166

Configure BizTalk Server 172

Generating a BizTalk Server Specification 176

Specification Generation Process 176

Generating a BizTalk Server Specification Document 176

Sending an IDoc to BizTalk Server 177

Sending an IDoc to SAP R/3 System 179

Additional Information 182

BizTalk Server 2000 182

SAP 182

Microsoft SQL Server 182

Microsoft Message Queue 182

PART THREE   Business-to-Business Integration **183**

Chapter 9   Integrating Business Partners into the Enterprise **185**

Why Electronic Commerce? 186

Types of Electronic Commerce Purchases 187

Challenges of Conducting Business Electronically 188

    Middleware 189

    Business-to-Business Integration 190

    Exchanging Data and Information 193

Chapter 10   Integrating BizTalk with EDI **197**

  Scenario 197

  Solution 198

  Tools and Technologies 199

    Hardware and Software Requirements 199

      File Transfer 200

      E-Business Software 200

      Trading Partner Interface 201

  Implementation 203

    Configuring for Internet Transmission 204

    Configuring for Routing Received Documents to MSMQ 207

    Planning for Growth and Scalability 209

Chapter 11   Automating Electronic Procurement **211**

  Scenario 211

  Solution 212

    Hub: Send Purchase Order to Supplier 213

    Supplier: Receive PO and Send Invoice to Hub 215

    Hub: Receive Invoice and Send Payment to Supplier 216

    Supplier: Receive Payment and Send Acknowledgement to Hub 218

    XLANG Schedule Activation 219

    E-Procurement XLANG Schedule Correlation 221

      Storing the Correlation Information 221

      Reading the Correlation Information 222

  Tools and Technologies 222

    Hardware and Software Requirements 222

    Using Microsoft Visual Studio .NET 223

      Creating XML Web Services 223

      Summary 228

Implementation 229

   Preliminary Setup 229

      Update the Global Assembly Cache 229

      Attach the SQL Server 2000 Databases 229

      Create the SQL Server 7.0 Databases 230

      Configure BizTalk Messaging Services 232

   Running the E-Procurement Sample 233

   Uninstalling the E-Procurement Sample 236

Additional Information 237

      Microsoft BizTalk Server 2002 237

      Microsoft SQL Server 237

      Microsoft Message Queuing 237

Chapter 12 Selling Through Trading Partners **239**

Scenario 241

   The Players 241

   Basic Interactions 242

   Different Purchasing Models 243

      Retail Web Site Purchasing Model 243

      Basic Supplier Purchasing Model 244

      Supplier Purchasing Model Using Remote Shopping 244

      Purchasing Model Summary 246

   Electronic Document Standards 247

   Scenario Summary 247

Solution 248

   Associated Technologies 248

   The Trading Partner's Buyer Application 249

   Catalog Publishing Solution 250

      Supported Document Formats 251

      Catalog Publishing Tasks 251

      Catalog Publishing Architecture 255

   Purchase Order Reception Solution 256

      Supported Document Formats 257

      Purchase Order Reception Tasks 258

      Purchase Order Reception Architecture 259

Remote Shopping Solution 262
    Supported Document Formats 263
    Remote Shopping Tasks 267
    Remote Shopping Architecture 269
Tools and Technologies 272
Implementation 272
    Basket Rendering Routines 273
        RemoteBasket.asp from Basket.asp 273
        InspectBasket.asp from RemoteBasket.asp 276
    New and Modified Files in the AFS Solution Site 283

Chapter 13   Using Web Services to Transfer Files 291

Scenario 291
Solution 291
Tools and Technologies 293
    Hardware and Software Requirements 293
    Install the Web Service File Transfer Utility 293
Implementation 294
    Operational Overview 294
    Configuring the Sending WSFT Utility 295
    Configuring the Receiving WSFT Web Service 296
Summary 297

PART FOUR   Business-to-Consumer Integration 299

Chapter 14   Reaching Consumers Using the Web 301

Microsoft Commerce Server 302
Microsoft Content Management Server 303
A Common Theme: Keeping Separate Jobs Separate 304

Chapter 15   Setting Up a Retail Storefront 307

Scenario 308
    The Shopper Perspective 308
    The Shopkeeper Perspective 311
    The Business Manager Perspective 312
    The Site Administrator Perspective 313
    The Site Developer Perspective 313
    Scenario Summary 314

Solution 314
   Microsoft Commerce Server Overview 316
      Commerce Server User Interfaces 316
      Commerce Server Web Site 319
      Commerce Server Objects 319
   Feature-by-Feature Solution Summary 321
      Navigation 321
      Product Catalogs 324
      Shopping Baskets 327
      Completing the Purchase 330
      Shopper-Centric Security 334
      Recommendations 336
      Improvements 341
      Privacy 344
      Different Languages and Currency 345
      Miscellaneous Shopper Features 345
      Shopkeeper-Specific Features 347
Tools and Technologies 347
Implementation 348
   Keyword Searches in the Retail Solution Site 349
      Main 349
      rsFreeTextSearch 350
      htmRenderFullTextSearchResults 352
      RenderSearchResults and RenderSearchResultRow 353
   Keyword Searches in the International Solution Site 353
      Search_Click 353
      Page_Load 354
      PerformSearch 355

Chapter 16　Managing Web Content **359**
Scenario 360
Solution 361
   The Basic Idea 362
   Concepts and Terminology 364
      Maintained in a Database 364
      Framed vs. Frameless Sites 365
      Templates 365
      Placeholders 366

Pages and Postings 367
Folders and Channels 368
Properties 369
Resources 369
Galleries 369
Roles 370
Rights Groups 370
Web Author 371
Site Builder 373
Connected Pages 375
Content Connector 375
Publishing API 375
URL Generation 376
Roles and Rights 376
Creating a Web Site 379
Content Connector for Commerce Server 2000 380
Simple and Rich Product Pages 380
Personalized Content Objects 381
Business Desk Extensions 382
User Authorization 383
Programming with Content Connector 383
Microsoft Solution for Internet Business 383
Programming with Content Management Server 384
Publishing API 384
Content Connector Framework API 387
Deploying Content Management Server 388
Site Deployment Manager 389
Site Stager 390
Content Management Server 2002 391
Site Programming Changes 391
Administration Changes 394
Authoring and Editing Changes 395
Miscellaneous Changes 395
Tools and Technologies 396
Implementation 397
COM Version of BuildTopNavTable 398
.NET-Based Version of BuildTopNavTable 399

PART FIVE   Wireless Integration **403**

Chapter 17   Integrating Location-Based Mobile Services **405**

Introduction 405
Location-Based Mobile Services Delivery 406
Building .NET Location-Based Mobile Services Solutions 411
    Mobile Internet Technology and Market Forces 411
    The LBMS View of Mobile Networks 411
    Location Technology and LBMS 414
    LBMS User Scenarios 421
    Market Segmentation 421
    Connectivity and Synchronization Requirements 422
  LBMS Protocol Standards 422
    The Standards Landscape 422
    MAGIC Services Protocol 423
  The Eight MAGIC Services 423
Solution Architectures 425
  Operating System and Enterprise Server Components 425
  Importance of the Lab 426
  Deployment Options 426
    Option 1: The Synchronous and Stateless Model 426
    Option 2: The Stateful Server Model 427
    Option 3: Sync-and-Go Model 427
Tools and Technologies 427
  Operating Environment and Scalability 427
    Hardware 429
    Software 429
    Gateway Server 430
    Transport Unpacking Server 430
    Accounting Server 430
    Core Navigation Server 430
Implementation 430
    Installing Microsoft Software 431
  Security Checklist 432
Additional Information 433

Chapter 18 Location-Based Mobile Services Architecture **435**

Scenario 435
Solution 435
  Key Design Considerations 435
    MSP, NSPs and Other Content Providers 437
    NSP, MSPs, and Other Customers 439
    MSP 2.0 in the Protocol Stack 440
  Transport Considerations 441
    HTTP 442
    SMTP 442
    TCP/IP 442
    Other Transports 443
  Navigation Service Provider Architecture 443
    Back-End – Front-End Division 443
    Space Publishing Server 447
  Service Delivery Targets 448
    Five Targets 448
    Delivery to Mobile Phones 450
    Delivery to In-Car Systems 451
    Delivery to a Mobile Service Provider 452
  Information Update 453
  Solution Parameters 453
    Wireless Connectivity 453
    Identifying Service Requirements 454
  Caching Options 454
  Solution Summary 455
    Mobile Phone 455
    In-Car 455
    Mobile Service Provider 455
    Space Publishing Server 455
    Position Proxy Server 456
Tools and Technologies 456
Implementation 456
  Implementing an NSP Delivery System 456
    Installing Microsoft Software 457
Additional Information 458

Chapter 19 Delivering Location-Based Mobile Services 459

Introduction 459
   MSP 2.0 Basics 460
      Session Service 460
      Context Service 461
      Semantics Service 462
      Query Service 463
      Mobility Service 465
      Positioning Service 466
      Rendering Service 466
      Update Service 467
      The Registry 468
      The API 469
   Session Service Example 470
      Session Service 470
   Space Publishing 472
      Scenarios 473
      Design 473
   Delivery to the Automobile 473
      Scenarios 473
      Design 474
   Delivery to the Mobile Phone 474
      Scenarios 475
      Design 477
   Delivery to MSP 477
      Scenarios 477
      Design 478
   Position Proxy Service 478
      Scenarios 478
      Design 479
   Summary 479
Additional Information 479

PART SIX The Future 481

Chapter 20 A Vision for the Future 483

.NET E-Business Servers Today 483
   E-Business Servers Today 484

Solutions 484
    HIPAA - Health Care Accelerator 485
    RosettaNet 486
    Accelerator for Suppliers (AFS) 487
    Microsoft Solution for Internet Business (MSIB) 487
  Enterprise E-Business Processes and Services 487
  Future Solutions and Accelerators 489
    BizOffice 489
    Financial Services Accelerator 489
.NET E-Business Servers Tomorrow 490

APPENDIX Sample Applications **493**
  Sample Host-to-Web Applications 493
    ASP.NET VB Host Program Access 493
    VB.NET Early Bound Host Program Access 494
    C# Early Bound Host Program Access 494
    VB.NET Host Program Access as Web Service 494
    VB.NET Host Program Access Web Service Web Client 494
    VB.NET Host Program Access Web Service Windows Forms Client 494
  SQL Server to DB2 Data Transfer–VB.NET 495
  SQL Server to DB2 Data Transfer– Visual Basic 6.0 495
  Customer Order Entry Application 495
  Customer Order Display Application 495
  VB.NET OLE DB Query Processor 495
  Connection String Manager 495
  Web Service File Transfer 496
  Automating Electronic Procurement 496

Glossary **497**

Index **511**

Overview

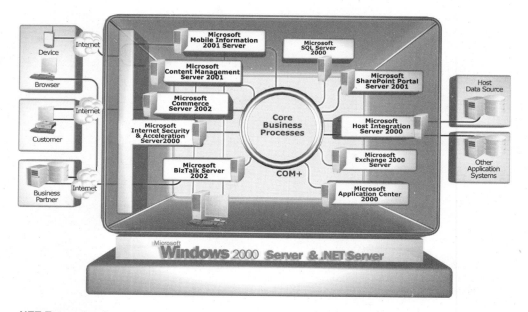

.NET Enterprise Servers

By James Wilson

Introduction

This book presents a practical guide that enables enterprise customers to take advantage of Microsoft® .NET Enterprise Servers. The focus is on providing solutions to common e-business problems faced by medium to large enterprises. Today, Microsoft .NET Enterprise Servers provide solutions to a broad array of scenarios. To address this large market segment, we compiled an anthology of scenarios under common e-business topics, such as Enterprise Application Integration (EAI), Business-to-Business (B2B) Integration, Business-to-Consumer (B2C) Integration, and Wireless Integration. To complete the picture, we close with a sneak preview of the emerging vision for the .NET e-business framework and the compelling solutions you can expect in the near future.

The figure on the inside cover of the book shows the customer's perspective of the .NET Enterprise Servers framework, and how these servers fit into your overall business processes. Throughout these pages we emphasize the customer's perspective and integrated solutions using .NET Enterprise Servers together.

Various authors and many technical experts contributed to this book. The format of each section and chapter is similar, while the content within each chapter varies in detail and style to illustrate a unique solution to a specific problem. This book is not intended to be read from start to finish. Part 1 gives you an introduction and an overview of the .NET Enterprise Servers. The remaining parts and chapters can be read according to your specific interests.

Each part begins with an introductory chapter that covers key issues and common problems encountered in developing e-business solutions. The following chapters in each part provide a discussion of a specific business scenario in a standard format. Each chapter begins with a *Scenario* that presents the business problem to be solved from the customer's perspective. The next section describes a conceptual *Solution* to the problem. A description of specific *Tools and Technologies* required to address the problem follows, showing you which server products to install, prerequisites and so forth. The *Implementation* section describes "what to do" to implement the solution. The details for how to configure each server product are left to the individual product documentation sets. For some scenarios, we provide sample code and snippets to demonstrate how you can quickly and easily implement solutions using the .NET Enterprise Servers and Microsoft® Visual Studio® .NET together. Finally, we provide pointers for where you can go for *additional information*.

Purpose

In order to understand how to use complex products and technologies together, you need a roadmap that shows you where to begin and where to go. We present the big picture, showing you which products and technologies you need to address specific scenarios. We purposely did not try to give an exhaustive description of how to implement a solution for broad topics such as supply chain management, which could easily fill a volume. Nor did we try to limit this discussion to conceptual material. The emphasis is on practical information that gives you a blueprint with some code samples to show you how to implement pieces of the puzzle, and lots of pointers to more information (e.g., product sites, product documentation, URLs, white papers, samples, etc.).

Audience

We chose scenarios that span horizontal markets to make this information relevant to a broad audience. For example, many companies are concerned with supply chain management, creating a retail Web site, setting up an automated e-procurement process, and so forth. The level of content is general enough to appeal to various disciplines within a large enterprise. At the same time, the detail is specific enough to add practical value to people who are tasked with implementing an enterprise-wide solution to a given business problem. Additionally, we targeted consultants, solution providers, application service providers, and independent software vendors to give them a framework they need to build solutions for their clients.

Information Technology and Business Managers

Information Technology (IT) managers and business managers need an easy-to-understand guide for how to use Microsoft's products and technologies together to build solutions that address urgent needs within their organizations. Each chapter begins with a scenario that describes a problem from the enterprise customer's perspective. The solution describes which products and technologies can be used together to address the scenario. This information helps decision makers to understand how to identify tools and technologies to address major projects in the coming year. Individual product documentation, by its very nature, cannot provide this view. The implementation and reference sections provide more detail to help you reach your goals successfully.

Information Technology Architects

Information Technology (IT) architects, system architects and system analysts will benefit from the blueprints provided in each chapter that relate to a specific scenario. The diagrams, figures, and overviews show you how to design integrated solutions to your problems. The *Implementation* section gives you code samples and ways to implement your design solution. Each chapter also contains references for where to go for more details on products, technologies, white papers, etc.

Consultants, Independent Software Vendors, Solution Providers, and Application Service Providers

Consultants, independent software vendors (ISV), Solution Providers (SP), and Application Service Providers (ASP) can gain insights into how the various .NET Enterprise Servers work together to provide integrated solutions for their clients. The practical guidance combined with detailed samples helps you understand how to successfully implement e-business projects.

Database Administrators, Application Developers, and System Integrators

Database administrators (DBA), application developers and system integrators need to understand how they are going to integrate new applications and technologies into their existing environments. The product overviews, integrated solutions, samples and references can help you learn how to merge existing applications and data within an e-business infrastructure.

Project Managers

Project managers need to understand how to use Microsoft's products together and how to plan for migrating to new platforms, technologies, and innovative solutions. The key concepts in this book enable you to build integrated solutions to common e-business scenarios from the project manager's perspective.

Scope

Microsoft .NET Enterprise Servers cover a broad array of applications and technologies to address enterprise customer needs. In this volume, we showcase three emerging products: Microsoft BizTalk Server 2002, Microsoft Commerce Server 2002, and Microsoft Visual Studio .NET. These exciting new products, along with the suite of e-business servers, form the heart of the book. The e-business servers are designed to work with the family .NET Enterprise Servers, many of which are described in the scenarios throughout the book. The second chapter, "Overview of .NET Enterprise Servers" provides a synopsis of servers that comprise the .NET Enterprise Servers family, and gives a more detailed account of the following servers:

- Microsoft® Application Center 2000

- Microsoft® BizTalk® Server 2002

- Microsoft® Commerce Server 2002

- Microsoft® Content Management Server 2001

- Microsoft® Exchange 2000 Server

- Microsoft® Host Integration Server 2000

- Microsoft® Internet Security and Acceleration (ISA) Server 2000

- Microsoft® SQL Server™ 2000

- Microsoft® Mobile Information 2001 Server

- Microsoft® SharePoint ™ Portal Server 2001

Major Focus: E-Business Servers

Since we had to limit the scope of this book, the major focus is on the e-business servers: Microsoft BizTalk Server, Microsoft Commerce Server, Microsoft Content Management Server, Microsoft Host Integration Server, and Microsoft BizTalk Adapters. The figure below shows the e-business servers highlighted within the framework of the .NET Enterprise Servers.

Chapter 1   Introduction

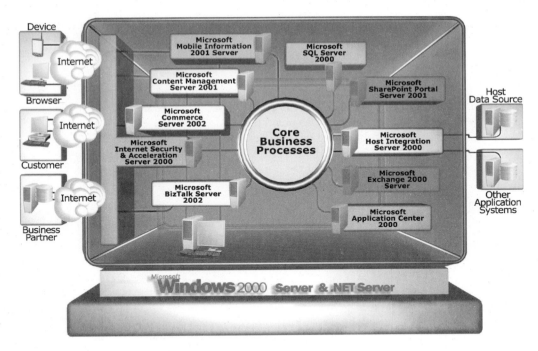

.NET Enterprise Servers: E-Business Servers

Minor Focus

Many of the scenarios involve Microsoft SQL Server, so we included descriptions of how SQL Server fits into the solutions for various problems. We left the details of how to install and configure SQL Server to the product documentation. The book also covers Microsoft Application Center, Microsoft Information Security and Acceleration Server (ISA), and Microsoft Mobile Information Server. These products and technologies are discussed in less detail than the e-business servers.

Beyond Scope

To limit the scope of this book, Microsoft Exchange Server and Microsoft SharePoint Portal Server are not included. We did not include Microsoft® bCentral™ solutions for small businesses. The Microsoft® Great Plains Business Solutions for medium size organizations is also beyond the scope of this book. Empowering employees using Exchange and SharePoint Portal Servers deserves an entire book. Solutions for small and medium sized businesses could each also fill a volume.

Plan of the Book

Leading companies are rapidly becoming virtual enterprises. Their business partners conduct transactions smoothly through automated interfaces, blurring the traditional boundaries across organizations. Customers are rapidly becoming technically astute, demanding instant information and online ordering. These trends and expectations are shaping the evolving e-business environment. Organizational effectiveness depends on a solid foundation that supports intelligent, secure sharing of information, and provides customers with what they want, when they want it, where they want it. This book's parts and chapters are arranged to provide a survey of practical ways to address some of these trends across an enterprise.

Part 1: Overview

This first chapter of the book gives you an outline of each part and defines the scope of the e-business market to be addressed. The second chapter explains .NET in plain English. Ending Part One, the third chapter gives you a bird's eye view of the .NET Enterprise Servers. These products are exceedingly complex, offering a multitude of functions and features. We provide you with tables, descriptions and diagrams that show you the major features of each server product. These first three chapters provide a framework to guide you through the rest of the book.

Part 2: Enterprise Application Integration

Enterprise Application Integration (EAI) encompasses a far-reaching subject that we cannot treat thoroughly here. We start with an overview of some of the major issues facing enterprises today. The following chapters each cover an EAI scenario, such as Web-to-host integration, data integration, and integrating BizTalk Server with SAP.

The distinction between EAI and B2B can be somewhat fuzzy. Often you need to address integrating with existing applications in order to automate the interfaces with your business partners. For example, if you create purchase orders in a financial software system such as SAP, you may need to integrate your SAP system with BizTalk Server first. Then you can send orders to your business partners over the Internet. The scenarios found in the EAI and B2B sections have some overlapping areas.

Part 3: Business-to-Business Integration

Large enterprises have been integrating with their business partners for years. Electronic Data Interchange (EDI) has worked for many companies, but the cost of being charged for each transaction can be substantial. By automating your orders and invoices using the Internet, you can eliminate the transaction charge and reduce your dependence on Value Added Networks (VANs).

In this part, we show you how BizTalk Server takes advantage of the Internet for B2B integration. The supply chain management integration chapter provides a description of automating processes across business partners. Some large enterprises require suppliers to interact with their e-marketplaces and e-procurement systems. The chapter "Selling Through Trading Partners" provides a good example of the products and tools available today to help you automate the interfaces with your suppliers. These chapters give you a broad overview of BizTalk Server, SQL Server, and BizTalk Accelerator for Suppliers (AFS), along with some code samples using Visual Studio .NET.

Part 4: Business-to-Consumer Integration

Integrating consumers can be vital to the success of a large enterprise. These business-to-consumer (B2C) chapters show you how you can make it easy for customers to do business with you. This part begins with a discussion of some common problems for businesses to address in order to integrate their customers. We show you how to set up a retail Web site using Commerce Server. Another scenario shows you how to use Content Management Server's powerful set of tools for building content-rich Web sites for Internet, extranet and intranet. Content Management Server helps business users manage large volumes of information for customers, partners, and employees.

Part 5: Wireless Integration

A discussion of solutions that make use of .NET Enterprise Servers would not be complete without mentioning integrating wireless applications into the enterprise. Microsoft Mobile Information 2001 Server is a recent addition to the family of .NET Enterprise Servers. Integrating wireless devices involves delivering information to very thin clients. Data aware devices already number in the hundreds of millions. This large population of connected and location-aware devices poses a very attractive target, but delivering location-based services is not an easy task. In these chapters we address how to build a server architecture that is capable of supporting location-aware applications. Most of the content shows you how to deliver core services to mobile applications via XML and SOAP. A Visual Studio .NET solution with a sample application is also included on the companion CD-ROM.

Part 6: The Future

Microsoft's e-business servers are rapidly evolving to address business process automation, application integration, product management, customer relationship management, content management, and business portal management. The future versions of this suite will take advantage of XML and SOAP to create a rich set of Web services that enable large enterprises to quickly implement solutions to complex business problems. Since these products are currently under development, we limit our discussion to the key areas of the emerging e-business vision.

Summary

At the time of writing in early 2002, Visual Studio .NET is just coming to market. The samples in various chapters feature Visual Studio .NET applications and code snippets to show you how quickly and easily you can create e-business applications. We included more samples on the companion CD-ROM to show you new features in Microsoft® Visual Basic® .NET, Microsoft® ADO.NET and Microsoft® Visual C#™ .NET. The Appendix Sample Applications section provides a more detailed listing of the CD-ROM contents.

Newer versions of BizTalk Server and Commerce Server recently came to market as well. Throughout this book we showcase these new products and technologies to help you navigate the complex maze of e-business solutions.

Microsoft has the tools and technologies available to enable large enterprises to build e-business infrastructures *today*. As the .NET architecture emerges, it will become easier to extend your e-business environment. Here, we provide you with the big picture (the .NET Enterprise Servers framework), a roadmap (scenarios, solutions), and signposts (tools and technologies, references, etc.). Enjoy the tour.

By William J. Harding

.NET in Plain English

For the past several years, Microsoft has been investing in the Internet. Technology developments, product developments, availability of technical information, and consumer marketing have been increasingly Internet-focused. In fact, it is hard to find any Microsoft technology or product that does not have a Web or Internet component or feature.

Attention to the Internet and the Web reached a high point in July 2000 when Microsoft announced its vision for future computing, calling it .NET (pronounced *dot net*). Ultimately influencing the entire product line, .NET represents one of the most important strategic initiative in Microsoft's history.

Many books and articles have been written about .NET, and many more are scheduled for publishing. This chapter presents an overview of the architecture and some components.

Microsoft® .NET does not describe any one product or service. Rather it is a vision for future computing that includes the way software is developed and what the user is able to do with various computing devices. Microsoft .NET includes a group of products and services to make that vision a reality.

The vision for future computing is XML Web services. XML Web services are the basic building blocks of distributed computing on the Internet. People and the computer applications they use are moving toward more communication and collaboration across networks and the Internet. Web services, using open standards, are becoming the method for creating computer applications that interact and communicate with each other over networks and the Internet. Applications can be constructed using multiple XML Web services from various sources that work together regardless of where they "live" or how they are implemented.

Microsoft .NET is based on open standards. .NET combines the presentation capabilities of HTML with the metadata capabilities of XML. HTML and XML are both a widely supported industry standard defined by the World Wide Web Consortium (W3C).

Microsoft .NET can be divided into the following technology areas:

- Microsoft® .NET Framework

- Microsoft® .NET Server Platforms

- Microsoft® .NET My Services

.NET Framework

The .NET Framework forms the foundation for application development. Microsoft® Visual Studio® .NET provides the tool set used to build XML Web services and applications using the .NET Framework and a common object-oriented programming model.

There are three major goals for .NET Framework:

- Simplify development of Web services and applications.

- Provide a set of developer tools and libraries that work across programming languages and computing devices.

- Make Microsoft® Windows® applications more reliable, secure, and easier to use.

Microsoft .NET Framework consists of a development environment which includes five key technologies:

- Visual Studio .NET development environment built from the ground up for XML Web services.

- Common language runtime that hosts running applications.

- Class libraries.

- Programming languages that make use of the common language runtime and class libraries.

- Microsoft® ASP.NET for developing Web applications and Web services.

Visual Studio .NET

Visual Studio .NET is the only development environment built from the ground up for XML Web services. By allowing applications to communicate and share data over the Internet, XML Web services enable businesses to transform the Internet into a true platform for integrating and delivering their core business products and services. Visual Studio .NET and XML Web services provide a simple, flexible, standards-based model that allows developers to assemble applications from new and existing code, regardless of the platform, programming language, or object model.

Microsoft is committed to providing the best development platform and tools for the Internet in a world of open standards, taking advantage of XML. .NET provides the tools and technologies you need to write applications that can communicate easily over the Internet (and any other network).

The following table describes several software development issues with .NET solutions.

Solving Software Development Problems using .NET

Current Problem	.NET Solution
Interoperability, integration, and application extensibility are too difficult and too expensive.	Using XML removes barriers to data sharing and software integration.
Competing proprietary software technologies complicate software integration.	.NET uses open standards and embraces all programming languages.
User applications are still too difficult to use. Applications cannot easily share data, making it difficult for users to act upon the data when they can access it.	Using XML makes data exchange and sharing uncomplicated. Software created using .NET gives users the ability to work with data when it is received.
Users working on the Web cannot control their personal information and data.	.NET provides a set of services that allow users to manage their personal information and control access to it.
Current computer applications and Web site services do not work well together and exist as islands of information.	.NET is designed to bring together features and services from multiple sites and companies into a coherent user experience.

Common Language Runtime

The common language runtime provides and manages several services at the time an application is executed. These services include enforcing security, and managing memory, processes, threads, and language integration. Language integration enables full integration of components and XML Web services, regardless of the programming language used. Microsoft provides four .NET programming languages, which are discussed in more detail below; however, a large number of non-Microsoft languages are also available for building .NET applications.

Most Windows executable programs (.exe) use unmanaged code, which makes no provision for security or memory management. Program code executing under the common language runtime is referred to as managed code, because it relies on the common language runtime to perform many low-level tasks such as memory management. Using managed code can provide a higher level of reliability and security than unmanaged code. The following figure shows a conceptual architecture of the common language runtime components.

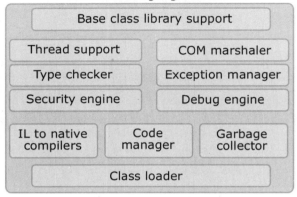

Common Language Runtime

Common language runtime components

To bridge the gap between managed and unmanaged code, and to take advantage of the enormous amount of conventional Windows code available to developers, common language runtime enables interoperability. For example, common language runtime enables managed code to call functions defined in unmanaged code.

> **Note** Applications that use such mixed code bases will not have the reliability and security benefits of pure managed code applications.

Common language runtime also has another important function as a virtual computer in addition to being a runtime system. Managed code applications are not compiled into executables in the same way as conventional Windows applications. Rather, they are distributed in an intermediate language called the Microsoft Intermediate Language, or MSIL. The common language runtime completes the compiling either when the application is installed or the first time the application runs. This operation is called "just in time compilation."

At the time of this writing, common language runtime is included with Visual Studio .NET and will ship as part of the Microsoft .NET Server products.

Class Libraries

The class libraries provide a standard set of system services. These libraries of code will replace and provide the same kind of functions as the Win32 API and the Microsoft Foundation Classes (MFC) for C++ or Visual Basic. The following figure shows the conceptual framework for the .NET class libraries.

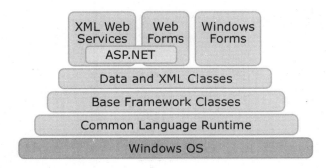

.NET class libraries

- The Base classes provide standard functionality such as input/output, string manipulation, security management, network communications, thread management, text management, and other functions.

- The Data classes support persistent data management and include SQL classes for manipulating persistent data stores through a standard SQL interface.

- XML classes enable XML data manipulation, searching, and translation.

- XML Web service classes support the development of lightweight distributed components, which will work even in the face of firewalls and network address translation (NAT) software.

- Web Forms include classes that enable you to rapidly develop Web graphical user interface (GUI) applications.

- Windows Forms support a set of classes that allow you to develop Windows-based GUI applications—facilitating drag-and-drop GUI development and providing a common, consistent, development interface across all languages supported by .NET Framework.

Programming Languages

Microsoft has introduced a new programming language, C# (pronounced *"C sharp"*), and reengineered three other languages to take advantage of the common language runtime and class libraries. Together they include:

- Microsoft® Visual C#™ .NET

- Microsoft® Visual Basic® .NET

- Microsoft® Visual C++® .NET

- Microsoft® JScript .NET

In addition, a number of other companies have announced support for .NET Framework in their programming languages. Whatever language you use, the Microsoft .NET Framework provides a rich set of application programming interfaces (APIs) for the Microsoft® Windows® operating system and the Internet.

Visual C# .NET

C# is a modern, object-oriented language that enables programmers to quickly build a wide range of applications. It provides tools and services that fully exploit both computing and communications.

Because of its innovative object-oriented design, C# is a great choice for architecting a wide range of components from high-level business objects down to system-level applications. Using straightforward C# language constructs, these components can be converted into XML Web services, allowing them to be invoked across the Internet, from any language running on any operating system.

More than anything else, C# is designed to bring rapid development to the C++ programmer without sacrificing the power and control that have been a hallmark of C and C++. Because of this heritage, C# has a high degree of compatibility with C and C++. Developers familiar with these languages can quickly become productive in C#.

Visual Basic .NET

In the new .NET architecture, Visual Basic has attained the stature of a first-class programming language. Visual Basic .NET allows full access to .NET Framework and provides language features like multithreading, event logging, and performance monitoring that were either impossible or extremely awkward in Visual Basic 6.0. Visual Basic programmers can now build a multithreaded queue processing service, explore advanced Web application techniques, and have full access to graphics.

Microsoft Visual Basic .NET is the next version of the Visual Basic development system, redesigned to enable uncomplicated development of next-generation XML Web services, while continuing its tradition of rapid application development for Microsoft Windows applications. Rather than simply adding some new features to Visual Basic 6.0, Microsoft has built Visual Basic .NET from the ground up on the .NET Framework. This enables you, as a Visual Basic developer, to take advantage of the enhancements in Visual Basic .NET to build enterprise-critical distributed *n*-tier systems.

With Visual Basic .NET, you now have access to a significantly richer and more powerful toolset than you had in previous versions of Visual Basic. Driven by strong customer demand, Visual Basic .NET delivers an extensive set of new features, including full object-oriented design capabilities, free-threading, and direct access to .NET Framework. In addition, the Visual Basic language has been streamlined, removing obsolete legacy keywords, improving type safety, and exposing the low-level constructs that advanced developers require. To deliver these features, several syntax changes and additions have been made to the language.

Visual Basic .NET now fully integrates with the other Microsoft Visual Studio .NET languages. You can develop application components in different programming languages, and your classes can now inherit from classes written in other languages. With the unified debugger, you can now debug multiple language applications, regardless of whether they are running locally or on remote computers.

Visual C++ .NET

Visual C++ .NET is a comprehensive tool set for creating Microsoft Windows-based and .NET-based applications, dynamic Web applications, and XML Web services, using the C++ development language. This robust development environment includes the Active Template Library (ATL) and Microsoft Foundation Class (MFC) libraries, advanced language extensions, and powerful integrated development environment (IDE) features that enable developers to edit and debug source code efficiently.

Visual C++ .NET provides developers with many professional-level features and enables them to create extremely powerful applications and components for Windows and the Web. From start to finish, the tool offers features that help streamline the process of C++ software development.

C++ is one of the world's most popular languages, and with Visual C++ .NET, developers benefit from a world-class C++ development tool. C++ is an interoperable, standards-based language, and C++ skills can be leveraged across multiple computing environments and communities.

JScript .NET

JScript .NET is the next generation of the Microsoft implementation of ECMA 262 language. Combining the existing feature set of classic JScript with the best features of class-based languages, JScript .NET gives you the best of both worlds. Improvements in JScript .NET, which are being developed in conjunction with ECMAScript Edition 4, include true compiled code, typed and typeless variables, classes (with inheritance, function overloading, property accessors, and more), packages, cross-language support, and access to .NET Framework.

JScript .NET is a true object-oriented scripting language. Even though JScript .NET can now use classes, types, and other industrial strength language features for writing robust applications, it still keeps its scripting feel, with support for typeless programming, expanded functions and classes, dynamic code execution (using **eval**), and more.

In addition to being a typeless language, JScript .NET can now be a strongly typed language. New primitive data types have been added to provide more flexibility than before. In the past, JScript was loosely typed since there was only one data type exposed to users. The variety of primitive data types did not exist. As a result, you did not need to declare the data types of variables.

There are many advantages of strong typing in a programming language. In addition to the benefit of using a data type that properly fits the data you are using, there are several other benefits, including:

- Improved execution speed

- Run-time/compile-time type-checking

- Code is more self-documenting

Finally, JScript .NET is not a slimmer version of another programming language, nor is it a simplification of anything. It is a solidly performing modern scripting language with a wide variety of applications.

ASP.NET

Microsoft ASP.NET is more than the next version of Active Server Pages (ASP); it is a unified Web development platform that provides the services necessary for developers to build enterprise-class Web applications. It takes the best from Active Server Pages (ASP), as well as the rich services and features provided by the common language runtime and adds many new features.

While ASP.NET is largely syntax-compatible with ASP, it also provides a new programming model and infrastructure that enables a powerful new class of applications. You can augment existing ASP applications by incrementally adding ASP.NET functionality to them.

The basis of ASP.NET is Web Forms. Web Forms are the User Interface (UI) elements that give your Web applications their look and feel. Web Forms are similar to Windows Forms since they provide properties, methods, and events for the controls that are placed on them. UI elements render themselves in the appropriate markup language required by the request, e.g. HTML. If you use Microsoft Visual Studio .NET, you will also get the familiar drag-and-drop interface used to create a UI for your Web application. The following figure shows an overview of how ASP.NET works.

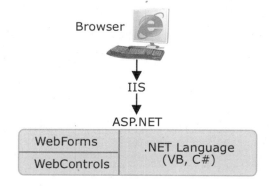

ASP.NET

Web Forms are made up of two components: the visual portion (the ASPX file), and the code behind the form, which resides in a separate class file.

Web Forms and ASP.NET were created to overcome some of the limitations of ASP. These new strengths include:

- Separation of HTML interfaces from application logic.

- A rich set of server-side controls that can detect the browser and send out appropriate markup language such as HTML.

- Less code to write due to the data binding capabilities of the new server-side .NET controls.

- An event-based programming model that is familiar to Microsoft Visual Basic programmers.

- Compiled code and support for multiple languages, as opposed to ASP, which was interpreted as Microsoft Visual Basic Scripting (VBScript) or Microsoft JScript.

- Allowing third parties to create controls that provide additional functionality.

.NET Server Platforms

The Microsoft .NET Enterprise Servers and the Microsoft® Windows® Server family, which includes the Windows .NET Server, make up the platforms and infrastructure for deploying, managing, and orchestrating XML Web services. These products are designed for mission-critical performance. They provide the enterprise business with the power, security, reliability, and scaling required for deploying and integrating business systems and applications. They also provide the flexibility to adapt to changing business requirements.

The Windows 2000 Server and Windows .NET Server offer a secure, scaleable foundation to run .NET Enterprise Servers and your next generation of business applications.

.NET Enterprise Servers, the subject of the next chapter, are listed here for convenience:

Microsoft® Application Center 2000

Microsoft® BizTalk® Server 2002

Microsoft® Commerce Server 2002

Microsoft® Content Management Server 2001

Microsoft® Exchange 2000 Server

Microsoft® Host Integration Server 2000

Microsoft® Internet Security and Acceleration (ISA) Server 2000

Microsoft® Mobile Information 2001 Server

Microsoft® SharePoint™ Portal Server 2001

Microsoft® SQL Server™ 2000

.NET My Services

Microsoft® .NET My Services brings new convenience and computing features to consumers by increasing the utility and value of devices, applications, and the Internet. Building upon the proven capabilities of Microsoft .NET Alerts and Microsoft .NET Passport, .NET My Services is a family of XML Web services that will allow users to store key personal information securely and control access to it. .NET My Services will allow businesses to increase customer satisfaction and build relationships by improving Web sites and Web services, offering operational efficiencies designed to cut costs and increase profits, and providing new business opportunities.

.NET My Services is a collection of XML Web services that are invoked over the Internet by means of industry-standard protocols including SOAP, XML, and Universal Description, Discovery, and Integration (UDDI). .NET My Services authenticates users, provides the ability to send alerts, and stores personal information, including contacts, e-mail, calendar, profile, lists, electronic wallet, physical location, document stores, application settings, favorite Web sites, devices owned, and preferences for receiving alerts.

Businesses can use .NET My Services to offer customers easier site sign-in, better personalization, auto-filled forms, streamlined e-commerce from desktop or mobile devices, effective appointment coordination, and location-based products and services. In addition, with the explicit permission of the customer, businesses can send alerts to the customer about events, offers, and promotions. Because customer information can be made available, businesses can use .NET My Services to identify each customer consistently across all venues of customer contacts.

From a consumer's perspective, .NET My Services is a digital safe deposit box in which personal information is stored. By default, personal information is only accessible to the user. Once information is placed in .NET My Services Digital Safe Deposit Box, users have complete control in choosing how to share information with friends, family, groups, or businesses. Additionally, users can sign up to receive alerts on any of a number of desktop or mobile devices.

Users benefit because .NET My Services eliminates the barriers that make it difficult and time-consuming to take advantage of the Internet and Web-enabled devices. .NET My Services addresses common problems, including manually entering information, using multiple passwords, scheduling problems, sharing personal information, and so forth.

.NET My Services is being used, according to current reports, by more than 165 million people using .NET Passport and over 36 million are ready to receive .NET Alerts.

Microsoft® .NET Passport is a suite of e-business services that makes using the Web and purchasing goods and services online easier, faster, and more secure for its members. .NET Passport provides its members with the Microsoft .NET Passport Single Sign-In and Microsoft .NET Passport Express Purchase service at participating sites. This reduces the amount of information that has to be remembered or retyped. .NET Passport protects the security of members' personal information and online transactions by using powerful encryption technologies and by requiring participating sites to adhere to comprehensive privacy policies that conform to accepted guidelines.

Microsoft® .NET Alerts gives businesses a powerful new communication tool that allows them to reach customers in ways that are relevant and actionable. .NET Alerts provides a service in which users sign up to receive alerts from a specific provider, so that they can quickly be notified of important events and act on that information. For example, rather than simply sending a customer an e-mail message that could sit in an inbox for days, a .NET Alerts provider can send a simple XML message to .NET Alerts service. This service then intelligently routes that message to a user's desktop, cellular phone, mobile device, or e-mail address—all based on the user's preferences. The user can then click on that alert and be directed back to the provider's site for more information.

Additional Information

We distilled information from several sources for this chapter:

- **White Papers**

    "Microsoft .NET for Manufacturing: Extending the Enterprise Through Open Protocols"

    http://www.microsoft.com/technet/itsolutions/net/plan/netmanu.asp

    ".NET in the Real World"

    http://www.microsoft.com/net/intro.asp

    ".NET Framework Product Overview"

    http://msdn.microsoft.com/netframework/prodinfo/overview.asp

    Other Whitepapers and articles are available on Microsoft Technet and MSDN.

You will find a range of information about .NET on the following Microsoft Web sites:

- **Microsoft.com .NET**

    http://www.microsoft.com/net

    This is the primary site for Microsoft .NET information. It includes information for developers, IT professionals, and businesses about the advantages of .NET. There are also links to more Microsoft Web sites focused on key .NET technologies, product offerings, and activities.

- **MSDN .NET Information**

  http://msdn.microsoft.com/net

  This Web site is the Microsoft source for .NET information, tools, and technologies for developers worldwide.

- **Visual Studio .NET home page**

  http://msdn.microsoft.com/vstudio

  This site contains product information about Visual Studio .NET.

- **SOAP**

  http://msdn.microsoft.com/soap

  This Web site consists of information about Simple Object Access Protocol (SOAP).

- **ASP.NET**

  http://www.asp.net

  This site contains information about ASP.NET, Microsoft's Active Server Pages programming tools for .NET.

- **GotDotNet**

  http://www.gotdotnet.com

  This Web site contains hundreds of tutorials and code samples that demonstrate ASP.NET and .NET Framework.

- **MSDN XML Information**

  http://msdn.microsoft.com/xml

  This site includes information about XML.

- **Microsoft .NET Enterprise Servers home page**

  http://www.microsoft.com/servers

  This Web site comprises product information about Microsoft .NET Enterprise Servers.

- **Microsoft .NET My Services home page**

  http://www.microsoft.com/myservices

  This site consists of information about Microsoft .NET My Services

- **Microsoft .NET Passport home page**

  http://www.passport.com

  This Web site covers information about .NET Passport.

By William J. Harding

Overview of .NET Enterprise Servers

The Microsoft family of .NET Enterprise Servers provides the enterprise business with a secure, scalable, and a high-performance platform on which to build integrated business software solutions. This chapter provides an overview of the Microsoft .NET Enterprise Server family of products, including:

- Microsoft® Application Center 2000
- Microsoft® BizTalk® Server 2002
- Microsoft® Commerce Server 2002
- Microsoft® Content Management Server 2001
- Microsoft® Exchange 2000 Server
- Microsoft® Host Integration Server 2000
- Microsoft® Internet Security and Acceleration (ISA) Server 2000
- Microsoft® SQL Server™ 2000
- Microsoft® Mobile Information 2001 Server
- Microsoft® SharePoint™ Portal Server 2001

Application Center 2000

Organizations use Microsoft® Application Center 2000 to deploy and manage applications. An Application Center 2000 application is a group of components that together make up a complete, distributed business solution. These components can include Web sites, COM+ components, and configuration settings. Using Application Center 2000, administrators can group components into an application and then deploy and administer that application. Doing so provides the following benefits:

- **Load balancing.** Application Center 2000 includes two software load balancing technologies that work with stateless middle-tier components, such as Web sites and COM+ applications. Network Load Balancing (NLB) balances IP requests across a cluster of servers on the Web tier, which serves HTTP clients. Component Load Balancing (CLB) balances the activation of DCOM requests, which serves DCOM traffic on the business logic tier.

  Application Center 2000 is also compatible with other load balancing devices and does not require a shared disk or special hardware. An Application Center 2000 cluster can serve intranet or Internet clients running thin-client software, such as Web browsers, or thick-client applications such as Microsoft® Visual Basic® programs.

  Application Center 2000 clusters are not the same as clusters created with Microsoft Windows® Clustering. The Windows Clustering model is designed to handle back-end applications, such as Microsoft® SQL Server™ 2000 databases or Microsoft Exchange 2000 Server stores; Windows Clustering uses a shared disk resource to coordinate between cluster members.

- **Centralized management.** The Application Center 2000 Integrated Management Console provides administrators with a single, unified image of the components that are deployed throughout a cluster. Specifically, administrators can use the Application Center 2000 management snap-in to configure load balancing, add and remove members, or configure a member to go offline when an application-level failure occurs. (Application Center 2000 monitoring tools detect hardware and software failures automatically and can trigger actions, such as running scripts or sending e-mail notifications, in response to a failure.) Administrators also have the option of managing Application Center 2000 clusters remotely through a browser or with a command-line tool.

Administrators can construct logical views of the applications and components deployed throughout a cluster and then manage them from a single location. Application Center 2000 can also provide cluster-wide views of performance trends, simplifying event management. Once an administrator defines an application, Application Center 2000 can keep the contents of that application synchronized across a cluster.

- **Software scaling.** Administrators can add members to and remove members from Application Center 2000 clusters without interrupting Web site availability. The deployment capabilities of Application Center 2000 enable administrators to use a staging server as a central content store from which to deploy applications to new servers within a cluster or to new clusters.

The following illustration highlights the load balancing, management, and software scaling capabilities of Application Center 2000.

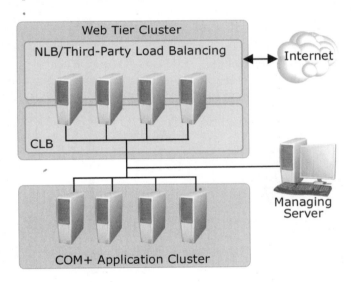

Application Center 2000

Application Center 2000 Documentation Resources

For more information about Application Center 2000, see the following documents and Web sites:

Application Center 2000 Documentation Resources

Document	Description	Location
Microsoft Application Center 2000 Product Documentation	Complete product documentation that describes how to install and administer Application Center 2000.	Included on the CD-ROM that contains Application Center 2000. Also downloadable from http://www.microsoft.com/applicationcenter/techinfo/productdocumentation/2000/ac2000.asp
Microsoft Application Center 2000 Resource Kit	Detailed guide about deploying, administrating, and designing Application Center 2000 solutions.	Order the Resource Kit at http://mspress.microsoft.com/books/4363.htm
Application Center 2000 on Microsoft TechNet site	Technical overviews of Network Load Balancing (NLB), Component Load Balancing (CLB), and the Application Center 2000 command-line tool.	http://www.microsoft.com/technet/acs/acsdocs/

BizTalk Server 2002

On the most basic level, Microsoft® BizTalk® Server 2002 transforms and routes data (in the form of XML-based messages) within and between organizations, including organizations that use a variety of software and hardware platforms.

Companies use the basic capabilities of BizTalk Server to build and deploy business processes of many types, such as:

- Transforming data between different formats, including XML, EDI, flat-file, and others.

- Managing the transmission, translation and routing of messages among trading partners, between applications, and between applications and systems.

- Integrating external data sources; and executing transactions over the network.

To make this possible, BizTalk Server provides a central, data-driven, integration server and a set of tools for performing Enterprise Application Integration (EAI) and business-to-business (B2B) transactions.

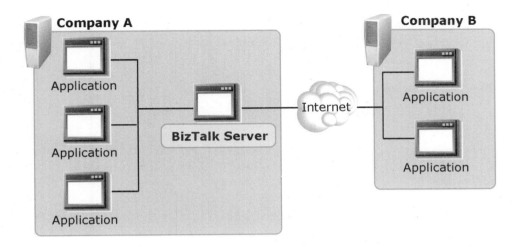

BizTalk Server 2002

BizTalk Server contains the following feature areas:

- **Administration.** Configure global server group properties, such as the location for the Shared Queue database and the Tracking database. Configure server settings. Configure and manage receive functions. View and manage document queues.

- **Document Tracking.** Track the progress of documents processed by Microsoft BizTalk Server 2000. Search for, display, view, and save complete copies of any interchange or document processed by BizTalk Server. Create queries to extract essential information from the Tracking database in an easy-to-view format. Extract, store, and analyze important user-defined data from within documents.

- **Orchestration Design.** Create drawings that describe business processes, and programmatically implement these drawings within an integrated design environment. Compile XLANG schedule drawings into XLANG schedules. Define the flow of data between messages within business processes.

- **Messaging Services.** Manage the exchange of data locally or remotely using BizTalk Messaging Manager. Create and manage channels, messaging ports, document definitions, envelopes, organizations, and distribution lists.

- **XML Tools.** Create and manage specifications. Create records and fields, and set their properties. Map records and fields from a source specification to records and fields of a destination specification. Use functoids to implement powerful data-transformation functionality. Functoids enable complex structural manipulations between elements.

BizTalk Server 2002 Documentation Resources

For more information about BizTalk Server 2002, see the following documents and Web sites:

BizTalk Server 2002 Documentation Resources

Document	Description	Location
BizTalk Server 2002 product documentation (online guides for BizTalk Server 2002 Standard Edition, Enterprise Edition, and Developer Edition)	How to get started and administer BizTalk Server 2002. Provides tutorials on modeling business processes, configuring BizTalk Messaging Services, and completing XLANG Schedules. Describes the tools, services, and COM objects used for creating BizTalk applications.	The books online are included on the CD-ROM that contains BizTalk Server 2002. Also available from the Microsoft TechNet site (see below).
BizTalk Server 2002 in the Microsoft Platform SDK	A guide for the developer to create applications that integrates with BizTalk Server 2002.	This guide can be found in the Microsoft Platform SDK
BizTalk Server 2000 on Microsoft TechNet site	Product documentation available online.	http://www.microsoft.com/technet/biztalk/btsdocs/
Microsoft BizTalk Server 2002 home page	Provides overview information, pricing and licensing, and downloadable trial copies of BizTalk Server 2002.	http://www.microsoft.com/biztalk

Commerce Server 2002

Microsoft® Commerce Server 2002 is used to host a business-to-consumer (B2C) or business-to-business (B2B) Web site with the following features:

- **Product Catalog System.** Create, update, import, export, search, and report on product catalogs.

- **Profiling System.** Manage millions of users, and build user and organizational profiles for use in content selection and targeting.

- **Business Analytics System.** Analyze site effectiveness by collecting data from the site, identify specific groups of users, trends, and offer cross-sell recommendations.

- **Targeting System.** Personalize Web sites with targeted merchandising that provides specific users with content, discounts, advertisements, and direct mail.

- **Business Process Pipelines.** Customize order, targeting, and merchandising processes, and define and link together the stages of a business process.

The following illustration shows how these features are related. In addition, the following definitions will help in understanding the diagram.

- **(Commerce Server 2002) Business Desk.** A Web-based site management tool used for managing and analyzing commerce sites.

- **Commerce Server 2002 Manager.** A Microsoft® Management Console-based system administration tool used for managing and configuring Commerce Server resources, sites, applications, and Web servers.

- **Commerce Server 2002 Data Warehouse.** A set of processes used by a system administrator for importing and maintaining site-usage data into databases for later analysis and reporting.

- **Catalog.** A way to organize products for sale. Commerce Server 2002 Business Desk helps create and organize catalogs by maintaining descriptions of catalog items.

- **Campaign.** A marketing program with a goal of producing a specific result. Commerce Server 2002 provides delivery mechanisms for online campaigns.

- **Order.** An online purchase request submitted to a Web site by a user.

- **Profile.** A set of characteristics that define any business-related item, such as a user, a company, or a business process.

The following figure shows an overview of Commerce Server's architecture.

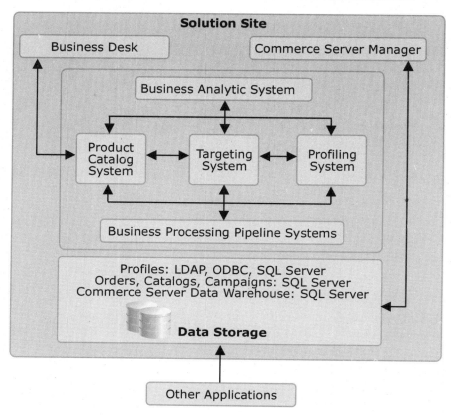

Commerce Server 2002

Commerce Server 2002 Documentation Resources

For more information on Commerce Server 2002, see the following documents and Web sites:

Commerce Server 2002 Documentation Resources

Document	Description	Location
Commerce Server 2002 product documentation on Microsoft TechNet Web site.	Product documentation available online.	http://www.microsoft.com/technet/comm/csdocs/

(continued)

Document	Description	Location *(continued)*
Commerce Server 2002 Developer Resources	Describes how to administer, troubleshoot, extend, and program with Microsoft Commerce Server 2002. Also describes how to develop, deploy, and manage commercial Web sites.	This can be found in the Microsoft Platform SDK
	Site contains white papers and technical articles, press releases, information on migrating from Site Server, and an online version of the developer documentation found in the Platform SDK. Also contains links to newsgroups, downloads of performance tools, and a way to order the Commerce Server 2002 Resource Kit.	http://msdn.microsoft.com/commerceserver
Commerce Server 2002 Solution sites	The Retail Solution site and Supplier Solution site are downloadable development reference sites that provide merchandising, catalog display, customer service, and order capture and receipt capabilities used for building e-commerce sites.	http://www.microsoft.com/commerceserver/downloads/solutionsites(fromCS2K).asp
Commerce Server 2002 home page	Contains product overview, pricing and licensing information, downloads of service packs, and trial copies of various versions of Commerce Server 2002.	http://www.microsoft.com/commerceserver/default.asp

Content Management Server 2001

Microsoft® Content Management Server 2001 is the enterprise Web content management system that enables companies to quickly and efficiently build, deploy, and maintain highly dynamic, content-rich Internet, intranet and extranet Web sites. Content Management Server plays an integral part in scenarios where customers have an abundance of information to communicate to customers, partners, or employees.

- **Comprehensive System for Managing Enterprise Web Content**. Features include content authoring templates, real-time content updates, revision tracking and page archiving, content scheduling, and flexible workflow. Additional features include dynamic server clustering, object caching, and SMP support.

- **Dynamic Content Delivery.** Deliver dynamic content for multiple audiences, devices, and purposes across enterprise Web sites. Personalize content to ensure a positive user experience for prospects, customers, employees, and business partners.

- **Rapid Time-To-Market for Enterprise Web Sites.** Quick software installation, sample templates and Web sites, flexible COM Application Program Interface (API), dynamic site mapping, .NET Server integration, and Windows Active Directory integration help deploy enterprise scalable dynamic e-business Web sites rapidly.

Content Management Server 2001 Documentation Resources

For additional information about Content Management Server 2001, see the following documents and Web sites.

Content Management Server 2001 Documentation Resources

Document	Description	Location
Content Management Server 2001 books online	Describe how to install, configure, and maintain Content Management Server 2001	It is also included on the CD-ROM that contains Content Management Server 2001.
Content Management Server 2001 Home Page	Provides overview information, technical resources, pricing and licensing information, trial copies, and links to product documentation, knowledge base articles, and white papers.	http://www.microsoft.com/cmserver

(continued)

Document	Description	Location *(continued)*
Content Management Server 2001 Documentation on Microsoft TechNet Web site		http://www.microsoft.com/technet/ /prodtechnol/cms/Default.asp

Exchange 2000 Server

Microsoft® Exchange 2000 Server unites users with knowledge anytime, anywhere. Exchange 2000 Server is designed to meet the messaging and collaboration needs of small organizations, large distributed enterprises, and everything in between. Exchange 2000 Server is seamlessly integrated with the Microsoft Windows® 2000 operating system.

Microsoft Exchange 2000 Server has the following features:

- **Active Directory Integration.** Use Microsoft Windows 2000 Active Directory to create a single management point for messaging systems.

- **Internet Information Services (IIS) Integration.** Tight IIS integration means high performance Internet mail and browser access to Exchange 2000 Server using Microsoft® Outlook®.

- **Windows 2000 Security Integration.** Integration with the Windows 2000 security means one security model serves both Windows 2000 and Exchange 2000 Server.

- **Storage Groups.** Manage a group of storage databases from a single administrative point. In addition, multiple storage groups and databases can provide an unlimited message store for users and data.

- **Clustering.** Clustering Exchange 2000 Server computers enables fail-over, improved availability, and load balancing.

- **Distributed Services.** Deliver scalability to tens of millions of users by storing subsystems on multiple servers.

- **Fault-Tolerant Message Routing.** Enhanced routing guarantees message delivery even when servers and network links are down.

- **Administration**. Integration with the Microsoft Management Console (MMC) provides a single point of administration. In addition, administration based on policies permits changes across mailboxes, servers, and folders in a single operation. A new monitoring infrastructure tracks usage and availability through a simple, filterable view of the system.

- **Unified Messaging Platform.** Use any device to access a single inbox containing e-mail, voice-mail, fax, and page messages.

- **Extended Messaging Services.** Additional services include instant messaging and chat services.

- **Multiple Client Access.** Use Outlook 2000 or Outlook Web Access to access e-mail, scheduling, contacts, and collaborative information.

- **Data, Audio and Video Conferencing.** Share applications, files, and participate in audio and video discussions and conferences. Track events and control access to conferences.

- **Development Platform**. Use Exchange 2000 Server to automate many types of workflow processes. Create applications that use OLE DB and ADO, and deliver structured data to the desktop via XML and HTTP. Use Web Forms to provide a powerful method for embedding Web applications with business logic, messages, and events.

Exchange 2000 Server Documentation Resources

For more information about Exchange 2000 Server, see the following documents and Web sites:

Exchange 2000 Server Documentation Resources

Document	Description	Location
Exchange 2000 Server product documentation.	Contains information used for building applications, introduces the data access features, describes core programming tasks, provides sample source code, explains the Exchange 2000 Server tool set, and includes an API and object model reference.	The online books are included on the CD-ROM that contains Exchange 2000 Server. Also available from the Microsoft TechNet site (see below).
Microsoft Exchange 2000 Server Resource Kit	Information to help deploy, manage, optimize, and troubleshoot Exchange 2000 Server.	http://mspress.microsoft.com/prod/books/4355.htm
Exchange 2000 Server in the Microsoft Platform SDK	A guide for the developer to create applications that integrate with Exchange 2000 Server.	This guide can be found in the Microsoft Platform SDK
Exchange 2000 Server on Microsoft TechNet site	Product documentation available online.	http://www.microsoft.com/technet/prodtechnol/exchange/proddocs

(continued)

Document	Description	Location *(continued)*
Microsoft Exchange 2000 Server home page	Provides overview information, pricing and licensing information, and downloadable trial copies of Exchange 2000 Server.	http://www.microsoft.com/exchange

Host Integration Server 2000

It is estimated that 70 percent of all enterprise corporate data is stored on host systems such as IBM mainframe and AS/400 computers. However, corporations are increasing the use of Web and Windows-based applications because they are typically seen as easier to learn and use, and faster to implement than comparable host-based applications.

Migrating host-based data and applications to Windows systems can be costly. To preserve investments in legacy systems, organizations can use Microsoft® Host Integration Server 2000 to *integrate* their host-based resources with Web and Windows-based solutions. Host Integration Server 2000 offers the following functionality:

- **Network Integration**. Companies can use Host Integration Server 2000 to integrate their Windows and mainframe networks without custom programming. This integration includes features such as terminal emulation, and Host Print Services that provides server-based 3270 and 5250 printer emulation, in which mainframe data is sent to a Windows-based printer over a LAN.

- **Data Integration**. Host Integration Server 2000 gives Windows computers the capability to access data in a mainframe database.

- **Application Integration.** Applications running on Windows computers can communicate with certain applications that run on mainframe computers.

The following illustration shows the capabilities that Host Integration Server 2000 offers:

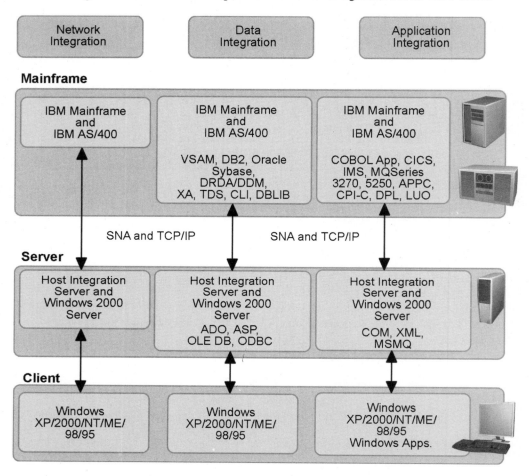

Host Integration Server 2000

Host Integration Server 2000 Documentation Resources

For more information on Host Integration Server 2000, see the following documents and Web sites:

Host Integration Server 2000 Documentation Resources

Document	Description	Location
Host Integration Server 2000 online books	Describe how to install, configure, maintain, and troubleshoot Host Integration Server 2000. Also includes the Host Integration Server 2000 *Programmer's Reference*.	The online books are included on the CD-ROM that contains Host Integration Server 2000
Host Integration Server 2000 product documentation on Microsoft TechNet Web site.	Product documentation available online.	http://www.microsoft.com/technet/host/hisdoc/default.asp
Host Integration Server 2000 Developer Resources	A guide that describes how to develop application-integration software, data-integration applications, and SNA applications. Also printer emulation, the development of link-support software, how to set up the client binaries and develop WMI applications for configuring and managing Host Integration Server 2000.	This can be found in the Microsoft Platform SDK, the Host Integration Server 2000 online books, and the Microsoft TechNet Web site.
Host Integration Server 2000 home page	Provides overview information Frequently Asked Questions page, pricing and licensing information, downloadable trial copies, and the Host Integration Server 2000 Developers Kit.	http://www.microsoft.com/hiserver
Host Integration Server 2000 Resource Kit with CD-ROM	Describes how to plan, install, maintain, and optimize Host Integration Server 2000. CDs include electronic copy of the book and tools, utilities, and sample code.	Microsoft Press (ISBN 0-7356-1182-3) Order online from http://mspress.Microsoft.com

Internet Security and Acceleration (ISA) Server 2000

Microsoft® Internet Security and Acceleration (ISA) Server 2000 provides firewall and caching features that organizations can use to secure their networks and improve network performance.

Using ISA Server 2000, organizations can implement security policies by configuring rules that specify which sites, protocols, and content can pass through the computer running ISA Server 2000. By monitoring requests and responses between the Internet and internal clients, ISA Server 2000 controls who can access specific computers on a corporate network. ISA Server 2000 also controls which computers on the Internet internal clients can access. The ISA computer or array of computers are located at the edge of the organization's network, which means they are well positioned to increase performance by caching data, whether this data is flowing from the Internet into the network or from the network to external clients.

The following points summarize the functionality of ISA Server 2000:

- **Security.** ISA Server 2000 includes a firewall service, application filters, a w3proxy Web proxy service, and Web (ISAPI) filters. The ISA firewall provides dynamic IP packet filtering, which evaluates packets, and Secure Network Address Translation (SecureNAT), which enables NAT clients to connect to the Internet through ISA Server 2000.

- **Caching.** ISA Server 2000 maintains a centralized cache of frequently requested Internet objects that all ISA Server 2000 clients can access. ISA Server 2000 also allows distributed content caching among multiple ISA Server 2000 hosts. Organizations can implement distributed caching with domain arrays, chains, or a combination of both.

- **Administration**. Administrators can configure ISA Server 2000 by using the ISA management tool or by invoking the ISA Server 2000 administration COM object through scripting.

The following illustration shows where ISA Server 2000 resides in a typical enterprise network.

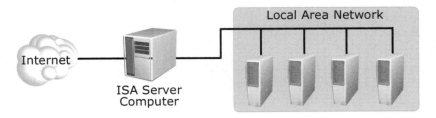

Internet Security and Accelerating Server 2000

Internet Security and Acceleration Server 2000 Documentation Resources

For more information about Internet Security and Acceleration Server 2000, see the following documents and Web sites:

ISA 2000 Documentation Resources

Document	Description	Location
Microsoft Internet Security and Acceleration (ISA) Server 2000 Software Development Kit	Describes how to configure ISA Server 2000 and how to how to extend it with custom application filters, Web filters, management tools, and user interface extensions. Also includes sample code.	You can find this guide in the Microsoft Platform SDK, or download it from http://www.microsoft.com/isaserver/techinfo/productdocumentation/2000/sdk.asp. It is also included on the CD-ROM that contains ISA Server 2000
Microsoft Internet Security and Acceleration Server 2000 on Microsoft TechNet Web site	Describe how to install, configure, maintain, and troubleshoot Microsoft ISA Server 2000.	http://www.microsoft.com/technet/isa/isadocs/default.asp
Microsoft Internet Security and Acceleration Server 2000 home page	Provides overview information, a product demonstration, pricing and licensing information, downloadable trial copies, and links to the ISA Server 2000 product documentation and Software Development Kit.	http://www.microsoft.com/isaserver/default.asp

SQL Server 2000

Microsoft® SQL Server™ 2000 consists of a family of components that satisfies the data storage and analysis requirements of the largest data processing systems and commercial Web sites. SQL Server 2000 offers:

- **SQL Server 2000 relational database engine** stores data in relational tables. Designed as a data-tier component for use in multi-tier applications, such as those built using Commerce Server 2000 or BizTalk Server 2000, the SQL Server 2000 relational database engine is capable of handling the data storage needs of the largest Web sites.

- **Microsoft SQL Server 2000 Analysis Services** provides tools for analyzing and mining the data stored in data warehouses and data marts. Analysis services aggregates and summarizes data into multidimensional cubes that can then be analyzed to yield critical business intelligence information. SQL Server 2000 Analysis Services also provides data mining capabilities. The data-driven analytical approach of data mining complements the model-driven analytical approach of OLAP.

- **SQL Server 2000 replication** enables copies of the same database on multiple computers to improve overall system performance, while at the same time keeping those copies synchronized. SQL Server 2000 can also replicate data to data warehouses, and to or from any data source that supports OLE DB access.

- **Data Transformation Services (DTS)** simplifies the process of extracting data from multiple OLTP systems and building it into an OLAP data warehouse or data mart. DTS works with any data source that can be accessed with OLE DB.

- **Microsoft Search Service** full-text search engine supports searches for words or phrases, words in close proximity to one another, and inflectional forms of verbs and nouns. Microsoft Search Service also supports searches that reference data in file systems outside of SQL Server 2000.

- **SQL Server 2000 English Query** gives developers and administrators the capability to turn their relational databases into English Query applications, which allow users to query the database by typing questions in English. The developer or end user does not need to know Structured Query Language (SQL).

- **Meta Data Services** provides a repository for storing, viewing, and retrieving descriptions of the objects in applications and systems. Companies can use Meta Data Services as a component of an integrated information system, a native store for custom applications that process meta data, or a storage and management service for sharing reusable models.

- **SQL Server 2000 administrative tools and wizards** enable administrators to:

  - Create, configure, and maintain databases and the objects within them, such as tables, views, and stored procedures.

  - Create, configure, and maintain data warehouses and data marts.

- Create and edit multidimensional cubes.

- Configure security by authorizing users to connect to an instance of SQL Server 2000 and view specific objects in databases and cubes.

- Work with data in databases and cubes, diagnose problems, monitor database performance, and audit user access.

Most of this functionality is of limited value until a company populates its databases and cubes with data and begins running applications that work with that data. The primary functionality of SQL Server 2000 is realized by running applications that use the data access mechanisms SQL Server 2000 supports.

This diagram is an illustration of the relationships between the major components of Microsoft SQL Server 2000.

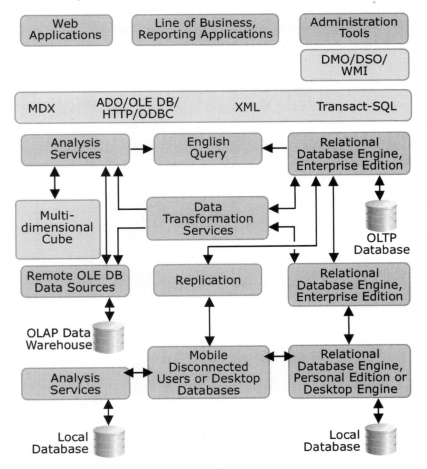

SQL Server 2000

SQL Server 2000 Documentation Resources

For additional information about SQL Server 2000, see the following documents and Web sites.

SQL Server 2000 Documentation Resources

Document	Description	Location
SQL Server 2000 Books Online	Describe how to install, configure, maintain, troubleshoot, and program SQL Server 2000 and Analysis Services.	http://msdn.microsoft.com/library/psdk/sql/portal_7ap1.htm. It is also included on the CD-ROM that contains SQL Server 2000
Microsoft SQL Server 2000 Resource Kit with CD-ROM	Describes how to plan, install, maintain, and optimize SQL Server 2000. CDs include a 120-day evaluation copy, electronic copy of the Resource Kit, selected topics from SQL Server 2000 books online, tools, utilities, and sample code.	Microsoft Press (ISBN 0-7356-1266-8). Order online from http://mspress.microsoft.com
SQL Server 2000 Home Page	A site that provides overview information about SQL Server 2000, technical resources, pricing and licensing information, downloadable trial copies of various versions of SQL Server 2000, and links to SQL Server 2000 product documentation, knowledge base articles, and white papers.	http://www.microsoft.com/sql
SQL Server 2000 Documentation on Microsoft TechNet Web site	The SQL Server 2000 Books Online.	http://www.microsoft.com/sql/techinfo/productdoc/2000/default.asp

Mobile Information 2001 Server

Microsoft® Mobile Information 2001 Server is the application server that extends the reach of Microsoft .NET Enterprise Servers, applications, enterprise data, and intranet content to the mobile user. It brings the corporate intranet to the latest generation of mobile devices, so users can securely access their e-mail, contacts, calendar, tasks, or any intranet line-of-business application in real time, wherever they happen to be. This overview addresses high-level information about Mobile Information 2001 Server.

- **Mobile-Enable the Enterprise**. Microsoft envisions a connected world, bringing mobile users and information together—any time, any place, and on any device. Mobile Information 2001 Server is the technology to accomplish this goal by connecting wireless applications and devices from multiple vendors and wireless carriers. Mobile Information 2001 Server integrates tightly with the Microsoft .NET Enterprise Servers and Microsoft Windows® 2000 Server to extend applications to multiple mobile devices.

- Enterprises demand carrier-class performance with high reliability, scalability, and performance. Mobile Information 2001 Server achieves this using clustering, replication, load balancing, and content delivery. In addition, Mobile Information 2001 Server provides secure and private wireless communications and data exchange by offering end-to-end security features for all wireless solutions.

The figure shows how Mobile Information Server fits into a corporate network.

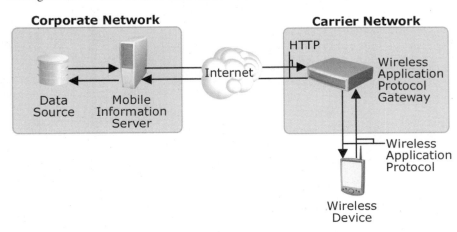

Mobile Information 2001 Server

- **Outlook Mobile Access**. The Outlook Mobile Access application that ships with Mobile Information 2001 Server, gives mobile users the same information they have using Microsoft Outlook in the office. Mobile users stay productive and efficient by using Outlook Mobile Access, which combines the freedom and convenience of wireless with the power of key enterprise information. Outlook Mobile Access is the mobile phone portal experience for browsing and receiving notifications from Outlook e-mail, calendar, tasks, and contacts. It extends the reach and utility of Microsoft Exchange 2000 Server.

- **Mobile Services and Solutions.** Mobile Information 2001 Server gives developers the ability to use their existing investment in the corporate intranet or a wire line computing solution by building connectors and services for any data server type or application. Developers can use existing skills and tools to create new wireless applications and content based on the highly extensible Mobile Information 2001 Server architecture. In addition, Mobile Information 2001 Server provides users with the ability to make the device that they already own become useful, by offering broad support for multiple mobile devices as well as flexibility for new generations of devices.

Mobile Information 2001 Server Documentation Resources

For additional information about Mobile Information 2001 Server, see the following documents and Web sites.

Mobile Information 2001 Server Documentation Resources

Document	Description	Location
Mobile Information 2001 Server books online	Describe how to install, configure, and maintain Mobile Information 2001 Server	It is also included on the CD-ROM that contains Mobile Information 2001 Server.
Mobile Information 2001 Server Home Page	Provides overview information, technical resources, pricing and licensing information, downloadable trial copies, and links to Mobile Information 2001 Server product documentation, knowledge base articles, and white papers.	http://www.microsoft.com/miserver
Mobile Information 2001 Server Documentation on Microsoft TechNet Web site		http://www.microsoft.com/technet/prodtechnol/mis/Default.asp

SharePoint Portal Server 2001

Microsoft® SharePoint™ Portal Server 2001 extends the capabilities of Microsoft Windows® and Microsoft® Office to organize, find, and share information. SharePoint Portal Server 2001creates corporate Web portals with document management, enterprise content indexing, and team collaboration features.

SharePoint Portal Server creates a Web portal known as the dashboard site. The dashboard site offers a centralized access point for finding and managing information. By using a browser to view the dashboard site, users can perform document management tasks and find information. The dashboard site allows users to:

- Browse through information by categories.

- Search for information.

- Subscribe to new or changing information.

- Check documents in and out.

- Review a document's version history.

- Approve documents for publication.

- Publish documents.

The dashboard site can provide access to information stored both inside and outside your organization, allowing users to find and share documents regardless of location or format. In addition, you can customize the home page of the dashboard site to display organizational news and other important information.

In addition to providing a default, organization-wide dashboard site, users can create customized personal dashboards to organize and present information that is especially relevant to them, such as project or workgroup-specific information. Users can add content to dashboards by creating Web Parts directly from Microsoft® Office XP or by importing Web Parts from a catalog.

SharePoint Portal Server 2001 Documentation Resources

For additional information about SharePoint Portal Server 2001, see the following documents and Web sites.

SharePoint Portal Server 2001 Documentation Resources

Document	Description	Location
SharePoint Portal Server 2001 books online	Describe how to install, configure, and maintain SharePoint Portal Server 2001.	It is also included on the CD-ROM that contains SharePoint Portal Server 2001.
SharePoint Portal Server 2001 Home Page	Provides overview information, technical resources, pricing and licensing information, downloadable trial copies, and links to SharePoint Portal Server 2001 product documentation, knowledge base articles, and white papers.	http://www.microsoft.com/ sharepoint
SharePoint Portal Server 2001 Documentation on Microsoft TechNet Web site		http://www.microsoft.com/technet/ /prodtechnol/sharepoint/ Default.asp

Summary

Information contained in this chapter was gathered from product documentation, product Web sites, Microsoft TechNet Web site, product resource kits and Microsoft Platform SDK.

These first three chapters provided the plan and scope of this book, an overview of the .NET framework, and a quick summary of the .NET Enterprise Server products. Now we turn to the major e-business scenarios. The following chapters provide you with conceptual information combined with some practical guidance for building solutions to common e-business problems.

PART TWO

Enterprise Application Integration

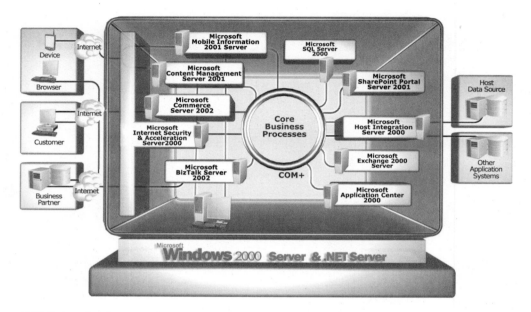

.NET Enterprise Servers

By Steven Baker

Integrating Applications into the Enterprise

In today's highly competitive business environment, organizations in all industries are challenged to be more productive with fewer resources. The move to integrate diverse applications within an organization is a response to this desire to do more with less. Enterprise application integration (EAI) is the term mostly commonly used to describe the process applied to integrating applications within a department, division, organization, or enterprise.

As companies have become more and more dependent on technology and computer systems for their business operations, the hardware resources and software applications used for operations have increased in number and variety. For most companies, the hardware and software systems used for business were procured over time. The computer hardware likely includes server and desktop products of various vintages and technologies from many different vendors. Similarly, the business software in use may include older legacy applications running on mainframes or minicomputers, client/server applications on UNIX and Windows systems, newer distributed applications based on components, and personal productivity software running on Windows desktop computers.

Most companies have already invested heavily in network and hardware infrastructure to allow any computer system within the organization to physically communicate with other computer systems. Enterprise application integration attempts to provide integration at the software level for all of the disparate applications used within an organization. These software applications are likely running on a variety of different operating systems and computer hardware. EAI also attempts to automate processes as much as possible, displacing manual user methods prone to error with software automation. The aims of this integration effort are to improve business performance and access to business information, while reducing administrative and operational costs. The objective is to create from these disparate software and hardware components the semblance of a single virtual enterprise application for users, operating as seamlessly as possible.

The Integration Challenge

For most companies of any size, the process of developing and implementing Enterprise application integration is a daunting task. The information technology (IT) infrastructure at most companies includes the following:

- A variety of different hardware platforms and operating systems

- Diverse software applications purchased over time

- Custom applications developed for specific purposes

- Packaged applications

Most organizations use a variety of hardware systems and software applications for critical business processes. Due largely to historical circumstances, these "back office" systems and applications represent purchases made over a considerable time, sometimes spanning several decades. This collage of software likely includes some packaged applications as well as custom applications developed in house or by vendors. Most custom applications were designed and built to accomplish a specific task well for a specific set of users, without much thought toward integration. These stovepipe systems, as they are often called, exist in most large organizations.

The applications used in an organization were likely built with different tools that leverage technologies available at the time. The mix of applications may include host applications running on IBM mainframes and minicomputers, distributed client/server applications, and newer component-based applications using distributed objects. The host applications may have been written in COBOL or PL/I to access transaction programs running on host computers and VSAM data files. Some of the client/server applications were written using proprietary fourth generation language (4GL) tools and C/C++ targeted at UNIX systems accessing a Relational Database Management System (RDBMS) using SQL. Others were based on Microsoft Visual C++ or Visual Basic and rapid application development (RAD) tools for accessing RDBMS systems such as Microsoft SQL Server on Windows. More recent applications based on distributed objects were written to operate using Microsoft's Distributed Component Object Model (DCOM), the Common Object Request Broker Architecture (CORBA), or the Java 2 Platform, Enterprise Edition (J2EE). DCOM, CORBA, and J2EE represent competing distributed object technologies. These distributed applications were developed using Visual Basic, C++, Java, or other languages. Internal web site development may include a number of scripted applications based on Visual Basic Scripting and Active Server Pages (ASP), JavaScript, Perl, Python, PHP, REXX, and the Common Gateway Interface (CGI) using UNIX shell scripts. Unfortunately, most of this software was not designed to easily integrate with other applications. For example, existing applications likely use a variety of different methods for authenticating users and providing appropriate levels of security and privacy for privileged data.

For most custom applications, it is likely that your organization has access to the source code for maintenance purposes. Integrating legacy applications may require changes to that source code, which can require extensive testing. Packaged software creates some significant additional problems. Without access to the source code and business logic (usually not an option for packaged applications), the primary options for integration are limited to those provided by the vendor.

In addition to back office applications, most organizations use a number of office productivity tools on desktop Windows or Macintosh computers as front office applications for email, document preparation, graphics, spreadsheets, small database applications, and other purposes. Very often, the information maintained in packaged desktop software applications grows over time to become critical to internal business processes and operations.

Acquisitions, mergers, and company reorganizations are only likely to have complicated this equation even more. Different companies or departments may well have followed very different development styles and cultures and used different technologies when implementing Information Technology (IT). For example, the finance division in one company was conservative and used host-based software on mainframes and minicomputers. In contrast, the human resources department may use software mostly on desktop Windows computers. Even for recent applications these differences are sometimes stark. For example, one company may have invested in custom applications based on DCOM and Visual C++, while another company may have based recent development on CORBA and Java. Now all of these software applications need to integrate with one another.

The following figure shows the requirements for increased communication across departments, along with the difficulty of integrating stovepipe application systems.

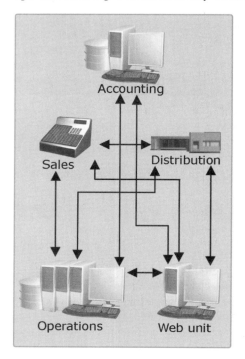

The chaos of applications in the enterprise

In hindsight, it is easy to say that these problems are a result of a lack of enterprise resource planning over time. But this is a vast simplification. When the core applications in some organizations were first developed a decade or two ago, who would have guessed that they would still be in use now. Last decade's developers could not have imagined and anticipated the distributed systems and distributed object technology we use today.

If money were no object, we would throw out all of the existing business software and start from scratch building applications using the latest and greatest technology so they can easily integrate. In the real world such a strategy is impossible (except for a few well-funded startups with no existing assets). Most organizations have made enormous investments in existing hardware and software that are too costly to replace anytime soon. These applications are essential for conducting business operations. Furthermore, company staff are trained and familiar with running business operations using these existing systems.

So, the challenge for EAI becomes accomplishing the integration process without requiring drastic changes to existing applications.

The Business Case for Integration

The benefits of integrating applications need to be worth the effort, given the cost and resources that are required. The business case for EAI is dependent on a thorough understanding of the business processes used in an enterprise. How do the current business processes used in your company or department function? Are there cases where users enter the same information into separate applications for different purposes? Would timely information from one application benefit another group of users and applications?

Some of the main benefits of enterprise application integration are to:

- Increase user productivity
- Reduce rates of error from redundant data entry
- Share timely information
- Provide a uniform interface for users

In most enterprises, it is quite common that some of the same information is entered into separate applications. Company personnel information is an example. Some of the same information is entered into the payroll system, human resource system, the business directory, and other software applications. Employees frequently change home addresses or have a name change. At a minimum, a change is needed in both the payroll system and human resources files. This information is possibly stored in various sales databases, organization charts, business directories, and emergency contact files. Since these are likely found in separate applications, this information is probably manually entered several times by different users. An employee is required to submit several separate forms (for example, one to payroll and one to human resources). An outcome from integrating these applications and automating this process is a reduction in forms processed and the staff time needed (increased productivity) accompanied by a reduction in accidental errors that are introduced and require correction.

Sales and manufacturing division information from the inventory system is easily shared to potentially boost sales and reduce manufacturing and inventory costs. Another benefit EAI can provide is building links for information sharing into existing applications. Some of these existing applications represent stovepipe systems that were adopted to meet a narrowly defined need in a department or division. Providing the semblance of an enterprise data store or data warehouse can facilitate information sharing.

EAI is also used as a mechanism to provide a more uniform look and feel (user experience) for diverse applications in an enterprise. Improving the user interface may well increase productivity, reduce errors, and reduce training costs. While providing some application consistency is generally not the primary reason to implement EAI, it is often a side effect of the process.

The costs and benefits of implementing EAI can vary dramatically based on the mix of existing applications and business processes currently in use. Companies and organizations differ. Some existing software applications are easier to integrate than others. For example, it is generally easier to integrate applications within a single operating environment (client/server applications in a distributed computing environment, for example) than within multiple software environments (the mainframe host environment, client/server, and distributed objects, for example). Companies that have been involved in mergers and acquisitions usually pose more difficult problems as a result of the complex, multiple environments that are likely to exist.

However, the potential benefits are usually greater in large enterprises with multiple environments. In these cases, EAI can provide substantial benefits precisely by reducing the amount of redundant information that is entered and by providing effective information sharing between applications.

EAI is often a prerequisite requirement for implementing business-to-business (B2B) applications. It makes little sense to embark on an aggressive plan to develop and deploy B2B processes if the existing internal applications lack integration.

Integration Approaches

A number of different approaches are successfully used for integrating applications. The differences between these types of EAI are based on where the integration occurs. The most common strategies and points of integration include the following:

- User interface

- Data sources

- Application Programming Interfaces (APIs)

- Business logic or methods

A plan for application integration within a company might well use several of these approaches as needed. Depending on the existing applications in use, some of these techniques are difficult or impossible.

Integration Using the User Interface

Business applications running on IBM mainframes and minicomputers continue to representative an enormous share of IT assets and business processes. These legacy applications remain in use because they still serve critical business functions well. Windows desktop computers running 3270 or 5250 emulation software typically provide the client and presentation layer.

The following figure shows integration based on the user interface, which represents the most primitive approach, used primarily with older legacy applications. For some host-based applications running on mainframes and minicomputers, the source code and development resources is no longer available. So the only point where integration can occur is through the user interface. Screen scraping is the only alternative for some older host applications until they are replaced.

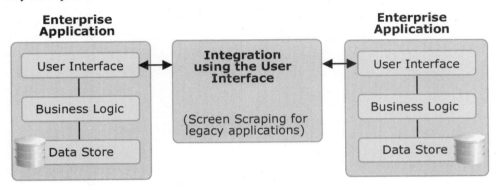

Integration based on the User Interface

Integration Using Data Sources

Integration based on using data sources takes advantage of the data store and data movement as the point of integration. Applications must store information in some form of persistent data store. Most recent applications, including many of the packaged software products, use a relational database system for this persistent data store. Older host-based applications may use Virtual Sequential Access Management (VSAM) files for the data store. Desktop productivity applications may use Windows or Macintosh database systems such as Microsoft Access, Microsoft FoxPro, or FileMaker Pro. Information is often extracted automatically from one data source, modified and transformed as needed to comply with business rules, and copied to other databases.

The reality of this concept is a bit challenging. In order to use data integration successfully, the structure of the metadata maintained in the application databases needs to be well understood. The database schema and the meaning of various data fields that are affected must be known. A simple update operation may require changes to several databases and many different tables. Sometimes, a limited understanding of the underlying business logic is necessary in order to comprehend all of the data fields that are affected by an operation.

To its advantage, the data integration approach is often less costly than more intrusive EAI methods. The tools and technologies needed for moving data between databases are well established and inexpensive compared with other EAI methods. The relational database products used for the data store often include the necessary features to support data movement and transformation. Since the existing applications are spared changes, the costs associated with modifying application source code, testing, and redeployment are avoided.

The following figure shows an overview of integration using data sources.

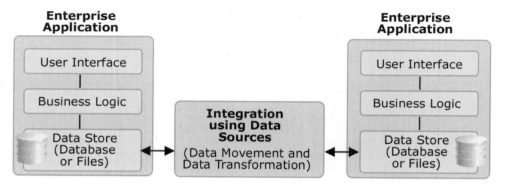

Integration using data sources

Integration Using Application Programming Interfaces

Integration at the Application Programming Interface (API) uses the interfaces provided by packaged and custom applications as the point of integration. Depending on the APIs exposed, access to business logic and processes are available as well as data. Developers can use these APIs to build glue between many applications so they can share business logic and data. This approach to EAI is most appropriate for large packaged applications containing complex business logic and complicated external database metadata that is undocumented or difficult to understand.

For example, SAP R/3 can use a number of external relational databases for its data store. But the database metadata is complex, making it difficult to integrate using just data sources without potentially jeopardizing the integrity of the SAP R/3 system. SAP provides a number of APIs that are used as the point of integration.

The primary drawback of this approach for packaged applications is that you are limited to what the vendor provides for APIs. Some packaged applications may expose rich interfaces that provide access to the complete business logic used internally. Other applications may only expose very limited interfaces that offer only access to data. Fortunately in order to stay competitive, most vendors are exposing more of the application logic through APIs for external use. While vendors may expose a number of APIs that are used for integration, it is often the case that these interfaces are of older design, complex to understand, and difficult to use correctly. For example, SAP traditionally exposed interfaces based on the Common Programming Interface for Communications (CPI-C), a legacy API used for program-to-program communications on IBM mainframes and minicomputers. While SAP now exposes other object-oriented interfaces for remote function calls, these other procedures may ultimately still call the older legacy APIs.

The following figure shows a conceptual overview of integration using APIs.

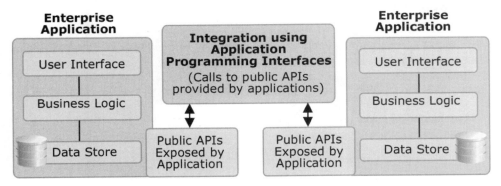

Integration using Application Programming Interfaces

Integration Using Business Logic

Integration based on using business logic or methods usually requires the most pervasive changes to existing applications. The goal is to share business logic that exists within the company. For example, updating information on customers probably occurs in several applications. Using shared business logic, a single method for updating customer information is shared by all applications that require this function. This strategy also simplifies maintenance and later updates. When changes are implemented to the business logic, the code only requires change in one place rather than in several separate applications. However, this power comes at a stiff price. All of the existing applications that need this feature would require modification to call the new shared method. As a consequence, this technique requires the most extensive changes to existing applications.

A number of approaches are available for implementing and hosting shared business logic. If a suitable method already exists within an application, it is possible in some cases to share this business logic by wrapping it as a distributed object using DCOM or CORBA. Then this business logic (object) can be called from other applications. An application server or transaction program (TP) monitor such as the Microsoft Distributed Transaction Coordinator (DTC) is used to host a repository of shared methods or business objects. The method is incorporated as part of a framework (the Microsoft .NET common language runtime, for example). Sharing methods is also based on using Web Services to host this business logic using the Simple Object Access Protocol (SOAP) for access.

The following figure shows an overview of integration using shared business logic and methods.

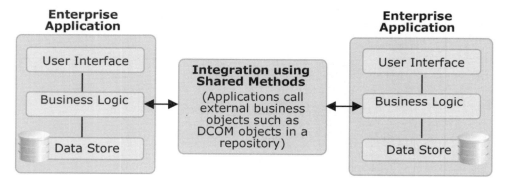

Integration using shared business logic and methods

Implementing Application Integration

Given the differences between the software assets and expertise in enterprises, it is inevitable that companies choose different approaches and implementation strategies for EAI. It is important to develop a well thought-out plan for implementing EAI that considers the costs and resources needed and the benefits that are accrued. A slow, methodical, piecemeal approach is most common, where applications are integrated gradually over time. It makes sense to single out some applications and use them as test cases in pilot programs to evaluate specific approaches, tools, and technologies.

The previous section about the different approaches to EAI implied the use of synchronous communication between existing applications. The image is that somewhere beneath the surface, the EAI components use some form of remote procedure call (RPC) to pass appropriate information from one application to others and participate in transactions when necessary. However, synchronous RPCs are not usually a requirement or even recommended for implementing many EAI strategies. Much of this sharing of information is handled effectively using asynchronous communication and messaging.

This process is illustrated by using personnel address information as an example. An employee needs to change home address information. A user enters this change into the primary application (perhaps this is the human resources system) that updates records in the primary data store for this system. Populating these changes to other applications such as the Payroll system probably does not need to be synchronous. The address in the Payroll system is most likely used twice a month or quarterly when checks are sent or W-2 forms are issued to employees. Some messaging or asynchronous process that guarantees updates to Payroll and other applications would work just as well, hence the popularity of message-oriented-middleware (MOM) and other messaging technologies as a tool for implementing EAI.

In other less common examples of EAI, synchronous behavior is a necessity. This is fortunate since a synchronous implementation would require that all participating applications run simultaneously and are able to communicate. For interactive use, this might require sub-second responses to meet design goals. It is possible that these applications operate on geographically dispersed systems by different divisions of the organization. Network outages, varying client loads, and other factors could well prevent a synchronous operation from completing successfully under these conditions.

While asynchronous communications is often the norm for EAI, it is still imperative that the messaging or other implementation strategies used can guarantee that the communication ultimately occurs successfully between applications. Consequently, transaction program (TP) monitors and other types of transactional middleware are often used to implement EAI.

Many of the technologies (traditional MOM and RPCs, for example) that are used to implement EAI represent point-to-point solutions. Changes in a particular human resources personnel database are integrated into a similar data store used by the Payroll system, for example. While this is a workable solution, keep in mind that as the numbers of these point-to-point connections increase (requiring configuration and maintenance), so does the complexity and brittleness of the EAI implementation. A more scalable approach in large enterprises is technologies such as publish and subscribe (for messaging) or a distributed object repository of shared business logic where far fewer point-to-point connections are configured and maintained.

The Extensible Markup Language (XML) is often discussed in the context of e-business applications. XML's greatest strength is that it provides a common text format for moving information between different businesses for B2B applications. While XML can and will undoubtedly be used as part of some EAI implementations, it offers much more to the B2B environment. In the context of EAI, the goal is accessing business logic and moving information between existing applications. It makes little sense to access this application information, format it as XML, move this information using some middleware layer, and then reformat the XML back to something the target applications can understand. Within the enterprise, the source and target applications should be well understood, mitigating the need for some common text format for this exchange. The middleware layer is already likely to provide and use some well-defined format for messaging or distributed object support. The cases where XML is useful in EAI implementations are where an existing application has better support for XML than any of the other points (external interfaces and metadata, for example) where integration can occur.

A large variety of products, tools, and technologies are used for implementing application integration. Various kinds of middleware are natural choices for the underlying technology for EAI. Middleware can provide the software infrastructure and glue to integrate separate applications while hiding the complexity of the process (different operating systems, APIs, and metadata, for example). As a solution for EAI, middleware is used more for its flexibility and power than for other features such as load balancing and scalability.

The middleware layer can use any of the following technologies:

- Remote Procedure Calls (RPCs)
- Messaging
- Data Access, Transformation, and Replication
- Transactional Support
- Components and Distributed Objects
- Application Frameworks

Consequently, a number of the middleware product categories are used for implementing EAI. These include message-oriented middleware (MOM), message brokers that support publish and subscribe, database middleware, transaction program monitors, application servers, and integration servers. Over time, many of the middleware products in these categories are evolving similar features to meet market demands.

A number of Microsoft products, tools, and technologies are used to implement EAI. Several of the .NET Enterprise Servers described in Chapter 3, "Overview of .NET Enterprise Servers," have a role to play in this process.

Note Separate Microsoft adapters are also available for BizTalk Server, providing access to IBM MQSeries messaging (Microsoft BizTalk Adapter for MQSeries) and SAP R/3 Systems (Microsoft BizTalk Adapter for SAP).

Some of the Microsoft technologies that are used in implementing EAI include the following:

Microsoft Technology	Use in EAI Implementations
.NET Framework common language luntime	Application framework, repository for distributed objects
Distributed Component Object Model (DCOM) and COM+	Distributed objects based on Component Object Model (COM)
COM Transaction Integrator for CICS and IMS (component of Host Integration Server 2000)	Distributed objects for accessing CICS and IMS transactions on IBM mainframes
Distributed Transaction Coordinator (DTC)	Transactional middleware
OLE DB Provider for SQL Server, Oracle, Access, FoxPro, and others (component of Microsoft Data Access Components)	Data access middleware (Windows and UNIX systems)
ODBC Drivers for SQL Server, Oracle, Access, FoxPro, and others (component of Microsoft Data Access Components)	Data access middleware (Windows and UNIX systems)

(continued)

Microsoft Technology	Use in EAI Implementations *(continued)*
OLE DB Provider for DB2 and ODBC Driver for DB2 (component of Host Integration Server 2000)	Data access middleware to DB2 systems on Windows, UNIX, AS/400, and IBM mainframes.
OLE DB Provider for AS/400 and VSAM (component of Host Integration Server 2000)	Data access middleware to AS/400 and VSAM files on AS/400 and IBM mainframes.
Data Transformation Services (component of SQL Server 2000)	Data movement and transformation supporting different data sources
Microsoft Message Queue (MSMQ)	Message-oriented middleware (MOM) on Windows and other platforms
MSMQ-MQSeries Bridge (component of Host Integration Server 2000)	Messaging to IBM MQSeries systems
AS/400 Data Queues	Messaging to AS/400 systems
BizTalk Messaging	Messaging, routing, and XML
Simple Object Access Protocol (SOAP) toolkit	Access to distributed objects using SOAP
Internet Information Server	Web service, FTP server, and SMTP server to support Web middleware and integration
Internet Explorer	Web browser for client presentation layer
Active Directory Services	Distributed directory and naming service
Host Security Integration (component of Host Integration Server 2000)	Single sign-on support on AS/400 and IBM mainframes
Advanced Program to Program Communications (APPC), Common Programming Interface for Communications (CPI-C), 3270 access (components of Host Integration Server 2000 SDK)	APIs to support programming on AS/400 and IBM mainframe computers

The Market for EAI

The demand for enterprise application integration by industry and government is growing rapidly. International Data Corporation (IDC) estimates that the market for EAI software reached $5 billion in 2000. IDC projections are that the market for EAI software will grow to over $54 billion by 2005, representing an average compound annual growth rate of 60%. These estimates for dramatic growth underscore the current and future demand for products and solutions targeted at implementing application integration in the enterprise.

Demand is strong for enterprise application integration because of the benefits to business that it promises: improved business performance and access to business information while reducing administrative and operational costs. The ambitious goal of EAI is to mold the software chaos that exists in most enterprises into the semblance of a single virtual application for users. This effort is still in its infancy, so there will be many lessons to learn. There will undoubtedly be many new products developed to target these challenges.

Illustrated in the following chapters are several common EAI scenarios likely to exist in many different companies and organizations. Each chapter is treated as a separate case study focused on using one of the EAI implementation strategies—data sources, application interfaces (APIs), or shared business logic and methods—to solve the highlighted integration problems. Each chapter illustrates how several existing Microsoft products and technologies are used together to solve the EAI challenge.

By Steven Baker

Integrating SQL Server with DB2

Most organizations have critical business data used by enterprise applications stored in a variety of databases and file systems. Furthermore, these data stores likely reside on a variety of computer and operating systems. Some of this system and data diversity may be from historical circumstances resulting from mergers and acquisitions. Some of this variety undoubtedly resulted from the gradual increase in computerized systems over time and the selection of different best-of-breed applications (and consequently an associated data store) for a particular purpose. In any case, it is not uncommon for large enterprises to have critical business data stored in Relational Database Management Systems (RDBMS) from different vendors, stored as host data in Virtual Sequential Access Management (VSAM) files on IBM mainframes or minicomputers, and stored in small database systems on personal computers using Microsoft FoxPro, Microsoft Access, or FileMaker Pro.

Now the charge is to use Enterprise Application Integration (EAI) to improve productivity and tie these disparate applications together into a more cooperative whole. The integration of data is a natural choice for many tasks. Data integration can bypass the necessity of making intrusive and costly changes to the existing application logic, user interface, or data structures.

Organizations often need to share business information among disparate applications. For example, custom reports, projections, and other analysis of sales or manufacturing data may be needed for making future business decisions. This critical sales and manufacturing data is often stored on host systems (IBM mainframe or IBM AS/400 systems) or on UNIX systems in a relational database management system. In fact, estimates are that the majority of corporate business data is still maintained on host systems. Yet the popular tools and personal productivity applications (Microsoft Word, Excel, and PowerPoint, for example) most commonly used to create custom reports and presentations run on the desktop. In some businesses, data used on the desktop for analysis and custom reporting may have to be manually entered from mainframe reports or files. So the challenge becomes integrating business applications using host data with productivity applications on the desktop. This application integration can enhance the options for custom reporting and analysis as well as eliminate costly and error-prone manual data entry. A popular approach for providing this integration bypasses the business applications and goes directly to the data source as the point of integration.

Microsoft provides a number of products and technologies that can be used to implement a data integration solution. Microsoft has developed two popular technologies that have become standards used for database middleware:

- Open Database Connectivity (ODBC)

- Object Linking and Embedding Database Providers (OLE DB)

Microsoft SQL Server 2000 and the older SQL Server 7.0 product include Data Transformation Services (DTS), a feature that can use ODBC Drivers or OLE DB Providers from Microsoft and other vendors to connect to heterogeneous database systems and transform and move data between systems. SQL Server also includes other features such as the Query Designer in Query Analyzer that make it relatively easy to analyze information and generate custom reports from the data stored in SQL Server.

A number of native ODBC drivers and OLE DB providers are included with SQL Server 2000 and with Microsoft Data Access Components (MDAC) on Windows. These OLE DB providers and ODBC drivers provide access to a variety of data sources including SQL Server, Oracle, Excel spreadsheets, Access databases, FoxPro/dBase database files, and flat text files. Microsoft Host Integration Server 2000 includes an OLE DB Provider for DB2 and an ODBC Driver for DB2 for accessing IBM DB2 on IBM mainframes, AS/400 computers, AIX, and Windows NT/2000 systems. A number of companies provide ODBC drivers and OLE DB providers for accessing other popular RDBMS and other database systems.

This chapter focuses on how these Microsoft products and technologies can be used together to provide a low cost data integration solution. This solution can be used for the simple task of generating custom reports and projections using desktop applications based on information in remote data sources. This solution can also be scaled and used for establishing a comprehensive data warehouse for online analytical processing (OLAP).

The chapter is divided into the following four sections:

- **Scenario**. This section describes the business problem to be solved in greater detail than the summary provided above.

- **Solution**. This section describes how Microsoft SQL Server 2000 Data Transformation Services in combination with ODBC drivers and OLE DB providers can be used to solve this business problem.

- **Tools and Technology**. This section focuses on the various tools and technologies involved in solving the business problem.

- **Implementation**. This section drills deeper into select portions of the implementation of the proposed solution, to give the reader a sense of the level of technical expertise required to implement the solution.

Scenario

How can an organization integrate personal productivity applications running on Windows used for custom reporting, analysis, and forecasting with relevant data from core business applications that operate on a variety of centralized or distributed systems? This business data may well be stored in several RDBMS systems such as Oracle, DB2, Informix, Sybase, or other popular database systems. The core applications could be used on an Intel-based server running Windows 2000, a RISC-based server running some version of the UNIX operating system (Sun Solaris, IBM AIX, HP-UX, SGI IRIX, Linux, or FreeBSD, for example), an IBM AS/400 system, or an IBM or compatible mainframe. In fact, critical business data in larger organizations is likely to be stored on several different hardware platforms and operating systems.

This is a general problem facing many organizations where a variety of computer information systems are in use. The challenge is to provide application integration as simply and inexpensively as possible. Companies have made very large investments in business applications over time. These software applications often manage critical business information and are essential for the operation of the department, division, or company. In addition, company staffs are trained on these systems and know how to use these business applications. It would be far too costly to replace these existing software applications in the near term. Integrating applications using the data sources can provide a low-cost way to provide application integration without making costly changes to these existing applications.

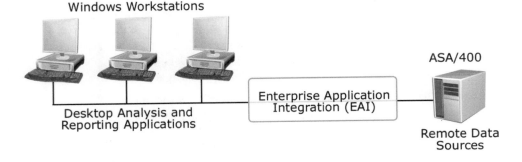

Integrating desktop reporting applications with remote data sources

To adequately understand the business problem and the solutions that is proposed in this chapter, it is important to review a number of related topics, including the database and operating systems involved, the interactions in question, and some of the different possible models for integration based on data transformation and movement.

In order to better focus our discussion and illustrate a conceptual solution, we assume that critical financial applications used by the sales department are running on an IBM AS/400 minicomputer using IBM DB2 for the data store. This scenario was chosen because it represents a common situation for many businesses involved in sales. Also, some of the issues raised related to data transformation from IBM DB2 systems are more difficult because of EBCDIC to ASCII and code page (language) conversions and the host data types supported by DB2.

For simplicity, this scenario assumes that the source of the data resides on a single RDBMS system running on a single AS/400 system. However, the discussion that follows would be just as applicable to an organization with several AS/400 systems running DB2 in many remote locations collecting data. In fact, this is often a common scenario for retail stores where each site uses a local AS/400 system and database to process local sales transactions. At some regular interval (each night or weekend, for example), the local data is migrated to a central data store.

The target for the data is a series of tables in an SQL Server database running on Windows 2000 Server. The Query Analyzer included with SQL Server 2000 can be used for generating custom queries from relevant business data for use in analysis, projections, and custom reports. SQL Server 2000 also includes English Query, which allows users to pose questions in English to create SQL queries. Desktop productivity applications such as Microsoft Word and Excel are able to easily import data from SQL Server for regular canned reports as well as custom reporting needs. The data can also be used in desktop graphics and presentation tools such as Microsoft PowerPoint for creating presentations.

This proposed scenario is a rather simple incremental approach using data integration to solve a specific EAI problem. It is a point-to-point solution where the data from a specific source location (or multiple source locations) is moved to a particular destination location for analysis and custom reporting. There are other more ambitious approaches using data integration that can provide a more comprehensive EAI solution, but at a much greater cost.

The concept of a "Federated Database" would allow all of the data (databases and data files) in an organization to be accessed using a single virtual database. The federated database would use database middleware to create the illusion of a single virtual database. Some of the tools and technologies discussed in this chapter could well be components of the database middleware used to create a federated database.

Several database vendors are promoting the concept of a "universal" database, a hybrid relational database of sorts that could handle text, audio, video, HTML, XML, objects, and other forms of data. This universal database would be able to meet the needs of all data in the enterprise. This universal database could be used to replace all of the existing data sources in the enterprise with a single huge database (that may well be physically implemented using parallel or distributed servers containing portions of the data, for example).

Obviously, EAI based on using a federated database or a universal database would be much more costly and time-consuming to plan, develop, implement, and maintain. Implementing a universal database, for example, would likely require changes to most applications in the enterprise. Yet a more comprehensive solution would also offer much greater benefits than the incremental point-to-point approach discussed in this chapter.

Understanding the Data

Application integration using data sources may sound simple, but first impressions can be deceiving. To use data sources effectively for integration, it is essential that EAI architects, developers, and administrators understand the database metadata and structures used by the underlying applications and how data flows. The metadata for the data sources must be well understood so that the appropriate fields are moved, transformed (when necessary), and interpreted correctly.

In the proposed scenario, the source of the data will be coming from DB2 tables on the AS/400. The metadata for the DB2 tables must be understood to identify the relevant fields used in analysis. It is only necessary to move data fields that are needed by the analysis and reporting applications on the desktop. The fewer database tables and columns of data from tables that need to be moved and transformed, the faster the process for data movement and transformation can proceed. The time required for this data movement and transformation may well limit the overall options for deployment and how frequently data can realistically be transferred.

Some of the data types supported by IBM DB2 are extensions to the SQL-92 standard (sometimes referred to as SQL-2) that most major database systems support. If these data types are used by the business applications in the DB2 tables, then columns in the tables will need to be mapped and transformed to appropriate data types supported by the destination data source, SQL Server 2000 in our example. For example, IBM DB2 supports several SQL data types listed below that may require mapping when transformed to other database systems such as SQL Server:

- BLOB - a binary large object
- CLOB - a large object containing single-byte character data
- DATE - Year, month, and day (the format for this data type in an RDBMS is often different)
- DBCLOB - a large object containing double-byte character data
- DECIMAL - a decimal number with fixed values for precision and scale
- GRAPHIC - a fixed-length string of double-byte characters (used to represent characters in some Asian languages)

- TIME - Hour, minute, and second (the format for this data type in an RDBMS is often different)

- VARGRAPHIC - a varying-length string of double-byte characters (used to represent characters in some Asian languages)

The GRAPHIC and VARGRAPHIC data types are specific to IBM DB2 and are for storing strings of double-byte characters used in several Asian languages. The large object types are not a part of the original SQL-2 standard. The BLOB and CLOB data types are included in the later SQL standards (often referred to as SQL-3) adopted by ISO in 1999 through 2001, but most database products are not yet conforming to these standards. Also, many database vendors used their own interpretation for the DATE and TIME SQL data types.

Understanding the Process

The destination application and process that uses the source data must also be understood. In our scenario, how often is there a need for analysis and custom reporting on the desktop? Are there times of the year (preceding quarterly reports, for example) when the demand for the latest data from sales or manufacturing is greater?

A decision needs to be made on how frequently data will be moved and transformed from the data source (IBM DB2 database tables) to the destination (SQL Server database tables). At what intervals do reports need to be generated? A common scenario is that this data movement happens once a day or once a week, usually occurring in the middle of the night or on weekends when the core business applications are shut down and the database is not involved with interactive use.

The frequency of data transfer can also be limited by the amount of data to move and transform and the amount of time this will take. In some organizations, the core business data may not be accessible from other applications for non-technical reasons during normal operating hours. System administrators may decide that concerns about the impact on response times for interactive users, database stability, and reliability issues justify making the DB2 or other RDBMS data off limits during normal or peak operating hours. Under these circumstances, data transfers may only be allowed when the critical interactive business applications are quiescent or off line for maintenance and batch operations.

It is often valuable to be able to support special one-time requests for analyzing the latest information for use in some special meeting and report. This may force data transfers to occur under less than ideal times.

Solution

Integration through the data sources makes it possible to provide application integration between heterogeneous systems. Using a database middleware layer, this integration can occur without making obtrusive and costly changes to the critical business applications. Data movement and transformation are well known technologies that can be used for this integration process.

In the proposed scenario, we will use ODBC or OLE DB for this database middleware layer. The Data Transformation Services (DTS) feature of SQL Server will be used for data transformation and movement between different data sources. DTS is a general-purpose tool for importing and exporting data between heterogeneous systems. DTS uses ODBC drivers and OLE DB providers to connect to heterogeneous systems to move and transform data. DTS is extremely flexible and is surprisingly fast. The DTS Import/Export Wizard included with SQL Server makes it easy to create a DTS package that is used to drive the process. All of the information needed for the data movement and transformation is stored in the DTS package. Using the DTS Wizard, it is easy to input and store any data type mappings or transformations that are needed. The DTS package can be stored in the SQL Server local repository, a metadata repository to be shared with other SQL Servers, or saved as a file accessible from Visual Basic. The DTS package can also be scheduled for later execution within the SQL Server scheduler.

For this scenario, we are assuming that the data sources exist as tables in an IBM DB2 database running on an AS/400 minicomputer used for core business applications. For simplicity, we will assume that only one AS/400 and DB2 data source is involved, but the scenario could just as easily be applied to multiple remote systems running DB2. The only difference would be that additional DTS packages would be required to access each different remote DB2 system. Host Integration Server 2000 includes the Microsoft ODBC Driver for DB2 and the Microsoft OLE DB Provider for DB2 that are needed to connect to DB2. Host Integration Server also provides the necessary network protocol support to connect to AS/400 and mainframe systems over either SNA or TCP/IP.

Many database administrators may be reluctant to allow access to the DB2 database containing critical business data from other applications that bypass the business application logic. In order to mitigate these concerns, the critical DB2 database and tables will not be accessed directly using DTS. The necessary information from DB2 will be copied to tables in a temporary (Temp) database (sometimes referred to as a staging table in the literature). DTS will only access these Temp or staging tables. These Temp tables will be generated automatically by the DB2 system when changes are made to the core data tables using triggers. These triggers can be considered special constraints placed on a database that can cause other events in DB2 to occur. In our scenario, a trigger will be created and attached to each core DB2 table that is to be made available to DTS. When the trigger event is activated by an insertion, deletion, or update of rows in a specific table, the change will be propagated to the Temp tables. Since SQL triggers are applied directly to the DB2 data tables, they do not require changes to the core business applications that use these data tables.

SQL Server can be used as the destination for the data movement, but this is not a requirement. The destination could just as well be an Oracle server or a series of Excel spreadsheets. The only requirement for using DTS is that the data source and destination can be accessed using an ODBC driver or OLE DB provider. In the proposed scenario, we will target an SQL Server database as the destination for the data. The destination SQL Server where the data is to be moved could be on the same Windows system where the DTS packages will be run or on a remote SQL Server somewhere in the enterprise. We will assume for simplicity that the destination SQL Server is same computer where the DTS packages will be run.

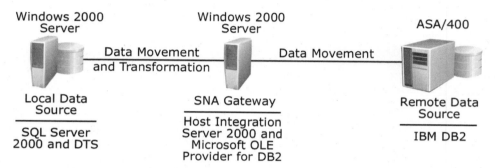

Using DTS for data transformation and movement

Once the data is transformed and moved into the SQL Server database, it can be accessed for analysis and reporting using a variety of methods including the following:

- SQL Server Query Analyzer (to build custom queries)

- English Query (to translate questions in English to SQL queries)

- SQL Server Analysis Services (to provide integrated and web-enabled analysis services using OLAP

- Excel import using the OLE DB Provider for SQL Server or the ODBC driver for SQL Server

- Visual Basic programs and Visual Basic for Application (VBA) scripts

- Data Transformation Packages that export the portions of the data to Excel spreadsheets for manipulation

Tools and Technologies

To implement the data integration solution using the Microsoft technologies described in this chapter, the following .NET Enterprise Server products are required:

- Microsoft® SQL Server™ 2000

- Microsoft® Host Integration Server 2000

SQL Server 2000 provides the Data Transformation Services (DTS) feature used for data transformation and movement between the data stores. DTS can use ODBC or OLE DB to connect to heterogeneous data sources. SQL Server can also be used as the repository for the data transformed and moved from the remote IBM DB2 system.

Host Integration Server 2000 provides the core networking connectivity over SNA or TCP/IP to AS/400 and mainframe systems as well as the Microsoft ODBC Driver for DB2 and the Microsoft OLE DB Provider for DB2.

Windows 2000 Server (Server, Advanced Server, or DataCenter Server) is a required prerequisite for installing SQL Server 2000 and Host Integration Server 2000. SQL Server 2000 and Host Integration Server 2000 can also be installed on Windows NT 4.0 with Service Pack 6a. However, Windows 2000 supports a number of new features that make it preferred.

Developers working on an implementation of this data integration scenario are likely to require Microsoft Visual Studio for any custom programming. The latest version, Microsoft Visual Studio .NET, released in February of 2002, is needed for development if new features such as the .NET Framework and managed code will be used. However, the older version of Visual Studio 6.0 can also be used for development, since the .NET Framework is not required in the implementation that is discussed in this chapter. Compared with many of the different scenarios discussed in this book, the data integration solution discussed in this chapter can be implemented with minimal programming.

This scenario assumes that critical business applications are running on an AS/400 computer using IBM DB2 for the data store. DB2/400 comes integrated as part of the OS/400 operating system for the AS/400 hardware platforms. With minor changes, this same scenario could be used with business applications on other platforms using DB2 as the data store.

IBM implements DB2 using the IBM Distributed Relational Database Architecture (DRDA). DRDA enables customers to access remote, distributed database systems across hardware platforms. DRDA supports most dialects of the Structured Query Language (SQL) for access to relational database management systems. IBM and other software vendors have implemented DRDA support into database systems, such as IBM DB2, and database tools on a wide range of operating systems. DRDA is an open, published, and widely supported protocol, which requires no additional license for development. This makes DRDA appealing to independent software vendors (ISVs), solution providers and large corporate development groups, as well as their customers.

Host Integration Server 2000 includes the following features for connecting with DB2 systems:

- Microsoft ODBC Driver for DB2
- Microsoft OLE DB Provider for DB2

Both the ODBC Driver for DB2 and the OLE DB Provider for DB2 included with Host Integration Server 2000 are implemented as an IBM DRDA application requester, which means it connects to popular DRDA-compliant DB2 systems.

The Microsoft OLE DB Provider for DB2 and the Microsoft ODBC Driver for DB2 can access the following DB2 systems through SNA LU 6.2 using Microsoft Host Integration Server 2000:

- DB2 for MVS Version 4 Release 1 (V4R1) or later
- DB2 for OS/390 Version 5 Release 1 (V5R1) or later
- DB2 for OS/400 (DB2/400) Version 3 Release 2 (V3R2) or later

The Microsoft OLE DB Provider for DB2 and the Microsoft ODBC Driver for DB2 can access the following DB2 systems directly using TCP/IP:

- DB2 for OS/390 Version 5 Release 1 (V5R1) or later
- DB2 for OS/400 (DB2/400) Version 4 Release 2 (V4R2) or later
- DB2 Universal Database for Windows NT Version 5 Release 2 (V5R2) or later
- DB2 Universal Database for AIX Version 5 Release 2 (V5R2) or later

Note that DB2 for OS/400 (DB2/400) Version 4 Release 3 (V4R3) requires that PTF SF99103 be applied. DB2 for OS/400 (DB2/400) Version 4 Release 4 (V4R4) requires that PTF SF99104 be applied.

IBM DB2 with DRDA support is available on a variety of other platforms. The OLE DB Provider for DB2 has not been tested with these other implementations.

The latest version of DB2 available at the present time is DB2 Universal Database Version 7.2 released by IBM in June 2001 for a number of platforms (Windows and UNIX). Note that one of the options proposed for implementation of this data integration scenario is based on using SQL triggers, a feature added in IBM DB2 Universal Database Version 6.0 and later. On the AS/400, these features were added with the release of DB2 Universal Database for OS/400, included as part of the OS/400 operating system in Version 5 Release 1. Prior to OS/400 V5R1, SQL triggers were not supported but system triggers could be used. System triggers are external programs written in RPG, COBOL, or ILE C that are attached to a physical or logical file that trigger on file system changes. Since DB2 tables are implemented as part of the file system on OS/400, system triggers can be used to implement the same effects as SQL triggers.

Implementation

Proper planning and design is essential to any enterprise application integration effort. Once a plan has been developed and adopted, then the implementation process can begin. The data integration solution proposed in this chapter can be accomplished with minimal or no programming. In fact, the challenge of this solution for implementers is the complex configuration of products and features required. This lack of the need for extensive programming is one of the inherent advantages of data integration in many EAI scenarios. So, most of the following discussion is focused on various issues and configuration details.

In order to implement the data integration solution described in this chapter, the following steps are required:

1. Install and configure the prerequisite hardware and software.

2. Prepare the IBM DB2 database and tables on the AS/400 for access.

3. Create the SQL Server Data Transformation (DTS) packages.

4. Schedule the DTS package to be run at specified dates and times or intervals.

These high-level tasks can be further broken down into sets of subtasks that will likely include some level of testing and evaluation.

This section provides some implementation details on these various tasks and points out issues to consider, particularly configuration options. We begin with a discussion on installing and configuring the prerequisite software.

Variations on a Model Solution

The Microsoft software to be installed and configured includes the Windows 2000 operating system, Host Integration Server 2000, and SQL Server 2000. The Microsoft OLE DB Provider for DB2 needed for connecting to IBM DB2 is included as part of Host Integration Server 2000. The OLE DB Provider for DB2 can be installed on Host Integration Server 2000 server computers as well as on Host Integration Server 2000 client systems. The model solution that will primarily be discussed in this section assumes that SQL Server 2000 and Host Integration Server 2000 will be installed on the same computer running some version of Windows 2000 Server software (Server, Advanced Server, DataCenter Server).

Host Integration Server 2000 provides core SNA gateway functions as well as data and application integration features such as the OLE DB Provider for DB2. The Host Integration Server 2000 server system can communicate with the AS/400 system using the System Network Architecture (SNA) protocols.

For this scenario, we assume that the Host Integration Server 2000 is to be installed on the same system as SQL Server 2000 so that the Microsoft OLE DB Provider for DB2 can be used with SQL Server Data Transformation Services.

Host Integration Server 2000 includes two clients for connecting to the server:

- End-User Client - The standard Host Integration Server 2000 client provides connectivity to the Host Integration Server 2000 Server SNA gateway, data access and application integration features. The End-User Client can operate on Windows 95, Windows 98, Windows Millennium Edition, Windows NT 4.0, Windows 2000, and Windows XP (Professional and Home Edition).

- Administrator Client - An enhanced Host Integration Server 2000 client that includes the capabilities of the End-User Client plus additional features. The enhancements include the ability to remotely manage Host Integration Server 2000 servers and the ability to run SNA transaction programs as services. The Administrator client can operate on Windows NT, Windows 2000, and Windows XP Professional.

Although it is not essential for the proposed scenario, it is useful to install the Host Integration Server 2000 Administrator Client on any computers running Windows 2000 Professional or Windows NT 4.0 Workstation that are used for administration. The Host Integration Server 2000 Administrator Client can be used to remotely configure and manage Host Integration Server installations.

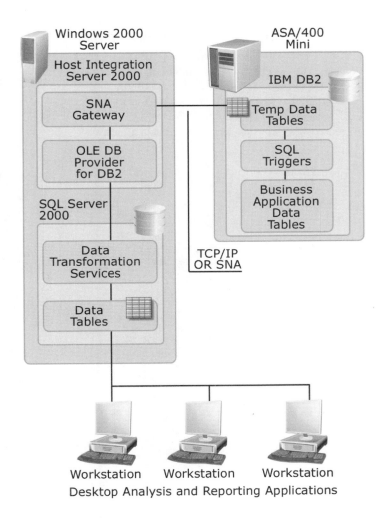

EAI solution combining servers for data transfer

Other model variations are possible for implementation. For sites with heavier data movement loads, it is possible to install Host Integration Server 2000 and SQL Server 2000 on a separate computer running Windows 2000 Server. For sites where the load from desktop users accessing data for analysis is more excessive and would impact data movement and transformation from DB2, it may make sense to use separate Windows 2000 Servers running instances of SQL Server 2000. Some SQL Server 2000 systems would be used primarily for data movement and transformation using DTS from the IBM DB2 system. Other SQL Server 2000 systems would be used as the local repository or data store for the data after it is transformed.

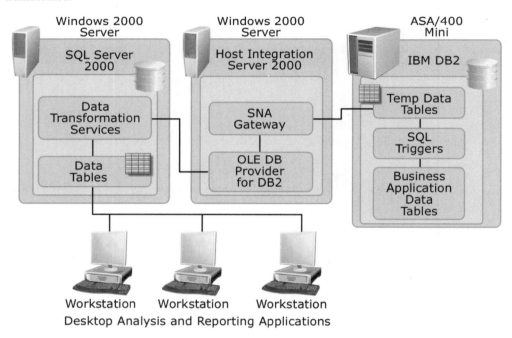

EAI solution for intensive data transfer

In internal testing at Microsoft using SQL Server 2000 DTS technology and Host Integration Server 2000 with the Microsoft OLE DB Provider for DB2, SQL Server 2000 and DTS were found to be the limiting factor for performance. Based on this testing on straight data movement tasks, three computers running SQL Server 2000, DTS packages, and the OLE DB Provider for DB2 were required to saturate the network capacity of a single instance of Host Integration Server operating as a SNA gateway. With the addition of data transformation to the SQL Server DTS workload, even more instances of SQL Server 2000 would likely be required to saturate the capacity of a single Host Integration Server.

Note that if communication to the AS/400 system uses TCP/IP rather than the SNA protocols, then the OLE DB Provider for DB2 can connect directly to the AS/400 system without using the Host Integration Server 2000 server system as a gateway. The choice of which protocol is used to connect with the AS/400 is often based on other considerations, such as security and support for transactions (which would favor SNA). In internal testing at Microsoft, DTS performance using the OLE DB Provider for DB2 was about 10% faster using SNA rather than TCP/IP. However, it is always best to run your own tests to better reflect the results for your particular environment, network infrastructure, and problems.

Windows 2000 Server and SQL Server Editions

The Windows 2000 Server family is available in several different versions differentiated by the maximum number of CPUs supported, maximum memory supported, and other features:

- Windows 2000 Server supports a maximum of 4 CPUs and 4 GB of memory.

- Windows 2000 Advanced Server supports a maximum of 8 CPUs and 8 GB of memory along with failover clustering and network load balancing. .

- Windows 2000 DataCenter Server supports a maximum of 32 CPUs and 64 GB of memory along with failover clustering and network load balancing.

Windows 2000 Advanced Server and Windows DataCenter Server include support for failover clustering and TCP/IP network load balancing that are lacking from Windows 2000 Server.

Similarly, SQL Server 2000 is available in two editions differentiated by the maximum number of CPUs supported, maximum memory supported, and other features:

- SQL Server 2000 Standard Edition supports a maximum of 4 CPUs and 4 GB of memory

- SQL Server 2000 Enterprise Edition supports a maximum of 8 CPUs and 8 GB of memory when installed on Windows 2000 Advanced Server and a maximum of 32 CPUs and 64 GB of memory when installed on Windows 2000 DataCenter Server. The Enterprise Edition also supports failover clustering and other enhanced features.

In contrast, Host Integration Server 2000 is available in a single version that can be run on any of the Windows 2000 Server family products.

The choice of which version of Windows 2000 Server and SQL Server 2000 to install should be based on the anticipated work loads and the numbers of users to be supported. If failover clustering or network load balancing is desired, then Windows 2000 Advanced Server or Windows 2000 DataCenter Server will be required with SQL Server 2000 Enterprise Edition.

Since data movement tends to be an intensive input/output task, adding more CPUs may not provide the consequent increase in performance expected. It may make more sense to add additional network cards to separate network communication with the AS/400 host computer using Host Integration Server from local network access to the SQL Server by desktop computers.

Installing and Configuring Software

In order to configure and use SQL Server Data Transformation Services, the OLE DB Provider for DB2 must already be installed and data sources configured. A normal progression for installation and configuration would be the following:

1. Install and configure Host Integration Server 2000.

2. Configure data sources for the Microsoft OLE DB Provider for DB2.

3. Prepare the IBM DB2 database and tables on the AS/400 for access.

4. Install and configure SQL Server 2000.

5. Create the SQL Server Data Transformation (DTS) packages.

6. Schedule the DTS package to be run at specified dates and times or intervals.

The installation of Host Integration Server 2000 and SQL Server 2000 are tasks that we will skim over. Detailed installation information is found in the product documentation. We will focus more on configuration issues since these are more challenging.

Configuring Host Integration Server

Once Host Integration Server 2000 is installed, link services need to be configured to connect with the AS/400 host. For connectivity using Ethernet or Token Ring hardware using the SNA protocols, the Data Link Control (DLC) protocol must be installed as part of Windows 2000 networking components. Other supported connection options include using X.25, Serial Data Link Control (SDLC), and other link services.

The SNA Manager is used to configure link services and create logical units (LUs) for connecting over SNA. A local LU for Advanced Program-to-Program Communications (APPC) must be configured on Host Integration Server to connect to a remote APPC LU configured on the AS/400 system. These APPC LUs can be considered as endpoints for conversations needed for this scenario using the SNA protocols.

Host Integration Server 2000 supports the concept of multiple servers running Host Integration Server working together in an SNA subdomain to provide core SNA gateway, application, and data services. Using multiple Host Integration Server 2000 servers offers enhanced reliability and failover capabilities. The member computers and users in an SNA subdomain can be different from those in a Windows 2000 domain. Host Integration Server supports two roles for servers to provide. One system is designated as the primary server and up to 14 other systems can be configured as backup servers. Backup servers replicate the configuration information from the primary server. The primary and backup servers can be configured to share application loads among the different servers. The SNA Manager application installed on the Host Integration Server 2000 servers is used to configure and manage Host Integration Server systems.

To provide enhanced reliability, SNA Manager allows LU pools to be created for use by applications. LU pools provide greater reliability allowing any LU from the LU pool to be used in a conversation. Consequently, LU pools are preferred for this implementation. The configuration process requires that local APPC LUs be defined and configured as well as the remote APPC LUs that reside on the AS/400 system. The SNA Manager used for configuring and managing Host Integration Server 2000 includes an AS/400 Wizard designed to easily create connections to AS/400 systems. This wizard walks users through the process of creating the necessary remote and local APPC LUs. The AS/400 Wizard can be invoked from the **Action** menu by selecting **All Tasks,** which will display this option. The **All Tasks** list of options can also be invoked by right-clicking the mouse on most of the items in the left pane tree view.

For this scenario, Host Integration Server 2000 is installed on the Windows 2000 system where SQL Server is installed. The Host Integration Server system should be designated as the primary server. The data integration features should be selected so the Microsoft OLE DB Provider for DB2 will be installed.

The Host Integration Server 2000 Administrator Client can also be used to remotely administer primary and backup Host Integration Server 2000 server systems. These administration capabilities include the ability to completely manage and configure remote Host Integration Server 2000 servers, including creating the APPC LUs needed in this scenario.

Configuring Data Sources for the OLE DB Provider for DB2

Microsoft OLE DB Provider for DB2 requires that data source information must be configured for any DB2 system that is to be accessed. A few default parameters are used when these parameters are not configured for each data source, but most parameters used for making connections to a specific DB2 system need to be configured.

The Microsoft Data Links, a core element of the Microsoft Data Access Components, provides a uniform method for creating file-persistent OLE DB data source object definitions in the form of Universal Data Link (UDL) files. Applications, such as the SQL Data Transformation Services used in this scenario, can open created UDL files and pass the stored initialization string to the OLE DB Provider for DB2 at run time.

UDL files are normally stored in a special system folder located at
`C:\Programs Files\Common Files\System\Ole DB\data links`

In order to use Microsoft OLE DB Provider for DB2 with an OLE DB application such as SQL Server DTS, the user must either (1) create a Microsoft data link (UDL) file and call this from the application, or (2) call the OLE DB provider from within the application using a connection string that includes the provider name ("DB2OLEDB") and any other needed parameters. For use in this scenario, we illustrate how to create a UDL file that can be used by DTS.

Creating Data Links for the OLE DB Provider for DB2

Host Integration Server 2000 includes a utility program (NewSNADS.exe) that enables users to easily create or modify data links. This tool is installed in the **System** folder below the subdirectory where Microsoft Host Integration Server 2000 is installed. This tool is installed in the following default location:
C:\Program Files\Host Integration Server\system\NewSnaDS.exe

A shortcut for this tool is added to the **Programs** menu under the
Host Integration Server\Data Integration folder with a name of **OLE DB Data Sources**. This shortcut is created when Microsoft Host Integration Server 2000 or the Host Integration Client 2000 is first installed and support for data access is selected.

A shortcut entitled the **OLE DB Data Source Browser** is also added to the **Programs** menu in the **Host Integration Server\Data Integration** folder. This shortcut opens Windows Explorer in the default directory where UDL files are stored:
C:\Programs Files\Common Files\System\Ole DB\data links

To create a new UDL file, run the NewSnaDS tool. Once a UDL file has been created using the NewSnaDS tool, the file can be changed to a more appropriate name and copied to other computers for use with the OLE DB Provider for DB2.

Configuring Data Links for the OLE DB Provider for DB2

The NewSnaDS tool can be used to open and modify an existing UDL file. Once a Data Link file is selected, the **Data Link Properties** dialog box appears with several property tabs:

- Provider
- Connection
- Advanced
- All

The properties of a Data Link file can also be edited using Windows Explorer by a right-clicking the mouse on the UDL file and selecting **Properties**. A **Properties** dialog box appears with the above OLE DB property tabs plus additional **General**, **Security**, and **Summary** tabs that provide access to standard file information (file location, file type, file size, file dates, file security permissions for access, etc.). The **General** tab has a text box with the name of the Data Link. This filename must end with the .UDL extension if the file is to be recognized as a Data Link file. Note that the **Security** and **Summary** tabs are available on NTFS files systems, not on the older FAT file systems. The **Provider**, **Connection**, **Advanced**, and **All** tabs provide access to the Data Link properties that need to be configured to connect to the DB2 system.

The Provider Tab

The **Provider** tab enables you to select the OLE DB provider (an alias to the provider name string) to use in the UDL file from a list of possible OLE DB providers. Select the Microsoft OLE DB Provider for DB2. The parameters and fields displayed in the remaining tabs (**Connection**, **Advanced**, and **All**) are determined by the OLE DB Provider that is selected.

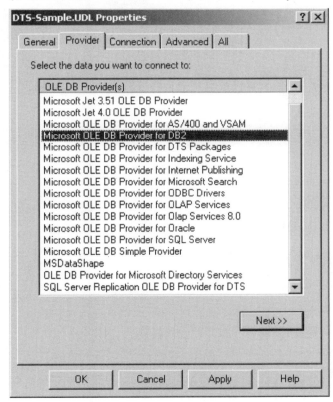

The Connection Tab

The **Connection** tab enables you to configure the basic properties required to connect to a data source. In the proposed solution, we will be connecting to the IBM DB2 system with the data tables that are to be accessed. The **Connection** tab dialog contains several sections:

- Data source and Network connectivity

- Authentication

- Database Properties

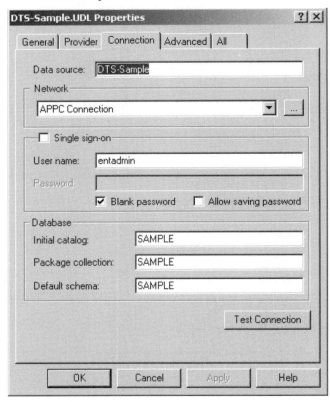

For the Microsoft OLE DB Provider for DB2, the **Connection** tab includes the following properties for Data source and Network connectivity values:

Property	Description
Data source	The data source is a property that can be used to describe the data source. Any descriptive text can be used.
Network	This drop-down list box allows selecting the type of network connection to be used. The allowable options are **APPC Connection** or **TCP/IP Connection**.
	If **APPC Connection** is selected (using SNA LU 6.2), click the **More Options** (…) button to open a dialog box for configuring APPC network settings. The properties you can configure include: the APPC local LU alias, the APPC remote LU alias, and the APPC mode name used for communication with the host. The default value for the APPC mode normally defaults to QPCSUPP. The local and remote LU alias fields do not have default values. The APPC mode name can be selected from the drop-down list box.
	If **TCP/IP Connection** is selected, click the **More Options** (…) button to open a dialog box for configuring TCP/IP network settings. The properties you can configure include the IP address of the DB2 host (or a hostname alias for this computer) and the Network Port (TCP/IP port) used for communication with the host. The default value for the Network Port is 446. The IP address of the host has no default value.

In the proposed scenario using SNA to connect to the AS/400 system, we are selecting an APPC Connection. This option requires that values be selected for the local APPC LU, remote APPC LU, and the APPC mode from drop-down lists. The local and remote APPC LUs should correspond with the values configured in Host Integration Server for connection with the remote AS/400 system. The APPC mode specifies the mode of communication used over SNA for this connection. The APPC mode for a Data Link defaults to the default value specified for SNA connections in Host Integration Server 2000. In most cases, it is unnecessary to change this value from the default of QPCSUPP.

For the Microsoft OLE DB Provider for DB2, the **Connection** tab includes the following properties for authentication information:

Property	Description
Single sign-on	Click this checkbox to enable using the Host Integration Security features providing a single sign-on to access this OLE DB data source. Note that single sign-on is only supported using the APPC Connection option (SNA LU 6.2). When this checkbox is selected, the **User name** and **Password** fields are unavailable. The **User name** and **Password** fields are set based on the login name used for the Windows 2000 domain login. When this checkbox is not selected, the **User name** and **Password** fields must normally contain appropriate values in order to access data sources on hosts.
User name	A valid User name and Password are normally required to access data sources on a host. These values are case-sensitive. Users must not check the **Single sign-on** option if a specific User name and Password are to be entered.
Password	A valid User name and Password are normally required to access data sources on hosts. These values are case-sensitive. The **Blank password** checkbox is only applicable for a Test Connection. In order to enter a password, the user will need to clear the **Blank password** check box if it is checked. If **Blank password** is checked, then a Test Connection with a blank password will not cause the OLE DB Provider to prompt for a password. Optionally, users can choose to save the password in the UDL file by clicking the **Allow saving password** check box. Users and administrators should be warned that this option saves the authentication information (password) in plain text within the UDL file.

The AS/400 requires that the **User name** and **Password** properties be in uppercase. When connecting to DB2/400, these parameters must be passed as uppercase strings. When connecting to DB2 on IBM mainframes, the **User name** and **Password** parameters can be in mixed case.

In the proposed scenario, it is possible to connect using a specific User name and Password defined in DB2 on the AS/400 system or use the single sign-on feature (often referred to as integrated Windows security). If a specific DB2 user name and Password is to be used, this information will likely need to be saved into the UDL file since this Data Link needs to be used with Data Transformation Services as part of a scheduled process. The user name and Password are saved in clear text in the UDL file. In this case, for security reasons it is imperative that the UDL file be protected with an Access Control List (ACL) that restricts access to all but system administrators. Saving the user name and Password also forces this UDL file to be updated whenever the Password associated with the user name is changed. So for a variety of reasons, specifying a User name and Password is not the preferred authentication option.

Single sign-on is the preferred authentication option, but this will require that the user account under which the DTS package will run must have the same User name and Password in the Windows domain as the remote DB2 database on the AS/400 system. Note that on most AS/400 systems, the User name and Password must be in uppercase.

For the Microsoft OLE DB Provider for DB2, the **Connection** tab includes the following properties for database property values:

Property	Description
Initial catalog	This OLE DB property is used as the first part of a 3-part fully qualified table name.
	In DB2/400, this property is referred to as RDBNAM. The RDBNAM value can be determined by invoking the WRKRDBDIRE command from the console to the OS/400 system. In DB2 Universal Database, this property is referred to as DATABASE.
	This is a required property and must not be blank.
Package collection	The name of the DRDA target collection (AS/400 library) where the Microsoft OLE DB Provider for DB2 should store and bind DB2 packages. This could be same as the Default Schema.
	The Microsoft OLE DB Provider for DB2 uses packages to issue dynamic and static SQL statements. Package names are not restricted and can be upper case, lower case, or mixed case.
	This is a required property and must not be blank.

(continued)

Property	Description *(continued)*
Default schema	The name of the Collection where the OLE DB Provider for DB2 looks for catalog information. The Default Schema is the "SCHEMA" name for the target collection of tables and views. The OLE DB Provider uses Default Schema to restrict results sets for popular operations, such as enumerating a list of tables in a target collection.
	For DB2/400, the Default Schema is the target COLLECTION name. For DB2 Universal Database (UDB), the Default Schema is the SCHEMA name.
	If the user does not provide a value for Default Schema, then the OLE DB Provider uses the USER_ID provided at login. Obviously, this default is inappropriate in many cases. Therefore, it is essential that the Default Schema value in the data source be defined.

For the proposed scenario, the Initial Catalog should contain the value of the RDBNAM or DATABASE on the remote DB2 system. The Default Schema may often be the same value as the Initial Catalog.

The OLE DB Provider will create DB2 packages dynamically in the location to which the user points using the Package Collection property. By default, the OLE DB Provider will automatically create one package in the target collection, if one does not exist, at the time the user issues the first SQL statement. The package is created with GRANT EXECUTE authority to a single <AUTH_ID> only, where AUTH_ID is based on the User ID value configured in the data source. The package is created for use by SQL statements issued under the same isolation level.

A problem can arise in multi-user environments. For example, if a user specifies a Package Collection value that represents a DB2 collection used by multiple users, but this user does not have authority to GRANT execute rights to the packages to other users (e.g., PUBLIC), then the package is created for use only by this user. This means that other users may be unable to access the required package. The solution is for an administrative user with package administrative rights to create a set of packages for use by all users.

The OLE DB Provider for DB2 ships with a program for use by administrators to create packages. The crtpkg.exe tool is a Windows GUI application for use by the administrator to create packages. This tool can be run using a privileged User ID to create packages in collections accessed by multiple users. This tool will create a set of packages and grant EXECUTE privilege to PUBLIC for all users. Once created, the packages are listed in the DB2 for OS/400 QSYS2.SYSPACKAGE, and the DB2 Universal Database (UDB) SYSIBM.SYSPACKAGE catalog tables.

The **Connection** tab also includes a **Test Connection** button that can be used to test the connection properties. The connection can only be tested after all of the required parameters are entered. The values for the Initial Catalog, Package Collection, and Default Schema parameters must not be blank or the test connection will fail. When this button is pressed, an APPC or a TCP/IP session will attempt to be established with the host DB2 system using the OLE DB Provider for DB2.

If a **Test Connection** fails, Host Integration Server 2000 supports several troubleshooting features. If the connection to the DB2 system is using a TCP/IP connection, the Host Integration Server 2000 tracing facilities (Trace Initiator and Trace Viewer) can be used to trace the connection process in detail. Be forewarned that if tracing is enabled for the OLE DB Provider for DB2 (referred to as the DB2 Network Library in Trace Initiator), then the User name and Password from the connection string are captured and viewable as plain text in the trace file. This is not an issue if Windows integrated security is used for authentication to the DB2 system since the Password field is empty and does not contain a real password. But if a dedicated User name and Password are used for authentication, then extreme care should be taken because of security concerns if other users are allowed access to these trace files. For security, an ACL should be placed on trace files used for troubleshooting DB2 connections that allow only system administrators to access these files.

The Advanced Tab

The **Advanced** tab allows users to select the character code set identifier used by the host, the PC code page used on the client, and some specific options when using the OLE DB Provider for DB2.

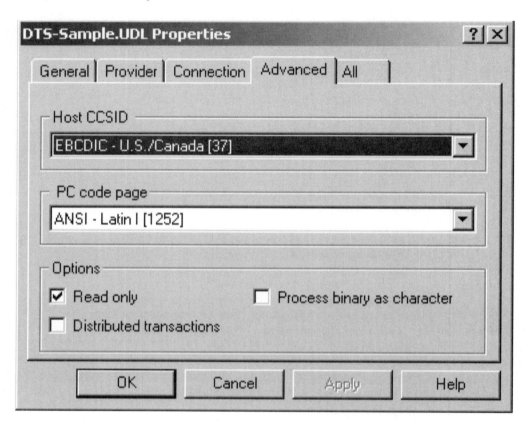

For the Microsoft OLE DB Provider for DB2, these properties include the following values:

Property	Description
Host CCSID	The character code set identifier (CCSID) matching the DB2 data as represented on the remote host computer. The CCSID property is required when processing binary data as character data. Unless the **Process Binary as Character** value is set to true, character data is converted based on the DB2 column CCSID and default ANSI code page.
	This property defaults to U.S./Canada (37).

(continued)

Property	Description *(continued)*
PC code page	The PC code page property indicates the code page to be used on the PC for character code conversion. This property is required when processing binary data as character data. Unless the **Process Binary as Character** checkbox is selected (value is set to true), character data is converted based on the default ANSI code page configured in Windows.
	This property defaults to Latin 1 (1252).
Read only	When this option is checked, the OLE DB Provider for DB2 creates a read-only data source by setting the Mode property to Read (DB_MODE_READ). A user has read access to objects such as tables, and cannot do update operations (INSERT, UPDATE, or DELETE, for example).
	This property defaults to a Mode property of Read/Write (DB_MODE_READ/WRITE).
Process binary as character	When this option is checked, the OLE DB Provider for DB2 treats binary data type fields (with a CCSID of 65535) as character data type fields on a per-data source basis. The Host CCSID and PC Code Page values are required input and output parameters.
	This property defaults to false.
Distributed transactions	When this option is checked, two-phase commit (distributed unit of work) is enabled. Distributed transactions are handled using Microsoft Transaction Server, Microsoft Distributed Transaction Coordinator, and the SNA LU 6.2 Resync Service. This option works only with DB2 for OS/390 V5R1 or later.

In the proposed scenario, the Host CCSID and PC Code Page would be selected from drop-down lists of supports character sets. The values for these parameters are only used if binary data fields with a CCSID value of 65535 on the DB2 system are to be treated as character data fields. In these cases, the Host CCSID selection should match the character set value used in the remote DB2 database for these binary data fields. Any PC Code Page can be selected that represents the preferred character set to be used on the SQL Server once the data has been moved and transformed. In most cases, these parameters are not used and data is converted based on the CCSID defined for each column in a DB2 table and default ANSI code page on the Windows system.

In the proposed scenario, the Read-only option should be checked to limit access to the DB2 tables to read access only. Since the DB2 data is to be used only for a data source, there is no need for read/write access. This read-only option can increase data access speed and protects the DB2 system from unintended changes.

The All Tab

The **All** tab allows users to configure essentially all of the properties for the data source except for the OLE DB Provider. The properties available in the **All** tab include properties that can be configured using the **Connection** and **Advanced** tabs as well as optional detailed properties used to connect to a data source.

Prepare the DB2 Tables on the AS/400

The goal of this solution is to copy and transform data from DB2 tables on the AS/400 system to similar data tables in SQL Server on Windows 2000. Many DB2 and AS/400 administrators may be reluctant to allow access to the DB2 database containing critical business data from other applications. There may be concerns about the impact of this external data access on interactive use and response times for these core business applications. There may be concerns about reliability and data integrity if external applications are allowed access to this critical business data.

In order to mitigate these concerns in the proposed solution, the critical DB2 database and tables will not be accessed directly using the OLE DB Provider for DB2 and DTS. The information from DB2 that needs to be accessed will first be copied to new tables in a temporary database in DB2. The OLE DB Provider for DB2 and DTS will only access these temporary or staging tables, not the core business data tables. DB2 can be configured to generate these temporary tables automatically using triggers when changes are made to the core data tables. These triggers are special constraints placed on a database that can cause other events in DB2 to occur. In our scenario, triggers will be created and attached to each core DB2 table that is to be made available to the OLE DB Provider for DB2 and DTS. When the trigger event is activated by an insertion, deletion, or update of rows in a specific table, the change will be propagated to the temporary tables.

IBM DB2 on the AS/400 supports two types of triggers:

- SQL Triggers - triggers configured as SQL statements on a database by the database administrator.

- System Triggers - triggers configured as external programs written in RPG, COBOL, or ILE C that are attached to a physical or logical file that trigger on file system changes. Since DB2 tables are implemented as part of the file system on OS/400, system triggers can be used to implement the same effects as SQL triggers.

The proposed solution uses SQL triggers, primarily because they are simpler to describe, create, and use. SQL triggers are a feature added in IBM DB2 Universal Database Version 6.0 and later. On the AS/400, these features were added with the release of DB2 Universal Database for OS/400 included as part of the OS/400 operating system in Version 5 Release 1.

Prior to OS/400 V5R1, SQL triggers were not supported but system triggers can still be used. The IBM documentation provided with DB2 provides details and source code examples of system triggers written in several languages.

An SQL trigger is a constraint configured on a database that can cause other DB2 operations to occur. SQL triggers provide a mechanism to actively monitor a database or group of tables for an occurrence when an insert, update, or delete operation is to be performed. The definition of the SQL trigger is stored in DB2 as part of the metadata associated with a database. SQL triggers on DB2 are created using the SQL CREATE TRIGGER statement applied to a data table. Any number of separate SQL triggers can be applied to a data table. The statements specified in the SQL trigger are executed each time an insert, update, or delete operation is performed on the table.

SQL Triggers must have a unique name. In DB2 Universal Database, SQL triggers have a two-part name similar to a table that includes the database name (SAMPLE.cust_trig4 in the SAMPLE database, for example). When creating triggers, the following properties must be specified:

- Trigger name - a unique name within a schema
- Triggering event - the type of operation that should invoke the trigger (an insert, update, or delete operation)
- Activation time - when the trigger is to be executed (either *before* or *after* the event occurs to the database)
- Granularity - whether the trigger should be activated only once based on an SQL statement causing the event (statement trigger) or for each row that is changed (row trigger)
- Transition variables - whether access to information on the specific changes to a database or row are needed in the form of variables to the trigger.

The body of the trigger can consist of one or more SQL statements. SQL triggers can also call DB2 stored procedures or DB2 user-defined functions to perform additional processing when the trigger is executed.

For the proposed solution, *after* triggers are used to activate for each row that is changed in a table. Three separate triggers are created for each data table in DB2 to be moved and transformed using DTS. The purpose of the triggers is to maintain a parallel set of data tables (temporary or staging tables) that are accessed using DTS.

The following triggers are needed:

- Insert trigger that inserts a new row of data to the corresponding temporary table.

- Update trigger that makes updates to an existing row of data in the corresponding temporary table

- Delete trigger that deletes an existing row of data in the corresponding temporary table

SQL triggers can be created using various tools provided with IBM DB2 for configuration and management. SQL triggers are saved in a Triggers folder under the database to which they are attached.

Recent versions of IBM DB2 include a SAMPLE database that will be used as the basis for developing an example SQL trigger. The SAMPLE database consists of several data tables including SALES, EMPLOYEE, etc. The SALES table has four columns: SALES_DATE, SALES_PERSON, REGION, and SALES. The SQL trigger defined below (sales_ins_trig in the DB2 SAMPLE database) is designed to trigger on inserts to the SALES table and insert a new row into a parallel TMPSALES data table.

```
CREATE TRIGGER sales_ins_trig
    AFTER INSERT on sales
    REFERENCING NEW as newrow
    FOR EACH ROW MODE DB2SQL
    INSERT INTO tmpsales(sales_date, sales_person, region, sales)
    VALUES(newrow.sales_date, newrow.sales_person, newrow.region, newrow.sales)
```

The name of the SQL trigger is specified as sales_ins_trig after the **CREATE TRIGGER** keywords. The fully qualified name of the trigger, SAMPLE.sales_ins_trig, includes the database name. DB2 Universal restricts database names to 8 characters and other name elements (the trigger name, for example) to 18 characters. These name-length restrictions are also dependent on the version of DB2 that is to be used.

The "AFTER INSERT" statement identifies sales_ins_trig as an *after* trigger where the triggering event occurs after an INSERT occurring on the SALES data table. The REFERENCING NEW syntax indicates that *newrow* is a transition variable that will be used by the trigger. The "FOR EACH ROW MODE DB2SQL" statement indicates the granularity of the trigger, in this case a trigger will activate for each row that is inserted. Finally the INSERT INTO and VALUES SQL statements indicate the action to be taken when this trigger occurs. In our example, the values of the fields (columns) in the new row being inserted in the SALES data table are also inserted into a new row that is inserted into the parallel TMPSALES data table.

SQL triggers for update and delete operations for the SALES data table also need to be created that will propagate changes to the TMPSALES data table. Similar SQL triggers would need to be created for each data table that is to be replicated in a temporary table.

SQL triggers are executed under the authentication of the user that created the trigger, not the user that may have executed the SQL statement that triggered the event. Consequently, DB2 administrators or other users with the appropriate authority must create the SQL triggers to maintain a set of temporary data tables proposed in this scenario. Administrative users or the owner of the TMPSALES database have the necessary authority to insert records.

Installing and Configuring SQL Server 2000

SQL Server 2000 can be installed on Windows 2000 Server, Windows 2000 Advanced Server, and Windows 2000 DataCenter Server. To support failover clustering, SQL Server 2000 Enterprise Edition is required and the operating system needs to be either Windows 2000 Advanced Server or Windows 2000 DataCenter Server. SQL Server 2000 Enterprise Edition supports the creation of server clusters that link up to four SQL server systems together as a virtual system.

Security on SQL Server 2000 fully supports Windows domain security allowing authentication based on Windows user and group accounts as well as SQL Server user accounts. When SQL Server is installed, you must choose the method to use for authentication:

- Windows domain accounts only

- A combination of Windows domain accounts and SQL Server user accounts (default)

Using only Windows domain accounts can simplify the management required when multiple SQL Servers are operated in a domain. Groups of users can be created in the Windows domain that are given different abilities to use and manage the instances of SQL Server.

The SQL Server (MSSQLServer) process that operates the database server and the SQL Server Agent (SQLServerAgent) used for scheduling tasks are configured to run as services on Windows 2000. An important decision that must be made during the installation process is the service account under which these services are run. The options are as follows:

- Local System account

- Specific Windows Domain user account

A disadvantage of using the Local System account is that while this account has administrative rights on the local Windows 2000 Server, the Local System has no privileges on other network computers in the Windows domain. This is particularly a problem if the SQL Server instance needs to operate tasks (run DTS packages or send e-mail on errors, for example) that depend on having privileges on other systems in the domain. So a domain account is a better choice for the proposed scenario. When using a Windows domain account, it is important that the user have administrative privileges on the local Windows 2000 Server where SQL Server is installed.

SQL Server 2000 supports the ability to integrate with Active Directory, the directory service in Windows 2000. Custom applications can use the OLE DB Provider for Microsoft Directory Services to access Active Directory information. This OLE DB Provider exposes both an LDAP interface and an SQL interface that can be used for queries.

SQL Server 2000 supports the option of running multiple instances of the SQL Server database engine on a single computer system. One instance of the database engine can be installed on a computer system as the default SQL Server instance, while additional named instances may also be installed. Each instance of the SQL Server database engine will include its own set of system and user databases and separate SQL Server and Server agent services. Additional instances can be created and added later to a system. This feature can be very useful, allowing a single computer to support several environments such as a production system in parallel with a separate test and development system.

The default collation sequence and character set to be used is determined when SQL Server 2000 is installed. While the collation sequence and character set can be specified on a per column basis in a data table, the defaults when these attributes are not specified are based on the selections made during installation.

SQL Server configuration information is stored in the local Windows registry as well as within various system tables maintained by the database engine. While many of these settings can be modified on a running system, some configuration settings such as the default collation sequence and the service account to use require a complete rebuild of the SQL system databases. A rebuild of the system database also deletes any data tables, so care should be taken to backup data before rebuilding SQL Server system tables.

A number of configurable parameters affect the performance of SQL Server 2000 including memory usage, CPU usage on multiprocessor systems, number of connections supported, threading, priorities, and fibers. If database performance is an issue, careful attention to these parameters can be used to tune the performance of SQL Server.

Configuring SQL Server DTS Packages

SQL Server Data Transformation Services (DTS) is designed to move and transform data between heterogeneous data sources. For the scenario described in this chapter, our goal is to move and transform data from an IBM DB2 database on an AS/400 system to data stored in SQL Server 2000 on a Windows 2000 system.

The DTS Import/Export Wizard provided with SQL Server is used to create DTS packages that control this process. DTS packages are sets of tasks for importing, transforming, and exporting data that can be reused and scheduled to operate as needed. DTS packages contain the following information:

- Connections - information on the source and destination of the data.

- Tasks - a description of operations to be performed as part of the package.

- Workflow procedures - information on processes that are to be executed on successful completion or failure of the task (send e-mail, for example).

- Data transformation procedures - detailed information on the transformation process used to convert data (sometimes referred to as data pumps in SQL Server documentation).

The connection information specifies the data provider to use for connecting to the source and the data provider to use for connecting to the destination. In our example, this would be the Microsoft OLE DB Provider for DB2 as the source and the Microsoft OLE DB Data Provider for SQL Server for the destination. Connection information also includes the database server or servers to connect to, logon and authentication information, and the specific database to access for the import/export operations.

The DTS process can be based on SQL queries against a database, scripts, or external commands as well as simple copies of data tables. So DTS tasks can consist of ActiveX scripts, SQL scripts, SQL queries, commands to transfer SQL Server objects, data-driven queries, bulk insert commands, and external processes to execute. The scenario described in this chapter is a simple task that copies and transforms some data tables in DB2 on the AS/400 to similar data tables in SQL Server on Windows 2000.

DTS packages can be stored in a variety of locations and formats including the following:

- Stored in SQL Server.

- Stored in an external DTS file using the COM (OLE) structured storage file format. This format is useful when the DTS package may need to be copied or e-mailed to other locations.

- Stored in external Visual Basic source files that can be used in Visual Basic programs.

A DTS package can be created on one computer and stored on a different computer running SQL Server or in one of the above external formats. The DTS package does not need to be stored on the SQL Server that will execute the package, but can be stored remotely on other computers running SQL Server.

The DTS Import/Export Wizard simplifies the complex task of initially creating a DTS package. The DTS Import/Export Wizard is usually started from **Microsoft SQL Server** folder off the **Programs** folder from the Windows **Start** button. The DTS Wizard is called **Import and Export Data** on the Microsoft SQL Server list of applications. The DTS Wizard can also be started from the SQL Enterprise Manager application used to configure and manage SQL Server 2000. Below each SQL Server instance in the Enterprise Manager treeview is a Data Transformation Services folder. Expanding the Data Transformation Services folder exposes the possible locations where DTS packages can be saved in SQL Server:

- Local Packages

- Meta Data Services Packages

- Meta Data

Right-clicking the Data Transformation Services folder brings up a menu with various options. The **Import** option or **Export** option off the **All Tasks** entry will start the DTS Import/Export Wizard.

The DTS Import/Export Wizard walks the user through the following steps:

1. Choose the data source.

2. Choose the destination.

3. Specify a type of operation (table copy and views or SQL query).

4. Select source tables and views and specify formatting and transformations.

5. Save, schedule, and replicate the DTS package.

Recent versions of IBM DB2 Universal Database include a SAMPLE database containing a number of data tables. The following illustrations are from the configuration of a DTS package to copy the SALES data table from the DB2 SAMPLE database to SQL Server. We start with the selection of the data source.

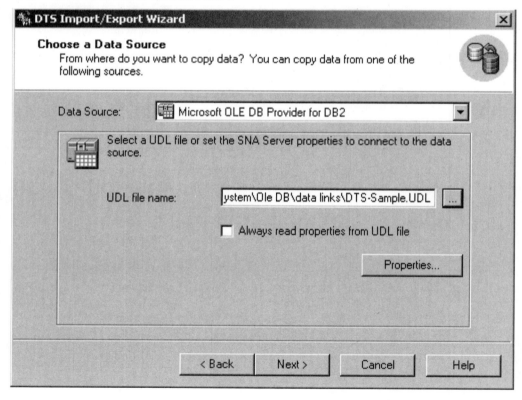

In our scenario, the Microsoft OLE DB Provider for DB2 was selected from the drop-down list of possible data sources. Once this provider was selected, the dialog was modified with the addition of a text field for the UDL file name to use for accessing the appropriate database and schema. This UDL file would have been previously created using the NewSNADS application included with the OLE DB Provider for DB2 on Host Integration Server 2000. The UDL file specifies the information required for accessing the appropriate DB2 database and tables on the AS/400 system. The button to the right of the text field for the UDL file name with three dots can be used to browse the file system for UDL files. It is useful to recall that data links are by default created in the following folder:
C:\Programs Files\Common Files\System\Ole DB\data links

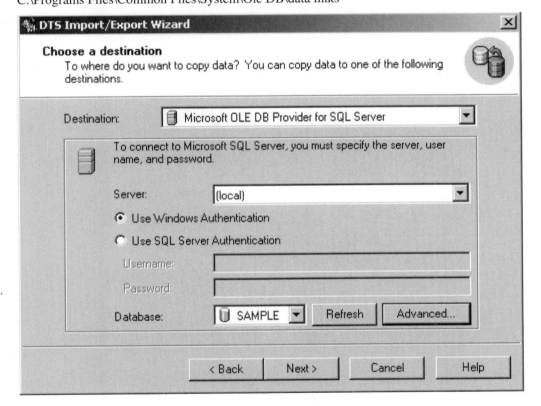

Selecting the destination for the DTS operation is simpler, since the target is SQL Server on the local system. The database to be targeted must have already been created in SQL Server using Enterprise Manager or an SQL script. The specific database to target is selected from the drop-down list. Windows authentication is preferred since a User name and Password do not need to be specified and saved in the DTS package.

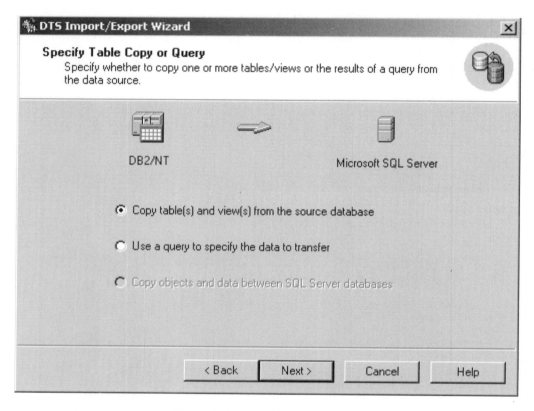

DTS supports copying data tables and views from a source database or using an SQL query to specify the data to transfer. For DTS operations between different instances of SQL Server, simple copying of objects and data is also supported. A DTS table copy supports transferring a subset of the columns in a table when the entire data table is not needed.

For the proposed scenario, a copy of tables is selected for this option. In a real data integration deployment, an SQL query may be preferred over a simple table copy if only a subset of the rows in a data table are of interest.

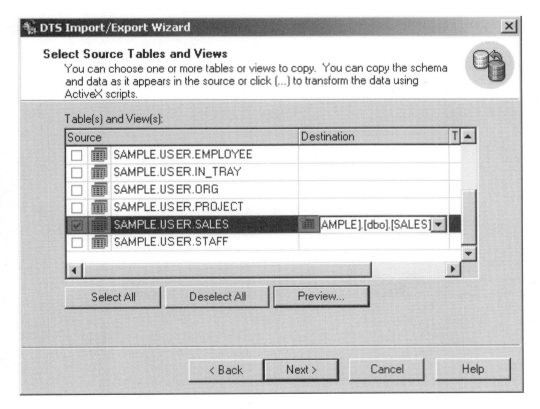

Once the data source, destination, and operation type are specified, the tables and views to be copied are selected from a list of data tables in the remote DB2 database. DTS uses the Microsoft OLE DB Provider for DB2 to query the remote DB2 system and return the data tables in the specified database. All of the tables in a remote DB2 database and schema can be specified, but it is more efficient to select only those tables that are needed. In the accompanying screen snapshot only the SALES table from the SAMPLE database has been selected for transfer.

Destination tables in SQL Server can be specified as well as any transformations that are to be applied to the columns in a data table. To the right of the Destination field in the grid is a Transform field that allows configuring specific transformations and mappings between columns in the source and destination data tables. Clicking the button with three dots in the Transform field launches the dialog for Column Mappings and Transformations. This dialog allows the user to view and modify how source data types are mapped and transformed to destination data types.

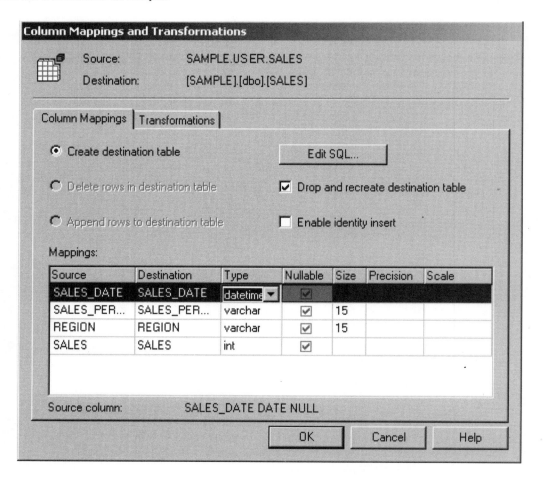

Using the DB2 SALES table in the SAMPLE database, the DTS wizard defaulted to map the DB2 "DATE" type used for SALES_DATE to the SQL Server "smalldatetime" type. Using column mapping, this conversion was changed to a "datetime" type in SQL Server. Any DB2 data types in the tables to be copied that are not supported by SQL Server would need to be mapped to some appropriate SQL Server data type.

The "Drop and recreate destination table" option should be checked if the copy operation is to occur repeatedly and replace the contents of the destination table on each copy. In the scenario for this chapter, this option should be selected for all tables to be copied.

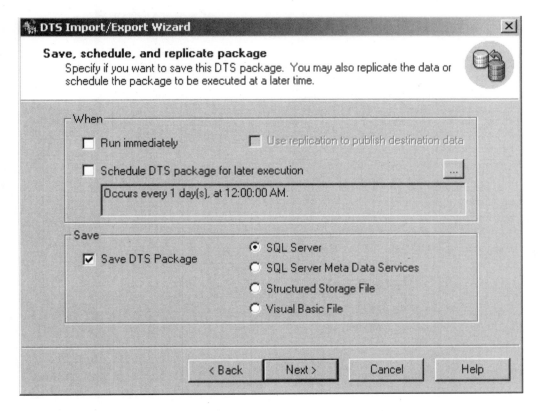

The DTS Import/Export Wizard allows the user to run the created DTS package immediately or schedule the package for later execution by the scheduler service (SQL Server Agent) in SQL Server. When initially creating a DTS package, the options to schedule or run the DTS package are better left unselected. The DTS package should be saved for later use first, and scheduled for execution after testing.

A DTS package can be saved in a number of locations and formats including the following:

- **SQL Server.** Saves the package to an SQL Server instance as a local package accessible for use only on the designated SQL Server.

- **SQL Server Meta Data Services.** Saves the package to the repository database on an SQL Server instance where the package can be shared using SQL Meta Data Services with other servers.

- **Structured Storage File.** Saves the package in an external DTS file using the COM (OLE) structured storage file format.

- **Visual Basic File.** Saves the package in an external Visual Basic source file as Visual Basic code that calls various DTS COM classes to accomplish the DTS process and tasks.

It is a good idea to initially save the DTS package to SQL Server or SQL Server Meta Data Services for use in preliminary testing. If the DTS package is saved to one of these SQL Server locations, it can be password protected to prevent unauthorized users from viewing or executing the package. After the DTS package has been tested and is operating properly, it also makes sense to save the package as a structured storage file so the package can be easily copied to other computers. The structured storage file format can contain multiple DTS packages and different versions of the same DTS package.

Once a DTS package is saved to one of the SQL Server formats or as a structured storage file, it is simple to open the package using the **DTS Designer** from **Enterprise Manager** and save the DTS package in other locations and formats.

The DTS package needs to be saved to a Visual Basic file if it will be used as part of an application program developed in Visual Basic. Note that the Visual Basic file that is created usually requires some minor changes before use (values needed for User name and Password to connect to a database, for example). The Visual Basic file also needs to be compiled using Visual Basic with the SQL DTS COM object classes in order to be used.

Working with DTS Packages

Once a DTS package has been created and saved, the package can be managed and executed using several SQL Server applications and tools:

- Enterprise Manager
- DTS Run Utility for Windows
- Dtsrun command

Enterprise Manager and DTS Packages

The Enterprise Manager can be used to view, modify, schedule, and execute DTS packages stored in SQL Server or Meta Data Services repository. Enterprise Manager can also open DTS packages saved as structured storage files. A Data Transformation Services folder is located in the left pane tree view of Enterprise Manager below each instance of SQL Server. Right-clicking the mouse on the Data Transformation Services folder provides options to create a new package or open an existing package for modification. The **Create Package** option starts the DTS Import/Export Wizard to create a new DTS package. The **Open Package** option allows you to open an existing DTS package file that was saved as a structured storage file and start the DTS Designer for making changes to the package. The DTS Designer provides a **Save As** option from the **Package** menu that can be used to save a DTS package in any of the DTS formats and locations.

Below the Data Transformation Services folder are separate folders for Local Packages and Meta Data Services Packages stored in SQL Server. Navigating to one of these folders and right-clicking an existing DTS package provides options to edit the package using the DTS Designer (called Package Design in the Windows title bar), schedule the package for later execution, or execute the package immediately.

While the DTS Import/Export Wizard simplifies the complex process of initially creating a DTS package, the DTS Designer used to modify an existing package is more challenging. The DTS Import/Export Wizard is a high-level tool that abstracts the DTS package creation process. In contrast, the DTS Designer is a very low-level tool that requires interaction with the DTS package at a very detailed level.

The **Disconnected Edit** option from the **Package** menu of the DTS Designer provides a two-pane control with a tree view in the left pane for displaying and editing the individual DTS objects and properties. The DTS objects include Connections, Tasks, Steps, and Global Variables defined in the DTS package. Each DTS object can have a large number of individual properties. For example, OLE DB Properties under the Connection object include about 80 individual properties that may be edited. Each DTS property has a minimum set of attributes that include Name, PropertyID, PropertySet (GUID), Value, and IsDefaultValue (a Boolean value indicating if the attribute value is the default). Because the granularity is so detailed in the DTS Designer, it is often easier to recreate a DTS package using the DTS Import/Export Wizard if a large number of changes are required.

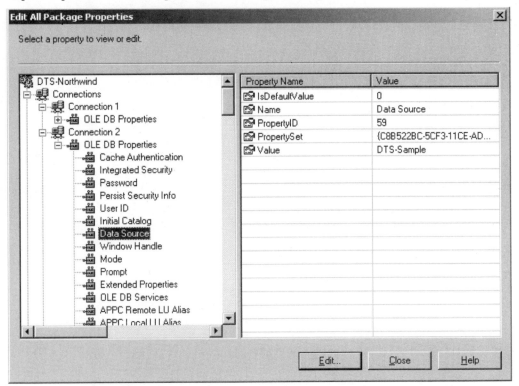

DTS Run Utility for Windows

When SQL Server is installed, a number of directories are added to the PATH environment variable that contain SQL Server applications and tools that can be executed from the command line.

The DTS Run Utility for Windows (dtsrunui.exe) can be used to execute and manage DTS packages. This application provides a graphical interface to run a DTS package immediately or schedule a package for later execution. This application is started from the command line by typing dtsruniu in a Command Prompt window. A shortcut can also be created to this executable under the Start Menu for convenience. The DTS Run Utility for Windows has a location box that allows the user to browse to and load the DTS package of interest. The package can be stored in SQL Server, SQL Server Meta Data Services, or as a DTS Structured Storage File.

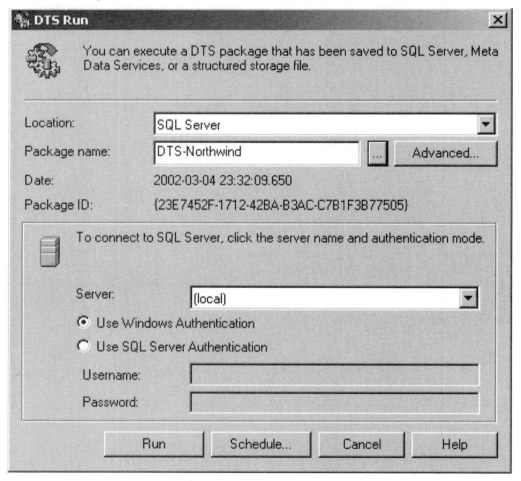

DTSRun Command

The DTSRun application (dtsrun.exe) can be used to manage packages from the Command Prompt. This application provides a command-line interface to run a DTS package immediately, delete a package stored in SQL Server or Meta Data Services, or load a package stored from SQL Server or Meta Data Services and store the package as an DTS structured storage file. This application is started from the command line by typing dtsrun in a Command Prompt window.

All of these different methods that run or schedule a DTS package for later execution support numerous options for logging the execution process to SQL Server, the Event log, or to external log files. Other actions can be triggered on successful completion or when errors occur including sending e-mail messages. In the proposed scenario for this chapter, it is appropriate to log the results of the execution process to the Event log and send e-mail to a system administrator.

Scheduling DTS Packages for Execution

Once the DTS package has been thoroughly tested for proper operation, it is appropriate to schedule the DTS package for regular execution. The DTS package can be scheduled for execution using the following methods:

- SQL Server – scheduled for regular operation from within SQL Server

- Windows 2000 Task Scheduler - scheduled for regular operation using the Windows Task Scheduler service.

The SQL Agent Service in SQL Server has the capabilities to schedule operations including the execution of DTS packages. As shown in the following illustration, the SQL Service supports the ability to schedule execution as a recurring job schedule on a daily, weekly, or monthly basis.

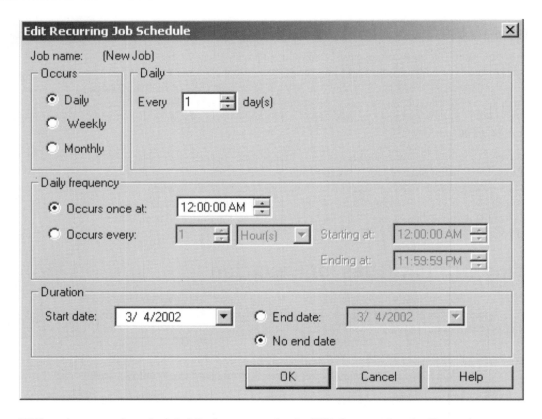

DTS packages can be scheduled for later execution in SQL Server using the Enterprise Manager or the DTS Run Utility for Windows. If the DTS package is to be scheduled for regular execution by SQL Server, then the DTS package should be saved to one of the internal SQL Server locations. If the DTS package is to be shared with other systems running SQL Server, then SQL Meta Data Services is the preferred location for saving the DTS package.

The Windows Task Scheduler is a general-purpose schedule service installed as part of Internet Explorer on Windows 2000. The Task Scheduler provides a COM-based programming interface and can be used to schedule tasks on local or remote computers. The Windows Task Scheduler offers more flexibility when scheduling a recurring job than the SQL Server scheduler. But in most circumstances, this greater flexibility is not needed.

In the scenario for this chapter, scheduling the execution of the DTS package in SQL Server would make sense. In order to not impact interactive users and the business applications on the AS/400, the DTS package can be scheduled to run once a day during late night hours.

Sample Applications Using DTS

On the CD-ROM accompanying this book are two sample applications in Visual Basic that are based on DTS packages that were created and saved to a Visual Basic file. The code samples are located in the "SQL Server 2000 to DB2 Data Transfer" folders. These samples use DTS to import the Northwind sample database and data tables included with SQL Server 2000 and export these data tables to IBM DB2. The Visual Basic source code exported from the DTS Import/Export Wizard has been modified with an initial dialog box that requests a pointer to UDL file to the SQL Server used for import and a UDL file to the DB2 system targeted for the export.

One sample directory contains a version of the source code and application using Visual Basic 6. The other directory contains a version of the code using Visual Basic.NET for the application. The sample code illustrates what a DTS package looks like when it is exported as Visual Basic source code for use in an application. The simple modifications to the exported DTS package show how easy it is to use DTS for developing custom applications for data integration.

An excerpt from these DTS samples in Visual Basic is listed below. The sample code illustrates the use of the DTS COM objects supported by SQL Server 2000 in an application. Most of the source code in these samples was generated by the DTS Import/Export Wizard. The sample code creates a new package then adds connection objects, DTS step objects, and DTS task objects and sets properties for these objects.

The following excerpt from the sample code defines the package, connections, and tasks in a DTS package.

```
Public goPackage As DTS.Package2
Public Sub Main()
    Set goPackage = New DTS.Package2
    goPackage.Name = "NWSQLS2DB2-Data"
    goPackage.Description = "Northwind - SQL Server to DB2"
    ' need to set other package properties

    ' create package connection information
    Dim oConnection As DTS.Connection2

    '------------- add new connection defined below for DB2.
    'For security purposes, the password is never scripted
    Set oConnection = goPackage.Connections.NewDataLink(App.Path & "\IBM-DB2.udl")
    oConnection.Name = "DB2 Connection"
    oConnection.ID = 2
    oConnection.ConnectionTimeout = 60
```

```
        oConnection.UserID = frmPackage.txtDB2User.Text
        oConnection.Password = frmPackage.txtDB2Password.Text
        ' Need to set other connection properties for the UDL to DB2


    goPackage.Connections.Add oConnection
    Set oConnection = Nothing

    '------------- a new connection defined below for SQL Server.
    Set oConnection = goPackage.Connections.NewDataLink(App.Path & "\SQLS2K.udl")
    oConnection.Name = "SQL Server Northwind DB"
    oConnection.ID = 1
    oConnection.ConnectionTimeout = 60
    oConnection.UserID = frmPackage.txtSQLUser.Text
    oConnection.Password = frmPackage.txtSQLPassword.Text
    ' Need to set other connection properties for the UDL to SQL Server

    goPackage.Connections.Add oConnection
    Set oConnection = Nothing

    ' create package steps information
    Dim oStep As DTS.Step2
    Dim oPrecConstraint As DTS.PrecedenceConstraint

    '------------- a new step defined below
    Set oStep = goPackage.Steps.New
    oStep.Name = "Copy Data from Categories to Categories Step"
    oStep.Description = "Copy Data from Categories to Categories Task"
    oStep.ScriptLanguage = "VBScript"
    oStep.AddGlobalVariables = True
    oStep.CloseConnection = False
    oStep.ExecuteInMainThread = False
    oStep.IsPackageDSORowset = False
    oStep.JoinTransactionIfPresent = False
    oStep.DisableStep = False
    oStep.FailPackageOnError = False
    ' Need to set other step properties for DTS Step 2

    goPackage.Steps.Add oStep
    Set oStep = Nothing
    ' Need to add and configure properties for other steps

    ' Create package tasks information
    '-----call Task_Sub1 for task Copy Data from Categories
    '     to Categories Task (Copy Data from Categories to Categories Task)
    Call Task_Sub1(goPackage)
    ' Need to call other tasks

    ' Save or execute package
```

```
'     To save a package instead of executing it, comment out the
'     executing package lines and uncomment the saving package line
'  goPackage.SaveToSQLServer "(local)", "sa", ""
   goPackage.Execute

  TracePackageError goPackage
    goPackage.UnInitialize
    Set goPackage = Nothing
End Sub
```

The following excerpt from the sample code defines one of the subtasks in a DTS package.

```
'------------- define Task_Sub1 for task Copy Data from Categories to Categories Task
(Copy Data from Categories to Categories Task)
Public Sub Task_Sub1(ByVal goPackage As Object)
    Dim oTask As DTS.Task
    Dim oCustomTask1 As DTS.DataPumpTask2
    Set oTask = goPackage.Tasks.New("DTSDataPumpTask")
    oTask.Name = "Copy Data from Categories to Categories Task"
    Set oCustomTask1 = oTask.CustomTask

    oCustomTask1.Name = "Copy Data from Categories to Categories Task"
    oCustomTask1.Description = "Copy Data from Categories to Categories Task"
    oCustomTask1.SourceConnectionID = 1
    oCustomTask1.SourceSQLStatement = _
        "select [CategoryID],[CategoryName],[Description],NULL AS [Picture] _
        from [Northwind].[dbo].[Categories]"
    oCustomTask1.DestinationConnectionID = 2
    oCustomTask1.DestinationObjectName = "CATEGORIES"
    ' Need to configure other properties for this task

    Call oCustomTask1_Trans_Sub1(oCustomTask1)

    goPackage.Tasks.Add oTask
    Set oCustomTask1 = Nothing
    Set oTask = Nothing
End Sub
```

The following sample code defines one of the transformation subtasks in a DTS package.

```
Public Sub oCustomTask1_Trans_Sub1(ByVal oCustomTask1 As Object)
    Dim oTransformation As DTS.Transformation2
    Dim oTransProps As DTS.Properties
    Dim oColumn As DTS.Column
    Set oTransformation = _
        CustomTask1.Transformations.New("DTSPump.DataPumpTransformCopy")
    oTransformation.Name = "DTSTransformation__1"
    oTransformation.TransformFlags = 63
    oTransformation.ForceSourceBlobsBuffered = 0
    oTransformation.ForceBlobsInMemory = False
```

```
oTransformation.InMemoryBlobSize = 1048576
oTransformation.TransformPhases = 4

Set oColumn = oTransformation.SourceColumns.New("Picture", 1)
oColumn.Name = "Picture"
oColumn.Ordinal = 1
oColumn.Flags = 112
oColumn.Size = 0
oColumn.DataType = 3
oColumn.Precision = 0
oColumn.NumericScale = 0
oColumn.Nullable = True

oTransformation.SourceColumns.Add oColumn
Set oColumn = Nothing

' Need to add and configure properties for other source columns

Set oColumn = oTransformation.DestinationColumns.New("PICTURE", 1)
oColumn.Name = "PICTURE"
oColumn.Ordinal = 1
oColumn.Flags = 116
oColumn.Size = 254
oColumn.DataType = 129
oColumn.Precision = 0
oColumn.NumericScale = 0
oColumn.Nullable = True

oTransformation.DestinationColumns.Add oColumn
Set oColumn = Nothing

' Need to add and configure properties for other destination columns

Set oTransProps = oTransformation.TransformServerProperties
Set oTransProps = Nothing

oCustomTask1.Transformations.Add oTransformation
Set oTransformation = Nothing
End Sub
```

Data Integration Using DTS

The scenario described in this chapter focuses on using data integration as a tool for providing application integration in the enterprise. Data tables are imported from DB2 on an AS/400 system and exported to SQL Server on Windows 2000. Once the data is stored in SQL Server, it can be easily accessed for analysis, projections, and custom reports. SQL Server supports a variety of query features for generating queries including Query Analyzer, English Query, and Analysis Services (OLAP). DTS can also be used to export data directly to Excel files or other formats. While this chapter has focused on importing data from DB2 to SQL Server, DTS supports transfer between any heterogeneous data sources using OLE DB or ODBC. The scenario could as easily be revised to provide data integration with Oracle, Sybase, Informix, or any data source supported by an OLE DB Provider or ODBC Driver. Combining SQL Server's Data Transformation Services with OLE DB and ODBC (database middleware) offers a powerful framework for data integration in the enterprise.

By Steven Baker

Integrating Employee Benefits Self-Service with SAP R/3

Modern business applications today are designed and implemented so they can be easily integrated with other applications within the enterprise. With the growth of networking, local intranets, and the World Wide Web, it has become important to be able to easily share information electronically between business processes. Consequently, the new paradigm for applications is essentially a collection of services and associated data that can readily be used by other applications.

However, many of the existing applications in use in an organization were not designed to plug into Enterprise Application Integration (EAI) architecture. Not long ago, each application was an island unto itself. Custom business applications were typically built as monolithic programs designed to solve a specific set of business problems. Packaged business applications, while having some configurable options, were also designed using similar models. These stovepipes, as they are often called, exist in most large organizations and reflect solutions purchased over time for specific problems. Even some of the largest packaged applications represent stovepipes of sorts that support rather limited ways to share information with other applications and processes. These applications may also reside on a variety of computer and operating systems.

Enterprise Application Integration is being promoted as a way to improve productivity and tie disparate applications together into a more cooperative whole. In the previous chapter, we discussed the integration of data as a natural choice for many tasks. Data integration can bypass the necessity of making intrusive and costly changes to the existing application logic, user interface, or data structures. But for many custom and packaged applications, data integration may not be appropriate as the point of integration. In some existing applications, the database metadata may be so complex or poorly documented that integration using the data would be difficult or impossible. Some packaged applications (SAP R/3, for example) function as application servers with integrated transaction processing, making it difficult to use data integration without affecting the reliability and transactional integrity of the data store.

Fortunately, many of these custom and packaged applications expose application programming interfaces (APIs) that can be used to access the business logic, processes, and data used by these programs. Leveraging these interfaces, enterprise planners and developers can bundle several separate applications into a more cooperative whole. The only limitations on using application integration are the specific interfaces and functions that a custom or packaged application exposes.

Organizations often need to share business information among their different applications. For example, information on company employees maintained by a human resources or personnel department includes employee wages, benefits, and other information needed by payroll and accounting software to write paychecks, properly withhold taxes, and issue forms required for compliance with the Internal Revenue Service.

A typical scenario in many large organizations regarding employee benefits is that an open enrollment period (typically the month of December) is available for employees to review and change their benefits. Employees receive handbooks that describe the medical, dental, life insurance, disability, and other benefits (401K plans, stock purchase options, etc.) to be offered in the following 12-month period. Employees also receive a paper form that must be submitted by the end of the open enrollment period with the benefits that they wish to select along with other needed information (dependents and insurance beneficiaries, for example). The information from this benefits enrollment form may be entered into some system maintained by the Human Resources department. A subset of this information must also be forwarded to the Payroll department to be entered by a data entry clerk into the payroll system. The scenario just described is the norm in many state government and university systems.

Now the goal is to automate existing business processes such as employee benefits enrollment to improve productivity, enhance employee satisfaction, and streamline the process. The scenario we will discuss in this chapter is based on automating the existing manual procedures described above for employee benefits enrollment with a Web-based self-service process using application integration. This EAI solution can easily include validation logic to check for problems and eliminate costly and error-prone manual data entry errors. The approach we will discuss for providing this integration uses Web-based middleware in conjunction with interfaces exposed by the payroll and benefits administration application as the point of integration.

Microsoft has developed several popular technologies that have become de facto standards used for Web-based middleware:

- Microsoft® Internet Information Server (IIS)

- Microsoft® Active Server Pages (ASP)

- Microsoft® Internet Explorer (IE)

Microsoft offers a number of products and technologies that could potentially be used to implement an application integration solution. These products and technologies include the following:

- Microsoft® BizTalk® Server 2000

- Microsoft® BizTalk® Adapter for SAP

- Microsoft® BizTalk® Adapter for MQSeries

- Microsoft® Message Queuing (MSMQ)

- Microsoft® MSMQ-MQSeries Bridge (MSMQ-MQSeries Bridge)

- Microsoft® SQL Server™2000

- Microsoft® Distributed Transaction Coordinator (DTC)

- Microsoft® Visual Studio®

- Microsoft® Visual Studio® .NET

- Microsoft® .NET Framework

This chapter will focus on how some of these Microsoft products and technologies can be used together to provide a low-cost application integration solution.

The chapter is divided into the following four sections:

- **Scenario**. This section will describe the business problem to be solved in greater detail than the summary provided above.

- **Solution**. This section will describe how Microsoft Internet Information Server in combination with other Microsoft products and technologies can be used to solve this business problem.

- **Tools and Technology**. This section will focus on the various tools and technologies involved in solving the business problem.

- **Implementation**. This section will drill deeper into select portions of the implementation of the proposed solution, to give the reader a sense of the level of technical expertise required to implement the solution.

Scenario

How can an organization integrate a Web-based self-service site for employee benefits with other applications that need this information? Employee benefits information is likely to be managed by a personnel or human resources (HR) department. Much of the information collected by HR needs to be maintained according to privacy conditions that severely limit access to this information by other employees. A subset of the information submitted by an employee during the benefits enrollment period needs to be transferred into other financial applications such as payroll and benefits administration. To further narrow this discussion, we will focus on the employee benefits enrollment process.

The typical process in many large organizations for handling employee benefits is a manual paper-based process. Employees submit a signed paper form during the open enrollment period to indicate the selections they wish to make for benefits in the following period (typically a year). This paper form is routed first to the personnel or human resources department where this information is checked and may be entered into an HR application. The benefits enrollment form includes the list of benefits to be subscribed (choice of medical plan, for example) plus other private information needed for benefits administration (names of spouse, dependents, and life insurance beneficiaries, for example). Then a subset of this form lacking the private employee information is sent to the Payroll department to be entered into payroll and other financial applications by a data entry clerk.

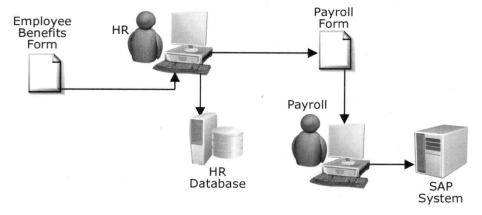

Existing manual process for handling employee benefits enrollment

This is a common scenario in many organizations where paper-based forms and manual data entry are part of the process for business applications. The challenge is to automate this process as simply and inexpensively as possible. Companies have made large investments in existing custom and packaged business applications. These software applications (payroll, for example) manage critical business information and processes that are essential for the operation of the company. Employees will express extreme displeasure if a payroll check is not issued on time. As a result, it would be far too costly to replace these existing software applications such as payroll and benefits administration in the near term. Integrating applications (payroll and benefits administration with human resources, for example) using online forms filled out and submitted by the employee can provide a low-cost way to automate this manual process without making costly changes to existing applications. The automation of the manual process can reduce errors, increase productivity, and enhance employee satisfaction.

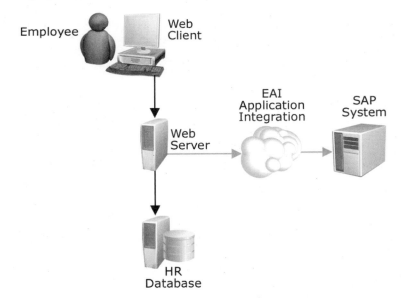

Integrating employee self-service with packaged applications

One of the approaches to automate this process is to use a self-service Web site for the employee to fill out and submit forms. The information collected from these electronic forms can then be integrated with HR, payroll, and benefits administration applications using interfaces exposed by these applications.

To adequately understand this business problem and the solutions that will be proposed in this chapter, it is important to review a number of related topics, including the specific custom or packaged applications involved, the interfaces that these applications expose, the interactions in question, and some of the different models possible for integration based on APIs.

In order to better focus our discussion and illustrate a conceptual solution, we will assume that the HR department uses a custom application for human resources management. We will assume that data from this human resources application is stored in a relational database management systems (RDBMS) on Windows 2000, UNIX, or as data files on an IBM AS/400 minicomputer or IBM-compatible mainframe system. Since the focus of this chapter will be more on integration with a packaged application used for the payroll system, we will assume for simplicity that the HR data is stored in SQL Server 2000 on Windows 2000. The HR data could as easily have been stored in Microsoft Access on Windows or one of the popular RDBMS systems on UNIX.

For this scenario, we will assume that payroll and other financial applications use a packaged application, SAP R/3 software. The SAP R/3 package was chosen since it represents the most popular Enterprise Resource Planning (ERP) suite with almost one third of total worldwide sales for ERP software. Most of our focus in this chapter will be on using the interfaces exposed by the SAP software for application integration.

SAP R/3 consists of some core components including an application server runtime and repository for business data plus a large suite of application modules that companies can use to handle business needs. Some of application modules available in SAP R/3 suite include applications for Financials, Material Management, Environment Health and Safety, Sales and Distribution, Fixed Asset Management, Quality Management, Plant Maintenance, Customer Relationship Management, Investment Management, and Human Resources. Companies can purchase and customize specific modules from the SAP R/3 suite to meet their business needs. The application module used for payroll in SAP R/3 is located under Human Resources. The specific component to be used for illustration is the PY-US module (U.S. Payroll) in the Payroll (PY) module under Human Resources. Benefits are handled as part of the Personnel Administration (PA) module under Human Resources. The specific component in SAP R/3 of interest in this scenario is the Benefits Administration (PA-BN) component under Personnel Administration.

SAP R/3 uses a relational database management system to store data used by the SAP applications. SAP can be used with a number of different RDBMS systems as the data store. A popular configuration for SAP R/3 is installation of the SAP applications on Windows 2000 Server using SQL Server 2000 as the database. SAP R/3 can also be installed on UNIX systems and configured to use any of the popular RDBMS systems (Oracle, Sybase, Informix, or IBM DB2, for example).

Data integration with SAP is not a viable option. The SAP R/3 database schema is far too complex to support an integration scenario using data sources. A typical SAP R/3 installation can use several thousand data tables within the SAP database. A complete installation of the SAP R/3 suite uses almost 23,000 data tables with cryptic names unrelated to the components they support. Furthermore, SAP R/3 operates as a sophisticated transaction processing system and application server that would preclude direct access to the data files without jeopardizing the transactional integrity and proper operation of the SAP packaged applications.

Fortunately, SAP R/3 does support a variety of well-defined interfaces that can be used for application integration. The scenario discussed here will be based on integration with the SAP R/3 system using these exposed interfaces over the network using TCP/IP. Consequently, the scenario discussed in this chapter is applicable whether SAP is deployed and installed on Windows 2000 or UNIX systems (Sun Solaris, AIX, HP-UX, for example). The choice of RDBMS used by SAP is also not a factor, since all access to the SAP application logic and data will be through public interfaces exposed by the SAP software. This is one of the advantages of basing integration on interfaces and APIs compared with data integration. Of course, data integration might well be a less costly and a less difficult approach if it were a viable option for integrating with SAP R/3.

Understanding the Process

In order to develop an appropriate solution, it is necessary to understand the process and data flows between applications. A self-service Web site for employee benefits enrollment information seems simple, but first appearances can be deceiving. The complications result from the necessity for encryption and authentication between all the processes involved and the need for transactional integrity. Encryption is needed to insure compliance with privacy requirements by preventing other users or processes from viewing sensitive data. Authentication is necessary to allow employees to change and modify only their own benefits records and prevent access to sensitive information on other employees. Authentication is also needed to prevent some system or user from masquerading as another employee or a process that sends or receives this information.

Using a Web browser on the local intranet, a user would connect to a benefits home page on the server. From this Web page, the user can request the online form for benefits enrollment. For privacy reasons, communications sent to or received from the user must be encrypted to protect information transmitted between the Web browser and the server. The user needs to be authenticated so that an employee can view and submit benefits changes only for himself or herself. The benefits Web site can also make available viewable online copies of various benefit options as well as printable copies of this information that can be downloaded.

Once the user completes entering data and hits the submit button, the data would be submitted to applications running on the Web server for validation. The logic on the middle-tier used for validation could check the input data for internal consistencies, obvious data entry errors, and illegal conditions (minimum and maximum range checks on amounts, for example). If the submitted information failed this validation logic, an error message would be returned to the user with information indicating which fields or values require corrections.

If the submitted form passed the validation checks, the information would be stored in the HR RDBMS system and the user would be notified that the process was successful. The information stored in the HR RDBMS system would also need to be sent to the SAP R/3 system and entered in the appropriate SAP application modules. The response times for employees submitting online information should be as short as reasonable. The best approach would be if the self-service Web site/HR database system were loosely coupled to the SAP R/3 system. The weak coupling to the SAP R/3 system allows the Web tier to function even if the SAP system happens to be offline for maintenance or inaccessible due to network problems. This loose coupling can be based on using transactional messaging handled as part of a distributed transaction. The distributed transaction should be such that both the update in the local HR database and the message acceptance in the outgoing message queue to the SAP R/3 system destination must both occur. If either of these transaction elements fails, then the entire transaction should be rolled back and the user informed that the benefits submittal process failed.

At another endpoint on the local intranet, an application should be waiting to receive messages in a special message queue. The outgoing messages should be sent to this destination queue using encryption for privacy. The message acceptance at the destination queue should depend on strong authentication so that the process is protected from unauthorized users submitting benefits messages for others into the destination message queue. The application removing the received message from the queue should call into the SAP R/3 system passing the necessary information from the message. The message receiving and message removal process and the call into SAP should also be handled as part of a distributed transaction so that all elements must succeed to guarantee integrity. The message receipt process could also send an email on success to the HR administrative staff and the employee as a secondary confirmation that the benefits enrollment process for the employee succeeded. This email would not contain any benefits information for the employee, since this could compromise privacy requirements.

Understanding the APIs

Application integration using exposed APIs and interfaces may sound simple, but the process is actually relatively complex. To use APIs effectively for integration, it is essential that EAI architects, developers, and administrators understand the application well enough to determine the appropriate interfaces to be used. The interface methods and parameters must be well understood so that the appropriate values are passed on input and retrieved on output.

SAP R/3 provides support for a variety of well-defined interfaces that can be used for application integration. Unfortunately, the interfaces exposed by SAP R/3 are complex and lack consistency in architecture and calling sequence. In many cases, several interfaces are exposed that provide very similar capabilities, making it more difficult to choose the approach to use in solving a business problem.

For use in EAI solutions, SAP reflects some problems common with many packaged and custom applications. SAP also has some issues unique to the product. Early versions of the SAP suite of applications were constructed as a monolithic stovepipe application lacking options for communication with external applications. Later versions of SAP (the R/3 release) adopted the classic client-server design using three layers:

- Presentation (user interface provided by SAPgui on client systems)

- Application (business logic layer provided by SAP runtime and SAP modules)

- Data (database layer provided by external RDBMS).

Newer SAP releases exposed interfaces for external communication targeted originally for exchanging information between SAP systems. Over time, these interfaces have been extended and enhanced for communication with external applications aside from other SAP systems.

SAP includes its own fourth-generation language (4GL), Advanced Business Application Programming (ABAP/4) language for internal development. All of the SAP application modules are written in ABAP and the SAP runtime consists of a runtime and interpreter for these ABAP applications. SAP R/3 also includes a collection of development tools (the ABAP Workbench) for developing applications or exposing custom external interfaces using the ABAP/4 language.

Some options available for accessing SAP R/3 from external applications include the following:

- Common Programming Interface for Communications (CPI-C)

- Remote Function Call (RFC)

- Business Application Programming Interface (BAPI)

- Intermediate Document (IDoc)

Traditionally, SAP used CPI-C for internal communications between function modules. CPI-C is one of the older programming APIs developed by IBM as part of its System Network Architecture (SNA). Industry standards were adopted for CPI-C interfaces as part of work done by the X/Open group. CPI-C applications are supported by Microsoft technology using Microsoft Host Integration Server 2000 and Visual C/C++. Although SAP still supports communication using CPI-C sessions, this method of external communication has been supplanted by other methods.

Remote Function Call interfaces were originally added to support communication between SAP systems. RFCs provide a synchronous remote procedure call (RPC) mechanism for external communication with other SAP systems and external applications. SAP exposes a number of external interfaces as remote function calls. SAP makes available an RFC SDK that can be used to call SAP Remote Function Calls from Visual C++, Visual Basic and Visual Basic for Applications (VBA), Java, Active Server Pages, VBScript, and JavaScript.

Business Application Programming Interfaces were added later to support object-oriented access to SAP business objects. BAPIs supply methods that encapsulate SAP business processes (business logic) and data, providing access to SAP business objects. BAPIs offer a layer of abstraction over the simpler RFC mechanism upon which they depend. SAP stores the BAPI objects including BAPI metadata in a Business Object Repository on the RDBMS system (data tier). Recent versions of SAP R/3 define almost 1,800 BAPI function methods for the entire SAP R/3 suite and include these BAPIs in the Business Object Repository on the SAP system. SAP supplies tools to access BAPI methods using Visual C++, Visual Basic and Visual Basic for Applications (VBA), Java, Active Server Pages, VBScript, and JavaScript. BAPIs have become a popular technique for integrating SAP with other applications.

RFCs and BAPIs are supported by development tools provided with the SAP R/3 system as part of the RFC SDK. The SAP R/3 DCOM Connector supplied as part of the RFC SDK includes tools to create proxy COM components exposing BAPIs and RFCs for use with external applications. The Object Builder tool included with the R/3 DCOM Connector allows the user to browse the Business Object Repository and select BAPI methods or RFC calls to add to a COM component. Once the BAPI methods are selected, the Object Builder can generate the source code for the COM components and build the COM proxy using Visual C++. The Object Builder also generates the interface definition language (IDL), include, and typelib (TLB) files to use the generated COM components with Visual Studio for developing external applications.

Conceptually, a SAP Intermediate Document (IDoc) is similar to the Electronic Data Interchange (EDI) standard. An Intermediate Document is a data container that is used to interchange information between any two processes that can understand the syntax and semantics of the data. It is the standard format adopted by SAP format for electronic data interchange between systems.

SAP includes almost 700 IDoc types in its repository. Each IDoc type represents a specific SAP format that is to be used to transfer the data for a business transaction. An IDoc type can transfer several message types, the "logical messages" that correspond to different business processes. An IDoc type is described using the following components:

- A control record that includes the source, destination, the IDoc type, and other control information (identical format for all IDocs types)

- One or more data records consisting of a fixed administration part and a data part or segment (the number and format of the segments can be different for each IDoc type)

- Status records which describe the processing stages that an IDoc can pass through (identical format for each IDoc type)

Several external RFC methods can be called that will retrieve an IDoc from a SAP system or send an IDoc to a SAP System. An IDoc is essentially passed as a large blob of data that must be parsed by the external application.

The IDoc types defined by SAP support a number of SAP business transactions, but IDocs provide access to only a subset of the SAP R/3 suite. RFCs provide a set of low-level methods for accessing SAP information. BAPIs provide an object-oriented abstraction to SAP business objects using RFCs under the covers. Currently, BAPIs provide the most extensive access to SAP for application developers looking to integrate with SAP R/3.

Challenges Specific to SAP

BAPIs can be browsed in SAP using the BAPI Explorer (called the BAPI Browser in older versions of SAP R/3). Once a particular business object or BAPI method is located in the repository, documentation and details about the specific BAPI can be viewed based on the metadata information stored in the repository. Similar tools are used to browse for RFCs or IDocs in the repository.

To call the BAPI Explorer, the user must make the following selections from the SAPgui menu after a successful logon to the SAP system:

```
Tools->Business Framework->BAPI Browser
```

Note that the BAPI Explorer is still called the BAPI Browser in the SAPgui menu system. The BAPI Explorer can also be called directly from the SAPgui menu using the Transaction BAPI command.

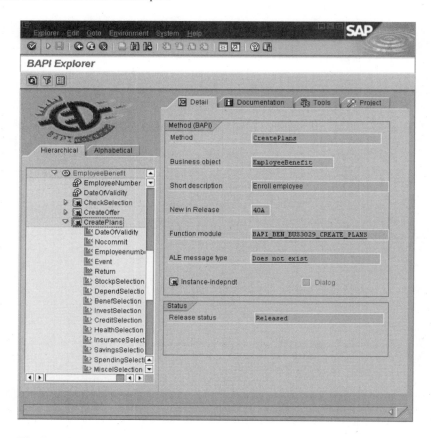

The BAPI Explorer user interface consists of a main window divided into two panes as follows:

- Hierarchy displayed in the left pane that displays all of the business object types and interface types for BAPIs that have been defined in the SAP system.

- Work area displayed in the right pane with a tabbed dialog for displaying details, documentation, tools, and projects for the object highlighted in the hierarchy display.

Once the SAP commands are mastered to browse through the list of BAPIs in the repository, the next problem is finding the appropriate BAPI that may be needed to solve your specific business problem. The way to locate an appropriate business object and BAPI method or RFC is to browse the list of business objects in the repository using the BAPI Explorer. The list of object names can be sorted hierarchically or alphabetically by name within the BAPI Explorer. To effectively use the hierarchy, the SAP application module name (Payroll or Personnel Administration, for example) most likely to contain the SAP information to be used must be known in advance. Otherwise, it may be easier to locate appropriate BAPIs by browsing for business object names beginning with keywords (benefits or employee, for example).

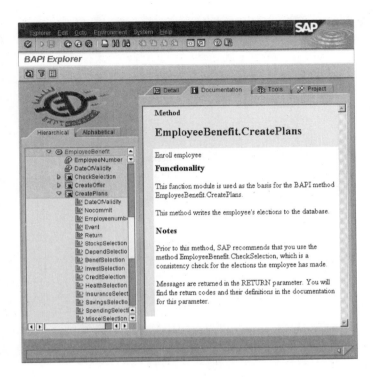

Once you locate a specific business object with an interesting name, the list of BAPI method names supported can be viewed. When a specific object, method, or method parameter name is selected in the BAPI Explorer, a Detail tab provides a short description of the BAPI object, method, or parameter indicating other attributes. The Documentation tab can be displayed to determine from the help text in the repository if the method is appropriate for solving a specific problem. A number of BAPI method names begin with "Get" as a prefix (the GetOpenEnrollmentPeriod method on the EmployeeBenefit object, for example) that read and return information from the SAP R/3 system. There appears to be less consistency in naming used for BAPI methods that write information to the SAP R/3, although some begin with "Create" as the prefix (the CreatePlans method on the EmployeeBenefit object, for example).

Solution

The goal of our solution is to replace existing manual processes with a self-service Web site for employees to use for benefits enrollment. The specific scenario calls for integration of a packaged application, SAP R/3, used for payroll and benefits administration with information maintained by the human resources (HR) or personnel department. This scenario can be visualized as two distinct building blocks that need to be connected as depicted below:

- A Web middleware layer including the Web server, business logic, and other application services to accept and process data from users. This Web tier handles interactive requests from employees using Web browsers (presentation layer) and stores information in separate human resources database. This tier needs the ability to reliably communicate some of this information to the application connector layer.

- An application connector layer handling the interface to a SAP R/3 system using exposed interfaces. This tier uses detailed information on the SAP interfaces to make calls to the SAP system, sending and receiving appropriate information. This tier needs a reliable way to receive communication from the Web middleware layer.

This arrangement with a separate building block for integration with each end-point is typical in many application integration scenarios. These application connectors, the Web middleware for input from Web clients and the SAP connector for integration with the SAP system, provide the specific glue needed to communicate with specific endpoint.

The middleware layer used for providing the self-service Web site is the first major building block in our scenario. A conceptual solution for the Web-based building block is straightforward. Microsoft Internet Information Server (IIS) can be combined with Active Server Pages (ASPs) for the Web-based middleware layer. The business logic is handled by the ASP code located on the server.

Using a Web browser, an employee connects to the benefits Web site to access the benefits Web page. The communication between the Web client and the Web server can use the secure sockets layer (https) to encrypt communication between client and server for compliance with privacy requirements. The Web server would need a public certificate registered by a well-known certificate authority so that the client can be assured of the identity of the server. Using features of Internet Explorer, the Web server can verify the user with Windows authentication.

ASP pages on the Web server implement the business logic for processing employee data entry. The application code can be written using VBScript, JavaScript, ISAPI, or other scripting languages. The ASP code can also make calls out to other components, Windows services, and applications. When information is received by the Web middleware layer, the database used by the human resources department needs to be updated. A subset of this information also needs to be written to the SAP system. The ASP pages need to coordinate a distributed transaction that will write information to the HR SQL Server 2000 data tables and at the same time send a limited subset of this information to the SAP R/3 system. ADO can be used from the ASP pages using VBScript to access and update the employee's records in the database.

The second building block in this scenario is the application connector layer containing the ability to send information to the SAP system and integrate with the appropriate SAP exposed interfaces. Several different solutions for this building block can be developed with Microsoft technologies and products based on the SAP interface or exchange mechanism to be used. Possible solutions include the following:

- Integration using BAPI methods and RFC methods

- Integration using IDocs

The application connector for integrating with SAP is best if it is loosely coupled with the Web middleware functions. By separating SAP integration from the Web middleware, both processes are isolated from problems resulting from network outages or off-line servers.

In the following sections, two of the approaches for the application connector will be discussed.

SAP Integration Using BAPI

SAP R/3 exposes a large number of BAPI method calls and RFCs that can be used for application integration. The BAPI Explorer included as part of the SAPgui Windows client allows a user to browse the Business Object Repository and locate appropriate business objects, the BAPI methods supported by the object, and details on the parameters and return values of a specific BAPI method. Since business objects represent the actual components used as part of the SAP system for communication between modules, this approach has the potential to provide broad support for application integration with SAP.

In our scenario, the application connector to the SAP system receives information from the Web middleware tier destined for the SAP system (see the following figure). Requests can be sent from the Web tier at any time. So the SAP application connector layer needs to provide a receive function that is running all the time. Consequently, the receive function of this application connector needs to be written as a Windows NT service that can be automatically started when the computer starts operation. Other components of the application connector layer can be integrated with this receive function service or can be separate applications that are started by the receive function when needed. This is a design decision to be made by system architects and application developers based on the particulars of a solution.

The communication between the Web middleware layer and the SAP application connector needs to provide loose coupling. Some form of messaging is a natural choice for this communication. Although it would be possible to develop a custom message service for use in this scenario, we chose to demonstrate how to integrate existing features and facilities.

The Microsoft Message Queue (MSMQ) service is included as part of Windows 2000 Server and provides a general-purpose asynchronous message service with guaranteed delivery. Applications would send messages to a queue defined in the MSMQ service on a local or remote server. These messages would be placed in the outgoing queue of the local server for delivery to the remote server. Other applications or processes can retrieve messages from these MSMQ queues at a later time. A message has no specific format to MSMQ and is considered a blob of bytes. So, a message can take any form that the developer chooses up to the size limit of a single message (4 megabytes). The only caveat is that both sender and receiver must understand the message format to be used in order to properly interpret the message. MSMQ messages can be encrypted simply by setting a property on a message. The MSMQ message can also provide authentication of the message sender and receiver.

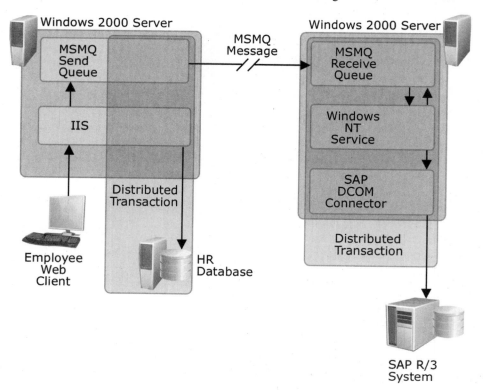

Integrating employee benefits Web site with SAP R/3 using BAPI

The application connector receive function can be developed as a Windows NT service that queries the appropriate MSMQ queue at some regular interval. If a message is found in the queue, the service can retrieve the MSMQ message from the Web middleware layer, parse the message for the parameters needed, and make the appropriate calls into the SAP system using BAPI methods and RFCs. These secondary functions could be packaged in a COM or COM+ DLL component or as an application that the service invokes with some specific parameters.

The Object Builder included with the SAP R/3 DCOM Connector can be used to create COM proxy objects for accessing BAPI methods and remote function calls in SAP. The Object Builder tool included with the SAP DCOM Connector can be used to browse the Business Object Repository and select BAPI methods and RFCs to be included in a COM object that will be created. Once the BAPI methods are selected, the Object Builder generates the necessary source code for the COM components and builds the COM proxy using Visual C++. In the scenario discussed in this chapter, it would make sense for simplicity to encapsulate all of the BAPI methods and RFC function module calls to be used into a single COM or COM+ component for accessing the SAP system. Since these calls will need to be handled as part of a distributed transaction, programming is likely to be easier with only a single DLL to deal with for the SAP integration code. This COM proxy should also contain appropriate code to establish a SAP logon session, since this session connection is required to issue BAPI method calls or RFCs. Bundling all of the SAP BAPI and RFC integration code in a single DLL should make it simpler to share a single SAP logon session than if a number of separate COM objects were generated using the SAP R/3 Object Builder.

When creating COM components using the Object Builder, three types of remote function calls to the SAP System are supported:

- Synchronous RFC - the application makes the function call to the R/3 system and waits for the call to complete. Some RFC function modules contain implicit or explicit commits, while others require the user to call the CommitWork method. This is dependent on the BAPI or RFC method, so the documentation should be checked.

- Transactional RFC - the same as a synchronous RFC but this type guarantees that each function issued is only executed once.

- Queued RFC - similar to the transactional RFC, but guarantees the order in which function calls will be processed in the SAP system.

Essentially all three of these RFC types still result in a synchronous remote procedure call to the SAP system, but the RFC type determines how the method call will be handled and processed once received by SAP.

In our scenario, the call into the SAP system must be part of a distributed transaction coordinated with the removal of an MSMQ message from an MSMQ queue. The MSMQ message should only be removed from the message queue if the BAPI and RFC method calls to the SAP system completed successfully. Otherwise, the MSMQ message should be left in the queue, and the process attempted again (roll back the transaction).

There may be cases where the queued RFC is needed if BAPI and RFC method calls are required in a specific order, but in our scenario this does not appear necessary. As a result, synchronous RFC is probably a reasonable choice.

Using the SAP Business Object Repository and exposed BAPI methods and RFCs can provide the broadest support for application integration with SAP. The scenario assumes a loose coupling of the Web middleware layer with the components used to make the appropriate BAPI method calls to the SAP System. This loose coupling is handled using MSMQ messaging. Loose coupling allows the benefits Web site to function properly even if the SAP system is off-line or network outages occur.

SAP Integration Using IDocs

BizTalk Server 2000 can be combined with the BizTalk Adapter for SAP to provide a solution based on using IDocs for integration with SAP R/3. There are several reasons why this approach may not be appropriate for the problem being discussed in this chapter. In the proposed scenario, the information flow is primarily from the user and the Web middleware layer into the SAP system. The predominant direction of these flows has an impact on the applicability of the BizTalk Adapter for SAP to the proposed scenario.

The current version of the SAP R/3 suite implements approximately 700 IDoc types that can be used by external applications for integration. If an IDoc does not exist for transferring the SAP information required in a specific EAI scenario, then using IDocs and the BizTalk Adapter for SAP is not a possibility. Since the IDocs provided with SAP R/3 cover only a subset of the full SAP R/3 suite, there will be some cases where integration using IDocs is not feasible.

The BizTalk Adapter for SAP uses RFC methods to connect to the SAP Business Object Repository and read the schema of all defined IDoc types. Based on knowledge of the IDoc formats, the BizTalk Adapter for SAP can use other RFC methods to request a specific IDoc from the SAP system. The IDoc returned from the RFC call is parsed knowing the structure of the IDoc format and the information is formatted as XML and passed to BizTalk Server for delivery to the requesting application.

In contrast, when the BizTalk Adapter for SAP is requested to send an IDoc, it expects to be handed a document formatted like an IDoc in XML. So in order to use the BizTalk Adapter for SAP in the scenario discussed in this chapter, the Web middleware layer would require a thorough understanding of the format of any IDocs to be used to write information to the SAP system. The Web middleware layer would need this information in order to format the equivalent IDoc for sending to the SAP system. Given the complexity of the IDoc format, this conversion is a complex task. While the conversion would be possible, the programming effort required is likely to be very substantial. To create a generalized solution that could interrogate the SAP repository for information on the IDoc format, the Web middleware layer would essentially be replicating the work accomplished by the BizTalk Adapter for SAP.

A later chapter in the business-to-business (B2B) section describes a more appropriate scenario for using BizTalk Server integrated with a SAP system.

Tools and Technologies

To implement the application integration solution described in this chapter, a number of Microsoft technologies are required, including the following:

- Microsoft® Internet Information Server

- Microsoft® Active Server Pages

- Microsoft® Internet Explorer

- Microsoft® Message Queuing

- Microsoft® Distributed Transaction Coordinator

- Microsoft® Visual Studio or Microsoft® Visual Studio® .NET

With the exception of Microsoft Visual Studio and Visual Studio .NET, all of these technologies are included with Windows 2000 Server.

The scenario also assumes that SQL Server 2000 is used for the human resources database, although this is not essential. The database could be any relational database management system (RDBMS) that offers an OLE DB provider or ODBC driver accessible using ADO, ODBC, or OLE DB.

If the human resources data is maintained on AS/400 minicomputers or IBM-compatible mainframes, Host Integration Server 2000 can be used to provide the core networking connectivity over SNA as well as the Microsoft ODBC Driver for DB2 and the Microsoft OLE DB Provider for DB2.

Windows 2000 Server (Server, Advanced Server, or DataCenter Server) is a required prerequisite for installing SQL Server 2000 and Host Integration Server 2000. SQL Server 2000 and Host Integration Server 2000 can also be installed on Windows NT 4.0 with Service Pack 6a. However, Windows 2000 supports a number of new features that make it preferred.

Either Microsoft Visual Studio or Microsoft Visual Studio .NET is required for this scenario. Visual Studio .NET is needed for development if new features such as the .NET Framework and managed code will be used. The .NET Framework is not required, so Visual Studio 6.0 can also be used in implementing the proposed scenario. Compared with the data integration scenario in the previous chapter, the application integration solution discussed in this chapter requires a substantial programming effort for implementation.

Implementation

This implementation of this scenario can be considered as two sets of application services that need to be loosely connected:

- Web middleware

- Application connector

The Web middleware includes the Web server and the associate business logic to handle interactive requests from employees. Associated with this building block is a local MSMQ outgoing queue where messages destined for the SAP system are stored until the messages are successfully delivered. In our scenario, all of the Web middleware services could be implemented on a single Windows 2000 server system.

Web Middleware

The Web middleware layer can be implemented as a collection of ASP or ASP.NET pages on Internet Information Server on Windows 2000 Server. Any Web pages on the benefits Web site used for benefits enrollment or other employee matters should be restricted so that the secure sockets layer (SSL) protocol is enabled to encrypt communications. Directory Security for the folder containing these pages should be set to require "Secure Communications" requiring a server certificate issued by a recognized certificate authority.

The more difficult aspects of the Web middleware layer have to do with using MSMQ for messaging and participating in a coordinated distributed transaction to handle MSMQ sends and database writes. There are several ways to program the Web middleware. One scheme is to package all of the application logic in VBScript on ASP pages. The VBScript code would make calls to the needed Windows and system APIs for handling messaging, transactions, and access to databases. Another approach would be to create COM or COM+ components using Visual C++ to handle the messaging, transactions, and data access and make calls to use these COM or COM+ components from the VBScript code on the ASP pages.

There is the possibility of performances issues with an all ASP solution since the ASP pages are interpreted at runtime. Compared with VBScript, Visual C++ provides greater flexibility and control when dealing with the transactions and messaging APIs. Consequently, the second approach is the one illustrated in this chapter.

One of the requirements for MSMQ in the proposed scenario is that Active Directory be used and that the MSMQ service be installed on the primary domain controller. This is a requirement because of the need for encryption and authentication for MSMQ messages sent and received between processes. MSMQ creates certificates used for encryption and digital signing and stores this information in MSMQ on the domain controller and in Active Directory.

The MSMQ message can be stored in either private or public queues, the distinction being whether the queue is advertised. In this scenario, either one will work. An application must know the name of any private queues so a private queue provides some limited security through obscurity. Real security will be provided by enforcing users (and processes invoked by users) to authenticate for access to the messages in a queue. These authentication issues are handled automatically by configuring properties on a queue when it is created. This requires that IIS and other server processes used be started under a domain user account, not the Local System account on a particular Windows server where the service is hosted. Encryption of messages is handled by setting a property before it is sent. The MSMQ messages also need to be marked as transactional in order to guarantee delivery.

To handle messaging, the MSMQ APIs can be called directly or COM+ queued components can be used. COM+ queued components are built on top of the MSMQ message service, so in either case the MSMQ service must be installed and configured properly and the appropriate MSMQ queues created.

One of the samples installed as part of the Platform Software Development can be used as a starting point for building the COM objects to handle messaging and database access. This sample is located under the samples\netds\messagequeuing\mqtrans folder below where the Platform SDK was installed. The MQTrans sample is a Visual C++ console application that demonstrates how to coordinated transactions that include sending or receiving MSMQ messages and database updates using ODBC. This sample illustrates how to set up a coordinated transaction to handle MSMQ message sends and database updates using the Distributed Transaction Coordinator (DTC).

MSMQ Message Body Format

One general issue still needs to be resolved regarding the Web middleware layer implementation. The MSMQ message sent to the SAP application connector tier has to contain the information needed to update the benefits and payroll information in the SAP system. MSMQ does not care what the message body contains, but the format of the message must be understood by both the sending and receiving applications. There are any number of options as to how this information should be structured in the message body, including the following:

- Comma-delimited text strings in a readable format

- Based on windows INF file format

- OLE/COM structured storage generated using the IStream interfaces

- XML generated using the MSXML library installed with Internet Explorer

- Records in a database file format such as Microsoft Access MDB format or the Microsoft Foxpro DBF

- Custom format

The primary consideration when selecting the message body format is whether the format is easy to prepare by the sending application and correspondingly easy to parse by the receiving application. Messaging containing readable text can be a useful tool for debugging during development. An option worth considering is to base the message format on the SAP COM proxies developed for the application connector layer. The Web middleware layer could use the same COM objects developed for the SAP application connector as the internal representation of how the middleware layer represents information.

SAP Application Connector

At least part of the SAP application connector software needs to be implemented as a Windows service installed under a domain user account. This Windows service would be set to check the incoming MSMQ queue at regular intervals for messages from the Web middleware layer. The interval for checking could be short (a few seconds, for example) so that under normal circumstances the SAP system is updated in almost real time. This interval could also be set much longer (an hour or a day, for example) so that updates to the SAP system would be closer to a batch process. If a long interval were selected, then the adapter connector layer could be implemented as an application rather than a service that is executed at some regular interval using the Task Scheduler.

Once a message is detected in the incoming queue, the message is retrieved and the information is sent to the SAP R/3 system. The removal of the message from the incoming queue and the successful update of the SAP system must be coordinated as a distributed transaction.

The Object Builder tool included with the SAP R/3 DCOM Connector is used to build COM proxies to the BAPI methods and RFCs needed to interface to the SAP system. The DCOM Connector, which forms a part of the SAP RFC SDK, must be installed on a development system that has Visual Studio 6.0 or Visual Studio .NET. The SAP R/3 DCOM Connector is based on a series of COM components and has a somewhat strange interface for users.

Before the SAP DCOM Connector can be used, the SAP COM for ABAP Service must be started. The shortcut to the SAP DCOM Connector is actually to a Web page loaded on the local computer during the RFC SDK install. This Web page is opened using Internet Explorer in order to start the DCOM Connector and gain access to the tools, A destination has to be configured to a SAP system where the developer has a SAP logon. Once a destination is configured, the Object Builder can be invoked from the DCOM Connector menu bar across the top of the page.

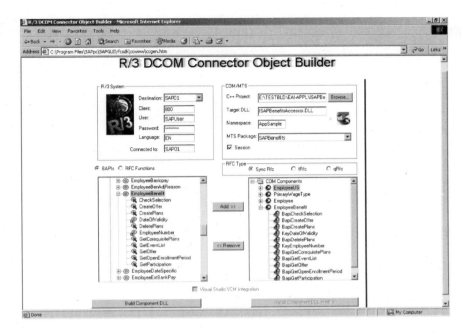

As shown in the illustration, the Object Builder allows you to select specific BAPIs or RFCs functions and add them to the list of COM proxies that will be generated. The tool allows you to select or browse to the C++ project where the source code and output from generating these COM proxies will be stored. Other options can be set including the target DLL name, the namespace in the source code to be generated, the MTS package name, the type of RFC mechanism to use, and whether a login session should be included in the code generated.

When all of the BAPIs and RFCs have been selected, the Build Component button will generate the source code to the COM proxies and build the COM components using Visual C++. Note that the VCVARS32.bat file from Visual C++ needs to be on your path or the environment variables from this file need to be set prior to starting the Object Builder tool. The Object Builder depends on parsing the VCVARS32 file or using environment variables to invoke the C++ compiler and find the needed include and library files.

After the COM DLL has been built successfully, the COM DLL can also be installed using the Object Builder. The IDL, include, and typelib files created for the COM DLL can be used to interface with these COM proxies to the BAPIs and RFC functions from other code. The process of creating these COM proxies to the SAP interfaces is simple once you get used to the tool interface.

Application Integration Using APIs and Interfaces

The scenario described in this chapter focuses on using integration using APIs and interfaces as a tool for providing application integration in the enterprise. It is interesting to contrast the application integration approach described in this chapter with the data integration scenario discussed in the previous chapter. The data integration scenario required very little programming, consisting mostly of configuring software. In contrast, the application integration approach depends mostly on programming to deliver a solution.

Although the scenario described in this chapter focused on integration with SAP, the general model can be applied to other large packaged application suites. The presentation layer is provided by employees using Web browsers. The Web middleware layer is implemented using IIS, ASP, and custom COM components. The application connector is implemented as a Windows NT Service using COM objects created with the Object Builder from the SAP DCOM Connector. These separate building blocks are loosely coupled using MSMQ messaging and distributed transactions.

This arrangement with a separate building block for integration with each end-point is typical in many application integration scenarios. The separate building blocks can be tailored to the scenario and provide the specific glue needed to communicate with a custom or packaged application. MSMQ can be used to provide loose coupling between the applications.

By William J. Harding

Integrating Host Data into the Web

Scenario

Corporate information drives the enterprise business. In many enterprise organizations, business critical information and data processing functions are on mainframe computing systems. In addition to the legacy host systems, today's enterprise also has a mix of highly specialized systems, many departmentally maintained. Each of these systems represents a significant investment and each is critical to successful business operations.

These organizations are finding an increased requirement to access and integrate these many computer systems. The problem is that these systems were never designed to work together, and they were not designed for Web operations (either internal to the organization or externally to the World Wide Web).

For years, IT departments have been trying to make information stored on one system available to other systems. Abandoning existing systems and starting from scratch to build a new enterprise-wide, one-system-fits-all data processing system is out of the question. The investment in mainframe legacy systems is too high. In addition, it does not make good business sense to abandon processing systems that are reliable and stable.

Enterprise Application Integration (EAI) by integrating legacy host systems with other data systems, in particular Microsoft Windows-based and Web systems is one solution to the problem. The ability to combine terminal-based host applications and databases with Windows-based applications is increasingly important to the overall data processing functions of the enterprise. When done successfully, legacy host integration eliminates the need to build laborious custom interfaces to link disparate applications and data. It addition, it also makes the host application completely invisible to the user.

Solution

One solution for integrating host application systems with Windows-based applications, including the Web, is by using Microsoft Transaction Integrator, Microsoft Component Object Model (COM) technology, and Microsoft® Visual Studio® .NET Application Integration Tools. This combination of technologies enables you to quickly build Web front-ends to host applications and data with little or no changes to the host code. The COM Transaction Integration (COMTI) technology is part of the Microsoft® Host Integration Server 2000 and integrates IBM mainframe-based transaction programs managed by the Customer Information Control Systems (CICS) and Information Management Systems (IMS).

The transaction integration technology enables data to be obtained from mainframe-based transaction programs (TPs), transferred, and used in component-based Windows® 2000 COM or distributed COM (DCOM) applications, when a synchronous or transactional solution is needed.

True integration of online transaction processing (OLTP) with COM-compliant systems means the integration of CICS and IMS with Windows-based solutions. CICS and IMS are widely used in the mainframe arena to create distributed OLTP solutions, such as customer tracking and order entry solutions. COMTI integrates CICS and IMS with COM by creating COM interfaces to the CICS and IMS transactions and running the CICS and IMS transactions on the mainframe from Windows.

COMTI preserves existing CICS and IMS TPs in either a three-tier client/server or Web-to-host computing environment. By using COMTI to invoke mainframe transactions, you can write programs in object-oriented environments and programming languages such as Visual Basic or C#, while still having access to host transactions.

Both SNA and TCP/IP connectivity is supported by COMTI. SNA connectivity is used if you need two-phase commit (2PC) type processing. TCP/IP connectivity is used if you need direct throughput. IBM has not implemented 2PC in the TCP/IP protocol, but for those cases where 2PC is not needed, TCP/IP can give you direct connectivity.

The following figure shows a conceptual overview of the COMTI architecture.

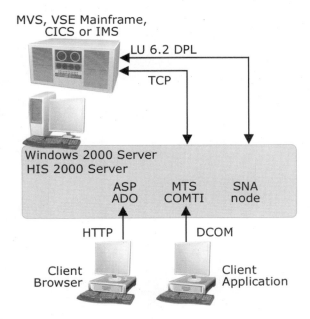

COMTI architecture

COMTI has two graphical user interfaces, COMTI Component Builder and COMTI Manager, and also contains the COMTI run-time environment that automatically handles the actual transaction integration. COMTI Component Builder is used to turn COBOL TPs into COMTI components (type libraries) that include COMTI run-time environment settings. COMTI Manager is used to configure and manage the following application integration services:

- COMTI components and their embedded COMTI run-time environment settings

- Remote environments in the SNA or TCP/IP network

- COM+ applications (or MTS packages)

A COMTI component in a COM+ application or older Microsoft Transaction Server (MTS) package works in concert with the COMTI run-time environment, Microsoft Distributed Transaction Coordinator (MS DTC), and the associated remote environment (RE) to drive a CICS or IMS Transaction Program (TP). Together, they accomplish these tasks:

- Activate the host (mainframe) TP

- Pass the parameters specified by the COMTI component to the TP

- Run the TP

- Return the results to the COMTI component

Once a COMTI component (a type library, .tlb file) is deployed in a COM+ application, that COM+ application becomes known as an automation server. When a client application calls for the services of (invokes) a method in that COMTI automation server, Windows automatically starts the COMTI run-time environment in the associated remote environment to invoke the mainframe transaction that is associated with that COMTI method. Component Services in Windows 2000 (or MTS in Windows NT 4.0) automatically handles any class factory, early or late binding, or other internal operations needed. The invoked mainframe transaction can call other transactions on the mainframe before returning the result to the COM-based client application through the COMTI Automation server.

Complete information on COMTI is available in the Host Integration Server 2000 documentation.

The Sample Application

This sample application simulates a fictitious bank (Cedar Bank) and demonstrates the major features of the .NET Framework and COMTI by retrieving customer account information using mainframe COBOL transactions by way of CICS or IMS. It also shows you how to call a COMTI Automation server from Web-based or other COM-based client applications. This sample application requires a live connection to a mainframe host environment. This sample application demonstrates:

- How to call COMTI automation servers from a Windows-based application or from an ActiveX component written in Microsoft Visual Basic .NET or C#.

- How to call COMTI automation servers from a client browser by using Visual Basic .NET and Active Server Pages (ASP).

- How to use ActiveX Data Object (ADO) recordsets.

The Cedar Bank sample application includes everything to put COMTI and Visual Studio .NET to work for you. Included are the following:

- Sample automation client applications, one written in each Visual Basic .NET and C#, along with the source code for these applications. (Instructions for compiling the code are given later in this chapter.)

- Eight different COMTI components that you can use to create eight different automation servers (one for each of the eight supported mainframe models). Each exposes the same COM interface.

- Sample COBOL transaction programs (TPs).

The following figure shows how COMTI is integrated with the .NET runtime environment, including interfaces to the mainframe environment.

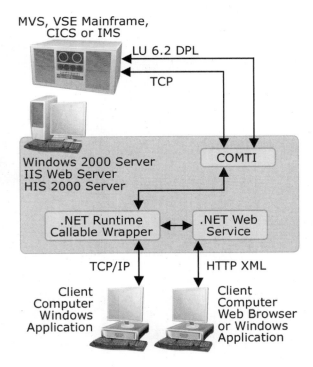

.NET Runtime COMTI integration

The sample Automation client application uses the methods of a COMTI Automation server to run COBOL-based mainframe TPs. The sample Automation client sends parameters to and receives results from each TP by calling the methods of a COMTI Automation server (a COMTI component deployed in a COM+ application or MTS package) by way of the COMTI run-time environment.

The COMTI Automation server's interface contains two methods (**getbal**, and **getaccts**) that any COM-based client application (the Automation client) can call to retrieve bank account information using mainframe COBOL transactions by way of CICS or IMS.

- The **getbal** method invokes the GETBAL COBOL transaction program on the mainframe, passes it a customer name and account number, and then returns the balance of the given account.

- The **getaccts** method invokes the GETACCTS COBOL transaction program on the mainframe, passes it a customer name and PIN, and then returns a number of account records, each containing a set of fields with information about one of the customer's accounts. The account records are returned as an ActiveX Data Object (ADO) recordset that you can call from a COM-based client application or that you can connect to a data-bound control in Internet Explorer from a Web-based client application.

The following diagram shows the connections between a .NET Windows client application, the .NET Runtime, and the COMTI methods, which then call the mainframe transaction programs.

Direct Client to COMTI

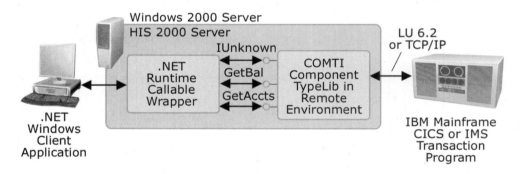

Direct client to .NET Runtime to COMTI to mainframe

The following diagram shows the connections between either a browser or a Windows client application, the .NET Server Web Service, the .NET Runtime, and the COMTI methods, which then call the mainframe transaction programs.

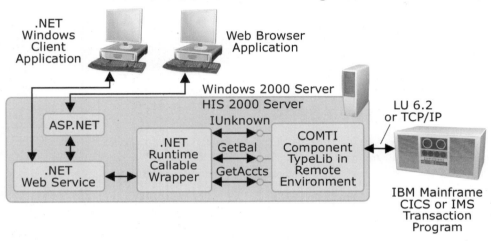

.NET Client to Web Server Hosting COMTI

Connecting the Web to the mainframe

The Cedar Bank sample application is designed to use host mainframe connectivity over TCP/IP or SNA (APPC/LU 6.2). COBOL source code is supplied to run COMTI over a live mainframe connection. Use this COBOL source code to create GETBAL and GETACCTS mainframe TPs, and then install them in CICS or IMS on your mainframe. See the "Running Cedar Bank with a Live Mainframe Connection" topic later in this chapter.

> **Note**   This sample application is based on the Cedar Bank Sample application that is installed with Host Integration Server 2000. The Cedar Bank sample application has been modified for the .NET Framework and requires not only Microsoft Host Integration Server 2000, but also Microsoft Visual Studio .NET as discussed later in this chapter.

The Cedar Bank Sample application supplied with Host Integration Server 2000 is programmed using Visual Studio version 6.0. The Host Integration Server 2000 documentation has complete information for the Cedar Bank sample application.

Tools and Technologies

This section describes the hardware and software requirements, and the components of the Cedar Bank sample application.

Hardware and Software Requirements

The Cedar Bank sample application is dependent on the Microsoft Host Integration Server 2000 product.

Microsoft Host Integration Server 2000

Microsoft Host Integration Server 2000 is one of the Microsoft .NET Enterprise Server products. An overview of Host Integration Server 2000 is located in the "Overview of .NET Enterprise Servers" chapter in Part One of this book.

Host Integration Server 2000 can be installed on computers running the following operating systems:

- All Windows 2000 Server and Windows NT 4.0 Server variations. (Windows NT 4.0 Server must have Service Pack 6a installed).

- The MSMQ-MQSeries Bridge requires Windows 2000 Server or Windows NT Server 4.0 Enterprise Edition.

- Installing Host Integration Server 2000 server on a Windows NT Workstation or Windows 2000 Professional is supported only for development use - production deployment requires installation on a Windows NT Server or Windows 2000 (Advanced/DataCenter) Server.

There are software dependencies for several Host Integration Server 2000 features. A complete list of these dependencies is available in the Host Integration Server 2000 documentation and Release Notes.

Some of the software dependencies required by Host Integration Server 2000 are software components that are shared across several Microsoft products and platforms. These shared components must be installed on the computer before Host Integration Server 2000 is installed.

Because these shared components are not under the control of the Host Integration Server 2000 development group, updated versions of these shared components should be obtained from the Microsoft Web site at http://www.microsoft.com/downloads.

Complete installation procedures for Host Integration Server 2000 are available in the product documentation.

Visual Studio .NET

Visual Studio .NET has the following system requirements. For the latest information, see the Visual Studio .NET Readme file.

- **Processor**: PC with a Pentium II-class processor running at least 450 MHz (Recommended: Pentium III-class, at 600 MHz)

- **RAM**: Windows NT 4.0 Workstation, 64 MB (Recommended: 96MB)

    Windows NT 4.0 Server, 160 MB (Recommended: 192MB)

    Windows 2000 Professional, 96 MB (Recommended: 128 MB)

    Windows 2000 Server, 192 MB (Recommended: 192 MB)

    Windows XP Professional, 160 MB (Recommended: 192 MB).

    Windows XP Home, 96 MB (Recommended: 160 MB).

- **Hard Disk Space:** 600 MB on system drive and 3 GB on installation drive

- **Operating System:** Windows 2000, Windows XP, and Windows NT 4.0.

- **Video:** 800 X 600 with 256 colors (Recommended: High Color 16 bit)

- **CD-ROM or DVD-ROM Drive:** Required

- **Mouse:** Required Microsoft mouse or compatible pointing device

Cedar Bank Files and Folders

The Cedar Bank Sample Application files are located on the companion CD-ROM to this book. The CD-ROM contains the folders listed in the following table. Except where noted, each folder contains all the files you need to run the Cedar Bank sample application using various host environment configurations, including the COMTI component type library (.tlb) file and the COBOL source code (.cbl) files that you need to install on your mainframe.

Sample Application Folders and Files

Folder Name	Description
ASP.NET VB Host Program Access	This sample program is written in Visual Basic .NET. It is an early bind to the Remote Environment component object and demonstrates the use of single data values and recordsets. This program uses the COMTI typelib and COBOL program for CICS MSLINK in the Cedar Bank tutorials folder associated with the Host Integration Server 2000 program files. This sample application requires that IIS, ASP.NET and Host Integration Server 2000 be installed and running on the same computer. The source code can be modified to use any one of several other Remote Environments.
VB.NET Early Bound Host Program Access	This client, written in Visual Basic .NET, is an early bind to the Remote Environment component object and demonstrates the use of single data values and recordsets. This means that the remote environment is selected and bound into the executable during compile time. Generally the early bind is more efficient than the late bind version. This program uses the COMTI typelib and COBOL program for CICS MSLINK in the Cedar Bank tutorials folder associated with the Host Integration Server 2000 program files. This sample application requires that IIS, VB.NET and Host Integration Server 2000 be installed and running on the same computer. The source code can be modified to use any one of several other Remote Environments.
C# Early Bound Host Program Access	This client, written in C#, is an early bind to the Remote Environment component object and demonstrates the use of single data values and recordsets. This means that the remote environment is selected and bound into the executable during compile time. Generally the early bind is more efficient than the late bind version. This program uses the COMTI typelib and COBOL program for CICS MSLINK in the Cedar Bank tutorials folder associated with the Host Integration Server 2000 program files. This sample application requires that IIS, C#, and Host Integration Server 2000 be installed and running on the same computer. The source code can be modified to use any one of several other Remote Environments.

(continued)

Folder Name	Description *(continued)*
Visual Basic .NET Host Program Access as Web Service	This sample program is written in Visual Basic .NET. It is an early bind to the Remote Environment component object and demonstrates the use of single data values and recordsets returned through a Web Service. This program uses the COMTI typelib and COBOL program for CICS MSLINK in the Cedar Bank tutorials folder associated with the Host Integration Server 2000 program files. This sample application requires that IIS, ASP.NET and Host Integration Server 2000 be installed and running on the same computer. The source code can be modified to use any one of several other Remote Environments.
Visual Basic .NET Host Program Access Web Service Web Client	This sample program, written in Visual Basic .NET, demonstrates a Web client application accessing the Web service. This program requires that the VB.NET Host Program Access as Web Service be set up and running.
Visual Basic .NET Host Program Access Web Service Windows Forms Client	This sample program, written in Visual Basic .NET, demonstrates a Windows forms client application accessing the Web service. This program requires that the Visual Basic .NET Host Program Access as Web Service be set up and running.

Cedar Bank Components and Remote Environments

Cedar Bank can use any of the following eight different host environment configurations, four in the CICS environment (two SNA and two TCP/IP) and four in the IMS environment (one SNA and three TCP/IP):

- CICS Link SNA (over LU 6.2)

- CICS SNA (over LU 6.2)

- CICS Concurrent (over TCP/IP)

- CICS MS Link (simulated CICS Link over TCP/IP)

- IMS SNA (over LU 6.2)

- IMS Implicit (over TCP/IP)

- IMS Explicit (over TCP/IP)

- IMS OTMA (over TCP/IP)

The following table includes a COMTI component for each of these eight host mainframe environments. Choose the COMTI component (.tlb) files that fit your particular mainframe environment, and create an instance of the remote environment (RE) type shown.

ProgID	RE Type	COMTI Component
CICS_Link.CedarBank.1	CICS LINK using LU 6.2	CICS_Link_CedarBank.tlb
CICS_LU62.CedarBank.1	CICS using LU 6.2	CICS_LU62_CedarBank.tlb
TCP_Concurrent.CedarBank.1	CICS and IMS using TCP/IP	CICS_TCP_Concurrent_CedarBank.tlb
TCP_MSlink.CedarBank.1	CICS and IMS using TCP/IP	CICS_MSLink_CedarBank.tlb
IMS_LU62.CedarBank.1	IMS using LU 6.2	IMS_LU62_CedarBank.tlb
IMS_TCP_Implicit.CedarBank.1	CICS and IMS using TCP/IP	IMS_TCP_Explicit_CedarBank.tlb
IMS_TCP_Explicit.CedarBank.1	CICS and IMS using TCP/IP	IMS_TCP_Implicit_CedarBank.tlb
IMS_TCP_OTMA.CedarBank.1	IMS using OTMA	IMS_OTMA_CedarBank.tlb

To configure the sample application to use a Remote Environment

1. Set up a Remote Environment using the procedures in the Host Integration Server 2000 documentation.

2. Using Visual Studio .NET, open either the Visual Basic or C# project along with its corresponding CedarBank.vb or the CedarBank.cs file.

3. Select the project in the Solution Explorer in Visual Studio .NET.

4. Click the **Project** menu, and then click **Add Reference.**

5. Browse to the typelib folder for the Remote Environment you set up in Step 1 above.

6. Select the typelib in the folder corresponding to the Remote Environment and click **OK**.

7. Find and Replace all instances of TCP_MSLINK with the name assigned in the project references section (such as CICS_LINK or IMS_OTMA.)

8. Compile and run the application.

COBOL Programs

If you run the Cedar Bank sample application over a live mainframe connection, you need to create and install the mainframe transaction programs (TPs). See the procedure "To set up the COBOL programs on your mainframe host computer" in the Implementation section. The COBOL source code is located on the respective Host Integration Server 2000 and the companion CD-ROM discs. For more information, see the Cedar Bank Files and Folders section above.

> **Note** All the COBOL programs provided are sample programs; they are not intended for use in production environments. They are provided to demonstrate techniques you can use to develop your own COBOL programs and servers for production use.

GetBal.cbl and Getaccts.cbl

The Cedar Bank COMTI component contains two methods (**getbal** and **getaccts**) that client applications use to retrieve bank account information for CICS or IMS. The **getbal** method accesses the getbal.cbl mainframe transaction program on the host, passing it a customer name and account number, and returning the account balance. The **getaccts** method accesses the Getaccts.cbl transaction program on the host, passing a customer name and PIN and returning a number of "account" records, each containing a set of fields with information about one of the customer's accounts. The **getaccts** method returns the account records as an ActiveX Data Object (ADO) recordset that can be accessed from your application code or connected to data-bound controls in Internet Explorer.

Once you configure Host Integration Server 2000 to communicate with your host system, you can use the COBOL source code files provided for each remote environment (RE) to create the getbal.cbl and Getaccts.cbl transaction programs and install them in CICS or IMS. The getbal.cbl and Getaccts.cbl files that you need are located in the same folder that contains the COMTI component (.tlb file).

See the procedure "To set up the COBOL programs on your mainframe host computer" below. Note that the actual procedure and the actual names of the COBOL programs are different for each RE to allow all RE types to work in a single CICS or IMS region.

Implementation

This section provides you a road map and the procedures for setting up the Cedar Bank sample application to be run using a live connection to your mainframe computer.

Running Cedar Bank with a Live Mainframe Connection

The Cedar Bank sample application comes with a COMTI component (.tlb) file and COBOL source code (.cbl) files for each of the four CICS remote environments (REs) and each of the four IMS REs. Each of the eight remote environments has a folder containing the files you need. COMTI Component Builder was used to build each of the eight COMTI components.

To connect to the mainframe, use the instructions in the "Making and Testing a Connection" topic under the "Installation and Configuration" section of Host Integration Server 2000 online Help. For an SNA (APPC/LU 6.2) connection to the mainframe, see the instructions about configuring Host Integration Server 2000 for LU 6.2. For a TCP/IP connection to the mainframe, refer to the following IBM documents for instructions about configuring the mainframe for TCP/IP:

- TCP/IP version 3R2 for MVS: CICS TCP/IP Socket Interface Guide (IBM Document #SC31-7131)

- TCP/IP version 3R2 for MVS: IMS TCP/IP Application Developers Guide (IBM Document #SC31-7186)

Use the following procedure to run the Cedar Bank sample application over a live mainframe connection:

To run Cedar Bank with a live mainframe connection

1. Install Host Integration Server 2000 using the installation instructions for Host Integration Server 2000. This will install COMTI at the same time.

2. Configure a live connection to your mainframe computer appropriate to your computing environment, using the configuration procedures in the Host Integration Server 2000 documentation.

3. Install Visual Studio .NET using the installation instructions for Visual Studio.

4. Create a folder to store the Cedar Bank files on the computer that contains Host Integration Server 2000. Suggestion: Create this folder in the same folder as Host Integration Server, \Program Files\Microsoft Host Integration Server\CedarBank

5. Copy all the files and folders from the companion CD-ROM to the CedarBank folder on your Host Integration Server 2000 computer.

6. Choose a host remote environment from the following table. The "RE Type" column gives you the type of remote environment (RE) that you need to create using COMTI Manager. The "Folder" column shows you where to find the COMTI component, recording file, and COBOL source code files for this host environment. The "Folder" column are those folders located at %systemdrive%\Program Files\Host Integration Server\System\Tutorials\CedarBank\All CedarBank Typelibs, and are installed when Host Integration Server 2000 is installed (see step 1 in the preceding section).

Use the following table to determine the RE type and corresponding folder for your host environment.

Host Environment	RE Type	Folder
CICS Link over an SNA (APPC/LU 6.2) network	CICS LINK using LU 6.2	\SNA CICS Link
CICS over an SNA (APPC/LU 6.2) network	CICS using LU 6.2	\SNA CICS
CICS Concurrent over a TCP/IP network	CICS and IMS using TCP/IP	\TCP CICS Concurrent
CICS MS Link over a TCP/IP network	CICS and IMS using TCP/IP	\TCP CICS MSLink
IMS over an SNA (APPC/LU 6.2) network	IMS using LU 6.2	\SNA IMS
IMS Implicit over a TCP/IP network	CICS and IMS using TCP/IP	\TCP IMS Implicit
IMS Explicit over a TCP/IP network	CICS and IMS using TCP/IP	\TCP IMS Explicit
IMS OTMA over a TCP/IP network	IMS using OTMA	\TCP IMS OTMA

7. Copy the COBOL source code programs (Cedrbank.cbl and Getaccts.cbl, and possibly Mscmtics.cbl) to the host mainframe in the CICS or IMS region that receives COMTI calls. Then use the source code to build and install the mainframe transaction programs on the host. See the procedure "To set up the COBOL programs on your mainframe host computer" in the next section.

8. Start COMTI Manager.

9. Create a remote environment (RE):

   - First, right-click **Remote Environments** in the console tree under the **COM Transaction Integrator** folder.

   - Next, point to **New**, and click **Remote Environment.**

   - Then, follow the prompts to create an instance of the type of RE that you need.

10. Create a new COM+ application (or MTS package):

    - First double-click **Component Services** (or **Microsoft Transaction Server**) in the console tree.

    - Next, select the **COM+ applications** (or **Packages Installed**) folder.

    - Then, on the **Action** menu, highlight **New**, and click **Application** (or **Package**).

11. Deploy the Cedar Bank COMTI component in your new COM+ application (or MTS package):

    - First, double-click the new COM+ application (or MTS package) in COMTI Manager.

    - Then, double-click the **Components** folder.

    - Next, use Windows Explorer to find the correct Cedar Bank COMTI component (.tlb file).

    - Then, drop the COMTI component into the empty details pane in COMTI Manager to deploy the COMTI component in the COM+ application (or MTS package) that you just created in step 8.

12. Set the new Cedar Bank COMTI component's properties:

    - First, right-click the new component, and click **Properties.**

    - Then, on the **Remote Environment** tab, click the remote environment that you created in step 7.

13. Run one of the Cedar Bank Automation client applications (VBCedarEB.exe, VBCedarLB.exe, VCCedarEB.exe, or VCCedarLB.exe), which is included on the companion CD-ROM Disc.

    These four client applications are already compiled. The source code is also available and can be compiled using Visual Studio .NET. See the procedure to follow.

14. Click **Go** under **Check Account Balance** to automate the mainframe transaction program using the default name and account number. (For this sample, the account balance is always 777.12.).

15. Click **Go** under **Show All Accounts** to see a list of the accounts returned by the mainframe transaction program.

To set up the COBOL programs on your mainframe host computer

Copy the COBOL source code for **cedrbank** and **getaccts** to the host; then compile, link, and install the programs. If you use RDO, use the following syntax:

- CEDA DEFINE PROGRAM (**cedrbank**)

- CEDA DEFINE PROGRAM (**getaccts**)

It is not necessary to define a transaction for these programs. **cedrbank** and **getaccts** are the default program names. You can use any names in place of these names. Note the names that you use because you will need to verify them when you import the **cedrbank** and **getaccts** method definitions.

To compile the Windows client applications using Visual Studio .NET

1. Start Visual Studio .NET

2. On the **Standard Menu** bar, click **File**, click **Open**, and then click **Solution**.

3. Navigate to one of the folders where you have copied the Cedar Bank files from the companion CD-ROM. (For example, the \VBCedarEB folder).

4. Click the file with the .sln extension. Visual Studio .NET Solution files have a .sln extension.

5. Press the **F5** key to compile the solution file using the debug option. Pressing **Shift-F5** compiles the file without the debug option. The solution file compiles and the program runs.

6. Click **Go** under **Check Account Balance** to automate the mainframe transaction program using the default name and account number. (For this sample, the account balance is always 777.12.).

7. Click **Go** under **Show All Accounts** to see a list of the accounts returned by the mainframe transaction program.

The following illustration shows the output you see when you run this sample application.

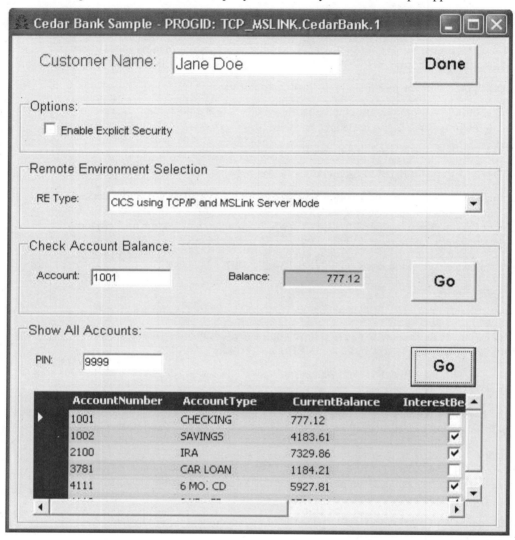

To compile the Web client applications using Visual Studio. NET

1. Start Visual Studio NET

2. On the **Standard Menu** bar, click **File**, click **Open**, and then click **Solution**.

3. Navigate to the \WebServices folder where you have copied the Cedar Bank files from the companion CD-ROM.

4. Click the file with the .sln extension. Visual Studio .NET Solution files have an .sln extension.

5. Press the **F5** key to compile the solution file using the debug option. Pressing **Shift-F5** will compile the file without the debug option. The solution file will compile and the program will run.

6. Click **Go** under **Check Account Balance** to automate the mainframe transaction program using the default name and account number. (For this sample, the account balance is always 777.12.).

7. Click **Go** under **Show All Accounts** to see a list of the accounts returned by the mainframe transaction program.

The Web client sample application illustration shows the output you see after running the sample.

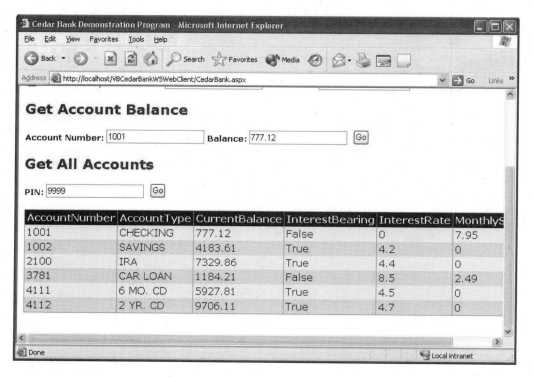

This chapter described how you could connect a Web client and Windows client to a host environment. Visual Studio .NET, along with the rich set of tools and products included in the .NET Enterprise Servers, can make this job easy.

Integrating BizTalk with SAP

Scenario

In this scenario, the company maintains all purchase order information electronically using SAP R/3 software from SAP AG Germany. Several of the vendors from whom this company buys supplies and/or raw materials have agreed to accept purchase orders electronically using XML documents.

The company needs a way to convert the SAP business document (purchase order) into an XML business document that BizTalk Server can process. Microsoft® BizTalk™ Adapter for SAP provides the necessary tool to solve this problem.

Solution

SAP is the world's largest inter-enterprise software company, and the world's third-largest independent software supplier overall. Today, more than 13,000 companies in over 100 countries run more than 30,000 installations of SAP software.

Because of the widespread usage of SAP software, Microsoft BizTalk Adapter for SAP was designed to integrate and transfer SAP data into BizTalk Server Business-to-Business models. This adapter includes tools for developers and IT administrators to access SAP R/3 IDoc structure details and convert them to XML for BizTalk Server processing. It also allows bi-directional and transactional support for SAP IDoc messaging.

Specifically, the BizTalk Adapter for SAP R/3 does the following:

- Provides BizTalk and SAP implementers a way to easily integrate IDoc data
- Provides tools that are customizable and straightforward to use
- Adheres to the BizTalk Server Framework 2.0

  Note BizTalk Adapter for SAP does not support other SAP data transmission technologies, including BAPI calls. Only IDocs are supported.

A typical business example using the BizTalk Adapter for SAP (Adapter for SAP) is shown in the following diagram. This example shows a process in which a purchase order generated by "Company A" is delivered eventually to "Company B."

To follow the process in more detail, refer to the numbers in the diagram with the matching description in the next section.

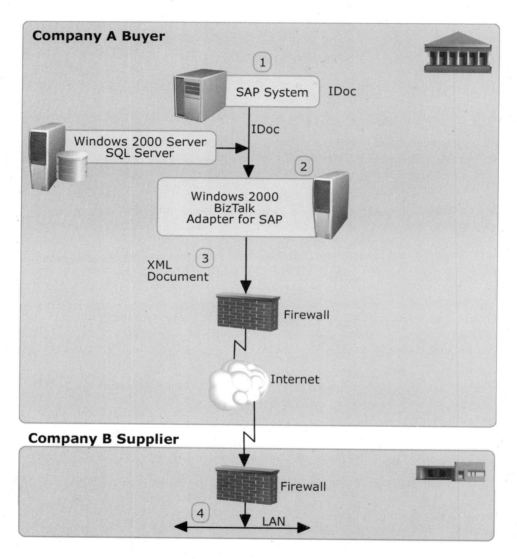

Document flow diagram

1. Company A creates a purchase order (in the form of an IDoc) using SAP R/3 system.

2. The Adapter for SAP receives the IDoc purchase order and transforms it into a data stream. Tracking information is also generated and stored in a SQL Server database.

3. The Adapter for SAP transfers the purchase order data to BizTalk Server. BizTalk Server converts the data stream into a XML document and sends it to Company B.

4. Company B receives purchase order as an XML document for processing.

This example is very simple and only shows a one-way path from SAP to BizTalk Server. The BizTalk Adapter for SAP data exchange process is bidirectional. It transfers IDocs sent by an SAP R/3 system to BizTalk Server (as described in the previous section), and transfers IDocs from BizTalk Server to SAP.

For more information on sending and receiving IDocs, see the sections on "Sending IDocs to BizTalk Server" and "Sending IDocs to SAP R/3 System."

Tools and Technologies

This section describes the hardware and software requirements, and the components of the Microsoft BizTalk Adapter for SAP.

Hardware and Software Requirements

BizTalk Adapter for SAP works in conjunction with other software including Microsoft® BizTalk™ Server 2000, Microsoft® SQL Server™ 2000, and others as discussed below. BizTalk Adapter for SAP does not require any additional resources not already required by BizTalk Server. Therefore, the minimum hardware requirements for a basic installation of Microsoft BizTalk Server 2000 include:

*   An Intel Pentium 300 Processor.

*   128 megabytes (MB) of RAM.

*   A 6-gigabyte (GB) hard disk.

*   A CD-ROM drive.

*   A network adapter card.

*   A VGA or Super VGA monitor.

*   A Microsoft or compatible pointing device.

    Note   Although the above configuration is sufficient to accommodate the software requirements shown below, you should consider additional resources (especially CPU processing and hard disk space) to improve performance.

Additional software must also be installed on the computer prior to installing the BizTalk Adapter for SAP. This software includes:

- Microsoft Windows 2000 Advanced Server with Service Pack 1.

- Microsoft SQL Server 7.0 or Microsoft SQL Server 2000.

- Microsoft Visio 2000 SR-1A or later.

- Microsoft Message Queue (MSMQ) 2.0.

- Microsoft BizTalk Server 2000. (See the BizTalk Server 2000 documentation for additional software prerequisites and installation procedures.)

- SAP DCOM Connector. The latest version is available from SAP and can be downloaded from http://www.sap.com/

> **Note**   The SAP DCOM Connector is compatible to run on any SAP R/3 system.

After installing the required software listed above, you can install the Microsoft BizTalk Adapter for SAP.

BizTalk Adapter for SAP Components

BizTalk Adapter for SAP is made up of the following components:

- Adapter for SAP Manager (Adapter Manager). The Adapter Manager is the program the system administrator uses to configure and control another part of the Adapter for SAP.

- IDoc Handler is the component that receives an IDoc from an SAP R/3 system and converts it to a data stream.

- Application Integration Component (AIC) is the component that sends an IDoc to an SAP R/3 system.

- Microsoft Message Queuing is used to queue IDocs until BizTalk Server can process them.

BizTalk Adapter for SAP Manager

BizTalk Adapter for SAP Manager (Adapter Manager) provides the interface for configuring and operating the Adapter for SAP components. In addition, the Adapter Manager:

- Retrieves IDoc structure.

- Generates XML schema.

- Defines routing.

See the "Configure BizTalk Adapter for SAP Manager" section for starting and configuring the Adapter for SAP.

IDoc Handler

The IDoc Handler is a COM object within BizTalk Adapter for SAP that processes IDocs sent from an SAP R/3 system. The IDoc Handler converts the IDoc into an ASCII IDoc delimited file and delivers it to a Microsoft Message Queue.

The IDoc Handler also guarantees successful IDoc delivery to the Message Queue by using a Transaction Identifier (TID) that conforms to the SAP Transactional Remote Function Call (tRFC). The IDoc Handler uses the TID to notify the SAP R/3 system either that the IDoc was received successfully, or to resend it.

Application Integration Component

Application integration components (AIC) are COM objects that BizTalk Server uses to deliver data to an application. BizTalk Adapter for SAP uses an application integration component (AIC) to send an IDoc delimited data stream from BizTalk Server (specifically BizTalk Messaging) to the SAP DCOM Connector. To complete the data transfer, the SAP DCOM Connector transfers the data to an SAP R/3 system.

A BizTalk Messaging Port must be configured to include the use of the Adapter for SAP AIC. When this configuration is completed in BizTalk Server, an instance of the AIC is created automatically and data (in this case, an IDoc delimited data stream) is transferred to it. The AIC then passes the data on to the SAP DCOM Connector.

Microsoft Message Queuing

Microsoft Message Queuing (MSMQ) technology enables applications running at different times to communicate across heterogeneous networks and systems that may be temporarily offline. Applications send messages to queues and read messages from queues. MSMQ provides guaranteed message delivery, efficient routing, security, and priority-based messaging. It can be used to implement solutions for both asynchronous and synchronous scenarios requiring high performance.

In BizTalk Adapter for SAP, MSMQ is used to queue IDocs for BizTalk Server processing.

For more information about MSMQ, visit http://www.microsoft.com/msmq/.

Implementation

Installing and configuring the BizTalk Adapter for SAP involves three processes. These must be done in the specific order shown:

- First: Install prerequisite software on a computer.
- Second: Install the BizTalk Adapter for SAP.
- Third: Configure the various components.

Installing Prerequisite Software

The prerequisite software is listed in the "Hardware and Software Requirements" section above. All prerequisite software must be installed before installing the Adapter for SAP.

Installing BizTalk Adapter for SAP

Follow these steps to install the BizTalk Adapter for SAP:

1. Install all prerequisite software as described in the "Hardware and Software Requirements" section.

2. Insert the Adapter CD.

3. The Welcome screen appears automatically. If it does not, double-click **setup.exe** on the CD-ROM.

4. To continue with installation, click **Next.**

5. Read the License Agreement. Select **I accept the License Agreement**, and then click **Next**.

6. Select the destination folder or accept the default settings, and then click **Next**.

7. Click **Next** to continue installation, or click **Back** to re-enter the installation information.

8. When installation has completed, click **Finish**.

Configuring Components

There are several manual configuration items that must be completed to successfully transfer IDoc information from an SAP R/3 system to BizTalk Server. This section describes the steps to configure these components. It is best to configure the system and components in the order given:

1. Configure SAP R/3 system

2. Configure DCOM Connector

3. Configure COM for ABAP

4. Configure MSMQ

5. Configure Adapter for SAP Manager

6. Configure BizTalk Server

Configure SAP R/3 System

This section describes the SAP R/3 system configuration and may be done by your SAP System Administrator. You need to configure an RFC Destination and a Transactional Remote Function Call (tRFC) port.

To configure SAP R/3 system

1. Associate the tRFC Port with the RFC Destination.

2. Target the RFC Destination with a specific COM for ABAP server. This is typically the same computer on which the SAP DCOM Connector and BizTalk Adapter for SAP are installed.

   This is done by using the **Program ID** field in the RFC Destination. The **Program ID** is the identifier used by SAP to establish a connection with the COM for ABAP server. The **Program ID** associated with your RFC Destination is used in one of the steps in "Configure COM for ABAP" below.

Configure DCOM Connector

This section describes the SAP Distributed Component Object Model (DCOM) Connector configuration procedures.

To configure DCOM Connector

1. Click **Start**, point to **Programs**, point to **SAP DCOM Connector**, and then click **SAP DCOM Connector**.

2. Click **Destinations** from the upper menu bar.

3. Click **Edit** from the middle menu bar (directly right of the **Connect** button).

4. Click **New** from menu bar.

5. Type a name for a new destination, and then click **OK**.

6. In the **Destinations** list, select the name you entered in the previous step.

7. In the **Connection** box, click **R/3 Connection** from the **Connection** drop-down list.

8. Click the dedicated server radio button.

9. In the **R/3 Hostname** box, type the name of your R/3 host server.

10. In the **System number** box, type the system number as supplied by your SAP System Administrator.

11. In the **Logon** box, type a Client number as supplied by your SAP System Administrator.

12. In the **Logon** box, enter an SAP R/3 system language code. For English, type **EN**.

13. In the **Security** box, type your SAP user name and password. SAP user names and passwords are case-sensitive.

14. Click **Save** from the menu bar, and then click **OK**.

Configure COM for ABAP

This section describes the procedures to configure the SAP DCOM Connector COM for ABAP service. This service is used to provide a communications conduit to an SAP R/3 system.

Configuring the COM for ABAP service involves identifying the SAP R/3 system from which IDocs will come, the name associated with the tRFC destination (Program ID), and the COM ProgID of the IDoc Handler COM object.

To configure the SAP DCOM Connector COM for ABAP service

1. Start the COM for ABAP Service. Click **Start**, point to **Programs**, point to **SAP DCOM Connector**, and then click **COM for ABAP Service**.
   When the ABAP Service starts, an icon for the ABAP Service appears in the Windows System Tray.

2. In the Windows System Tray, double-click the **COM for ABAP Service** icon.

The following display appears:

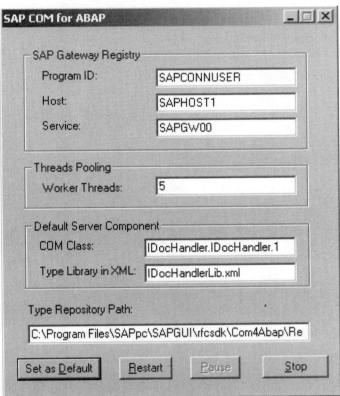

3. Click **Pause** to stop the COM for ABAP service. This allows the fields to be edited.

   Note Steps 4, 5, and 6 require information that may be supplied by your SAP Administrator. The values shown in the screen display above are used only as examples. Your information will be different.

4. In the **SAP Gateway Registry** box, in the **Program ID** field, enter a name that will be used as the program ID.

5. In the **Host** field, type the name of your SAP R/3 system host server.

6. In the **Service** field, type the name of the service.

7. Specify the number of threads needed to handle your specific workload. When determining the number of threads for your environment, 2 times the number of processors is a good starting point. This example shows 5 in the Worker Threads field.

   Note In steps 8, 9, and 10, the exact, specified values for **COM Class**, **Type Library in XML**, and **Type Repository Path** must be typed into the appropriate fields.

8. Type **IDocHandler.IDocHandler.1** as **COM Class**.

9. Type **IDocHandlerLib** as **Type Library in XML**.

10. Search your system disk drives for **IDocHandlerLib**. Type the directory path (not including the filename) of the **IDocHandlerLib** file as the **Type Repository Path**.

11. Click **Set as Default** to make these your default settings.

12. Click **Restart**.

13. Exit the program.

Configure Microsoft Message Queuing

This section describes the Microsoft Message Queue (MSMQ) configuration.

The procedure below configures a private queue. Configuring a public queue will also work.

To configure Message Queuing

1. Click **Start**, point to **Programs**, point to **Administrative Tools**, and then click **Computer Management**.

2. Under **Computer Management (Local)**, expand **Services and Applications**, and then expand **Message Queuing**.

3. Right-click the **Private Queues** folder, point to **New**, and then click **Private Queue**.

4. Type a name for the new Private Queue.

5. Select **Transactional**.

6. Click **OK**.

Configure BizTalk Adapter for SAP Manager

This section describes the configuration of the BizTalk Adapter for SAP Manager.

Three areas require configuration using the Adapter Manager. They are:

- Select R/3 Destination
- Select Message Queue
- Define Routing Keys

Note   Any configuration changes in the BizTalk Adapter for SAP Manager will not take effect in the components (IDocHandler and SendAIC) until the COM+ Application for BizTalk Adapter for SAP is shut down and restarted.

To start the Adapter Manager

- Click **Start**, point to **Programs**, point to **BizTalk Adapter for SAP**, and then click **BizTalk Adapter for SAP**.

    The following display appears:

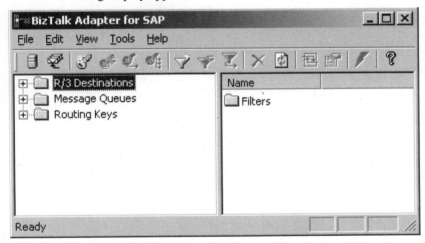

Selecting an R/3 Destination

The BizTalk Adapter for SAP Manager provides a list of available R/3 systems from which a destination can be selected. R/3 destinations can also be used to identify required schemas. Configured R/3 destinations are located in the R/3 Destinations folder. New destinations can be added and existing destinations can be renamed.

To select an R/3 destination

1. Start the **Adapter for SAP** Manager.

2. Right-click **R/3 Destinations**, and then click **Select Destinations**.
   The following **Select R/3 Destinations** screen appears. The top box lists available R/3 destinations. The bottom box lists selected R/3 destinations.

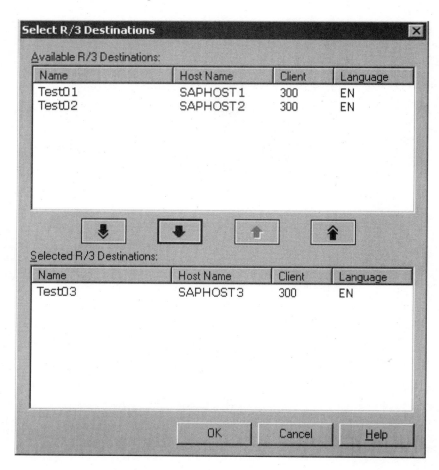

3. In the Available R/3 Destinations section, select a destination.

Click the arrow to move it to the **Selected R/3 Destinations** section. Clicking the arrow moves all available destinations to the **Selected R/3 Destinations** section.

4. Click **OK**.

Selecting a Message Queue

As with the R/3 destinations, new queues are selected from a list of available queues. The queue is used as a temporary storage place for IDocs that are sent by an SAP R/3 system. BizTalk Server then retrieves the IDoc from a MSMQ Queue.

To select a Message queue

1. Start the BizTalk Adapter for SAP Manager.

2. Right-click **MSMQ Queues,** and then click **Select MSMQ Queue**.
   The **Select MSMQ Queues** screen appears. The top box lists available Message Queues.
   The bottom box lists selected MSMQ Queues.

3. In the **Available MSMQ Queues** section, select a queue.

   Click the arrow to move it to the **Selected MSMQ Queues** section. Clicking the arrow moves all available queues to the **Selected Queues** section.

4. Click **OK**.

Filtering IDocs

Filters can be used to select the desired Message and IDoc Types for viewing or converting to BizTalk Server. Filters can be renamed.

To create a new filter

1. Start the **Adapter for SAP** Manager.

2. Expand **R/3 Destinations**, expand a specific R/3 destination, right-click **Filters**, and then click **Create Filter**.

   The following screen appears:

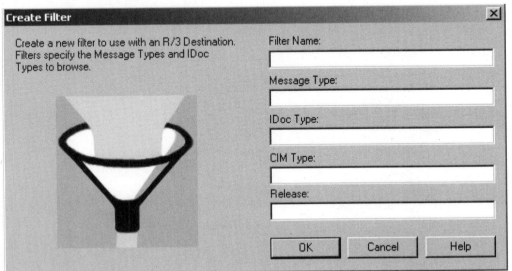

3. In the Create Filter dialog box, type the following information:
   Filter Name
   Message Type
   IDoc Type
   CIM Type
   Release

4. Click **OK**.

To associate a filter with an R/3 destination

1. Start the **BizTalk Adapter for SAP** Manager.

2. Expand **R/3 Destinations**, select and right-click an R/3 destination, and then click **Associate Filter**.

3. In the **Available Filters** section, select one or more filters from the list.

4. Click the ⬇ arrow to move it to the **Selected Filters** section. Clicking the ⬇ arrow moves all available destinations to the **Selected Filters** section.

5. Click **OK**.

Generating a BizTalk Server Specification Based on an IDoc Type

A BizTalk Server specification must be generated for each IDoc Type. Once a BizTalk document specification is created, multiple IDocs of the same type can be generated and sent to BizTalk Server for processing.

To generate a BizTalk Server specification

1. Start the BizTalk Adapter for SAP Manager.

2. Expand R/3 Destinations, select and expand an R/3 destination, and then expand Message Types.

3. Select an IDoc (for example, ORDERS).

4. Under IDoc Types, select and right-click an IDoc (for example, ORDERS01), and then click Generate BizTalk IDoc Specs.

   When the Generate BizTalk IDoc Specification screen appears, click Generate.

5. When the Status column displays Generation Successful, click Close.

Creating Routing Keys

A Routing Key is used to store the routing information for an IDoc. Creating Routing Keys prevents defining the routing each time an IDoc is generated. Instead, an IDoc type can be associated with its Routing Key, which then sends it on to its defined destination. For example, a Routing Key (named "KEY01") is created in which is stored the information for routing the IDoc "INVOIC01". When an IDoc is generated with the name "INVOIC01", and is submitted to either the IDoc Handler or the Application Integration Component (AIC), it is automatically sent to the destination defined in the Key. Routing Keys can also be renamed.

When a Routing Key is created, it is associated with a valid MSMQ Queue. If the Queue is then deleted, the routing is broken.

To create a routing key

1. Start the **BizTalk Adapter for SAP** Manager.

1. Right-click **Routing Keys**, and then click **Create New Routing Key**.

2. In the **Create a New Routing Key** dialog box, type a name for the **Routing Key Name**.

3. Select **IDoc Version**.

4. In the **Control Field** section, select a row and type an entry for the **Value**.

5. Click **OK**.

After the routing keys are created, you must associate a routing key with an R/3 destination or a queue.

To associate a routing key with an R/3 destination or Messaging Queue

1. Start the BizTalk Adapter for SAP Manager.

2. Expand **R/3 Destinations**, select and right-click an R/3 destination, and then click **Associate Routing Keys**.

3. In the **Available Routing Keys** section, select one or more keys from the list.

Click the arrow to move it to the **Selected Routing Keys** section. Clicking the arrow moves all available routing keys to the **Selected Routing Keys** section.

4. Click **OK**.

A valid destination must be associated with a routing key for the key to successfully transfer the IDoc. If two or more routing keys are created for the same IDoc type but the first key does not have a destination, the IDoc will be transferred using the first routing key in the list with a valid destination.

Tracing

Tracing is a tool used for troubleshooting a system. You must create a Routing Key for the tracing utility to work. The files created by a trace provide detailed information about the sequence of events occurring within the Adapter for SAP system. The ideal way to use tracing is when you have isolated and reproduced a problem. Tracing can produce large log files that occupy disk space and may delay application response time.

If you want to trace the IDoc Handler component, consider running the trace after you select the message type. Running the trace on all message types will create a large log file.

Configure BizTalk Server

This section describes the procedures to configure the BizTalk Server and includes the following:

- Creating Document Definitions/Envelopes
- Creating Organizations
- Creating a Port
- Creating a Channel
- Creating Receive Function

For more information on configuring BizTalk Server, see Microsoft BizTalk Server 2000 documentation. The BizTalk Server procedures shown below are also available in the BizTalk Server documentation, but are reproduced here for your convenience.

Creating Document Definitions/Envelope

Document definitions in a channel represent the inbound and outbound documents that are processed by BizTalk Server. An envelope encapsulates electronic business data to be transported.

To create Document Definitions/Envelope

1. Click **Start**, point to **Programs**, point to **Microsoft BizTalk Server 2000**, and then click **BizTalk Messaging Manager**.
1. If a configuration dialog box appears, click **Cancel**.
2. Click **File**, point to **New**, and then click **Envelope**.
3. Type a name appropriate to its purpose.

4. Select **FLATFILE** from the **Envelope format** drop-down list.

5. Select the **Envelope Specification** check box, and browse for the XML document.

6. Click **OK**.

7. Click **File**, point to **New**, and then click **Document Definition.**

8. Type a name for the **Document Definition**.

9. Select the **Document specification** check box and browse for the XML document.

10. Click **OK**

Creating an Organization

The organizations that you create by using BizTalk Server Messaging Manager represent the trading partners with whom you exchange documents.

To create an organization

1. Click **Start**, point to **Programs**, point to **Microsoft BizTalk Server 2000**, and then click **BizTalk Messaging Manager**.

2. Click **File**, point to **New**, and then click **Organization.**

3. Type a name for the trading partner organization.

4. Click **OK** to finish the definitions needed for Organizations.

Creating a Port

A port is a named location using a specific communication technology (such as Message Queuing or BizTalk Messaging). In BizTalk Orchestration Designer, a port is defined by the location to which messages are sent or from which messages are received, and the technology that is used to implement the communication

To create a port

1. In BizTalk Messaging Manager, on the **File** menu, point to **New**, and then point to **Messaging Port**.

2. Click **To an Organization** to create a messaging port to a trading partner organization.

3. The New Messaging Port Wizard opens.

4. Type a name for the port, and then click **Next**.

5. Browse for the **Organization Name**.

6. Browse for the **Primary Transport Address** to display the **Primary Transport** dialog box.

7. Select **File** as transport type.

Note For inbound IDocs, select Application Integration Component as transport type. Browse for the Component name and select SendIDocAIC SendIDoc, and then click OK.

8. Type a file path address.

9. Create this folder on your system drive if it does not exist. If it does, delete all the files in the folder.

10. Click **OK** on the **Primary Transport** dialog box.

11. Click **Next**.

12. Select an envelope from **Envelope information**.

13. Click **Next**.

14. Click **Create a channel** for this messaging port and select **From an organization**.

15. Click **Finish** to start the New Channel Wizard.

16. Complete the procedures in the **Create Channel** section below.

Creating a Channel

A channel is a set of properties that you can use to configure BizTalk Messaging Services to process a document that it receives. Channels can be created for a messaging port. Once a channel has processed a document, the document is transported to the destination specified in the associated messaging port.

To create a channel

1. Completing the New Messaging Port Wizard automatically starts the New Channel Wizard.

2. Type a name for the channel name, and click **Next**.

3. Browse for the specific **Organization** name, click **OK**, and then click **Next**.

4. Browse for the specific **Inbound documentation** name, click **OK,** and then click **Next**.

5. Browse for the specific **Outbound documentation** name, click **OK** and then click **Next**.

6. Click **Next** again, and then click **Finish**.

Creating Receive Function

The BizTalk Server receive function retrieves files stored in a folder and submits them to BizTalk Server. The receive function is configured using the BizTalk Server administration console. Using the console, a folder can be designated as the location where the receive function will poll for the existence of files. If files are present, the receive function transfers the files to BizTalk Server.

To create a receive function

1. Click **Start**, point to **Programs**, point to **Microsoft BizTalk Server 2000**, and then click **BizTalk Server Administration**.

2. Expand **Microsoft BizTalk Server 2000**, and then expand the server group for which you want to add a receive function.

3. Click **Receive Functions**.

4. On the **Action** menu, point to **New**, and then click **Message Queuing Receive Function**.

   The **Add a Message Queuing Receive Function** dialog box appears.

5. In the **Name** box, type the name of the Message Queuing receive function.

6. In the **Comment** box, add a brief description (optional).

7. In the **Server on which the receive function will run** list, click the name of a server in the group.

8. In the **Polling location** box, type the server and Message Queuing names that this receive function uses as the receive location.

   For example:

   Direct=OS:<servername>\<queuename>

   Select the processing server on which the queue resides. Transactional messaging is only supported by local queues.

9. In the **Preprocessor** list, click the custom preprocessor.

   Leave this blank if you are not using a custom preprocessor.

10. In the **User name** and **Password** boxes, type a valid user name and password to connect to Message Queuing.

    This is required only when the receive location is not on the server processing interchanges and documents.

11. Click **Advanced**.

12. Select an **Envelope name**.

13. Select a **Channel name**.

14. Click **OK**, and then click **OK** again.

Now that you have successfully configured all necessary components, you can generate an XML BizTalk Server Documentation Specification.

Generating a BizTalk Server Specification

This section describes the process and the procedures to generate a BizTalk Server document specification (XML document schema) from an IDoc structure.

Specification Generation Process

The following illustration shows the process of generating a BizTalk Server specification (XML schema) document from an IDoc structure.

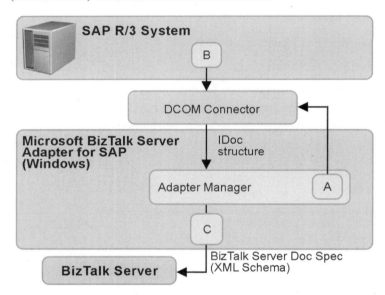

BizTalk Server document specification generation process

A. **BizTalk Adapter Manager** uses **DCOM Connector** to access an IDoc structure from an SAP R/3 system.

B. **DCOM Connector** passes the IDoc structure to the **BizTalk Adapter Manager**.

C. **BizTalk Adapter Manager** converts the IDoc structure to a BizTalk Server document specification and stores it to a file for BizTalk Server to process.

Generating a BizTalk Server Specification Document

The following procedures need to be completed for each IDoc structure that is to be converted to an XML schema. Once an XML schema is created, multiple IDocs of the same type can be generated and sent to BizTalk Server.

For example, follow these procedures to convert the IDoc Structure for a purchase order to an XML schema. The XML schema can be used for all purchase orders sent to BizTalk Server. This procedure will not need to be completed again for the purchase order type IDoc unless something in the original IDoc structure changes (such as a new revision).

To generate a BizTalk Server specification document

1. Start the **BizTalk Adapter for SAP** Manager.

2. Expand **R/3 Destinations**, choose and expand an R/3 destination, and then expand **Message Types**.

3. Select an IDoc (for example, **ORDERS**).

4. Under **IDoc Types**, select an IDoc (for example, **ORDERS01**), right-click, and then click **Generate BizTalk IDoc Specs**.

5. Select the IDoctype, and then click the **Edit Type Info** button.

   Note   You must first select the **IDoctype** to activate the **Edit Type Information** button.

6. In the **IDoc Type Information** screen, type the correct **Release** and **Version**, and then click **OK**.

   Note   For a successful schema generation, be certain you have the correct release and version information. You may verify the release and version information from the SAP Frontend application using the **/n we60** command prompt. This is found on the **Documentation for IDoc Types** screen.

7. The **Generate BizTalk IDoc Specification** screen appears, click **Generate**.

8. When the **Status** column displays **Generation Successful**, click **Close**.

Now you are ready to send the IDoc to BizTalk Server.

Sending an IDoc to BizTalk Server

This section describes the data flow of an IDoc from an SAP R/3 system to BizTalk Server.

A BizTalk Server specification (XML schema) must already exist for the IDoc to be sent to the SAP R/3 system. To generate a specification, see the section "Generating a BizTalk Server Specification Document."

The following illustration shows the process.

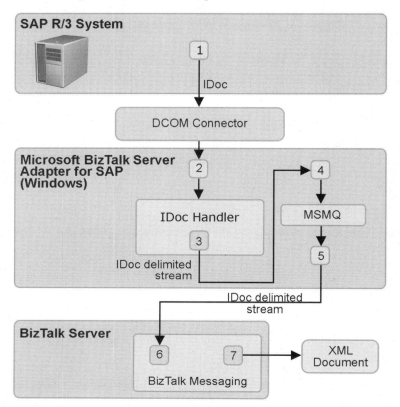

Transferring an IDoc from SAP to BizTalk Server

1. The SAP R/3 system delivers an IDoc to the SAP DCOM Connector.

2. The SAP DCOM Connector delivers the IDoc, along with a transaction identifier (TID), to the IDoc Handler component of the BizTalk Adapter for SAP.

3. The IDoc Handler component converts the IDoc to an IDoc delimited stream.

4. The IDoc Handler transfers the IDoc delimited stream to an MSMQ Queue.

5. BizTalk Messaging retrieves the IDoc delimited stream from MSMQ.

6. The IDoc data stream is validated against the BizTalk Server Specification document (XML schema).

7. An XML document is created and sent to BizTalk Server for any additional processing.

   Note   This process is initiated by the SAP R/3 system.

To confirm the transfer process

Look for a file in the folder on your BizTalk Server computer that was configured to receive files transferred from the R/3 system. Any files present have been received by the Adapter for SAP and validated by BizTalk Server against the BizTalk Server Specification document (XML schema).

Sending an IDoc to SAP R/3 System

This section describes the data flow of an XML document through BizTalk Server to SAP.

A BizTalk Server specification (XML schema) must already exist for the IDoc to be sent to the SAP R/3 system. To generate a specification, see the section "Generating a BizTalk Server Specification Document."

The following illustration shows the process:

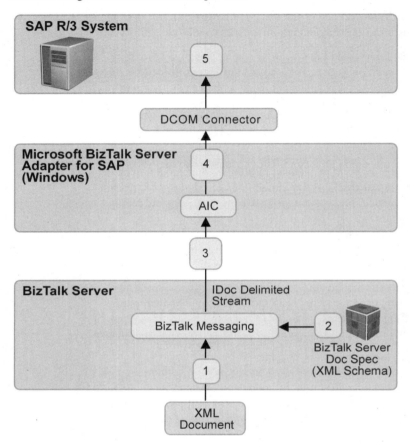

Transferring an IDoc from BizTalk Server to SAP

1. BizTalk Server is presented with an XML document.

2. BizTalk Messaging retrieves the XML document and the BizTalk Server document specification and produces an IDoc delimited stream.

3. The IDoc delimited stream is sent to the Application Integration Component (AIC) of the BizTalk Adapter.
   A BizTalk Tracking ID is also sent to the AIC. (This will be used as the SAP TID.)

4. The AIC delivers the IDoc delimited stream and the BizTalk Tracking ID (the SAP Transaction TID) to the SAP DCOM Connector.

5. The SAP DCOM Connector sends the IDoc to the SAP R/3 system.

Once the various components of BizTalk Server and the Adapter for SAP have been configured using the configuration step in this document, the process of transferring an IDoc is automatic.

To send an IDoc to SAP

1. Copy the XML document file to the folder created and designated as the folder where the BizTalk Server receive function will pick it up. (See the section about creating a BizTalk receive function).

2. The file will disappear from the folder. The BizTalk Server receive function polls the folder, pulls the file, and processes it as shown in the illustration above.

Additional Information

This section provides additional resource information.

BizTalk Server 2000

- BizTalk Server 2000 Web site http://www.microsoft.com/biztalk/
- BizTalk Server Frame work overview Web site http://www.biztalk.org/
- BizTalk Server online documentation

SAP

- SAP Web site http://www.sap.com
- SAP Frontend online documentation
- SAP DCOM Connector online documentation

Microsoft SQL Server

- Microsoft SQL Server Web site http://www.microsoft.com/sql
- Microsoft SQL Server online documentation

Microsoft Message Queue

Microsoft Message Queue Web site http://www.microsoft.com/msmq/

PART THREE

Business-to-Business Integration

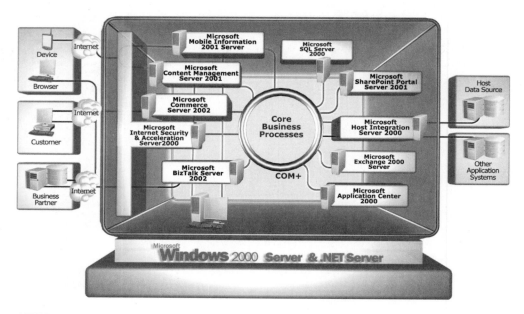

.NET Enterprise Servers

By William J. Harding

Integrating Business Partners into the Enterprise

No business or industry operates in a vacuum. A business of any type or size maintains relationships with other businesses. The efficiency with which one business creates and maintains these relationships can have a direct impact on the success of the business. One type of business relationship is the buying and selling of goods and services between businesses. And to be able to buy and sell electronically is one of the most important technological advances to improve the efficiency of business-to-business relations.

Electronic commerce can mean different things depending on your perspective of the business situation. In general, electronic commerce strives to improve the way business transactions are done using a variety of electronic devices. In the past, these electronic devices have typically been the telephone and fax machine. More recently, the use of computers and computer networks, including the Internet is increasing.

Electronic commerce can generally be divided into two distinct areas: business-to-business and business-to-customer. Some would argue that there is a third category, that of commerce within an enterprise business. Certainly there is also some overlap between business-to-business and business-to-customer when one business becomes the end customer of the goods or services of another business.

History shows that when organizations combine technological changes and the organizational restructuring to take advantage of the technology, large gains in productivity and even gains in market share can result. Business is conducted more efficiently. However, in order to take full advantage of the benefits that electronic commerce offers, organizations must be willing to change business practices, procedures, and processes. Also, it is not unusual that new business opportunities can be created.

Worldwide, businesses are changing the way they do business. With the rapid growth of technology, the emergence of global economy, and increasing use of the Internet as a viable and necessary part of business-to-business communication, the importance of forming new relationships with trading partners (suppliers and customers) while maintaining existing ones has become critical to remain competitive. Electronic commerce helps to improve customer interaction, improve business processes and procedures, and exchange information both within and between enterprise organizations.

Why Electronic Commerce?

Ultimately, the reason to use electronic commerce is based on the classic business equation:

Profit = Revenue - Costs

Businesses use electronic commerce to either lower operating costs or increase revenue, or both.

Electronic commerce can reduce operating costs through transaction management by:

- Better coordination between sales, production, and distribution (that is, supply chain management, customer relationship management (CRM), etc.).

- Consolidating operations and reducing overhead.

Electronic commerce can increase revenue by:

- Creating new markets for old products.

- Creating new information-based products.

- Establishing new service delivery mechanisms to better server customers.

To be more specific, business-to-business computer applications are developed to facilitate the management of the areas outlined in the following table.

Management Areas

Area	Management Improvements
Inventory	Shorten the order-ship-bill cycle.
	Overall levels can be reduced.
	Reduce turn-around time.
	Reduce out-of-stock occurrences.
Supplier	Rreduce the number of suppliers.
	Reduce Purchase Order (PO) processing costs and time.
	Increase the number of PO's processed in the same amount of time.
	Increase PO processing accuracy.
	Reduce the number of people required to process POs.

(continued)

Area	Management Improvements *(continued)*
Distribution and channel	Better tracking of goods from supplier to consumer
	Better tracking of documentation
	Better information distribution to trading partners
Payments and funds transfer	Payments sent and received electronically
	Reduced clerical errors
	Lower transaction costs

Types of Electronic Commerce Purchases

Now that we have computer and communication systems to facilitate the management of the areas outlined previously, the question becomes: What is being purchased? The following chart outlines the different types of purchases that an organization makes.

What businesses are buying

Type	Definition	Example
Direct materials	Raw materials and components that end up being part of the organization's final product.	Aluminum and other parts to make an airplane; fabric for a clothes manufacturer; computer parts for a computer maker.
Capital equipment	Items that have substantial value and an extended life.	Computers, machinery, office furniture.
Operating supplies	Supplies consumed for business purposes, but not used in the manufacture of the final products or the maintenance of facilities.	Paper, toner, office supplies, travel expenses.
Maintenance and repair supplies	Supplies consumed to maintain the manufacturing process, equipment, and facilities.	Lubricants, motors, janitorial supplies, filters, paint.
Services	Labor provided to the organization by people who are not employees of the organization.	Contract legal, IT, and other professional and temporary people.

(continued)

Type	Definition	Example *(continued)*
Facilities and equipment rental and lease.	Facilities and equipment that are rented or leased for an extended period of time.	Warehouse space, additional office space, vehicles, large equipment items.
Other	General category.	Sale or purchase of surplus items or infrequent spot purchases.

Challenges of Conducting Business Electronically

Integrating business partners into the enterprise poses several technical challenges, including:

- The rapid pace of technology advances.

- The use of technology to transfer information from one place to another within the same organization and between organizations.

- Choosing a technology to meet the needs of the business.

- Integrating existing (and often different) technology already being used in an organization.

Information can be represented in many different forms and exchanged in many different ways. Regardless of its form, data must be communicated fast, reliably, and securely between a business and its trading partners. As the number of trading partners increase, so do the demands placed on the enterprise to provide a means of communicating, such as an increase in the number of different systems, different data formats, and different processing requirements. Businesses must respond to these demands or risk losing an opportunity.

The challenges of business-to-business integration can be divided into two areas: computer systems and platforms, and data. It can be very difficult to separate a particular computer system and the data formats associated with that system.

In addition, it is becoming increasingly important for systems between organizations to be bound at both the data and the process levels. Exchanging only data and information is fine, but it is only a start. There is an increased need to share business rules, processes, and procedures.

The Microsoft .NET Framework enables organizations to design, build, and implement integrated business-to-business applications. The chapters in this part of the book describe what organizations can do today to integrate with their business partners. Middleware represents one key area to facilitate business-to-business integration.

Middleware

Middleware can take various forms and can be implemented on various levels. Middleware is a mechanism (software, hardware, or both) that enables one system to communicate with another. The "system" in this definition may be a data file, an application, a database, or an entire computer implementation.

The business-to-business solutions discussed in this book involve some type of middleware. As such, middleware hides the complexities of differing computing systems and platforms, operating systems, and networks, and facilitates the integration of the various parts within and between enterprises.

Middleware can be as simple as a software process that "adapts" or converts the data format used by one application to the data format used by another application. ("Simple" is relative. Although the concept of converting (or translating) one data format to another is simple, in practice, the actual conversion process can be very complex, depending on the data formats being converted.) Middleware can also be as complex as supplying a level of business logic in addition to the data conversion and computer system connections.

Middleware has become so important that even a new business opportunity has resulted. A type of middleware sometimes called "message broker," has allowed an entire "middleware" business to be created. Such a business can broker information and data in the form of messages between two or more target systems. The target system may be other business systems. A message broker can be positioned between any number of source and target systems. Message brokers can accommodate differences in application semantics and can process information by transforming the structure or format to the needs of the target system receiving it.

Some of the services a message broker can provide include:

- Message translation
- Intelligent routing
- Rules processing
- Message queuing
- Flow control
- Directory Services
- Adapters and APIs

The ability of a message broker to integrate between two different systems without changing those systems is a tremendous value to B2B integration.

Business-to-Business Integration

One of the biggest and most obvious problems associated with business-to-business electronic integration is trying to connect one business with one kind of platform, to another business operating with a different platform.

There are several ways to automate business transactions, including:

- Value Added Networks
- Business-to-business marketplaces and exchanges
- Direct, or Point-to-Point

Value Added Network (VAN)

A value-added network is a private network provider (sometimes called a turnkey communications line) that is hired by a company to facilitate electronic data interchange (EDI) or provide other network services. Before the World Wide Web, some companies hired VANs to move data to other companies. With the arrival of the World Wide Web, many companies found it less expensive to move their data over the Internet instead of paying the monthly fees and per-transaction charges found in typical VAN contracts. In response, contemporary value-added network providers now focus on added services, such as EDI translation, encryption, secure e-mail, and management reporting. The primary benefits of a VAN include a secure, reliable, and traceable means to exchange data between partners.

However, VANs are expensive to set up and use. The high cost may be an obstacle to a business trying to maintain competitiveness by lowering operating expenses. And the high cost may make it impractical or impossible for smaller partners to participate. Finally, VANs exist outside the enterprise, making businesses rely on a third party for the management and transmission of mission critical data.

Business-to-Business Marketplaces and Exchanges

One of the more innovative and successful Internet-based e-commerce efforts is the business-to-business marketplace. The B2B marketplace is designed to bring buyers and sellers together in one location, allowing them to buy and sell from each other. At the time of this writing, hundreds of marketplaces exist focusing on nearly every vertical and horizontal business segment. The basic idea of a marketplace is to use the Internet to match buyers and sellers as effectively as possible along the entire length of the value chain.

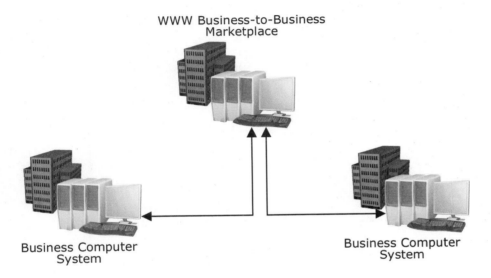

WWW Business-to-Business Marketplace

Business Computer System   **Business Computer System**

B2B marketplace

Regardless of the size of the business, a B2B marketplace promises to add value mainly in two ways.

- B2B sites hope to better match buyers and sellers of products and services. This should enable buyers to purchase at lower prices and allow sellers to broaden customer reach. In addition, B2B sites hope to lower administration costs associated with the procurement process for both buyers and sellers.

- B2B sites can add value by facilitating fulfillment services before and after a sales transaction. Such services may include providing for payment and credit arrangements, coordinating distribution and logistics schedules, integration with financial systems, settling and clearing transactions, settling disputes between participants, and even the inspections of goods.

The decisions involving whether or not a business participates in B2B marketplaces, how to participate, and at what level of involvement are complex and not going to become easier. Companies must evaluate how B2B marketplaces can help improve procurement and supply chain efficiency. Executives must be specific about what will work for their organizations.

It is even possible that joining a B2B marketplace could undermine the current competitive position a company may have. For example, if Company A were to join a marketplace for sourcing and find that its competitors are also members, the competitors could stand to gain greater benefit from the cost savings.

A business exchange represents another type of marketplace. As shown in the diagram, the business exchange accepts documents from a variety of sources and in a variety of formats. The exchange reformats the documents if necessary to meet the requirements of the receiver, and then routes them on to the appropriate receiving business. The business exchange also handles some of the business logic required to ensure messages and documents are formatted and routed correctly.

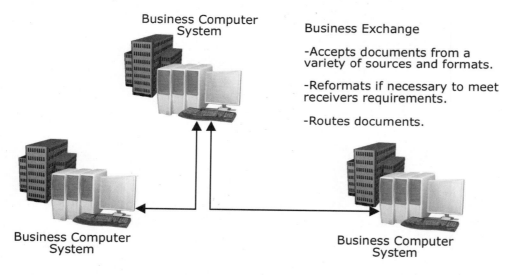

Business document exchanges as a mediator between two other businesses engaged in B2B

Direct or Point-to-Point

The ideal electronic commerce relationship between two businesses exists where the data generated using the computer system of Company A is transmitted over the Internet to Company B, and vice versa. The goal is to have complete confidence in both business systems, and that the data, information, and transactions transmitted and received by both organizations is correct and the processing of that data is also correct.

Exchanging Data and Information

Because different businesses are operating on different computer platforms using different data formats, translation from one format to another is almost always necessary. Many data formats exist. Some are proprietary.

Exchanging Data Using EDI

One of the first efforts to implement B2B electronic commerce was the use of Electronic Data Interchange. EDI requires specialized computer systems and software to translate data from internal computer systems into one of several competing "standard" document formats, which are then transmitted electronically.

In summary, EDI has the following characteristics, (both good and bad):

- EDI solves a lot of problems by standardizing exactly how information should be formatted and in what way the data messages should be packaged. However, the rigid standard and the variety of ways it was implemented also created some of its problems.

- Implementation is slow and expensive.

- Competing standards exist such as ANSI X12, used mostly in North America, and UN/EDIFACT (United Nations Electronic Data Interchange for Administration, Commerce, and Transport).

- The Internet is not typically used. Instead, EDI documents are exchanged using a Value Added Network (VAN), which is a form of business information exchange. VANs are proprietary and expensive.

- EDI is a one-for-one replacement for paper documents. The same manual processes and procedures are needed to manage the data and documents. No functionality was added to the computer data processing systems.

- The EDI formats are proprietary and difficult to read.

Recent efforts are underway to implement EDI on the public Internet. To do this, the EDI document format is first converted to an XML document. The chapter "Integrating BizTalk with EDI" discusses a solution for this problem.

Exchanging Data Using XML and Middleware

The Extensible Markup Language (XML) as defined by the XML Working Group of the World Wide Web Consortium (W3C) is a markup language designed specifically for delivering information over the World Wide Web. Because there are many books written about XML, we do not go into the details here. Rather, we briefly outline XML's ability to answer many of the problems discussed previously.

One of the main benefits of XML is that it is self-describing. XML documents not only contain the actual data, but also contain the information about the data. This "data about the data" is called metadata. The ability to combine the data and the metadata in the same document allows applications and even databases to exchange the information without having to know anything else about each application or database. As long as the two systems understand how to read an XML document, or have a middleware program translate into and out of XML, they can communicate.

Because XML is relatively simple and text-based, it provides individual industries with the ability to define a common metadata for the industry. For example, the aircraft industry metadata definition would be quite different from the metadata definition of the super market or large grocery store industry.

Two of the challenges of using XML involve defining and using a common metadata definition for an industry, and adapting existing legacy systems to use XML documents. Defining a common metadata definition or schema involves not only with developing the definition. Also users of XML must agree to use the same definition.

Middleware typically not only provides the transport mechanism between two different systems, but also provides (or assists in) the conversion of proprietary data formats into XML documents and schemas.

The combination of XML and middleware provides business-to-business integration where applications and computer systems are not under the control of one organization. When a majority of businesses can agree upon XML and the common metadata standards, XML becomes a valuable tool moving information into and out of the enterprise.

The Solution: Web-Based Services Using XML

Microsoft offers several products and technologies to help enterprise customers to integrate with their business partners, using XML Web-based services. The major products featured in this part of the book include BizTalk Server, BizTalk Accelerator for Suppliers (AFS), BizTalk Adapter for transferring large data files over the Internet, and SQL Server. Since the BizTalk Framework Initiative addresses some of the common problems in B2B integration, we included a brief introduction here.

BizTalk Framework Initiative

The **BizTalk Framework Initiative** as created by Microsoft, is designed to be open to everyone and use open standards. The BizTalk Framework Initiative has three parts:

- **BizTalk Framework:** A document that is a set of specifications to allow different organizations and applications communicate reliably.

- **BizTalk.org:** A web site that provides information about message exchange and integration technologies. It is also a repository for XML schemas.

- **BizTalk Server:** Microsoft BizTalk Server is the technology created by Microsoft to use the BizTalk Framework. BizTalk Server is summarized in chapter "Overview of .NET Enterprise Servers."

Although XML is a core component of BizTalk, BizTalk is much more. BizTalk is designed to solve several business-to-business application integration issues, some of which are:

- Bridge the gap between applications running on different platforms and in different companies.

- Create a common XML message format that can be agreed on and used by many organizations.

- Provide a common technology infrastructure that will become a B2B application integration standard.

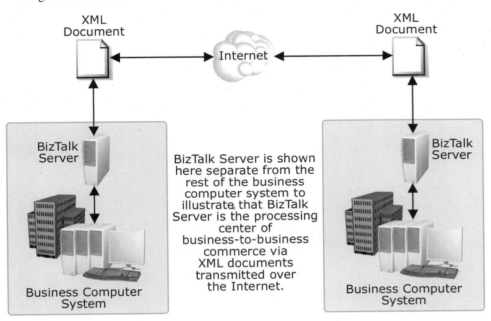

B2B using BizTalk Server and XML documents

The following chapters describe some ways to help you integrate your business partners into your enterprise. The scenarios cover integrating BizTalk Server with existing EDI platforms, automating electronic procurement, selling through trading partners, and using Web-based XML services to transfer large data files over the Internet.

By William J. Harding

Integrating BizTalk with EDI

Scenario

Microsoft conducts a great deal of business electronically. To achieve this, Microsoft devised a business-to-business system that focuses on operational soundness, operational control, and business document tracking. In addition to the complex and specific end-user applications (such as MS Market and MS License), and custom applications for tracking and control, Microsoft primarily uses two server products to integrate business processes and exchange business documents among applications and business partners, namely Sterling Commerce GENTRAN: Server NT and Microsoft® BizTalk® Server 2002.

Microsoft uses GENTRAN to process and transport Electronic Data Interchange (EDI) and Compatibility, Integration and Interoperability (CII) business documents, such as purchase orders and invoices, over a Value Added Network (VAN) to business partners. Microsoft also uses BizTalk Server to process and transport XML business documents over the Internet to other business partners. BizTalk Server is also used for many other functions as discussed in this and other chapters of this book.

Because of the problems associated with EDI, as discussed in the business-to-business introductory chapter, Microsoft is using more XML documents and using BizTalk Server to process and transmit EDI documents. The benefits of migrating to BizTalk Server and XML include:

- Existing business applications do not need to be replaced.

- BizTalk Server can convert EDI documents to XML documents.

- Using XML documents can reduce or eliminate VAN costs by using the Internet to transfer business documents.

- BizTalk Server can reduce the time to set up electronic organization profiles and trading policies.

Solution

The solution to Microsoft's existing EDI implementation involves migrating from GENTRAN to BizTalk Server. The figure shows the e-business infrastructure currently in use at Microsoft. The process starts when a Microsoft employee uses an application (MS Market, MS License, SAP, and others) to generate a business document such as a purchase order.

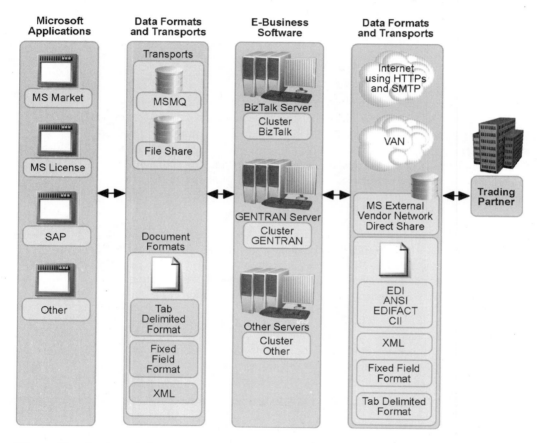

Microsoft's e-business infrastructure

The business application generates a file in one of three formats: tab-delimited, fixed field, or XML, and transfers the file to either a Microsoft Messaging Queue (MSMQ) or a shared folder. The file is then picked up by either the GENTRAN system or the BizTalk Server system depending on which is assigned to monitor the message queue or the shared folder. A GENTRAN or BizTalk Server processes the file and transmits it to a designated business partner.

GENTRAN is used to process EDI documents and transmit them to designated business partners over a value added network. BizTalk Server is used to process XML documents and transmit them to designated business partners via Hyper Text Transfer Protocol Secure sockets (HTTPS) over the Internet using BizTalk Framework 2.0 reliable messaging.

One solution to the problem discussed above is to transfer EDI documents from GENTRAN to BizTalk Server where they can be transmitted over the Internet. BizTalk Server can also convert EDI documents into XML documents.

An additional part of this solution is the custom applications that have been created to track and control the document transfer process, provide alert messages, and keep a historical database of all transactions.

Tools and Technologies

This section describes hardware and software requirements and the components needed to integrate Microsoft BizTalk Server with GENTRAN.

Hardware and Software Requirements

This section is a generalized list of the hardware and software requirements of the system as shown in the figure above. This items listed represent the minimum requirements necessary. The actual number of installations required depends on many factors, such as the number of users on the system, the number of documents being generated, the number of trading partners involved, and other variables.

Microsoft uses both Web-based and Windows-based end-user client/server applications.

- Web-based applications such as MS Market are accessed by the end-user (client) using a computer running a Windows Operating System and a Web browser, specifically Microsoft® Internet Explorer 5.5 or later.

- The server component of the Web-based application uses a computer running Windows 2000 Server. Microsoft® Internet Information Server™ (IIS) is included with the Microsoft® Windows® 2000 Server products. Extensive Web programming may be involved using Active Server Pages, CGI scripts, or other techniques. Microsoft® Commerce Server and Microsoft® SQL Server™ can be used to create this part of the application.

- Windows applications can be created using a variety of tools and languages available with Microsoft® Visual Studio®.

File Transfer

Referring once more to the figure above, notice that after the business application has created a business document (such as a purchase order), it is placed into either a Microsoft Messaging queue or a file share point. The absolute minimum requirement is a computer running Windows 2000 Server with Microsoft® Message Queuing (MSMQ) installed and shared folders configured.

Files are then pulled from the queue and shared folder into either BizTalk Server or GENTRAN. At the same time, transactions are tracked and a history database is updated. In order to do this:

- Microsoft has created a custom Visual Basic application that monitors the message queue and the shared folder, pulls all files that have been placed there, and delivers them to BizTalk Server or GENTRAN.

- This application also interfaces with Microsoft SQL Server to track the transaction and to keep a transaction history database.

- This application creates alert messages for events, such as when files are placed in the shared folder, or when shared folder space is low.

Another file transfer method is used in the specific case of integrating SAP systems with BizTalk Server. For a complete description of integrating SAP systems with BizTalk Server and the BizTalk Server Adapter for SAP, see the online documentation for BizTalk Adapter for SAP.

E-Business Software

Microsoft primarily uses two e-business software solutions. They are

- Microsoft BizTalk Server

- Sterling Commerce GENTRAN: Server NT

Both solutions are defined, and their usage is explained in the following paragraphs.

BizTalk Server 2002

Microsoft® BizTalk® Server 2002 unites, in a single product, enterprise application integration (EAI) and business-to-business (B2B) integration. It provides a complete set of messaging and orchestration services that you can use to automate business and data-exchange processes.

BizTalk Server also provides a powerful Web-based development and execution environment that integrates loosely coupled, long-running business processes, both within and between businesses. The server provides a standard gateway for sending and receiving documents across the Internet, as well as providing a range of services that ensure data integrity, delivery, security, and support for the BizTalk Framework and other key document formats.

The minimum hardware requirements for a basic installation of Microsoft BizTalk Server include:

- An Intel Pentium 300 Processor.

- 128 megabytes (MB) of RAM.

- A 6-gigabyte (GB) hard disk.

- A CD-ROM drive.

- A network adapter card.

- A VGA or Super VGA monitor.

- A Microsoft or compatible pointing device.

Although the above configuration is sufficient to accommodate the software requirements shown below, you should consider additional resources (especially CPU processing and hard disk space) to increase performance.

Additional software must also be installed on the computer prior to installing the BizTalk Server. This software includes the following:

- Microsoft® Windows® 2000 Advanced Server with Service Pack 1.

- Microsoft® SQL Server™ 7.0 or Microsoft SQL Server™ 2000.

- Microsoft® Visio™ 2000 SR-1A or later.

- Microsoft® Message Queue (MSMQ) 2.0.

GENTRAN

GENTRAN is a series of e-business software products produced and marketed by Sterling Commerce (Dublin, OH, USA). GENTRAN specializes in data exchange using standards-based Electronic Data Interchange (EDI) transactions.

For complete information on Sterling Commerce and GENTRAN, see the Sterling Commerce Web site at http://www.sterlingcommerce.com.

Trading Partner Interface

Microsoft uses four methods to transmit business documents from the e-business software to business partners. The transport method depends on the type of document to be sent, the e-business software processing the document, and the capability of the trading partner. The capability also involves business agreements between the trading partner and Microsoft. These methods are summarized in the following diagram.

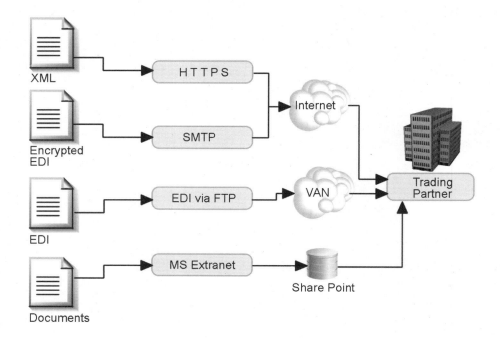

File transport methods

XML Documents coming from BizTalk Server are transmitted to a trading partner directly over the Internet using HTTPS protocol. For outbound data this is accomplished by using BizTalk Server to post messages (data) to a page (ASP or CGI, etc.) on the trading partner's Web site that is capable of receiving posted data. A sample page for doing this is included with BizTalk Server.

For data inbound to Microsoft, a Web page is published for the trading partners' use in posting their data in a similar manner. Microsoft Information Technology Group (MSITG) uses BizTalk Framework 2.0 with reliable receipts. This standard helps to insure the successful transport of data between BizTalk servers.

Trading partners who do not use BizTalk Server only have the ability to create a BizTalk Framework reliable receipt. This is a standardized SOAP message that can be generated based upon data in the inbound message.

Direct Share allows trading partners to establish a direct connection into a private vendor network, which Microsoft has created outside the Microsoft corporate network, (also called the Extranet). Here, Microsoft has created secure, shared folders (directories) and user accounts for the trading partner. The file formats that can be traded include both standard and proprietary formats. A trading partner can access the private vendor network using dial-up remote access services (RAS) or T1, and PPTP to retrieve documents from and deliver documents to Microsoft.

EDI documents from Microsoft's GENTRAN servers are transferred using FTP over a T1 line to a Value Added Network (VAN). A trading partner can retrieve the documents through the VAN.

Encrypted EDI documents can be transmitted over the Internet using Simple Mail Transfer Protocol (SMTP). This transport method uses a software product called Templar by CI Solutions.

Implementation

Integrating BizTalk Server into existing GENTRAN installations can solve the business problems of:

- Reducing or eliminating the costs associated with using a VAN to transfer business documents between business partners.

- Reducing the time and complexity of setting up and configuring automated electronic transmission of business documents between trading partners.

Integrating BizTalk Server into existing GENTRAN installations also brings about the benefits of these added features:

- EDI to XML translation.

- Using the Internet and HTTPS protocols to securely transmit XML documents to business partners.

This implementation section will focus only on the integration of BizTalk Server and GENTRAN systems. As the following diagram illustrates, the process involves placing files and data processed by GENTRAN on a file share. BizTalk Server then retrieves the files from the share and either transmits them to a business partner over the Internet or makes them available for other internal processing by placing the files in a Microsoft Messaging Queue (MSMQ).

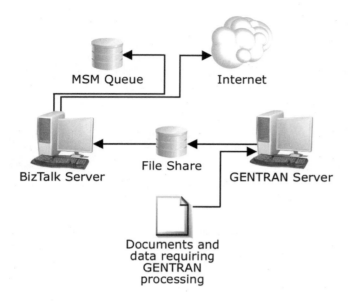

MSM Queue

Internet

File Share

BizTalk Server

GENTRAN Server

Documents and
data requiring
GENTRAN
processing

GENTRAN to BizTalk file transfer

Configuring for Internet Transmission

The following procedure can be used to configure GENTRAN: Server NT to transfer data to BizTalk Server, which in turn, then transmits the data over the Internet via HTTPS protocol. This procedure is very general and represents the major steps in the configuration process. Each of these steps may involve one or more detailed procedures. The detailed procedures can be found as part of the product documentation.

In order to send data via HTTPS, the receiving site must have a site certificate installed for their URL in order for HTTPS to function. Certificates can be obtained from commercial certificate authorities.

To configure GENTRAN: Server NT

1. Configure your outbound trading partner relationship. This is a normal GENTRAN procedure.

2. Create a mailbox using the GENTRAN file system gateway, which will be used to send data. The simplest way is to create one mailbox for each trading partner.

3. Create a folder on your GENTRAN server named BIZTALK and share that folder so that the UNC path is \\GENTRANServerName\BIZTALK\.

4. Create a subfolder to your BIZTALK share as follows: \\GENTRANServerName\ BIZTALK \HTTPS_out.

5. Configure the mailbox to transfer the messages sent to the mailbox to the file share where your BizTalk Server will pick them up. (This file share will be configured in the BizTalk Server procedures below.) For this example, we will use the folder created in step 4: \\GENTRANServerName\ BIZTALK \HTTPS_out.

6. Configure the mailbox to either append all messages to a single file or keep each message as an individual file. This decision will depend upon how your trading partner expects to receive the data. For this example, append all messages to a single file and name it **TP1outbound.tmp**

7. Using the GENTRAN Partner Editor, assign the trading partner to use this mailbox.

8. Create a GENTRAN **session & event** for processing and sending the data. The session should have the following pseudo code. The actual import file name will depend upon your own installation and file naming conventions. Here we have used ImportFile.DAT.

```
Import        \\GENTRANServerName\GENSRVNT\Imports\ImportFile.DAT
File_Delete        \\GENTRANServerName\GENSRVNT\Imports\ImportFile.DAT
Send/Receive Partnerkey & Document If Documents Exist in Outbox
File_Rename            \\GENTRANServerName\GENSRVNT\BizTalk\HTTPS_out\TP1outbound.tmp to
                      \\tkebisgnt31\BizTalk\HTTPS_out\TP1outbound.dat
```

9. Notice the rename step in the pseudo code renaming **TP1outbound.tmp** to **TP1outbound.dat.** This step is important because you do not want BizTalk Server polling for a file as it is being created. By renaming the file, you guarantee that the file is complete before BizTalk Server retrieves it.

10. Test the process by sending a sample message through GENTRAN for this trading partner and using your session to export it. It should end up in the shared folder \\GENTRANServerName\ BIZTALK \HTTPS_out.

The GENTRAN configuration is now complete.

To configure BizTalk Server

The following steps use BizTalk Messaging Manager:

1. Create an Organization for the trading partner to whom you will be sending documents. For this example we will use TP1 (Trading Partner 1).

2. Create an application under your default home organization for the source application (if one does not exist already). This is the application from which data is being sent.

3. Create a BizTalk Port to an Organization (trading partner) and include their HTTPS URL.

   HTTPS is preferred for data that may be confidential or proprietary but requires that the trading partner have a site that is capable of supporting HTTPS sessions. For this example, we will name this port HTTPS:TP1. Some trading partners may require a user name and password in order to connect to their site. Please see the BizTalk Server Documentation for information on configuring user names and passwords for HTTP ports.

4. Create a Null Document Definition (NullDocDef). This is a document definition without a schema and will be used latter.

5. Create a channel that uses the application, organization, port and NullDocDef created in steps 1-4. For this example, we will name it HTTPS:TP1.

6. Using BizTalk Server Administration tool, select the BizTalk group and receive functions. Then create a new BizTalk File receive function to poll the share you created in the GENTRAN setup. In our example this is \\GENTRANServerName\ BIZTALK \HTTPS_out.

   You can name it to your own standards. For clarity, use something similar to "HTTPS:TP1:Transport" so that you can reference the process for the trading partner in supporting the system.

7. Select the server on which the receive function will run.

8. Under **File Types to Poll for,** enter the following mask: TP1*.dat. You will want to set up one receive function for each trading partner.

9. Under **Polling location**, enter the share you created: \\GENTRANServerName\ BIZTALK \HTTPS_out.

10. Enter a username and password if they are required to access the share.

11. Click **Advanced,** and then select **Submit** with a pass-through flag.

12. Under channel, select the HTTPS:TP1 channel that you created above. This will cause all data submitted to this channel to process through the selected channel.

13. **Save** the receive function.

Configuration of BizTalk Server is now complete. When you saved the receive function (step 13), after about 60 seconds it begins monitoring the share for files. When a file arrives, the BizTalk receive function processes the file. This results in the test file, which was created in the GENTRAN setup, now being processed from the share and having been sent to the trading partner's Web site defined in the BizTalk Port.

Configuring for Routing Received Documents to MSMQ

The following procedure can be used to configure GENTRAN: Server NT to transfer data to BizTalk Server, which in turn, then transfers the data to an application program using Microsoft Message Queuing. This procedure is very general and represents the major steps in the configuration process. Each of these steps may involve one or more detailed procedures. The detailed procedures can be found as part of the product documentation.

To configure GENTRAN: Server NT

1. Configure your inbound trading partner relationship. This is a normal GENTRAN procedure.

2. Create a folder on your GENTRAN server to be used to write messages inbound to MSMQ. For example: \\GENTRANServerName\ BIZTALK \MSMQ_QueueName

3. Set the relationship to have an export file name of MSMQ_App1data.tmp and write the data to a shared folder. For this example, the shared folder name is \\GENTRANServerName\ BIZTALK \MSMQ_QueueName

4. Create a GENTRAN Session and Event to export data and set the **Partner** and **Transaction** you want to export. Since you defined the file name in the relationship, you do not have to enter a file here. Pseudo code for the GENTRAN session is as follows:

```
Process_File    \\GENSRVNT\BIN\INBOUNDFILE.DAT
File Delete     \\GENSRVNT\BIN\INBOUNDFILE.DAT
GDW_Export      partnerkey & Document If Documents Exist.
File Rename     \\tkebisgnt31\Biztalk\MSMQ_QueueName\MSMQ_App1data.tmp
\\tkebisgnt31\biztalk\MSMQ_QueueName\MSMQ_App1data.dat
If a .tmp files exists.
```

5. Notice the rename step in the pseudo code renaming **MSMQ_App1data.tmp** to **MSMQ_App1data.dat.** (This file is generated from the GENTRAN relationship that you configured in step #3.) This step is important because you do not want BizTalk Server polling for a file as it is being created. By renaming the file as a last step, you guarantee the file is completed before BizTalk retrieves it.

6. Test the process by sending a sample message through GENTRAN for this trading partner and using your session to export it. It should end up in the shared folder \\GENTRANServerName\ BIZTALK \MSMQ_QueueName.

7. The GENTRAN configuration is now complete.

To configure BizTalk Server

The following steps use BizTalk Messaging Manager:

1. Create an Organization for the trading partner from whom you will be receiving documents. For this example we will use TP1 (Trading Partner 1).

2. Create an application under your home organization for the destination application (if one does not exist already). This is the application to which data is being sent.

3. Create a BizTalk Port for the application, which includes the MSMQ Queue. For this example, we will name this port MSMQ:App1.

4. Create a Null Document Definition (NullDocDef). This is a document definition without a schema and will be used latter.

5. Create a channel that uses the application, organization, port and NullDocDef created in steps 1-4. For this example, we will name it MSMQ:App1.

6. Using BizTalk Server Administration tool, Create a new BizTalk File receive function to poll the share you created in the GENTRAN setup. In our example this is \\GENTRANServerName\ BIZTALK \MSMQ_QueueName

7. You can name it to your own standards. It is suggested for clarity you use something similar to "MSMQ:App1:Transport" so that you can reference the process for the application in supporting the system.

8. Select the server on which the receive function will run.

9. Under **File Types to Poll for,** enter the following mask: MSMQ*.dat. You will want to set up one receive function for each trading partner.

10. Under **Polling location**, enter the share you created: \\ServerName\ BIZTALK \MSMQ_QueueName.

11. Enter a username and password if they are required to access the share.

12. Click **Advanced** and select **Submit** with a pass-through flag.

    Under channel, select the MSMQ:App1channel that you created above. This will cause all data submitted to this channel to process through the selected channel.

13. **Save** the receive function.

Configuration of BizTalk Server is now complete. When you saved the receive function (Step 13), the system begins monitoring the share for files. When a file arrives, the BizTalk receive function processes the file. The result is that test file you created in the GENTRAN setup should now be processed from the share and has been sent to the MSMQ Queue defined in the messaging port created in Step 3 above.

Planning for Growth and Scalability

The examples shown will work in an environment where the number of trading partners is small or volume of data is relatively low. However, it gives a good outline for integrating the two products for transport purposes.

For scaling and high volume implementations, develop a common XML or flat file routing record that identifies the document, sender, receiver document type, and a control number. An example of an XML routing record is shown below.

```
<routing ReceiverKey="Sojourn Information Systems" SenderKey="e*BIS" DocumentName="StandardPO"
ControlNumber="X57394" />
```

Additional routing records can be created for flat files or other formats of data besides XML depending upon your needs. Routing records provide all the information necessary for a component or receive function to process "self-routing" documents into BizTalk Server. Doing this can make your deployment scalable because you do not have to set up multiple BizTalk Server receive functions.

You can find recommendations for developing custom envelopes for routing data and further details about meeting your specific needs in the BizTalk Server documentation.

Automating Electronic Procurement

Scenario

This scenario represents a business situation in which your company is purchasing products from several different suppliers. We will focus on setting up a business solution by using Microsoft BizTalk Server 2002 to automate the procurement process that takes place between your company and its suppliers over the Internet. We call this solution e-procurement.

In this scenario you set up a purchasing hub for your company. The hub handles all the inbound and outbound documents that are exchanged between your company and the suppliers. For the purposes of this scenario, a business transaction between your hub and the suppliers uses four different documents. A transaction starts when a purchase order (PO) is sent from the hub to the supplier. Upon receipt of the PO, the supplier generates an invoice for that PO, which is returned to the hub. When the hub receives an invoice for an outstanding PO, the hub sends a payment to the supplier. Finally, the supplier sends a payment acknowledgement to the hub and the e-procurement transaction is complete. The following illustration shows the business transaction used in this sample.

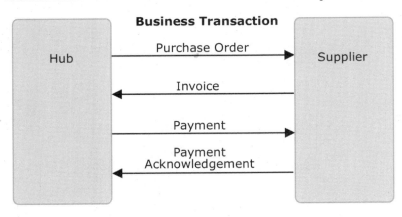

E-procurement scenario data flow

The documents in this transaction are transmitted to their destinations over the Internet by using XML Web services created with Microsoft Visual Studio .NET. All of the custom components used in this scenario are written in the Microsoft Visual C# .NET (C sharp) programming language.

Solution

Microsoft BizTalk Server 2002 provides a rich set of features to use in implementing an automated e-procurement system. On both the hub and the supplier systems, BizTalk Server XLANG schedules are used to implement the business processes and logic required to complete a business transaction.

The following topics describe the flow of documents through both systems, as shown in the preceding illustration.

- Hub: Send Purchase Order to Supplier

- Supplier: Receive PO and Send Invoice to Hub

- Hub: Receive Invoice and Send Payment to Supplier

- Supplier: Receive Payment and Send Acknowledgement to Hub

The following topics describe how BizTalk Server 2002 features are used in this scenario:

- XLANG Schedule Activation

- E-Procurement XLANG Schedule Correlation

Hub: Send Purchase Order to Supplier

The following illustration shows the purchase order flow through the hub system.

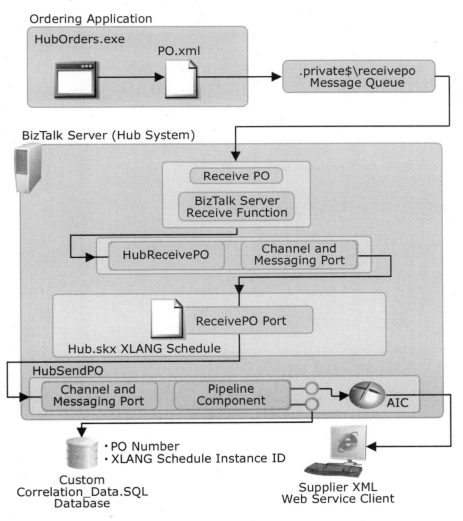

Hub system initiates a business transaction

A business transaction is initiated when the ordering application generates a purchase order (PO) named PO.xml, and delivers it to the receivepo message queue, which is monitored by the Receive PO receive function. The document is submitted to a BizTalk Messaging Services channel configured for PO processing. The HubReceivePO messaging port activates a new instance of the XLANG schedule Hub.skx, and then delivers the document to the ReceivePO port on that XLANG schedule. The schedule contains some business logic to apply a simple approval process to the purchase order. For this scenario, the purchase order is automatically approved if the total value is less than $1,000.00. If the PO.xml document is approved, it is sent to the HubSendPO channel for further processing. When the processing completes and the correlation information is written to a database, the purchase order is sent to the supplier by means of an application integration component (AIC) that functions as a client to the supplier's XML Web service.

Notes If the PO.xml document is denied, the schedule terminates, and no further documents are processed for the business transaction.

The purchase order \Microsoft .NET Server Solutions for the Enterprise\E-Procurement\Application\PO.xml is used as a template document by the ordering application. This document is populated with a purchase order number and purchase order total when the user submits the order.

Supplier: Receive PO and Send Invoice to Hub

The following illustration shows the incoming purchase order and the resulting invoice flow through the supplier system.

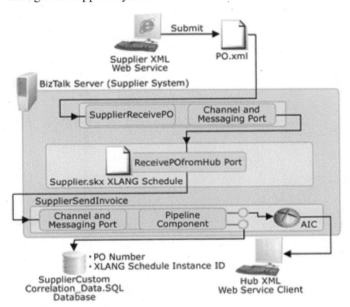

Supplier system receives a purchase order and sends back an invoice

The supplier's XML Web service accepts the incoming purchase order. The XML Web service submits the PO to a BizTalk Messaging Services channel configured for PO processing. The SupplierReceivePO messaging port then activates a new instance of the XLANG schedule Supplier.skx, and delivers the document to the ReceivePOfromHub port on that XLANG schedule. The schedule contains some business logic to apply a simple approval process to the purchase order. For this scenario, the purchase order is automatically rejected if the total value is less than $300.00. If the PO.xml document is approved, it is sent to a component that transforms the purchase order into an invoice document. Then the invoice is sent to the SupplierSendInvoice channel for further processing. When the processing completes and the correlation information is written to a database, the invoice is sent back to the hub by means of an AIC that functions as a client to the hub's XML Web service.

Notes The transform component used in the supplier schedule simulates the function of a sales or accounting application that accepts purchase order documents and generates the corresponding invoice documents.

The transform component is written in C#, and is bound to the supplier XLANG schedule through the interop assembly for accessing managed code through COM.

Hub: Receive Invoice and Send Payment to Supplier

The following illustration shows the invoice and the resulting payment flow through the hub system.

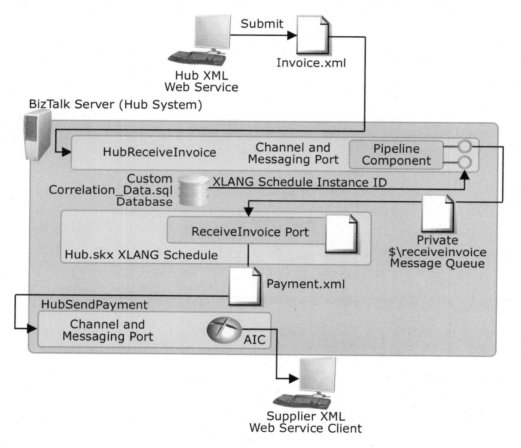

Hub system receives an invoice and sends back a payment

The hub's XML Web service accepts the incoming invoice. The XML Web service submits the invoice to a BizTalk Messaging Services channel configured for invoice processing. Then the pipeline component on that channel correlates the incoming document with an XLANG schedule instance identifier. This correlation information is obtained by reading the key-pair values from the custom correlation database. The invoice is sent to the correlated XLANG schedule instance, and resumes processing on the ReceiveInvoice port. After the document is back in the schedule, it is sent to a component that transforms the invoice into a payment. The payment is sent to the HubSendPayment channel for further processing. When the processing completes, the payment is sent to the supplier by means of an AIC that functions as a client to the supplier's XML Web service.

Note   The transform component used in the hub schedule simulates the function of an ordering or accounting application that accepts invoice documents and generates the corresponding payments.

Supplier: Receive Payment and Send Acknowledgement to Hub

The following illustration shows the payment and the resulting acknowledgement flow through the supplier system.

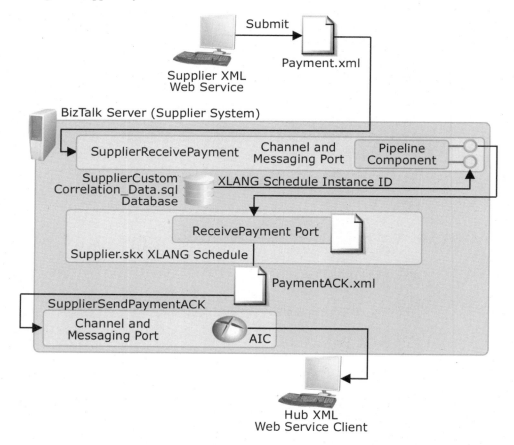

Supplier system receives a payment and sends back an acknowledgement

The supplier's XML Web service accepts the incoming payment for the invoice that it issued. The XML Web service submits the payment to a BizTalk Messaging Services channel configured for payment processing. Then the pipeline component on that channel correlates the incoming document with an XLANG schedule instance identifier. This correlation information is obtained by reading the key-pair values from the supplier custom correlation database. The payment is sent to the correlated XLANG schedule instance, and resumes processing on the ReceivePayment port. After the document is back in the schedule, it is sent to a component that transforms the payment into a payment acknowledgement. The payment acknowledgement is sent to the SupplierSendPaymentAck channel for further processing. When the processing completes, the payment acknowledgement is sent back to the hub by means of an AIC that functions as a client to the hub's XML Web service. At this point, the supplier XLANG schedule for this transaction completes.

The XLANG schedule instance on the hub system completes after it receives the payment acknowledgement, correlates it to the correct purchase order, and writes the acknowledgement document to the folder \Microsoft .NET Server Solutions for the Enterprise\E-Procurement\Application\eprocurement\PaymentAckReceived.

XLANG Schedule Activation

BizTalk Server messaging ports activate the XLANG schedules used in this scenario. However, the first actions within the schedules are bound to **Message Queuing** shapes, rather than **BizTalk Messaging** shapes, so that per-instance message queues are not created. This helps to optimize the performance of the schedule by preventing the creation, and subsequent deletion, of a message queue used only for initiating the schedule. The following illustration shows the hub XLANG schedule drawing.

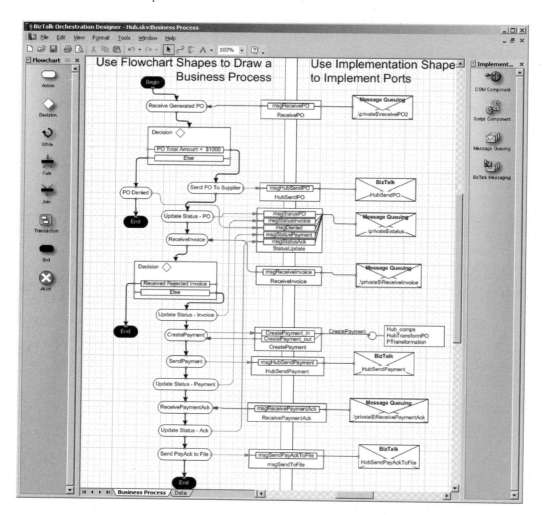

E-Procurement XLANG Schedule Correlation

This scenario uses two databases to store and retrieve information that correlates the documents exchanged in a business transaction to the correct XLANG schedule instances. Without this mechanism, documents would not be properly synchronized when multiple orders are processed simultaneously. This could result in a payment being issued on the wrong invoice. One database exists on the hub system to correlate the documents processed by the Hub.skx XLANG schedule, and one database exists on the supplier system for documents processed by the Supplier.skx XLANG schedule. The BizTalk Server channel called by the XLANG schedules uses a custom pipeline component to save and recall correlation information in these databases. The correlation information consists of two parts:

- The globally unique identifier (GUID) of the XLANG schedule instance. This value is stored in the database in the SkedInstanceGUID column.

- A user-defined transaction identifier. This value is stored in the database in the TransactionID column.

The XLANG Scheduler Engine automatically generates the XLANG schedule GUID when the XLANG schedule begins. The TransactionID is a unique identifier contained within a specific document instance, such as a purchase order number or invoice number. The hub TransactionID for a purchase order is obtained from the **Number** field on the hub ordering application. The user can modify this value before submitting a purchase order. By contrast, the supplier TransactionID for an invoice is automatically generated by the SQL Server stored procedure **usp_InsertCorrInfo** that is associated with the SupplierCustomCorrelation database.

Storing the Correlation Information

In this scenario, when the hub receives a new purchase order from the ordering application, the GUID of the XLANG schedule is extracted and stored in the CustomCorrelation database along with the PO number as a TransactionID. When the supplier receives the purchase order and activates an XLANG schedule of its own, the GUID of the supplier's XLANG schedule is stored along with the invoice number as the TransactionID. The supplier system stores this pair of values in its own SupplierCustomCorrelation database. These initial correlation values are used to associate the remaining incoming and outgoing documents to the correct running XLANG schedule instance as the transaction progresses until the XLANG schedule completes.

Reading the Correlation Information

The correlation of a document to its running XLANG schedule instance begins when the hub receives an invoice associated with a purchase order. At this point, BizTalk Server queries the invoice for the TransactionID (PO number) and looks up the associated XLANG schedule GUID in the CustomCorrelation database. The invoice document is passed to the Hub.skx schedule instance that matches the GUID, and the schedule continues running.

Similarly, when the supplier receives a payment from the hub, BizTalk Server queries the payment for the TransactionID (invoice number) and looks up the associated XLANG schedule GUID in the SupplierCustomCorrelation database. The payment document is passed to the Supplier.skx schedule instance that matches the GUID, and the schedule continues running.

Finally, when the hub receives the payment acknowledgement, BizTalk Server queries the acknowledgement for the TransactionID (PO number) and looks up the associated XLANG schedule GUID in the CustomCorrelation database. The payment acknowledgement is passed to the Hub.skx schedule instance that matches the GUID, and the schedule continues running.

Tools and Technologies

This section describes the hardware and software requirements for running the e-procurement sample included on the CD-ROM provided with this book.

Hardware and Software Requirements

This sample assumes that you have the following installed on the computer that is running BizTalk Server:

- Microsoft BizTalk Server 2002
- Microsoft Visual Studio .NET
- Microsoft SQL Server
- Message Queuing (also known as MSMQ)
- Microsoft Internet Information Services (IIS)

Note   It is recommended that you run the sample on a clean installation of BizTalk Server in a nonproduction environment. If you would like to quickly delete all the BizTalk Server objects (ports, channels, and so on), you can run the cleanbtm.vbs script that is located in the \Microsoft .NET Server Solutions for the Enterprise\E-Procurement\Application\eprocurement folder. If you would like to manually delete all of the BizTalk Server objects created by the setup script, a list of these objects is provided at the end of this chapter.

Important   The cleanbtm.vbs script removes all configuration information from the BizTalk Messaging Management database. This script should only be run in a testing environment.

Using Microsoft Visual Studio .NET

The components and XML Web services used in the e-procurement scenario were created by using Microsoft Visual Studio .NET. These components and services use a set of primary interop assemblies (PIAs) to access the COM-based BizTalk Server 2002 application programming interfaces (APIs).

For more information about using PIAs to access any BizTalk Server 2002 API from managed code, download the BizTalk Server 2002 Toolkit for Microsoft .NET from the Microsoft Developer Network.

Creating XML Web Services

This section contains information about creating the XML Web services used in this scenario. These XML Web services provide a mechanism for accepting incoming documents through SOAP. The documents are sent from a client to the host running an XML Web service. The client obtains a reference, also called a proxy, to the remote host by specifying the URL of the XML Web service. After the proxy is established, the client can use the methods provided by the XML Web service.

In this scenario, the BizTalk messaging ports contain an application integration component (AIC) that uses a proxy to the appropriate remote XML Web service method call. For example, the messaging port on the supplier system that sends an invoice contains an AIC with a proxy to the XML Web service method **Process_invoice**(*invoice*) provided by the hub system. Note that the *invoice* argument passed to the method represents a strongly typed object corresponding to the CommonInvoice.xml document schema.

The XML Web services provide methods to accept a specific document type, such as a purchase order or invoice, and submit that document directly to a BizTalk Server 2002 channel for further processing.

Converting a BizTalk Document to a C# Class

For every document that is passed to an XML Web service, you need to create a corresponding C# class. The following steps illustrate this process:

1. On the **Start** menu, point to **Programs**, point to **Microsoft BizTalk Server 2002**, and then click **BizTalk Editor**.

2. On the **File** menu, click **Retrieve from WebDAV**.

   The **Retrieve from WebDAV** dialog box appears.

3. Browse for an XML document schema, and then click **Open**.

4. On the **Tools** menu, click **Export XSD Schema**.

   The **Export XSD Schema** dialog box appears.

5. Type a name for the XSD file in the **File name** box, and then click **Save**.

6. Close BizTalk Editor.

7. On the **Start** menu, point to **Programs**, point to **Microsoft Visual Studio .NET**, point to **Visual Studio .NET Tools**, and then click **Visual Studio .NET Command Prompt**.

   The **Visual Studio .NET Command Prompt** window appears.

8. Run the XSD program to create a C# class from the XSD file you created previously by typing:

   XSD *filename***.xsd /c**

   This command creates a new C# class named *filename*.cs.

9. Edit this C# class file to add a namespace declaration. For example:

```
namespace namespacename {
<contents of file>
}
```

10. Update the XML element information.

    For example, using the following output:

```
/// <remarks/>
[System.Xml.Serialization.XmlRootAttribute("Seller", Namespace="", IsNullable=false)]
public class Seller {

    /// <remarks/>
    [System.Xml.Serialization.XmlElementAttribute("Address", typeof(Address))]
    [System.Xml.Serialization.XmlElementAttribute("ContactInfo", typeof(ContactInfo))]
    public object[] Items;
}
```

Remove the public object[] Items statement, and add new declarations, shown in **bold**:

```
/// <remarks/>
[System.Xml.Serialization.XmlRootAttribute("Seller")]
public class Seller {

/// <remarks/>
[System.Xml.Serialization.XmlElementAttribute("Address", typeof(Address))]
public Address[] Address;

[System.Xml.Serialization.XmlElementAttribute("ContactInfo", typeof(ContactInfo))]
public ContactInfo[] ContactInfo;
}
```

11. Make the changes in the preceding step to all XML element declarations in the file.

12. Create a new Web Service project in Visual Studio .NET.

13. Add the C# (.cs) file created from the document specification to the Web Service project.

14. Add a custom method to the XML Web service code. For example:

```
[WebMethod]
public string Process_invoice(CommonInvoice invoice)
{
    StringWriter sw = new StringWriter();
    XmlSerializer serializer = new XmlSerializer(typeof(CommonInvoice));
    serializer.Serialize(sw, invoice);

    Interop.BTSInterchangeLib.InterchangeClass BTSObj = new
Interop.BTSInterchangeLib.InterchangeClass();
    string result =
BTSObj.Submit(Interop.BTSInterchangeLib.BIZTALK_OPENNESS_TYPE.BIZTALK_OPENNESS_TYPE_NOTOPE
N,
        sw.ToString(), // the document body
        null, // docname
        null, // sourcequalifier
        null, // sourceid
        null, // destqualifier
        null, // destid
        "HubReceiveInvoice", // channel
        null, // filepath
        null, // envelope
        0); // passthrough

    BTSObj = null;
    return result;
}
```

Notes The [Webmethod] declaration must be added to the method to make it externally available.

StringWriter and **XMLSerializer** classes are used to convert the passed-in object into an XML string.

Test the XML Web service page to ensure that it works. Also note the URL of the XML Web service to reference in the client program.

At this point, the client program can add a reference to the XML Web service method that you just created. This allows you to call the XML Web service from an application integration component (AIC), which is bound to a BizTalk Server messaging port. As a result, BizTalk Server can process a document and then deliver it directly to the XML Web service.

Calling an XML Web Service from an AIC

This section describes the steps required for an AIC to call an XML Web service.

Update the resource file

Create a C# class project in Microsoft Visual Studio .NET for the AIC that calls the XML Web service. View the Reference.cs file to ensure that the XMLRoot information contained in this class is correct, and that the structure matches the class in the original .cs file created for the XML Web service.

To view and update the Reference.cs file

1. In the **Solution Explorer**, click **Show All Files**.

2. Expand **Web References**, expand the name of the XML Web service host, expand **Reference.map**, and then double-click **Reference.cs**.

3. Every element in the XML file has been converted to a public class. Search for the root element in the XML file.

   The root element appears as:

   ```
   [System.Xml.Serialization.XmlAttribute("Namespace=http://tempuri.org")]
   public class RootElementName {
   ```

4. Change this to the following:

   ```
   [System.Xml.Serialization.XmlRoot("RootElementName")]
   public class RootElementName {
   ```

   Where *RootElementName* is the name of the document's root element.

5. Repeat steps 3 and 4 for every element in the document.

Add a reference to the XML Web service

The AIC project must contain a reference to access the XML Web service remotely. After this reference is made, the project acts as a client to that XML Web service. For example:

```
// Reference to the hub XML Web service
using Supp_send_invoice.localhost;
```

Implement the IBTSAppIntegration.ProcessMessage method

To indicate that the project is an AIC, the code must implement the **ProcessMessage** method on the **IBTSAppIntegration** interface.

The following example is from the supplier's client code that sends an invoice to the hub XML Web service:

```
string IBTSAppIntegration.ProcessMessage(string strDocument)
{
// The incoming string is CommonInvoice, convert the
// xml string into an object by deserializing it
    CommonInvoice invoice;
    XmlSerializer serializer = new XmlSerializer(typeof(CommonInvoice));
    TextReader stringstream = new StringReader(strDocument);
    invoice = ((CommonInvoice)serializer.Deserialize(stringstream));

// Open up the hub XML Web service
    Hub_services web_service = new Hub_services();

// Process the order
    string result = web_service.Process_invoice(invoice);

    web_service = null;
    return result;
}
```

Register the AIC for use with COM

When creating your AIC project in Microsoft Visual Studio .NET, you might want to use a fixed GUID value to maintain binary compatibility. Otherwise, the GUID for the component changes every time you compile the code. In that case, any references to this component would have to be rebound in your XLANG schedules.

The following procedure assigns a static GUID value to the component and registers the AIC for COM interoperability:

1. Add the following reference to your project:

```
using System.Runtime.InteropServices;
```

2. Just before the class declaration in your project, add the GUID declaration (shown in bold):

```
[Guid("")]
public class AIC_name : IBTSAppIntegration
```

> **Note** The "Guid" literal string shown above is case-sensitive.

3. On the **Tools** menu, click **Create GUID**.

   The **Create GUID** dialog box appears.

4. Select option 4, **Registry Format**, click **Copy**, and then click **Exit**.

5. Place your cursor between the quotes in the **[Guid("")]** declaration and paste in the GUID value.

6. In the **Solution Explorer** pane, right-click the project and then click **Properties**.

   The project **Property Pages** dialog box appears.

7. Click the **Configuration Properties** folder in the left pane.

8. On the **Configuration** drop-down menu, click **All Configurations**.

9. Change the value of the **Register for COM interop** property to **True**.

Summary

In this section, you learned how to use Microsoft Visual Studio .NET to:

- Convert a BizTalk document specification into a C# class

- Create an XML Web service

- Call the XML Web service from a BizTalk Server AIC

- Register the component for COM interoperability

All of the source code for the examples in this section is included on the CD-ROM provided with this book. To view the source code, open the file \Microsoft .NET Server Solutions for the Enterprise\E-Procurement\Application\eprocurement\Build_everything.sln. The next section explains how to configure and run the e-procurement sample.

Implementation

Before you can run the e-procurement sample, you must register components, attach the correlation databases, and configure the BizTalk Messaging objects on the hub and supplier systems. In this scenario, both the hub and the supplier are configured on one BizTalk Server installation. In an actual production environment, the hub and the supplier would be two separate entities connected to the Internet.

Important   The instructions in this sample assume that this sample and BizTalk Server 2002 are installed on the same drive.

Preliminary Setup

The steps in this section explain how to configure your system to run the e-procurement sample provided on the CD-ROM that accompanies this book. After you run the CD-ROM setup, the e-procurement sample is located on the installation drive in the folder \Microsoft .NET Server Solutions for the Enterprise\E-Procurement.

Note   Before proceeding with the setup, verify that your system meets the conditions specified in the Hardware and Software Requirements section earlier in this chapter.

Update the Global Assembly Cache

The primary interop assemblies required for BizTalk Server 2002 must be added to your Microsoft .NET global assembly cache (GAC). This provides a single access location for components using the assemblies, so that multiple local copies of the assemblies are not required. To update the GAC with the BizTalk Server 2002 assemblies, run the following script:

\Microsoft .NET Server Solutions for the Enterprise\E-Procurement\Application\setup_eproc.cmd

Attach the SQL Server 2000 Databases

In this procedure you set up the correlation databases that are used with the e-procurement sample. You should use these instructions if you are using Microsoft SQL Server 2000 in your BizTalk Server installation. If you are using Microsoft SQL Server 7.0, use the instructions in the following topic titled "Create the SQL Server 7.0 Databases" instead of this one.

The following instructions assume that SQL Server 2000 is installed on the same computer as BizTalk Server. If SQL Server is installed on a different computer, you will need to modify these instructions so that they will work in your environment. The hub database files (CustomCorrelation_Data.*) are located in the \Microsoft .NET Server Solutions for the Enterprise\E-Procurement\Application\eprocurement\hub_database folder, and the supplier database files (SupplierCustomCorrelation_Data.*) are located in the \Microsoft .NET Server Solutions for the Enterprise\E-Procurement\Application\eprocurement\supplier_database folder.

1. On the **Start** menu, point to **Programs**, point to **Microsoft SQL Server**, and then click **Enterprise Manager**.

   The **SQL Server Enterprise Manager** appears.

2. Expand **Microsoft SQL Servers**, expand **SQL Server Group**, and then expand the server on which you want to attach the database.

3. Click **Databases**.

4. On the **Action** menu, point to **All Tasks** and click **Attach Database**.

   The **Attach Database** dialog box appears.

5. Click the browse button (**...**).

   The **Browse For Existing File** dialog box appears.

6. Browse to the folder **\Microsoft .NET Server Solutions for the Enterprise\E-Procurement\Application\eprocurement\hub_database**.

7. Click **CustomCorrelation_Data.MDF**, and then click **OK**.

   A message box appears indicating that the process was successful.

8. Repeat the steps in this procedure to attach the file **SupplierCustomCorrelation_Data.MDF** located in the folder **\Microsoft .NET Server Solutions for the Enterprise\E-Procurement\Application\eprocurement\supplier_database**.

Create the SQL Server 7.0 Databases

You should use the following procedure if you are using Microsoft SQL Server 7.0 in your BizTalk Server installation. If you are using Microsoft SQL Server 2000, use the instructions in the preceding topic titled "Attach the SQL Server 2000 Databases" instead of this one.

1. On the **Start** menu, point to **Programs**, point to **Microsoft SQL Server 7.0**, and then click **Enterprise Manager**.

   The **SQL Server Enterprise Manager** appears.

2. Expand **Microsoft SQL Servers**, expand **SQL Server Group**, and then expand the server on which you want to attach the database.

3. Click **Databases**.

4. On the **Action** menu, click **New Database**.

   The **Database Properties** menu appears.

5. In the **Name** field, type **CustomCorrelation** as the name of the database.

6. Click **OK**.

7. On the **Action** menu, click **New Database**.

   The **Database Properties** menu appears.

8. In the **Name** field, type **SupplierCustomCorrelation** as the name of the database.

9. Click **OK**.

10. Close the **SQL Server Enterprise Manager**.

11. On the **Start** menu, point to **Programs**, point to **Microsoft SQL Server 7.0**, and then click **Query Analyzer**.

    The **Connect to SQL Server** menu appears.

12. Ensure that the correct information to connect to SQL Server is entered. Click **OK**.

13. On the menu bar, make sure that the value in the **DB** field is **CustomCorrelation**. If it is not, click the **DB** drop-down list box and select **CustomCorrelation**.

14. On the **File** menu, click **Open**.

15. Browse to the folder **\Microsoft .NET Server Solutions for the Enterprise\E-Procurement\Application\eprocurement\hub_database**.

16. Click the **CustomCorrelationTable.sql** file.

17. On the **Query** menu, click **Execute**.

    This will process the **CustomCorrelationTable.sql** file. If the SQL file has been run, you will see a message stating: **The command(s) completed successfully**.

18. Repeat the steps in this procedure for the **SupplierCustomCorrelationTable.sql** file located in the folder **\Microsoft .NET Server Solutions for the Enterprise\E-Procurement\Application\eprocurement\supplier_database**.

19. Close **Query Manager**.

Configure BizTalk Messaging Services

In this procedure you run the setup application to configure the BizTalk Messaging Services for the hub and the supplier to run the e-procurement sample.

The e-procurement setup application performs the following tasks:

- Creates these message queues:

   .\private$\receiveinvoice

   .\private$\receivepayment

   .\private$\receivepaymentack

   .\private$\receivepo

   .\private$\receivepo2

   .\private$\supplierreceivepo

   .\private$\supplierreceivepo2

   .\private$\status

   The queues are used to transfer data between the business partners represented by the running hub and supplier XLANG schedules. The status queue is used to provide dynamic updates to the application used to submit orders from the hub.

- Creates the channels and ports

   Each channel is configured to override the messaging port default values and associate the message with a specific XLANG schedule instance by using the message label.

- Registers the COM components

- Creates the Message Queuing receive function

- Creates the XML Web services

- Moves the document specifications to the WebDAV folder

- Configures the BizTalk Messaging Management database

- Registers the necessary DLLs

Prior to running the setup application, verify that none of the message queues listed above exist. If any of these queues exist, the e-procurement sample setup might fail.

To set up the e-procurement sample

1. In Windows Explorer, browse to the folder **\Microsoft .NET Server Solutions for the Enterprise\E-Procurement\Application\eprocurement\Setup**.

2. Double-click **eProcSetup.exe**.

    A setup dialog box appears.

3. Click **Setup**.

    A status field in the dialog box displays the progress of the setup until it completes.

Running the E-Procurement Sample

The e-procurement sample demonstrates how to exchange documents through XML Web services and correlate user-defined fields in an XLANG schedule. This sample allows you to use a data value that uniquely identifies a document, such as a purchase order number, and associate that identifier with a running XLANG schedule instance to process a document through the steps of a business transaction.

To run this sample

1. In Windows Explorer, browse to the folder **\Program Files\Microsoft BizTalk Server\SDK\XLANG Tools**.

2. Double-click **XLANGMon.exe**.

    The XLANG Event Monitor appears. Running the XLANG Event Monitor allows you to view the progress of the hub and supplier XLANG schedules as they progress through the transaction. This is an optional step.

3. In Windows Explorer, browse to the folder **\Microsoft .NET Server Solutions for the Enterprise\E-Procurement\Application\bin\Debug** on the BizTalk Server installation drive.

4. Double-click **HubOrders.exe**.

The Hub Order Application appears.

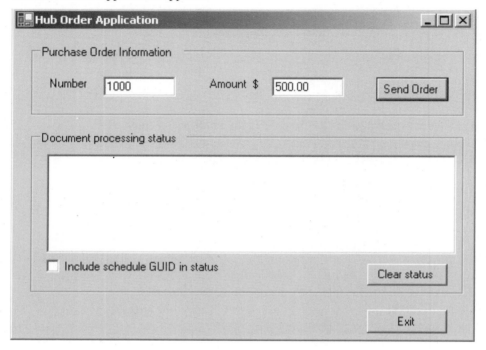

5. Enter values in the purchase order **Number** and **Amount** fields if desired.

   Notes The purchase order number must be unique, or the XLANG schedule will fail. After an order is submitted, this field is auto-incremented, and it cannot be edited until the application is run again. If the hub ordering application is run more than once, you can ensure a unique value by editing the purchase order number to a new value that hasn't been used previously. If you prefer, you can also ensure a unique purchase order number value by using the SQL Server Enterprise Manager to manually delete the previous entries from the tblCorrelation table in the CustomCorrelation database.

   Values above $1,000.00 and below $300.00 will not be fully processed, because either the hub or the supplier system will reject them.

6. Click **Send Order**.

   An order is submitted to the e-procurement system, and the progress of the order is displayed in the **Document processing status** area.

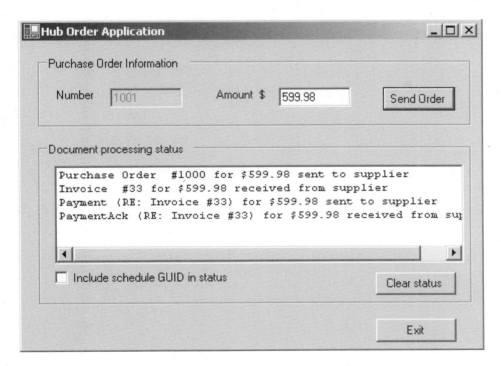

7. To verify that the transaction completed successfully, browse to the folder **\Microsoft .NET Server Solutions for the Enterprise\E-Procurement\Application\eprocurement\PaymentAckReceived**. This folder should contain a payment acknowledgement XML file that uses the following naming convention: payack_[GUID].xml. This document contains the purchase order number and dollar amount for which the payment was issued.

If you are using the XLANG Event Monitor to view the schedules, the hub schedule appears first in the folder of running schedules, followed by the supplier schedule. Eventually, the supplier schedule finishes and moves to the completed folder, followed by the hub schedule.

To run the sample and have the purchase order denied on the hub, change the purchase order **Amount** field to a value greater than $1000.00. To run the sample and have the purchase order denied by the supplier system, change the purchase order **Amount** field to a value less than $300.00.

Uninstalling the E-Procurement Sample

A script is not provided to remove the files and BizTalk Messaging Configuration objects, such as messaging ports and channels, that are created by running the setup application. The following list contains the BizTalk Messaging Configuration objects, files, folders, and libraries used by this sample. These can be manually deleted when you are finished running the sample.

Channels

HubReceivePO, HubSendPO, SupplierReceivePO, HubReceiveInvoice, SupplierSendInvoice, HubSendPayment, SupplierReceivePayment, SupplierSendPaymentAck, HubReceivePaymentAck, HubSendPayAckToFile

Messaging ports

HubReceivePO, HubSendPO, SupplierReceivePO, HubReceiveInvoice, SupplierSendInvoice, HubSendPayment, SupplierReceivePayment, SupplierSendPaymentAck, HubReceivePaymentAck, HubSendPayAckToFile

Organizations

Hub, Supplier

Document definitions

ECommonInvoice, ECommonPayment, ECommonPO, EPaymentAck, EStatus

Receive functions

Receive PO

Private messaging queues

receiveinvoice, receivepayment, receivepaymentack, receivepo, receivepo2, supplierreceivepo, supplierreceivepo2, status

BizTalk Server repository files (WebDAV)

ECommonInvoice.xml, eCommonPayment.xml, ECommonPO.xml, ePaymentAck.xml, eStatus.xml

Registered libraries

db_common.dll, hub_send_payment.dll, hub_send_po.dll, hub_comps.dll, hub_correlation.dll, supp_send_invoice.dll, supp_send_payack.dll, supp_comps.dll, supplier_correlation.dll

Primary Interop Assemblies

BTSComponentsLib.dll, BTSInterchangeLib.dll, MSCSCoreLib.dll, PipeCompLib.dll

XML Web services

E_Proc_Hub_WS, E_Proc_Supplier_WS

Additional Information

This section provides additional resource information.

Microsoft BizTalk Server 2002

- BizTalk Server 2002 Web site http://www.microsoft.com/biztalk/
- BizTalk Server Framework overview Web site http://www.biztalk.org/
- BizTalk Server online help
- BizTalk Server 2002 Toolkit for Microsoft .NET on the Microsoft Developer Network (MSDN) Web site http://msdn.microsoft.com

Microsoft SQL Server

- SQL Server Web site http://www.microsoft.com/sql
- SQL Server online documentation

Microsoft Message Queuing

Message Queuing Web site http://www.microsoft.com/msmq/

By Jim Christensen

Selling Through Trading Partners

In order to remain competitive, some businesses are faced with a decision to switch from existing paper-based processes to an electronic system for conducting commerce. One of the main factors driving this shift is the adoption of electronic procurement systems by large buying organizations. In order to realize the benefit of purchasing electronically, buyers need to have suppliers online as well. As a result, these buyers, or trading partners, have begun requiring their suppliers to trade with them electronically. As more customers realize the advantages offered by electronic procurement, the competitive advantage can definitely shift to those suppliers able to interact electronically. Sometimes, buying organizations will set a deadline beyond which all ongoing suppliers must have upgraded their processes in this way.

In other scenarios, suppliers have realized that by switching to electronic processes, they can actually sell more effectively to their existing customers and at the same time expand their customer base, perhaps by acquiring customers from a competitor who is not as technologically advanced. In some cases, suppliers can also significantly lower their cost of doing business, which in turn allows them to provide more competitive prices.

Some opposing factors have prohibited mass adoption of electronic trading by suppliers. Some suppliers are concerned that if human interaction is removed or minimized by moving to a completely automated process, their products can become commoditized. They are concerned that purchasing decisions will be made based solely on the lowest price. To combat these concerns, suppliers need a system that not only reduces their costs, but also enables them to continue to expose their brand and value proposition. Such a system would keep price as just one of several factors that buyers need to consider. Microsoft has adopted the generic name "remote shopping" for this functionality, and it is also known by names such as Punchout, Tap Out, and RoundTrip/Open Catalog Interface (OCI) within the industry.

Regardless of whether a supplier experiences one of these scenarios or some other variation, Microsoft can help. A new product, Microsoft BizTalk Accelerator for Suppliers (AFS), released in the fall of 2001, pulls together the functionality of a powerful set of other Microsoft .NET Enterprise Servers into a solution that specifically addresses a supplier's need to switch from paper-based processing of business documents to standards-based electronic processing. These other products are:

- **Microsoft BizTalk Server**. This server is used to transform and transport the electronic business documents.

- **Microsoft Commerce Server**. This server is used for its product catalog management functionality, its extensible business manager user interface, and its infrastructure for supporting remote shopping.

- **Microsoft SQL Server**. Both BizTalk Server and Commerce Server use this server for storing their respective data.

- **Microsoft Windows server operating systems**. This server provides the operating system platform upon which the other servers run.

This chapter focuses on how these .NET Enterprise Servers can be brought together by AFS to provide a low-cost solution for suppliers looking to switch to electronic trading. The chapter is divided into the following sections:

- **Scenario**. This section describes the solution to a business problem in greater detail than the previous summary.

- **Solution**. This section describes how Microsoft Content Management Server can be used to solve this business problem.

- **Tools and Technology**. This section focuses on the various tools and technologies involved in solving the business problem.

- **Implementation**. This section drills deeper into select portions of the proposed solution, to give the reader a sense of the level of technical expertise required implementing the solution.

This chapter progresses from a high-level discussion of the business problem and Microsoft's solution to it, to a more granular discussion of some coding examples in the "Implementation" section. If you are looking for more of an overview, you may want to skip the last section.

Scenario

Simply stated: How can suppliers use technology to reduce costs, increase revenue, and differentiate themselves from their competition without incurring high costs and long deployment cycles?

To adequately understand this question and the solution that will be proposed in this chapter, it is important to review a number of related topics, including the businesses and people involved in the interactions, the different purchasing models, and some of the electronic document standards commonly used.

The Players

Let us begin by clarifying the exact meaning of the terms Supplier, Trading Partner and Customer as used in this chapter, so as to distinguish this business problem from other commercial interactions involving customers.

- **Supplier**. For the purposes of this chapter, a "supplier" is a company that sells product or services directly to another business. In this context we are not focusing on the business aspects of selling directly to a consumer. Through the rest of this chapter we will focus on how a supplier can sell more effectively to other businesses by taking advantage of electronic commerce via the Internet.

    Note   While this chapter focuses on business-to-business (B2B) interactions, suppliers often do market their products directly to consumer and business customers using retail Web sites, conventional paper catalogs, and/or a physical storefront.

- **Trading partner**. For the purposes of this chapter, "trading partners" are other companies that sell products on behalf of a supplier. Trading partners might be companies that are offering these products to their own employees, using a procurement system and are, in effect, buying the products themselves. Or trading partners might be companies that are offering the supplier's products to other companies and/or individuals. In any event, with respect to electronic product catalogs and purchase orders, suppliers interact directly with their trading partners, and only indirectly with the "customers" who are buying the products.

    In order for a trading partner to know what products and/or services a supplier is selling, the supplier must provide the trading partner with an electronic version of their product catalog. When a customer uses a trading partner's buyer application to make a purchase from the supplier's catalog, the trading partner sends the supplier an electronic version of a purchase order, which the supplier fulfills using established procedures.

- **Customer**. For the purposes of this chapter, a "customer" is the person who is ultimately choosing a product for purchase. The customer might be an employee of the trading partner company, and uses an internal procurement application to purchase office supplies or computers. Or, the customer might be an individual or employee of another company that makes purchases through the trading partner company's Web site because it offers a wide variety of products, sometimes competing products, from multiple suppliers.

  In the scenario where the customers are the employees of a trading partner, it is very common for there to be a set of processes that are used to control and track purchasing. For example, a manager might need to approve the purchase request of an employee. And when an employee makes a purchase, the accounts payable department needs to know about it, so that they can resolve bills they receive with actual orders placed.

In general, this chapter discusses the interactions that occur between the supplier and a trading partner. It is important to keep this terminology straight as you continue reading.

A critical aspect of the interactions between the supplier and the trading partner is an established relationship. This relationship must have consequences for the customer. For example, the relationship might specify that only a particular subset of the products is available for purchase by a customer, or perhaps it involves special prices. This scenario needs to be distinguished from other scenarios in which the same customer might purchase the same product directly from the supplier, such as through a retail Web site. Scenarios of the later type can also be classified as business-to-consumer (B2C), even though the customer is making the purchase on behalf of a business.

Basic Interactions

Consider the following two interactions:

- **Choosing products or services**. Trading partners, and ultimately customers, need to know what products or services a supplier is selling. They need enough detail about the products or services and their prices to make a purchasing decision. Product catalogs are a common mechanism through which this information can be communicated. Traditionally, product catalogs tend to be paper-based and distributed through postal mail. Now, with the Internet, product catalogs can be completely electronic, and viewed on a Web site or other equivalent technology.

- **Placing orders**. Once the customer has determined which products to purchase, a mechanism is needed for communicating their choices from the trading partner to the supplier. Any additional business processing, such as approvals, needs to occur before those choices are forwarded to the supplier. If the choices are not approved, the order is rejected and is never sent to the supplier.

It is also important to understand that suppliers and trading partners use different types of software for these interactions. Customers interact with buyer applications, also known as procurement applications, hosted by a trading partner. The trading partner might be the company that the customer works for, or it might be an electronic marketplace that specializes in hosting a buyer application. For more information about buyer applications, see the section "The Trading Partner's Buyer Application" later in this chapter. Note that Microsoft does not currently sell procurement applications for trading partners.

Suppliers require software that will interact with procurement applications, by providing electronic product catalogs to the procurement application and accepting purchase orders from the procurement application. Microsoft .NET Enterprise Servers, bound together with AFS, provide this software functionality.

Different Purchasing Models

This section discusses three different purchasing models, the first of which is not related to the subject of this chapter, but is shown here for contrast. The second and third models show two distinct ways in which suppliers and trading partners can interact.

Retail Web Site Purchasing Model

For contrast, first consider the type of purchasing model associated with a typical retail Web site. The following figure illustrates this model, wherein the customer uses only a browser to interact with a retail Web site that, in this case, is run by a company that is also a supplier. The company (supplier) running the Web site maintains the catalog, the shopping basket, and the resulting order.

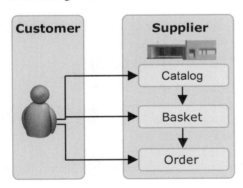

Retail Web site purchasing model

Basic Supplier Purchasing Model

The most straightforward supplier and trading partner purchasing model, which allows for customer order workflow to be performed, involves the supplier sending an electronic version of their product catalog to the trading partner. The trading partner provides the infrastructure through which the customer interacts with the catalog, basket, and order (the infrastructure could be a Web site or an equivalent procurement application). The following figure illustrates this model, and shows how the supplier's role is limited to sending the product catalog and receiving orders after the order workflow has successfully occurred. As opposed to the retail scenario, the trading partner maintains a copy of the catalog (at some level of detail), the only instance of the basket, and the original version of the order.

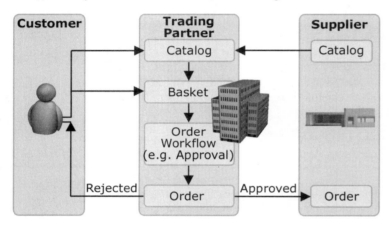

Basic supplier purchasing model

Supplier Purchasing Model Using Remote Shopping

Another purchasing model that is reasonable for the supplier and trading partner scenario involves remote shopping. In this scenario, where customers access the product catalog is not as critical as the requirement for the shopping basket, order workflow, and order to be managed within the trading partner environment. As long as the products chosen for purchase end up in a basket that is managed within the trading partner system, the trading partner remains in control of whatever additional steps are required before the order is actually placed with the supplier. The following figure illustrates this model, and shows how the customer interacts with the catalog and basket on the trading partner system, and with the catalog and a temporary "remote basket" on the supplier system. Ultimately, the supplier Web site returns the customer to the basket managed by the trading partner before completing the purchase.

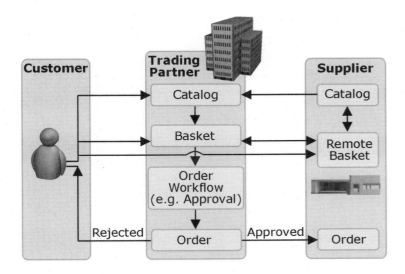

Remote shopping purchasing model

Note that the catalog supplied, if at all, to the trading partner presumably has less detail than the catalog made available through the supplier's Web site. How much less detail can vary. At one extreme, there might not be any individual products in the trading partner's version of the catalog, making it hardly a catalog at all. In this case, the catalog simply has a list of product names and URLs to the complete product detail in the supplier's Web site. In terms of browsing for products, the trading partner buyer application is basically a list of links to these sites.

At the other extreme, the catalog published to the trading partner might be missing only some specialized configuration options. The details of a computer's configuration, such as the amount of RAM and the size of the hard disk, are a classic example. In this scenario, the supplier's remote shopping Web site may look less like a traditional retail Web site with a shopping basket and so on, and more like a configuration wizard.

Regardless of how the supplier and trading partner agree to split the responsibility for product presentation in this scenario, the key point is that the trading partner maintains the only persistent instance of the basket and the original version of the order, and the supplier temporarily maintains a secondary, remote basket.

Purchasing Model Summary

These two supplier and trading partner purchasing models offer different advantages. With the basic model, suppliers can have reduced overhead because they do not need to build and manage a Web site for remote shopping. On the other hand, because it is entirely up to the customer to display the supplier's products on a Web site or another type of buyer application, the supplier is no longer in control of how their products are presented, and whether they are presented in the complete context of the associated support and services. For example, customers might display similar products from different suppliers side-by-side, emphasizing price differences and thus suggesting that the products are nothing more than commodities.

With the remote shopping purchasing model, the supplier incurs higher overhead because they must build and maintain a Web site through which product information is provided. However, because this Web site is in their control, they are able to promote their products and associated services, helping to prevent customers from making purchasing decisions based solely on price. Depending on how much of the shopping experience is pushed back to the supplier's Web site, the trading partner's Web site or procurement application could be simplified. In the extreme, it might just contain links to each supplier's site, perhaps with a high-level description of the type of products offered.

Many suppliers will want to use the remote shopping purchasing model, regardless of the increased cost, because it offers them the following advantages:

- The supplier remains in control of the detail shown for their products, and can include images, detailed descriptions, and so on.

- The supplier can provide better product configuration because they can customize their own Web site as required for their products. Often, they have this rich functionality anyway, for use on their retail Web site.

- The supplier can retain and exploit their brand name, which, depending on the brand, can be worth a lot.

- The supplier can provide a personalized shopping experience by remembering customers from previous visits, customizing content according to their preferences, and so on.

- The supplier can make sure their product information is current with respect to such factors as price and inventory, reducing their dependence on the catalog upload frequency supported by a particular trading partner.

In any event, the purchasing model chosen by a particular trading partner/supplier pair needs to be negotiated. From the perspective of the customer, who initiates a purchase, the systems run by the trading partner and the supplier need to work as one integrated system.

Electronic Document Standards

Another issue related to the process of transitioning to electronic document exchange concerns the document standards to be used. Although large corporations have been using Electronic Data Interchange (EDI) for a number of years, the costs (per transaction, and for infrastructure and maintenance) have been prohibitive for many companies. The emergence of the Internet, and especially Extensible Markup Language (XML), in the last few years have brought the possibility of affordable exchange of electronic business documents into the realm of possibility for small- and medium-sized businesses. But XML does not, by itself, define the format of electronic business documents, such as product catalogs and purchase orders. Rather, it provides a meta-language in which such formats can be created. There are many different XML standards for describing business documents. For the most part, these standards are tied to specific vertical markets. Exploring all of these standards is beyond the scope of this chapter, therefore we will focus on two standards that are not specific to a particular vertical market, and that have enjoyed wider adoption than many others. These standards are:

- **Commerce Extensible Markup Language (cXML).** This standard defines a relatively streamlined format for the exchange of XML-based business documents. It was originally developed by Ariba, but has since been proposed as a public standard. For more information, see http://www.cxml.org.

- **XML Common Business Library (xCBL).** This standard defines a relatively robust format for the exchange of XML-based business documents. It was originally developed by Commerce One, but has since been proposed as a public standard. For more information, see http://www.xcbl.org.

As with the purchasing model, the supplier and trading partner must agree on which XML format to use, which will most often be dictated by the trading partner. Given this, the most successful suppliers are likely to be the ones that are most flexible in this regard.

Scenario Summary

In summary, to remain competitive in the coming years, many suppliers will need to support the exchange of electronic business documents with their customers. There are a couple of purchasing models under which the primary interactions involved in shopping, choosing products, and placing orders, can occur. In addition, the format of the electronic business documents will vary based on the (XML) standard adopted. Because customers, as opposed to suppliers, will typically be driving decisions about shopping models and document formats, suppliers who can support multiple and changing models and formats with multiple customers will be best positioned for success.

Solution

Using the Microsoft.NET Enterprise Servers and other Microsoft products, suppliers have been building robust and flexible supplier solutions. To help accelerate the development of these types of solutions, Microsoft introduced a new product in the fall of 2001, called Microsoft BizTalk Accelerator for Suppliers (AFS). The goal of this product is to accelerate the deployment of a supplier solution by providing the common pieces of a supplier solution, as well as the guidance to customize and extend the solution. By providing the foundation of a supplier enablement solution, suppliers can have a quicker time to market in a less cost-prohibitive way. As the name also suggests, Microsoft BizTalk Server plays a central role in the solution AFS offers.

Associated Technologies

As previously mentioned, the solution relies on BizTalk Server to provide certain key aspects of its functionality, namely, the transformation and transportation of XML documents, as described in the following:

- **Transformation**. XML document transformation concerns the process of transforming, say, a product catalog from one XML format to another semantically equivalent, but syntactically distinct, XML format.

- **Transportation**. XML document transportation concerns the process of sending and receiving XML documents between the supplier and its trading partners.

The solution also relies on Microsoft Commerce Server in the following important ways:

- **Product catalog**. The Commerce Server Product Catalog System serves as the catalog management tool that hosts the online catalog for Web browsing and remote shopping, and that supports the process of publishing product catalog information to trading partners.

- **Order processing**. The Commerce Server Business Processing Pipelines System serves as the order-processing engine for purchase orders received from trading partners.

- **Remote shopping Web site**. The Commerce Server Retail Solutions Site serves as the basis for the extensions that support the remote shopping that may be required, depending on the purchasing model being implemented.

- **Extensible user interface**. The Commerce Server Business Desk application provides an extensible architecture that has been adopted by AFS to provide interfaces for publishing product catalogs, managing trading partners, and processing orders.

The solution also relies on Microsoft SQL Server as the data repository, both directly through new tables and extensions to existing Commerce Server tables, and indirectly because both BizTalk Server and Commerce Server use SQL Server.

Finally, depending on deployment choices, a couple of other Microsoft .NET Enterprise Servers might be used in an AFS deployment. Microsoft Internet Security and Acceleration Server (ISA) can be used as the firewall in a secure deployment, and Microsoft Application Center is available for managing multi-server Web site configurations (Web farms).

The Trading Partner's Buyer Application

In order to understand the operational requirements for the software on the supplier's system, it is important to review the functionality of the trading partner's buyer application. In this context, "buyer application" is being used to describe the entire class of such applications with which the supplier's system may interact. Buyer applications include:

- **Procurement applications**. A procurement application is an application used by a business to manage the process of buying products and services. The procurement application provides an interface through which a buyer can choose items and initiate the purchasing process. After the purchase is initiated, additional processing is generally required, such as routing the purchase order to the appropriate party (or parties) for approval and informing the accounts receivable department. How many of these additional steps are performed within the procurement application itself will vary from business to business. A procurement application may or may not be Web-based, though the trend is in that direction.

- **Marketplaces**. A marketplace is a business that specializes in consolidating the product offerings of multiple suppliers into a single location from which they can be purchased. Third-party businesses and, in some cases, individuals can shop in a marketplace, placing products from a variety of suppliers in their baskets, and then checking out as a single purchase. Various details about such transactions, such as how billing is handled, or whether all products are available to all shoppers, will vary from marketplace to marketplace.

Regardless of the type of buyer application, the basic interactions between the supplier and the trading partner systems will be the same. In most cases, product catalogs, at some level of detail or another, will move from the supplier system to the trading partner system. And purchase orders will move from the trading partner system to the supplier system.

If remote shopping is used, the level of detail supplied in the product information may be less, with the difference being taken up through a remote shopping session directly on the supplier's Web site. Whatever detail is not provided in the product catalogs will need to be provided during the remote shopping session, and a minimum amount of information will need to end up back in the trading partner system so that the shopping basket can be displayed and the purchase order can be constructed. The amount of information required in the trading partner system can vary, but will generally include at least a product ID or stock-keeping unit (SKU), a product description, a quantity, the unit price, and perhaps an image.

Also, if remote shopping is used, interactions between the supplier and trading partner systems will be significantly more complex. Depending on the XML format being used, a different sequence of messages for the initiation and termination of the remote shopping session are required.

Catalog Publishing Solution

Product catalogs change over time: new products are added, old products are removed, prices change, and so on. This means that catalog publication is very rarely a one-time operation. Almost always, product catalogs will need to be published and then published again on some periodic basis. Any reasonable catalog publishing solution must take this into account.

The catalog publishing solution provided by AFS can be divided into the following areas, each of which is discussed in its own sub-section:

- **Supported document formats**. Whenever documents are exchanged electronically between two parties, the format of the documents is obviously something upon which both parties must agree. This section discusses the product catalog document formats supported by AFS.

- **Tasks**. Publishing catalog data involves a number of different tasks, some of which are performed once, or at least only occasionally, and some of which are performed routinely. This section discusses both types of tasks.

- **Architecture**. The catalog publishing architecture of AFS uses BizTalk Server and Commerce Server and, as is frequently the case with the .NET Enterprise Servers, SQL Server behind the scenes. This section provides a high-level look at this architecture and how catalog data flows through the architecture and eventually to the trading partner.

Supported Document Formats

Out of the box, AFS is capable of publishing product catalogs in the 3.0 version of the xCBL format and in the 1.1 and 1.2 versions of the cXML format, which together provide interoperability with several dominant marketplace and procurement application vendors: Commerce One, Ariba, and Clarus. Possessing this capability amounts to including pre-built BizTalk Server maps for transforming the source format into each of these three destination XML formats. These maps include XSLT code for mapping elements and attributes of the source document to elements and attributes of the destination document. Developers can edit the maps to support additional formats and new versions of these formats using the BizTalk Mapper application.

Because Commerce Server includes a powerful catalog management system, AFS chose the Commerce Server Catalog XML format as the source format. Specifically, version 1.5 of that format, available in Commerce Server 2000 Service Pack 1 (SP1) and later, serves as the source XML format for AFS.

In summary, AFS provides maps for the following product catalog transformations:

Source XML Format	Destination XML Format
Commerce Server Catalog XML v1.5	cXML 1.1 Catalogs and Punchout Catalogs
Commerce Server Catalog XML v1.5	cXML 1.2 Catalogs and Punchout Catalogs
Commerce Server Catalog XML v1.5	xCBL 3.0 ProductCatalog

Catalog Publishing Tasks

Some tasks associated with catalog publishing need to be performed only once, or at most, infrequently. Other tasks need to be performed more frequently, based on a balance between the overhead involved and the need to update trading partners with changes that have been made to the catalog. This section discusses both types of tasks.

Setup, One-Time, and Infrequent Tasks

This section discusses the catalog publishing tasks that need to be performed only once in order to set up a catalog for publication, or in some cases, when some relevant change is made, such as to the catalog schema or to the trading partner URL to which published catalogs are sent. These tasks are:

- **Preparing catalog data for publication**. As delivered, AFS is designed to publish catalog data that exists in the Commerce Server Product Catalog System. Obviously, suppliers who are already using this catalog system will have a simpler time publishing their catalog data, but there are other options. Suppliers have several options for preparing their catalog data for initial publication and maintaining it for subsequent publications, based on where the catalog data is stored:

  - If the supplier is already using the Commerce Server Product Catalog System to maintain their catalog data, they need to make sure that they have installed Commerce Server SP1 or later, and that their catalog supports the required properties.

  - If the supplier intends to start using the Commerce Server Product Catalog System to maintain their catalog data, perhaps as part of building a new e-commerce Web site, they need to use Commerce Server SP1 or later. To initially populate the catalog system, electronic catalog data can probably be manipulated into one of the formats that can be imported into Commerce Server, either XML or comma-separated values (CSV), or they can enter it by hand using the catalog modules of the Commerce Server Business Desk application.

  - If the supplier uses a different catalog system to maintain their catalog data, they can either come up with a way to periodically import that data into the Commerce Server Product Catalog System, or they can create one or more of their own maps for converting from some other BizTalk Server–compatible source format into the appropriate destination format(s).

    The former option means that the import processing must essentially become the first step in periodic catalog publication. The later option will probably involve significantly more effort, including the modification of the Catalog Publisher Business Desk module that comes with AFS.

- **Working with BizTalk Server maps**. Another one-time or infrequent task concerns the product catalog schema. The maps supplied with AFS assume that the default Commerce Server catalog scheme is being used. If a supplier is using the Commerce Server Product Catalog System and has changed the default schema, they may need to modify, or create new versions of, the appropriate map(s). If this is required, the **ExportXML** method of the **CatalogManager** object can be used to create an XML-Data Reduced (XDR) file that captures the current Commerce Server catalog schema in the form of a version 1.5 XDR file. Such XDR files can be used with BizTalk Mapper for recreating maps that take Commerce Server catalog schema changes into account. Whenever the product catalog schema is modified, it may be necessary to update the corresponding maps.

- **Performing other BizTalk Server configurations**. In order to process documents, BizTalk Server requires a number of different "artifacts" to be created. These artifacts contain the BizTalk Server information that constitutes trading partner organizations, applications, document definitions, message envelopes, channels, and messaging ports. For the most part, AFS automatically creates the BizTalk Server artifacts that it requires. One exception, that applies when the published catalog is supposed to be posted to a URL supplied by the trading partner, is the transport messaging port and corresponding transport channel. Essentially, this is how you tell BizTalk Server where to deliver a document. When necessary, a supplier should use BizTalk Messaging Manager to create these custom artifacts, and then select the new transport channel when creating a trading partner profile in AFS (see the following task).

- **Creating a trading partner profile**. For each trading partner to whom a supplier is going to publish a catalog, the supplier must create a trading partner profile for that trading partner in the Trading Partner Manager module in Business Desk (the Trading Partner Manager module is one of three new modules provided in the AFS Solution Site). A trading partner profile consists of the following information:

  - A unique name for the trading partner.

  - A shared secret that is used in cXML for authentication.

  - The catalog format to be used (cXML 1.1, cXML 1.2, or xCBL 3.0).

  - The BizTalk Server transport channel associated with the trading partner.

  - For xCBL 3.0 only, the URL that the trading partner has established to receive (purchase) OrderResponse messages.

- **Creating a Catalog Publication**. For each catalog within the Commerce Server Product Catalog System that is going to be published to a specific trading partner, the supplier must create a catalog publication in the Catalog Publisher module in Business Desk (the Catalog Publisher module is another one of the three new modules provided in the AFS Solution Site). A catalog publication consists of the following information:

  - The name of the catalog to be published.

  - The trading partner to which the catalog is to be published, as established by creating a trading partner profile for that trading partner.

  - The supplier's identifier in a particular credential domain. For example, a nine-digit Dun & Bradstreet Data Universal Numbering System (D-U-N-S) number.

  - The credential domain in which the supplier's identifier is unique. For example, Dun & Bradstreet.

Ongoing Tasks

This section discusses the catalog publishing tasks that need to be performed on a routine basis, excluding normal server maintenance such as backups. There is really only one such task, publishing the product catalog, though in some scenarios, several steps may be required.

If the supplier maintains their product catalog data in the Commerce Server Product Catalog System, the act of publishing a catalog consists of a few simple steps:

1. Open the Catalog Publisher module in Business Desk.

2. Select the appropriate catalog publication (which associates the catalog to be published with the trading partner to which it should be published).

3. Click the **Publish** button on the toolbar.

As suggested previously, if the supplier does not maintain their product catalog data in the Commerce Server Product Catalog System, there are several alternative choices, as follows:

- If there is an effective way in which the catalog data can be routinely converted to a format that can be imported into the Commerce Server Product Catalog System (XML or CSV), which could be done each time before following the steps previously specified.

- If the catalog data is available in a BizTalk Server–compatible format other than Commerce Server Catalog XML v1.5, a new map could be created to map that format to the appropriate destination format.

The question of how often catalogs should be published is something to be negotiated with the trading partner, and depends on a couple of factors that may need to be balanced against one another:

- **The trading partner's ability to process catalogs that it receives**. Depending on the size of the catalog, the specific task involved, and the number of catalogs being received by the trading partner (potentially from a number of suppliers), the trading partner may place restrictions on the frequency of catalog updates.

- **The supplier's ability to perform the steps required to publish the catalog data**. If the catalog data is maintained in the Commerce Server Product Catalog System, this will not be a concern. However, if the clicking of the **Publish** button is just the final step of a much longer process, it could be a factor.

- **Changes made to the catalog data by the supplier**. The more frequent these changes, the more frequently the supplier is likely to want to update their trading partners. If the scenario involves remote shopping, it may be important to synchronize local updates to the catalog with the act of updating the trading partner's version of the catalog. Otherwise, the customer might become confused when the two versions of the catalog data do not correspond.

Catalog Publishing Architecture

Viewed from a high level, the architecture of catalog publishing in AFS consists of getting the product data into a catalog in the Commerce Server Product Catalog System, using BizTalk Server to transform that data into a format that can be interpreted by the trading partner, and then sending the transformed data to the trading partner using a previously agreed upon method.

The following figure illustrates the steps involved at the next level of detail. The numbered arrows in the figure correspond to an explanation of the steps following the figure.

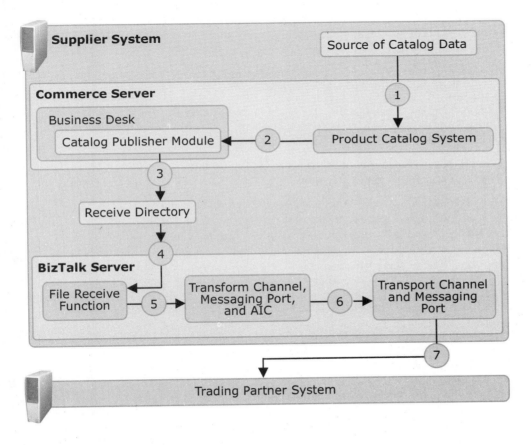

Catalog publishing architecture

The steps involved in publishing a catalog, as shown in the previous figure, are:

1. The source of the catalog data is used to populate the Commerce Server Product Catalog System. Hopefully, the catalog data is available in an electronic format that can be manipulated into a format that is compatible with the catalog system's import process. If not, the catalog data can always be entered manually using the Catalog Editor module in Business Desk.

2. When a catalog publication is selected and the **Publish** button is clicked in the Catalog Publisher module, the catalog data is exported from the Commerce Server Product Catalog System in the Commerce Server Catalog XML v1.5 format.

3. After the catalog data export is complete, the Catalog Publisher module wraps the catalog data and a few other items of information in a BizTalk Server envelope and writes the resulting XML to a directory on the BizTalk Server.

4. A file receive function in BizTalk Server retrieves the envelope-wrapped catalog data from the directory where the catalog data was written in step 3.

5. Based on the name of the file containing the envelope-wrapped catalog data, the file receive function invokes the correct BizTalk Server channel, messaging port, and AIC to transform the catalog data to the appropriate destination format.

6. After the AIC strips the envelope from the transformed catalog data, it invokes the transport channel that was passed in the envelope.

7. The transport channel and messaging port send the transformed catalog data to the configured location. Although the default transport messaging ports included in AFS specify that the transformed data should be written to a local file, many trading partners will provide the supplier with a URL with which to create a new messaging port that will post the catalog data to the trading partner using HTTP.

Purchase Order Reception Solution

The whole point of a supplier publishing their catalog to a trading partner is to generate sales. The trading partner needs to present the supplier's products to its customers so that those customers can purchase them, resulting in the trading partner sending a purchase order back to the supplier. Not only is it important for a supplier to receive purchase orders, but also they need to fulfill the orders in a timely manner and bill the appropriate party. Any reasonable purchase order reception solution must take this into account.

The purchase order reception solution provided by AFS can be divided into the following areas, each of which is discussed in its own sub-section:

- **Supported document formats**. Whenever documents are exchanged electronically between two parties, the format of the documents is obviously something upon which both parties must agree. This section discusses the purchase order document formats supported by AFS.

- **Tasks**. Receiving purchase orders involves a number of different tasks, some of which are performed once, or at least only occasionally, and some of which are performed routinely. This section discusses both types of tasks.

- **Architecture**. The purchase order reception architecture of AFS uses BizTalk Server and Commerce Server and, as is frequently the case with the .NET Enterprise Servers, SQL Server behind the scenes. This section provides a high-level look at this architecture and how purchase orders flow through the architecture from the trading partner to the supplier's order processing system.

Supported Document Formats

Out of the box, AFS is capable of receiving purchase orders in the 3.0 version of the xCBL format and in the 1.1 and 1.2 versions of the cXML format, which together provide interoperability with several dominant marketplace and procurement application vendors: Commerce One, Ariba, and Clarus. Possessing this capability amounts to including pre-built BizTalk Server maps for transforming each of these three source formats into the destination XML format. Developers can edit the maps to support additional formats and new versions of these formats using the BizTalk Mapper application.

Because Commerce Server includes a rich transaction database, AFS chose the Commerce Server Order XML format as the destination format. Specifically, version 1.0 of that format, available in Commerce Server 2000 and later, serves as the destination XML format for AFS.

In summary, AFS provides maps for the following purchase order transformations:

Source XML Format	Destination XML Format
cXML 1.1 OrderRequest	Commerce Server Order XML v1.0
cXML 1.2 OrderRequest	Commerce Server Order XML v1.0
xCBL 3.0 Order	Commerce Server Order XML v1.0

Purchase Order Reception Tasks

Some tasks associated with purchase order reception need to be performed only once. Other tasks need to be performed more frequently, on an as-needed basis. This section discusses both types of tasks.

Setup, One-Time, and Infrequent Tasks

In general, the setup tasks associated with purchase order reception are minimal compared to catalog publication. This section discusses the tasks that must be performed, beyond successfully completing the installation of AFS. These tasks are:

- **Providing an order reception URL to trading partners**. In order to receive purchase orders from trading partners, those trading partners must know the URL to which they should post the purchase order documents. In the AFS Solution Site, the name of the page to which purchase orders should be posted is ReceivePO.asp, with which the relevant URL should end, (The beginning part of the URL will depend on the supplier's domain name.)

- **Creating a trading partner profile**. For each trading partner from whom a supplier is going to receive purchase orders, the supplier must create a trading partner profile for that customer in the Trading Partner Manager module in Business Desk (the Trading Partner Manager module is one of three new modules provided in the AFS Solution Site). A trading partner profile consists of the following information:

  - A unique name for the customer.

  - A shared secret that is used in cXML for authentication.

  - The order format to be used (cXML 1.1, cXML 1.2, or xCBL 3.0).

  - The BizTalk Server transport channel associated with the customer.

  - For xCBL 3.0 only, the URL that the customer has established to receive (purchase) Order Response messages.

  Note that this profile might already have been created while setting up to publishing catalogs to the trading partner.

- **Assessing processing performance**. Depending on individual business requirements, a supplier should confirm that the processing performed in the Business Process Pipelines System meets their needs. For additional information about configuring and altering the Order Processing pipeline, see the Commerce Server documentation.

Ongoing Tasks

This section discusses the purchase order reception tasks that need to be performed on a routine basis. Under normal circumstances, purchase orders received using AFS are processed automatically, ending up as orders in the Transactions database. These orders can be viewed using the Orders Manager module in Business Desk (the Orders Manager module is one of the three new Business Desk modules included in the AFS Solution Site).

The ongoing tasks associated with received purchase orders will vary from supplier to supplier, but there are two broad categories of activities in which all suppliers will participate. These are:

- **Fulfillment**, or getting the ordered products to the customer.

- **Billing**, or getting paid for the ordered products.

AFS does not dictate how these activities occur, but it does provide the fields **Order Status** and **Fulfillment Status** for each order in the Transaction database. The **Order Status** field is configurable – new order status codes can easily be added to account for specific business needs. The **Fulfillment Status** field includes the following fulfillment status values:

- **Auto**. Indicates that the order should be processed automatically.

- **Auto24**. Indicates that the order should be processed automatically within 24 hours of receipt.

- **Manual**. Indicates that manual intervention is required before the order is processed.

- **Fulfilled**. Indicates that the order has been fulfilled.

- **Rejected**. Indicates that the order has been rejected.

When using the Orders Manager module in Business Desk, these fields can be used when searching for orders, allowing that module to be used more effectively by the supplier employees tasked with order fulfillment and billing.

AFS also includes supplementary documentation that describes how AFS can be integrated with existing backend systems such as Great Plains and SAP. Such integration could prove useful for the tasks associated with fulfillment and billing.

Purchase Order Reception Architecture

Viewed from a high level, the architecture of purchase order reception in AFS consists of:

- Receiving a purchase order from a trading partner.

- Using BizTalk Server to transform the purchase order to a format compatible with Commerce Server.

- Using the Commerce Server Business Process Pipelines System to process the order and save it to the Transactions database.

The following figure illustrates the steps involved at the next level of detail. The numbered arrows in the figure correspond to an explanation of the steps following the figure.

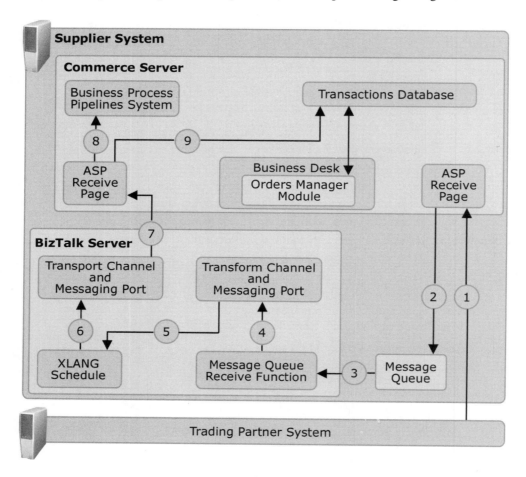

Purchase order reception architecture

The steps involved in publishing a catalog, as shown in the previous figure, are:

1. The trading partner uses HTTP to post the purchase order to an ASP page in the supplier's Web site. As implemented in the AFS Solution Site, the name of this page is ReceivePO.asp.

2. In the page ReceivePO.asp the purchase order undergoes preprocessing so that BizTalk Server can properly transform it; this preprocessing is different for each format. Next, the XML comprising the purchase order is enclosed in a BizTalk Server envelope, and the trading partner name from the query string is stored as an envelope property. The purchase order XML document is then placed in one of three different Microsoft Message Queues, based on the protocol passed in the query string.

   For xCBL 3.0 purchase orders, the HTTP response to the posting contains only the HTTP status indicating whether the purchase order was successfully received and passed to the message queue. The OrderResponse message is constructed and placed in another envelope property, and posted back to the trading partner later in the process.

   For cXML 1.1 and 1.2 purchase orders, the HTTP response to the posting also includes the OrderResponse message.

3. One of three different BizTalk Server Message Queuing receive functions retrieves the purchase order from its corresponding message queue. This is the start of BizTalk Server processing.

4. The Message Queuing receive function passes the purchase order to the corresponding transform channel.

5. Using the provided BizTalk Server map, the transform channel converts the purchase order from its source XML format (xCBL 3.0, cXML 1.1, or cXML 1.2) to the Commerce Server Order XML v1.0 format, and the transform messaging port passes the transformed XML document to an instance of the XLANG schedule.

6. As delivered, the XLANG schedule performs only a single action: (HTTP) posting the transformed XML document to the configured ASP receive page (_recvpo.asp) in the AFS Solution Site. This is accomplished by passing the transformed XML document to a transport channel and messaging port.

   The XLANG schedule is included at this stage so that specialized business processes can be added to the purchase order processing within BizTalk Server.

7. The transport channel and messaging port forward the transformed XML document to the ASP receive page _recvpo.asp without performing any processing on it.

8. After removing the envelope, the ASP receive page (_recvpo.asp) in the AFS Solution Site uses the Business Process Pipelines System to process the order.

   This page also retrieves the trading partner name from the envelope and verifies the trading partner, automatically creating an organization profile for the trading partner if necessary.

9. If the Business Process Pipelines System successfully processed the order, it is saved to the Transactions database.

   If the order originated in xCBL 3.0 format, the OrderResponse message is also retrieved from the envelope and, if the Business Process Pipelines System successfully processed the order, the OrderResponse message is posted back to the trading partner at this point in the processing.

Although it is not strictly part of the automated processing of purchase orders in AFS, the previous figure also illustrates how the Orders Manager module in Business Desk accesses orders in the Transaction database to view and update their status.

Remote Shopping Solution

Sometimes a supplier and a trading partner will determine that some portion of the customer's shopping experience should actually take place on a Web site built and managed by the supplier rather than the trading partner. The customer begins shopping in the trading partner's buyer application, and then at some point the customer is lead directly to the supplier's Web site to perform some aspect of the shopping that is presumably more detailed in nature. For example, the customer may choose the size and color of an article of clothing or configure a computer system. After this detailed aspect of the shopping session is complete, the customer returns to the trading partner's buyer application to complete the purchase.

When this type of shopping paradigm is implemented properly, it should provide the customer with a smooth, intuitive experience. This can be a challenge. The trading partner's buyer application needs to provide a user interface for "jumping" to the supplier's Web site that won't confuse the customer, and the supplier's Web site needs to welcome the customer directly into the next step in their shopping experience. For example, if customers are brought to the supplier's Web site to configure computer systems, they should see a page that shows the system they have chosen and has the controls they need to choose their CPU speed, hard disk size, and so on.

Ideally, when customers complete their tasks on the supplier's Web site, they should not be surprised about returning to their shopping basket in the trading partner's buyer application. Much of the smoothness of interaction between the sites can be achieved through proper naming of the user interface controls (and their associated text) that lead from one application to the other. For example, the button (or other control) in the supplier's Web site that returns the customer to the trading partner's buyer application should not be named **Check out**. Depending on the scenario, it would be better if the button were named **Return to Buyer Application**, or something similar.

Both of the business document standards cXML and OCI define a protocol of messages that can be exchanged to implement a remote shopping experience, although they are each known by different names. While Microsoft has adopted the generic name "remote shopping" to describe this type of shopping paradigm, it is known as Punchout within the cXML standard and as RoundTrip by the Commerce One implementation of the OCI standard. (The Clarus implementations of cXML refer to remote shopping as Tap Out.)

The remote shopping solution provided by AFS can be divided into the following areas, each of which is discussed in its own sub-section:

- **Supported document formats**. Whenever documents are exchanged electronically between two parties, the format of the documents is obviously something upon which both parties must agree. The documents related to remote shopping are more complicated, and less intuitive, than those used for product catalogs and purchase orders. This section discusses the sequences of document exchanges supported by AFS that initiate and terminate remote shopping sessions.

- **Tasks**. Implementing and supporting remote shopping involves a number of different tasks, some of which are performed once, or at least only occasionally, and some of which are performed routinely. This section discusses both types of tasks.

- **Architecture**. The remote shopping architecture of AFS uses Commerce Server and, as is frequently the case with the .NET Enterprise Servers, SQL Server behind the scenes. (Unlike product catalog publication and purchase order reception, BizTalk Server is not used in the AFS implementation of remote shopping.) This section provides a high-level look at this architecture and how information flows through the architecture when remote shopping is initiated in the trading partner's buyer application and terminated in the supplier's Web site.

Supported Document Formats

Out of the box, AFS supports remote shopping for cXML. Support for the xCBL version of remote shopping, and thus the Commerce One buyer applications, is not quite as straightforward. This is because xCBL itself does not define a document protocol for remote shopping. Instead, Commerce One has adopted a particular version of protocol defined by SAP called the Open Catalog Interface (OCI 2.0b). This protocol uses HTTP rather than XML to pass the information required to initiate and terminate remote shopping sessions. Support for both types of remote shopping consists of significant additions to the Commerce Server 2000 Retail Solution Site, creating a new solution site known as the AFS Solution Site that is included in AFS.

For product catalog publication and purchase order reception, BizTalk Server is used to transform product catalogs and purchase orders between the native Commerce Server XML formats for these documents and the corresponding documents in the cXML and xCBL formats. There is no corresponding transformation performed for remote shopping, for a couple of different reasons. First, Commerce Server does not handle remote shopping on its own, as it handles product catalogs and purchase orders. Second, the protocol of documents exchanged for remote shopping is more complex, and varies between cXML and xCBL more than the simpler document exchanges involved in product catalogs and purchase orders. Indeed, as mentioned previously, xCBL uses the SAP OCI 2.0b method of remote shopping initiation and termination, which does not even use XML.

In any event, as discussed in more detail in the following remote shopping architecture section, the AFS implementation of remote shopping consists of extensions to the Commerce Server 2000 Retail Solution Site – new pages that implement the cXML and xCBL document exchanges directly.

The documents used by cXML and OCI are different enough to warrant their presentation in separate sub-sections.

cXML Documents for Remote Shopping

The cXML remote shopping protocol defines the following XML documents to control the initiation and termination of remote shopping sessions:

cXML Document	Description
Punchout Index Catalog	The Punchout Index Catalog document is not strictly one of the remote shopping session documents, but it does define the format for a product catalog document for which remote shopping is meant to be used. In other words, it defines the format of product catalog documents that will inform the buyer application that the included products require a remote shopping session in order to be purchased.
	Note that a cXML catalog can be mixed in that some of the products can be specified such that they are purchased without a remote shopping session, while other products can be specified such that they require remote shopping.

(continued)

cXML Document	Description *(continued)*
PunchOutSetupRequest	The PunchOutSetupRequest document is used by the trading partner's buyer application to initiate a remote shopping session. It is sent to a particular URL in the supplier's Web site and must include enough information for the supplier's Web site to construct a URL that is specific to the remote shopping session being initiated, including information about the customer and about the products for which the remote shopping session is being initiated.
	This document must also include a URL at which the trading partner's buyer application is expecting the PunchoutOrderMessage to be sent at the conclusion of the remote shopping session.
	The **PunchOutSetupRequest** element in the XML document includes an *operation* attribute that has a significant impact on the nature of the remote shopping session. There are four legal values:
	• **Create**. The create operation indicates the start of a brand new remote shopping session.
	• **Edit**. The edit operation is used to make changes to products chosen or configured in a previous remote shopping session, and includes the product details from the previous session. This is most significant to supplier Web sites that maintain some type of record of remote shopping sessions, and need to track any changes made.
	• **Inspect**. The inspect operation is used to examine, but not modify, the products chosen or configured in a previous remote shopping session, and includes the product details from the previous session. When such operations are initiated after the supplier has received the corresponding purchase order, it would benefit the customer to have the status of the order displayed as well.
PunchOutSetupResponse	The PunchOutSetupResponse document is constructed by the supplier's Web site in response to receiving a PunchOutSetupRequest message, and is returned to the trading partner's buyer application in the HTTP Response stream. It includes a URL that the buyer application can use to start the remote shopping session on behalf of the customer.
PunchoutOrderMessage	The PunchoutOrderMessage document is constructed by the supplier's Web site when the customer concludes their shopping, or configuration, or some other task, and clicks the **Return to Buyer Application** button. It is used to communicate the contents of the remote shopping "basket" back to the trading partner's buyer application.
	For reasons that are too complex to mention here, this XML document is sent as the contents of a particular hidden form field in an HTTP POST operation.

OCI Documents for Remote Shopping

The OCI 2.0b protocol for remote shopping, defined by SAP and adopted by Commerce One to supplement their xCBL implementations, uses HTTP by itself for initiating and terminating remote shopping sessions, without embedding XML documents within the HTTP documents. The relevant HTTP documents defined by OCI 2.0b are:

OCI Document	Description
Outbound Request	The Outbound Request document is an HTTP GET request that communicates the required information in its query string parameters. This includes information about the customer and the trading partner, including the URL at which the trading partner is expecting the Inbound Request to be posted.
	Note that, unlike its cXML counterpart, the Outbound Request does not provide a way to specify a particular product.
Inbound Request	The Inbound Request document is an HTTP POST request that communicates the results of the remote shopping session from the supplier's Web site back to the trading partner's buyer application. It uses one or more sets of form fields to communicate information about the products chosen, using field names of the following forms (where "n" is replaced by ascending numbers beginning with "1"):

- NEW_ITEM-QUANTITY[n] – number of this product ordered – required.

- NEW_ITEM-UNIT[n] – unit in which this product is sold– required.

- NEW_ITEM-PRICE[n] – price of this product – required.

- NEW_ITEM-CURRENCY[n] – currency of product's price – required.

- NEW_ITEM-DESCRIPTION[n] – product description – optional, if EXT_PRODUCT_ID is provided.

- NEW_ITEM-EXT_PRODUCT_ID[n] –supplier's product identifier – optional, if DESCRIPTION is provided.

Remote Shopping Tasks

Some tasks associated with remote shopping need to be performed only once. Other tasks need to be performed more frequently, on an as needed basis. This section discusses both types of tasks.

Setup, One-Time, and Infrequent Tasks

By far the largest one-time task associated with remote shopping is the creation of a Web site that provides the appropriate remote shopping support. There are several possible starting points from which this might begin:

- **The supplier does not have an existing retail Web site**. In this case, the entire Web site infrastructure will need to be introduced so that customers who are engaged in remote shopping on the site can access the required functionality. The required functionality will depend on the nature of the remote shopping to be implemented. It might be essentially the same functionality as a retail Web site, with the ability to browse a product catalog and manipulate a shopping basket. On the other hand, it might be something quite specific, such as a series of Web pages that implement a wizard for configuring a product chosen in the trading partner's buyer application.

  If the required functionality is more like the former example, the AFS Solution Site could provide an effective starting point for Web site development, and offers the advantage of also being able to serve as an effective starting point for a convention retail Web site as well. If the required functionality is more like the latter example, a custom-designed Web site is probably required, although many of the brand new routines in the AFS Solution Site could be reused. See the "Implementation" section at the end of this chapter for more information about the AFS Solution Site and the new code that distinguishes it from the prior Solution Sites.

- **The supplier has an existing Web site that is based on one of the Commerce Server Solution Sites**. In this case, development effort will be required to integrate the AFS modifications from the AFS Solution Site into the supplier's Solution Site. Given that the supplier will have almost certainly made a number of modifications to the original Solution Site code base, the best way to view the new code in the AFS Solution Site would be to use a tool like WinDiff (which is included in various Microsoft developer products like Microsoft Visual Studio) to compare the Retail Solution Site for Commerce Server 2000 with the AFS Solution Site. See the "Implementation" section at the end of this chapter for more information about the AFS Solution Site and the new code that distinguishes it from the prior Solution Sites.

- **The supplier has an existing Web site that is not based on the Commerce Server Solution Sites**. In this case, development time will be required to add the remote shopping functionality to the site in a way that is compatible with the design of that site. In any event, the files in the AFS Solution Site that were modified from the Retail Solution Site will still be instructive to study and copy, and contain some brand new stand-alone routines that may prove useful in another implementation. And the files in the AFS Solution Site that are brand new are remote shopping–specific, and are bound to contain routines that are useful in another implementation, used as is or modified to better integrate with the design of the other Web site.

The brief descriptions of these scenarios may seem to indicate that creating a supplier solution that includes remote shopping is fairly simple. On the contrary, including remote shopping in the solution significantly increases the amount of effort required to get the solution up and running. And if the supplier did not previously run a Web site as part of their business, support for remote shopping will change that.

Any other one-time tasks associated with remote shopping are part of creating, testing, and maintaining a remote shopping Web site, for example, interacting with trading partner(s) to exchange information about the URLs that will be used to initiate remote shopping.

Ongoing Tasks

The ongoing tasks associated with running a remote shopping Web site are more or less the same as for running a retail Web site. The supplier needs to keep the catalog up-to-date and perform periodic clean-up tasks, such as deleting abandoned baskets. If data is being gathered for analysis in the Commerce Server Data Warehouse, this data needs to be periodically imported into the Data Warehouse. Thorough enumeration to these tasks is beyond the scope of this chapter, but is covered extensively in the Commerce Server documentation.

Remote Shopping Architecture

Viewed from a high level, the architecture of remote shopping in AFS consists of a trading partner's buyer application switching a customer into the basket page interface of the AFS Solution Site, and upon a signal from the AFS Solution Site, switching them back into the buyer application. After returning to the buyer application, the contents of the customer's basket in the buyer application must reflect any shopping activity that occurred in the AFS Solution Site.

The following figure illustrates the steps involved at the next level of detail. The numbered arrows in the figure correspond to an explanation of the steps following the figure. Note that the figure depicts remote shopping in a generic way, and deviations by either the cXML protocol or the OCI protocol will be explained for each step.

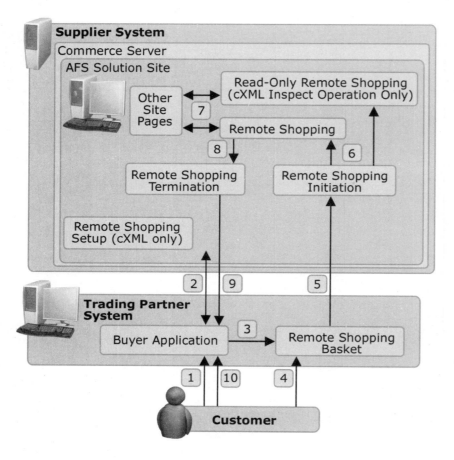

Remote shopping architecture

The steps involved in supporting a remote shopping session, as shown in the previous figure, are:

1. The customer interacts with the trading partner's buyer application, and then performs an action, such as clicking a button, that initiates a remote shopping session.

2. For cXML, but not for OCI, the buyer application exchanges a pair of messages with the supplier's Web site using a well-known URL (PunchOutSetupRequest and PunchOutSetupResponse). Authentication and basket initialization are performed at this point, and the URL used in step 5 is returned to the buyer application.

3. The buyer application uses a standard browser for the customer's remote shopping session. If the buyer application is browser-based, it might just redirect to the appropriate URL, or it might open a new browser window for the remote shopping session. If the buyer application is not browser-based, it must open a browser window for the remote shopping session.

4. The customer is now interacting with a browser window that is dedicated to the remote shopping session.

5. The remote shopping browser uses the appropriate URL to begin the remote shopping session. For cXML, the URL returned in step 2 is used, which corresponds to the page RemoteBasketNav.asp.

   For OCI (xCBL), the URL of the page OCIAccept.asp is used, with the appropriate query string arguments appended. This page then redirects to the page RemoteBasketNav.asp.

6. Regardless of the protocol being used, the page RemoteBasketNav.asp is used to dispatch the customer's browser session to the appropriate visible page. For cXML, this can be the basket page or a product page, and will be different versions depending on whether the specified operation allows modifications to be made to the contents of the basket (one of the four pages RemoteBasket.asp, InspectBasket.asp, product.asp, or InspectProduct.asp).

   For OCI (xCBL), the user always ends up on the page RemoteBasket.asp, because OCI does not support the concept of a remote shopping session targeted at a specific product or the concept of a read-only remote shopping session.

7. Now that the customer is in the remote shopping session, they can, in general, freely navigate the supplier's Web site, and assuming that basket modifications are allowed, perform operations that alter the contents of their basket.

8. Eventually, the customer will decide to end the remote shopping session and click the **Return to Buyer Application** button (or its equivalent). This results in the page FormPostRemoteBasket.asp being run.

9. The page FormPostRemoteBasket.asp packages up the contents of the remote shopping basket according to the protocol in use, and posts the corresponding form to the URL provided during the initiation of the session.

10. The customer is now back in the trading partner's buyer application, where the basket should reflect changes made during the remote shopping session, if any. Under normal circumstances, the customer will eventually check out, initiating the approval process that will eventually lead to either the rejection of the purchase order, or the sending of the purchase order to the supplier using the process outlined in the previous section "Purchase Order Reception Solution."

Tools and Technologies

To implement a supplier solution using the Microsoft technology described in this chapter, the following .NET Enterprise Server products are required:

- Microsoft BizTalk Accelerator for Suppliers (AFS)
- Microsoft BizTalk Server
- Microsoft Commerce Server
- Microsoft SQL Server

Note the lack of version/year numbers in the previous list. As this book is going to press, new versions of several of these products are being released. When AFS was first released in the fall of 2001, it supported BizTalk Server 2000 with Service Pack 1a, Commerce Server 2000 with Service Pack 1, and SQL Server 2000. Since then, BizTalk Server 2002 has been released and Commerce Server 2002 is due to be released in the spring of 2002. An update to AFS will follow shortly after that. Interested suppliers should refer directly to the Microsoft Web site (www.microsoft.com) for more precise information about software requirements and version compatibility.

In addition, developers working on an implementation of AFS might want Microsoft Visual Studio to make developing solutions easier. As with Commerce Server and BizTalk Server, a new version of Visual Studio is due to be released soon. Suppliers who choose to implement their solution using the latest versions of the .NET Enterprise Servers might want to use the new version of Visual Studio and the .NET Framework so that they can use the .NET-enabled features in these products.

Finally, depending on the deployment scenario and the firewall requirements of the supplier, Microsoft Internet Security and Acceleration Server (ISA) might be another product to consider.

Implementation

How much developer effort will be required to implement a supplier solution will depend on whether or not the supplier is going to implement a remote shopping Web site, and if so, whether or not the AFS Solution Site comes close to meeting their needs. If the answer to the first condition is yes, that remote shopping is part of the scenario, and the answer to the second condition is no, that the AFS Solution Site is not the right implementation, then a significant amount of implementation effort will be required. Unfortunately, the scope of that effort and the various directions it might take are far beyond what can be effectively discussed here.

Instead, this section provides a glimpse at what was involved in converting the Commerce Server 2000 Retail Solution Site into the AFS Solution Site by using two distinct approaches. The first approach, in the following sub-section, will examine the routine **htmRenderBasket** that is found in three different pages in the AFS Solution Site. The second approach, in the next sub-section, will provide an overview of the files that were modified and the new files that were added in the course of converting the Retail Solution Site to the AFS Solution Site.

Basket Rendering Routines

In the course of converting the Retail Solution Site into the AFS Solution Site, the page basket.asp was not changed. However, making copies of basket.asp and then making a relatively small number of modifications created two other pages. These two new pages are RemoteBasket.asp and InspectBasket.asp. The page RemoteBasket.asp is used to display the contents of the remote shopping basket for OCI-based remote shopping sessions and for cXML-based remote shopping sessions when the specified operation is "create" or "edit." The page InspectBasket.asp is used to display the contents of the remote shopping basket for cXML-based remote shopping sessions when the specified operation is "Inspect." The page InspectBasket.asp is essentially a read-only version of the page RemoteBasket.asp; the basket contents can be viewed but not changed.

In order to provide a sense of the type of changes that were required to create these two new variations of the basket page, this section will examine the changes that were made to the routine **htmRenderBasket**, first in the course of creating the version in the page RemoteBasket.asp from the version in the page basket.asp, and then in the course of creating the version in the page InspectBasket.asp from the version in the page RemoteBasket.asp.

Note that this examination is only a brief discussion of the changes that were made in the course of creating the AFS Solution Site, but hopefully they will provide some sense of the types of code modifications that need to be made to add remote shopping functionality to any retail Web site.

Also note that a different design approach, in which a lot of conditional code is added to a single basket page, could have been taken. For the AFS Solution Site, the designers apparently determined that the duplicate code on the three separate versions of the basket page was worth savings in logic complexity that would have been required in the single basket page approach.

RemoteBasket.asp from Basket.asp

When the new page RemoteBasket.asp was created from a copy of the page basket.asp, a number of changes where made to the routine **htmRenderBasket**. This section examines those changes by presenting an annotated version of the modified code in the page RemoteBasket.asp.

When reading through this code, note the following conventions:

- Annotations added to explain the changes are in italic font.

- Code that is new in the RemoteBasket.asp version of **htmRenderBasket** is shown in bold font.

- To avoid the reading difficulty associated with wrapped lines of code, those lines have been truncated and are indicated with a bold ellipsis (**...**) at the point the line was truncated.

- To save unnecessary reading and trees, some whole sections of code that were not changed have been omitted, and are indicated by a vertical ellipsis and an annotation, as follows:

  .
  . *Code that was not changed has been removed here.*
  .

- Some reformatting with respect to linefeeds has been done to enhance readability.

The new version of the routine **htmRenderBasket** that is used in the page RemoteBasket.asp is functionally very similar to the original version in the page basket.asp. The only difference is that the new version does not support discount processing. The annotated, abbreviated version of the routine **htmRenderBasket** follows:

```
Function htmRenderBasket(mscsOrderGrp, oOrderFormDisplayOrder)
    Dim sOrderFormName, mscsOrderForm, dictItem, listAggregatedItems, ...
    Dim i, urlLink, urlAction, bDiscountApplied, sProdCode, htmLinkText
    Dim htmBasketHeaderRow, htmBasketDataRow, htmQtyCol, htmProdCode, ...
    Dim arrData, arrParams, arrParamVals, arrDataAttLists
```

The following bold code, added to the page RemoteBasket.asp, defines two new variables for calculating the item totals and the basket total without using any discount processing. It also initializes the basket total variable to zero in preparation for tallying.

```
    Dim fItemTotalWithNoDiscount, fBasketTotalWithNoDiscount

    ' NOTE: Discounts are not applicable to Remote shopping baskets -
    ' Code rendering discount info below is commented
    ' and kept commented for future use...

    fBasketTotalWithNoDiscount = 0

    bDiscountApplied = False

    Set listAggregatedItems = Server.CreateObject("Commerce.SimpleList")
    For Each sOrderFormName in oOrderFormDisplayOrder
        Set mscsOrderForm = mscsOrderGrp.Value(ORDERFORMS).Value(sOrderFormName)
```

The following bold code, commented out in the page RemoteBasket.asp, prevents discounts from ever being applied to the contents of a remote shopping basket.

```
'If mscsOrderForm.Value("_winners").Count > 0 Then
  'bDiscountApplied = True
'End If
For Each dictItem In mscsOrderForm.Items
    Call listAggregatedItems.Add(dictItem)
Next
Next
```

.
.   *Code that was not changed has been removed here.*
.

```
arrParams = Array(CATALOG_NAME_URL_KEY, CATEGORY_NAME_URL_KEY, ...
arrParamVals = Array(dictItem.Value("product_catalog"), ...
urlLink = GenerateURL(MSCSSitePages.DeleteItem, arrParams, arrParamVals)
htmLinkText = RenderText(mscsMessageManager.GetMessage( ...
htmRemoveCol = RenderLink(urlLink, htmLinkText, MSCSSiteStyle.Link)
```

The following bold code, added to the page RemoteBasket.asp, does a simple calculation to determine the total item price (quantity times price), and adds to the running total price for the entire remote shopping basket.

```
' Discounts are not applicable to Remote shopping baskets - only show
' product's adjusted list price and its actual extended total.

fItemTotalWithNoDiscount = dictItem.quantity * _
                           dictItem.Value("_cy_iadjust_currentprice")
fBasketTotalWithNoDiscount = fBasketTotalWithNoDiscount +
fItemTotalWithNoDiscount

    If bDiscountApplied Then
```

.
.   *Code that was not changed has been removed here.*
.

```
    Else
        ' "name" and "description" are required product properties
        ' and cannot have null values.
        arrData = Array(_
            htmQtyCol, _
            htmProdCode, _
            dictItem.Value("_product_name"), _
            dictItem.Value("_product_description"), _
            htmRenderCurrency(dictItem.Value("_cy_iadjust_currentprice"))), _
```

The following bold code, modified in the page RemoteBasket.asp, adds a formatted version of the item total to the array that specifies the values for the current row in the basket page table. In the page basket.asp, this line is:

```
       htmRenderCurrency(dictItem.Value("_cy_oadjust_adjustedprice")), _

              htmRenderCurrency(fItemTotalWithNoDiscount), _
          htmRemoveCol)
       End If

       htmRenderBasket = htmRenderBasket & RenderTableDataRow(arrData, arrDataAttLists, _
                                              MSCSSiteStyle.TRMiddle)
    Next

    urlLink = GenerateURL(MSCSSitePages.DeleteAllItems, Array(), Array())
    htmLinkText = RenderText( _
                     mscsMessageManager.GetMessage("L_RemoveAll_HTMLText", sLanguage), _
                     MSCSSiteStyle.Body _
                              )
    arrData = Array( _
                 NBSP, _
                 mscsMessageManager.GetMessage("L_BASKET_SUBTOTAL_COLUMN_TEXT", ...
```

The following bold code, modified in the page RemoteBasket.asp, adds a formatted version of the basket total to the array that specifies the values for the final, sparse row in the basket page table. In the page basket.asp, this line is:

```
              htmRenderCurrency(mscsOrderGrp.value.saved_cy_oadjust_subtotal), _

              htmRenderCurrency(fBasketTotalWithNoDiscount), _
          RenderLink(urlLink, htmLinkText, MSCSSiteStyle.Link))
```

•

• *Code that was not changed has been removed here.*

•

```
    htmRenderBasket = RenderForm(urlAction, htmRenderBasket, HTTP_POST)
End Function
```

InspectBasket.asp from RemoteBasket.asp

When the new page InspectBasket.asp was created from a copy of the page RemoteBasket.asp, a number of additional changes where made to the routine **htmRenderBasket**. This section examines those changes by presenting an annotated version of the modified code in the page InspectBasket.asp.

The same conventions were used when annotating this version of the routine **htmRenderBasket** as were used in the previous section. Specifically:

- Annotations added to explain the changes are in italic font.

- Code that is new in the InspectBasket.asp version of **htmRenderBasket** is shown in bold font.

- To avoid the reading difficulty associated with wrapped lines of code, those lines have been truncated and are indicated with a bold ellipsis (**...**) at the point the line was truncated.

- To save unnecessary reading and trees, some whole sections of code that were not changed have been omitted, and are indicated by a vertical ellipsis and an annotation, as follows:

  .

  .   *Code that was not changed has been removed here.*

  .

- Some reformatting with respect to linefeeds has been done to enhance readability.

The new version of the routine **htmRenderBasket** that is used in the page InspectBasket.asp is based on the version in the page RemoteBasket.asp. The various differences are all based on the need to make the new version read-only. The versions of the routine **htmRenderBasket** that are in the pages basket.asp and RemoteBasket.asp contain a number of different controls and links that allow the contents of the basket to be altered. The main content of the basket page is rendered in an HTML table, where all of the rows other than the first row (the header row) and the last row (the sub-total row) are used to display individual products that are in the basket. Each of these product rows contains the following ways in which the contents of the basket can be altered:

- The text box that displays the quantity of the product can be edited and the associated update button can be clicked.

- The cell that displays the product ID is a link to the corresponding product page. Once on a product page, the entire catalog can be browsed, and new products can be added to the basket.

  Note that code in the routine **RenderBasketPage** in the page InspectBasket.asp has been changed such that the left-side navigation link to the product catalog is not displayed.

- The final cell in each row displays a remove link that can be used to remove the corresponding product from the shopping basket.

The final row in the table, in addition to displaying the sub-total for the basket, displays a remove all link that can be used to completely empty the shopping basket.

The modifications to the routine **htmRenderBasket** in the page InspectBasket.asp were all made to remove these various ways of altering the contents of the shopping basket. The annotated, abbreviated version of the routine **htmRenderBasket** follows:

```
Function htmRenderBasket(mscsOrderGrp, oOrderFormDisplayOrder)
    Dim sOrderFormName, mscsOrderForm, dictItem, listAggregatedItems, sName, sBtnText
```

.

. *Code that was not changed has been removed here.*

.

The following bold code, modified in the page InspectBasket.asp, is used to render the column headings for the table that displays the basket contents. Although the "no discounts" modifications discussed previously have been inherited from the page RemoteBasket.asp, for completeness this page includes modifications for both the discount and no discount versions of the table. Because the page InspectBasket.asp implements a read-only view of the remote shopping basket, the table no longer includes the final column used for the links that would remove the corresponding item from the basket. In the pages basket.asp and RemoteBasket.asp, the additional column is rendered using the following line as the last element in the array:

```
mscsMessageManager.GetMessage("L_BASKET_REMOVE_COLUMN_TEXT", sLanguage))
```

Note that in the actual code, the removed line is commented out rather than removed, as has been done here for clarity.

```
If bDiscountApplied Then
    arrData = Array( _
        mscsMessageManager.GetMessage("L_BASKET_QUANTITY_COLUMN_TEXT", sLanguage), _
        mscsMessageManager.GetMessage("L_ProductCode_HTMLText", sLanguage), _
        mscsMessageManager.GetMessage("L_Product_Name_DisplayName_HTMLText", ...
        mscsMessageManager.GetMessage("L_Product_Description_DisplayName_HTMLText", ...
        mscsMessageManager.GetMessage("L_BASKET_UNITPRICE_COLUMN_TEXT", sLanguage), _
        mscsMessageManager.GetMessage("L_BASKET_DISCOUNT_COLUMN_TEXT", sLanguage), _
        mscsMessageManager.GetMessage("L_BASKET_MESSAGES_COLUMN_TEXT", sLanguage), _
        mscsMessageManager.GetMessage("L_BASKET_TOTALPRICE_COLUMN_TEXT", sLanguage))
```

```
Else
    arrData = Array( _
        mscsMessageManager.GetMessage("L_BASKET_QUANTITY_COLUMN_TEXT", sLanguage), _
        mscsMessageManager.GetMessage("L_ProductCode_HTMLText", sLanguage), _
        mscsMessageManager.GetMessage("L_Product_Name_DisplayName_HTMLText", ...
        mscsMessageManager.GetMessage("L_Product_Description_DisplayName_HTMLText", ...
        mscsMessageManager.GetMessage("L_BASKET_UNITPRICE_COLUMN_TEXT", sLanguage), _
        mscsMessageManager.GetMessage("L_BASKET_TOTALPRICE_COLUMN_TEXT", sLanguage))
End If

htmRenderBasket = htmRenderBasket & RenderTableHeaderRow(arrData, Array(), ...
```

*The following bold code, modified in the page InspectBasket.asp, is used to establish non-default column alignments for the data rows in the table, which are rendered within the **For** loop that follows. Again, although the "no discounts" modifications discussed previously have been inherited from the page RemoteBasket.asp, both versions of the column alignment are modified here. It is the centered alignment of the final "remove item" column that has been removed in the page InspectBasket.asp. In the pages basket.asp and RemoteBasket.asp the alignment of the final, remove item column is established using the following line as the last element in the array:*

```
MSCSSiteStyle.TDCenter)
```

Note that in the actual code, the removed line is commented out rather than removed, as has been done here for clarity.

```
If bDiscountApplied Then
    arrDataAttLists = Array( _
        MSCSSiteStyle.TDCenter, _
        MSCSSiteStyle.TDLeft, _
        MSCSSiteStyle.TDLeft, _
        MSCSSiteStyle.TDLeft, _
        MSCSSiteStyle.TDRight, _
        MSCSSiteStyle.TDRight, _
        MSCSSiteStyle.TDLeft, _
        MSCSSiteStyle.TDRight)
Else
    arrDataAttLists = Array( _
        MSCSSiteStyle.TDCenter, _
        MSCSSiteStyle.TDLeft, _
        MSCSSiteStyle.TDLeft, _
        MSCSSiteStyle.TDLeft, _
        MSCSSiteStyle.TDRight, _
        MSCSSiteStyle.TDRight)
End If
```

```
For i = 0 To listAggregatedItems.Count -1
    Set dictItem = listAggregatedItems(i)

    sName = PRODUCT_QTY_URL_KEY & "_" & dictItem.Value("_poname") & "_" & ...
```

The following bold code, modified in the page InspectBasket.asp, is used to disable the ability to modify the quantity of a given item in the remote shopping basket. In the pages basket.asp and RemoteBasket.asp, the following lines of code are used to render a quantity text box and an associated update button for the quantity table cell associated with each item in the basket:

```
htmQtyCol = RenderTextBox(sName, dictItem.quantity, 3, 3, MSCSSiteStyle.TextBox)
sBtnText = mscsMessageManager.GetMessage("L_Update_Button", sLanguage)
htmQtyCol = htmQtyCol & RenderSubmitButton(SUBMIT_BUTTON, sBtnText, ...
```

In the page InspectBasket.asp, these cells in the table are also populated with the item quantity, but as plain, unalterable text, with the associated update button.

```
htmQtyCol = RenderText( dictItem.quantity, MSCSSiteStyle.Body)

arrParams = Array(CATALOG_NAME_URL_KEY, CATEGORY_NAME_URL_KEY, ...
arrParamVals = Array(dictItem.Value("product_catalog"), ...
```

The following bold code, modified in the page InspectBasket.asp, changes the page to which the text in the product code column links. It was changed from product.asp to InspectProduct.asp, the latter of which is a read-only version of the former. In the pages basket.asp and RemoteBasket.asp, this line is:

```
urlLink = GenerateURL(MSCSSitePages.Product, arrParams, arrParamVals)

urlLink = GenerateURL(MSCSSitePages.InspectProduct, arrParams, arrParamVals)

sProdCode = dictItem.Value("product_id")
If Not IsNull(dictItem.Value("product_variant_id")) Then
    sProdCode = sProdCode & "-" & dictItem.Value("product_variant_id")
End If

htmLinkText = RenderText(sProdCode, MSCSSiteStyle.Body)
htmProdCode = RenderLink(urlLink, htmLinkText, MSCSSiteStyle.Link)

arrParams = Array(CATALOG_NAME_URL_KEY, CATEGORY_NAME_URL_KEY, ...
arrParamVals = Array(dictItem.Value("product_catalog"), ...
```

The following bold code, modified in the page InspectBasket.asp, eliminates the code that generates the link for the remove item cell for each item in the remote shopping basket. As it turns out, these lines could have been removed altogether because the variables are not used anywhere after the assignment of the empty strings. In the pages basket.asp and RemoteBasket.asp, these lines are:

```
urlLink = GenerateURL(MSCSSitePages.DeleteItem, arrParams, arrParamVals)
htmLinkText = RenderText(mscsMessageManager.GetMessage(...
htmRemoveCol = RenderLink(urlLink, htmLinkText, MSCSSiteStyle.Link)
```

Note that in the actual code, the removed portions of the lines are commented out rather than removed, as has been done here for clarity.

```
urlLink = ""
htmLinkText = ""
htmRemoveCol = ""

' Discounts are not applicable to Remote shopping baskets - only
' show product's adjusted list price and its actual extended total.

fItemTotalWithNoDiscount = dictItem.quantity * _
                              dictItem.Value("_cy_iadjust_currentprice")
fBasketTotalWithNoDiscount = fBasketTotalWithNoDiscount + fItemTotalWithNoDiscount
```

The following bold code, modified in the page InspectBasket.asp, no longer displays the remove item link as the final cell in each row. This corresponds to the removal of the header for this column, as seen earlier in the routine. In the pages basket.asp and RemoteBasket.asp the remove item link is rendered as the final cell in each row using the following line as the last element in the array:

```
htmRemoveCol)
```

Note that in the actual code, the removed line is commented out rather than removed, as has been done here for clarity. Also note that the modified code in the If condition will never be run, given the changes made when creating the page RemoteBasket.asp out of the page basket.asp.

```
If bDiscountApplied Then
    ' "name" and "description" are required product properties
    ' and cannot have null values.
    arrData = Array(_
        htmQtyCol, _
        htmProdCode, _
        dictItem.Value("_product_name"), _
        dictItem.Value("_product_description"), _
        htmRenderCurrency(dictItem.Value("_cy_iadjust_currentprice")), _
        htmRenderCurrency(dictItem.Value("_cy_oadjust_discount")), _
        dictItem.Value("_messages"), _
        htmRenderCurrency(dictItem.Value("_cy_oadjust_adjustedprice")) )
```

```
        Else
            ' "name" and "description" are required product properties
            ' and cannot have null values.
            arrData = Array(_
                htmQtyCol, _
                htmProdCode, _
                dictItem.Value("_product_name"), _
                dictItem.Value("_product_description"), _
                htmRenderCurrency(dictItem.Value("_cy_iadjust_currentprice")), _
                htmRenderCurrency(fItemTotalWithNoDiscount) )
        End If

        htmRenderBasket = htmRenderBasket & RenderTableDataRow(arrData, ...
    Next
```

The following bold code, modified in the page InspectBasket.asp, is responsible for setting up the final, sub-total row of the table such that it does not display the remove all button in the (now missing) final column. The actual code on the page is a bit of a mess because it comments out the old code rather than removing it, and it uselessly sets the urlLink and htmLinkText variables to empty strings even though it does not ever use them again.

In the pages basket.asp and RemoteBasket.asp, the original lines of code are:

```
urlLink = GenerateURL(MSCSSitePages.DeleteAllItems, Array(), Array())
htmLinkText = RenderText(mscsMessageManager.GetMessage("L_RemoveAll_HTMLText", ...
arrData = Array(_
    NBSP, _
    mscsMessageManager.GetMessage("L_BASKET_SUBTOTAL_COLUMN_TEXT", sLanguage), _
    htmRenderCurrency(fBasketTotalWithNoDiscount), _
    RenderLink(urlLink, htmLinkText, MSCSSiteStyle.Link))

If bDiscountApplied Then
    arrDataAttLists = Array(" COLSPAN='6'", MSCSSiteStyle.TDLeft, ...
Else
    arrDataAttLists = Array(" COLSPAN='4'", MSCSSiteStyle.TDLeft, ...
End If

htmTotalRow = RenderTableDataRow(arrData, arrDataAttLists, MSCSSiteStyle.TRMiddle)

urlLink = ""
htmLinkText = ""
arrData = Array(_
    NBSP, _
    mscsMessageManager.GetMessage("L_BASKET_SUBTOTAL_COLUMN_TEXT", sLanguage), _
    htmRenderCurrency(fBasketTotalWithNoDiscount) )
```

```
If bDiscountApplied Then
        arrDataAttLists = Array(" COLSPAN='6'", MSCSSiteStyle.TDLeft,
MSCSSiteStyle.TDRight )
    Else
        arrDataAttLists = Array(" COLSPAN='4'", MSCSSiteStyle.TDLeft,
MSCSSiteStyle.TDRight )
    End If

    htmTotalRow = RenderTableDataRow(arrData, arrDataAttLists, MSCSSiteStyle.TRMiddle)
```

The following bold code, modified in the page InspectBasket.asp, eliminates any action URL from being associated with this form. This was done because the update quantity buttons that used to be associated with form submittal are no longer being rendered. In the pages basket.asp and RemoteBasket.asp, the action URL for the form is generated using the following line:

```
    urlAction = GenerateURL(MSCSSitePages.EditItemQuantities, Array(), Array())
```

Note that in the actual code, the removed line is commented out rather than removed, as has been done here for clarity.

```
    htmRenderBasket = htmRenderBasket & htmTotalRow
    htmRenderBasket = RenderTable(htmRenderBasket, MSCSSiteStyle.BasketTable)
    urlAction = ""
    htmRenderBasket = RenderForm(urlAction, htmRenderBasket, HTTP_POST)
End Function
```

New and Modified Files in the AFS Solution Site

The AFS Solution Site is a modified version of the Retail Solution Site that shipped with Commerce Server 2000. A small percentage of the existing files in the Retail Solution Site were modified for the AFS Solution Site, and a similar number of new files were added. This section reviews each of these files, discusses their purpose, and where appropriate, discusses their potential for reuse in any remote shopping Web site.

_additem.asp (modified)
>   This page is used to add an item to the shopping basket and then logs the action as a Commerce event.

The routine **Main** in this page was modified for the AFS Solution Site.

_delall.asp (modified)
>   This page is used to delete all of the items from the shopping basket.

The routine **Main** in this page was modified for the AFS Solution Site.

_delitem.asp (modified)

This page is used to delete an item from the shopping basket and then logs the action as a Commerce event.

The routine **Main** in this page was modified for the AFS Solution Site.

_editqty.asp (modified)

This page is used to change the quantity of an item in the shopping basket.

The routine **Main** in this page was modified for the AFS Solution Site.

_recvpo.asp (modified)

This page is used to receive a purchase order from BizTalk Server (performing AFS processing), transform the data into a **Dictionary** object, add it to the order group, run the pipeline\recvpo.pcf pipeline and, on validation, save the new order.

The routines **OnTransactionAbort** and **VerifyOrganization** in this page were added for the AFS Solution Site.

The routines **Main** and **RunOrderPipeline** in this page were modified for the AFS Solution Site.

CS2K_PO.xml (new)

This file defines the schema for Commerce Server Order XML version 1.0.

Suppliers will probably find this file to be useful for Web sites other than the AFS Solution Site.

cXML1.1_PO_to_cXML1.1_POR.xsl (new)

This file defines the XSL transformation for creating a cXML 1.1 purchase order response (POR) out of a cXML 1.1 purchase order.

Suppliers will probably find this file to be useful for Web sites other than the AFS Solution Site.

cXML1.2_PO_to_cXML1.2_POR.xsl (new)

This file defines the XSL transformation for creating a cXML 1.2 purchase order response (POR) out of a cXML 1.2 purchase order.

Suppliers will probably find this file to be useful for Web sites other than the AFS Solution Site.

FormPostRemoteBasket.asp (new)

This page is used to build and post the protocol-specific XML document that terminates a remote shopping session.

This new page includes the routines **CheckBasket**, **CloseSession**, **errorHandler**, **htmRenderBasketWarnings**, **InitializeBasketPage**, and **Main**.

With sufficient design planning, suppliers may find many of the routines in this file to be useful for Web sites other than the AFS Solution Site.

global.asa (modified)

This file is used to create and initialize global objects and variables and place them in Application scope.

InspectBasket.asp (new)

This page is used to render the read-only basket page used for cXML-based remote shopping sessions when the operation is "Inspect."

This new page includes the routines **CheckBasket, CreatePOIndexes, htmRenderBasket, htmRenderBasketWarnings, htmRenderCheckoutButton, htmRenderDiscountMessageGroup, htmRenderDiscountMessages, htmRenderDiscountsApplied, htmRenderPredictions, InitializeBasketPage, Main, PredictedPropToHREF**, and **RenderBasketPage**.

With sufficient design planning, suppliers may find many of the routines in this file to be useful for Web sites other than the AFS Solution Site.

InspectProduct.asp (new)

This page is used to render the read-only product page used for cXML-based remote shopping sessions when the operation is "Inspect."

This new page includes the routines **htmRenderBuiltInProperties, htmRenderUserDefinedProductProperties, htmRenderVariantsList, listGetVariantPropertiesToShow, Main, PeekField**, and **sGetPropertyDisplayName**.

With sufficient design planning, suppliers may find many of the routines in this file to be useful for Web sites other than the AFS Solution Site.

newaddr.asp (modified)

This page is used to add, edit, and delete address book addresses.

This page now also includes the page include\const.asp.

OCIAccept.asp (new)

This page is used to accept initiation of OCI-based remote shopping sessions.

This new page includes the routines **Main, ShowRemoteBasketError**, and **ValidateOCIFormFields**.

With sufficient design planning, suppliers may find many of the routines in this file to be useful for Web sites other than the AFS Solution Site.

opt-out.asp (modified)

This page is used to add the user to the opt-out list of a direct mail campaign.

The routine **Main** in this page was modified for the AFS Solution Site.

pipeline\recvpo.pcf (modified)

This pipeline configuration file is used to configure the Order Processing pipeline (OPP) that enables the Web site to receive orders using AFS. A **Scriptor** pipeline component was added to the pipeline to compute the proper subtotal for the order.

product.asp (modified)

This page is used to display the details for a given product.

The routine **Main** in this page was modified for the AFS Solution Site.

punchout.asp (new)

This page is used to accept initiation of cXML-based remote shopping sessions.

This new page includes the routines **AddPunchoutItemsToRemoteBasket**, **GetCXMLVersion**, **GetItemsPresentInRequest**, **Main**, **SendPunchoutSetupResponse**, and **ValidatePunchoutRequest**.

With sufficient design planning, suppliers may find many of the routines in this file to be useful for Web sites other than the AFS Solution Site.

rc.xml (modified)

This file is used to define localizable string constants.

A number of new, localizable strings were added, and some existing strings were modified for the AFS Solution Site.

ReceivePO.asp (new)

This page is used to accept xCBL and cXML purchase order documents from trading partners to begin AFS purchase order reception processing.

The routine **Main** in this page was modified for the AFS Solution Site.

RemoteBasket.asp (new)

This page is used to render the read/write basket page used for xCBL-based remote shopping sessions and for cXML-based remote shopping sessions when the operation is either "create" or "edit."

This new page includes the routines **CheckBasket**, **CreatePOIndexes**, **htmRenderBasket**, **htmRenderBasketWarnings**, **htmRenderCheckoutButton**, **htmRenderDiscountMessageGroup**, **htmRenderDiscountMessages**, **htmRenderDiscountsApplied**, **htmRenderPredictions**, **InitializeBasketPage**, **Main**, **PredictedPropToHREF**, and **RenderBasketPage**.

With sufficient design planning, suppliers may find many of the routines in this file to be useful for Web sites other than the AFS Solution Site.

RemoteBasketNav.asp (new)

This page is used to determine the proper page to render during remote shopping sessions.

This new page includes the routines **GetRemoteBasketSessionStartPage**, **GetRemoteBasketSessionUserID**, **Main**, **PrepareTimeOutResponse**, and **SetRemoteBasketSessionUserID**.

With sufficient design planning, suppliers may find many of the routines in this file to be useful for Web sites other than the AFS Solution Site.

services\include\render_common.asp (modified)

 This page contains common rendering functions.

The routine **sReConstructPageURL** in this page was modified for the AFS Solution Site.

template\layout1.asp (modified)

 This page provides the HTML display layout for the page content along with an advertising banner, navigation bar, menu bar, discount banner, and footer.

A META REFRESH element was added to cancel the remote shopping session whenever the customer's Auth Ticket times out.

template\menu.asp (modified)

 This file is used to prepare and display the menu bar.

The routines **GetURLToCancelRBSession** and **htmRenderRBUserLogoffSection** in this page were added for the AFS Solution Site.

template\navbar.inc (modified)

 This file is included by the file layout1.asp to display the navigation bar.

The routine **RenderNavbar** was modified for the AFS Solution Site such that HTML fragment caching is not used for remote shopping sessions and, when remote shopping, the basket link leads to the remote shopping basket instead of the normal basket.

unpack.vbs (modified)

 This Microsoft Visual Basic script file is used when a site is unpacked using Commerce Server Site Packager. It sets up the error\500error.asp page to be a custom error handler for the site, as well as certain App Default Config resource properties.

This file was changed such that the names and virtual roots for the AFS Solution Site and its associated Business Desk are different than the names and virtual roots used for the Retail Solution Site.

xCBL3.0_PO_to_xCBL3.0_POR.xsl (new)

 This file defines the XSL transformation for creating an xCBL 3.0 purchase order response (POR) out of an xCBL 3.0 purchase order.

Suppliers will probably find this file to be useful for Web sites other than the AFS Solution Site.

error\500error.asp (modified)

 This page is used to display messages for any 500 error that occurs during page processing.

The routine **RenderPostData** in this page was modified for the AFS Solution Site.

include\afs_common_lib.asp (new)

This page contains general-purpose routines for use with AFS.

This new page includes the routine **ValidateAndGetTradingPartnerID**.

With sufficient design planning, suppliers may find the routine in this file to be useful for Web sites other than the AFS Solution Site.

include\afs_error_lib.asp (new)

This page contains error-handling routines for use with AFS.

This new page includes the routine **WriteAFSLogMesg**.

include\afs_PO_Const.asp (new)

This page contains constants used for purchase order processing within AFS.

This page defines constants that are specific to the purchase order reception functionality within the AFS Solution Site.

include\afs_PO_util.asp (new)

This page contains routines for processing purchase orders within AFS.

This new page includes the routines **AddProductName**, **CompareMsgId**, **CreateOrderResponseDetailRecord**, **doPurchaseOrderResponse**, **EncodeString**, **GetISO8601TimeStampEx**, **GetSiteConfigField**, **GetURL**, **PostToSite**, **ReadPOMsgAck**, **sFormatString**, **sGetComputerName**, **sGetMsg**, **TransformPO**, **ValidateOrderQuantity**, **ValidateSharedSecret**, **WriteEventLog**, **WritePO2MSMQ**, **WriteToFile**, **xCBLOrderResponse**, and **ZeroPrefix**.

With sufficient design planning, suppliers may find many of the routines in this file to be useful for Web sites other than the AFS Solution Site.

include\const.asp (modified)

This page provides a location for constants to be defined when extending the Solution Site, and contains a number of AFS-specific constants.

This file now contains a small number of constants that are specific to AFS.

include\global_internationalization_lib.asp (modified)

This page contains functions used to retrieve country/region name and code lists, and to work with alternate currencies.

This file is showing up as modified in comparison tools like WinDiff, although the difference is not visible.

include\global_main_lib.asp (modified)

This page contains the routine **Main** that is called by the global.asa file to create, initialize, and place in Application scope many of the objects supplied by Commerce Server.

The routine **Main** in this page was modified for the AFS Solution Site such that it also sets an application variable named TimeZoneDiff by calling the routine **js_GetTimeZoneDiff**.

include\global_siteconfig_lib.asp (modified)

This page contains routines used to retrieve site configuration information, join a Web farm, and build the dictPages data structure.

The routines **GetSecurePagesDictionary** and **iGetWebServerPort** in this page were modified for the AFS Solution Site.

include\global_timezone_lib.asp (new)

This page contains routines related to time zone processing for use with AFS.

The Microsoft® JScript® routine **js_GetTimeZoneDiff** in this page was added for the AFS Solution Site.

With sufficient design planning, suppliers may find the routine in this file to be useful for Web sites other than the AFS Solution Site.

include\setupenv.asp (modified)

This page is used to set up framework variables, retrieve information about the user, and call the routine **Main** in the file that has included it.

The routines **ClearRemoteBasketOrderForms** and **RedirectToBasket** in this page were added for the AFS Solution Site.

include\std_profile_lib.asp (modified)

This page contains routines used to create a new profile, retrieve and update a current profile, check whether the user has a profile, and check whether profiling is enabled on the site.

The routine **EnsureUserProfile** in this page was modified for the AFS Solution Site such that it allows remote shopping customers to not have a profile, even though they are authenticated.

include\std_remotebasket_lib.asp (new)

This page contains routines related to remote shopping for use with AFS.

This new page includes the routines **ConvertToDecimalCurrency**, **CreateNewUserSession**, **CreateRemoteBasket**, **doSplitString**, **GencXMLPayloadHeader**, **GenerateGUID**, **GenPunchoutOrderHeader**, **GenPunchoutOrderItems**, **Get_cXMLItemTemplate**, **Get_cXMLOrderMesgTemplate**, **Get_cXMLSupplierUserAgent**, **GetISO8601TimeStamp**, **GetRemoteBasket**, **GetRemoteBasketOrderTotal**, **GetSiteLocaleLanguage**, **HTMLEncodeAndEscapeString**, **htmRenderRemoteBasketCheckoutForm**, **htmRenderRemoteBasketSubmitForm**, **InitializeRemoteBasket**, **RenderOCISubmitFormContent**, **RenderPunchoutSubmitFormContent**, **RenderRBCheckoutErrMesg**, **RenderRemoteBasketFormContent**, **SignOffRemoteBasketSession**, and **ZeroPrefix**.

With sufficient design planning, suppliers may find many of the routines in this file to be useful for Web sites other than the AFS Solution Site.

include\std_xml_lib.asp (new)

This page contains routines used for XML manipulation within AFS.

This new page includes the routines **GetRootBodyPartFromMIME**, **ParseRequestForm**, **SafeGetAttributeText**, **SafeSelectSingleNodeAttributeText**, and **SafeSelectSingleNodeText**.

With sufficient design planning, suppliers may find many of the routines in this file to be useful for Web sites other than the AFS Solution Site.

By William J. Harding

Using Web Services to Transfer Files

Scenario

As previously stated, one of the most common problems businesses are trying to solve is how to transfer data to other businesses reliably and securely over the Internet. The scenarios that require a business to send data and information to another business are almost endless. They include:

- Large companies that need to exchange data and information with small partners. Small companies usually have access to the Internet via a Web browser and ISP-based e-mail, but not much beyond that. Even though these small business partners are not sophisticated in their use of EAI and business-to-business integration, they still need to exchange data with a larger partner securely and reliably.

- Businesses that usually need to send and receive information in various formats. Some of these include EDI, XML, ASCII, and binary formats.

- Businesses that have the need to send large amounts of data. The ability to send files larger than 1 GB over the Internet reliably may mean the difference between updating a Web-based catalog today, or days from now.

A solution, which we present in this chapter, can do all these things and more.

Solution

In this section we present a sample application that can be used to exchange data between business partners securely, reliably, and with non-repudiation. Also contained in this section are hardware and software requirements for the utility, installation procedures, and implementation configurations. The sample application, which we will name the Web Service File Transfer (WSTF) utility, is available on the companion CD-ROM, in the \Code\Web Service File Transfer folder. The information about installing and using the WSFT is given below.

The features of the WSFT sample application are:

- **WSFT is based on industry standards.** The WSFT uses industry standards for exchanging data. SOAP (Simple Object Access Protocol) is used with HTTP over the Secure Sockets Layer (HTTPS) to ensure secure and reliable data transfer through corporate firewalls.

- **WSFT is built on Microsoft .NET.** WSFT is built entirely with .NET technologies and uses the Web services of .NET.

- **Data chunking.** WSFT breaks large documents and files into smaller units (hence the term "chunking"). These smaller units of data are then transmitted over the Internet in parallel. At the destination, the segments are re-assembled in proper order to recreate the document or file.

- **Data flow control.** A receiving partner may not be able to receive data as fast as a sending partner can send it. WSFT allows the receiving partner to tell the sending partner what the maximum transfer rate should be. WSFT will then automatically adjust the data transmission rate to ensure the maximum rate is never exceeded. In addition, WSFT will automatically detect network congestion and slow the data transmission rate accordingly. When the congestion is cleared, it will automatically speed up data transmission again.

- **Restart transmission.** When transmitted over the Internet, the more the document's size increases, the greater the chance of an interruption in the transmission. WSFT has the ability to restart the transmission at the point where the interruption occurred, rather than starting from the beginning again.

- **Secure transmission.** WSFT can provide secure and reliable transmissions by requiring authentication and authorization. Authentication is enforced by the use of user identification and password, and a digital signature. WSFT also has the ability to determine user authorization. By supporting digital signatures, WSFT can also support document non-repudiation.

  Data confidentiality can be ensured by data encryption. Data encryption can be accomplished by using data keys between the two trading partners or by using the HTTPS protocol.

- **Scalability.** WSFT can support a varied system range from very small installations that use a single processor computer to very large installations that use clusters of multi-processors systems. WSFT is designed to receive message segments by different processes on different machines simultaneously.

- **Performance.** Initial tests have shown that WSFT is able to maintain a constant data transmission and receive rate regardless of the size of the document.

Tools and Technologies

This section describes the hardware and software requirements for using Web Service File Transfer utility.

Hardware and Software Requirements

The Web Service File Transfer utility requires the following hardware and software.

- A computer capable of running Windows 2000 Server or Windows .NET Server.

- Windows 2000 Server or Windows .NET Server.

- The.NET Framework Redistributable. This is available on the companion CD or on the Web at:
  http://msdn.microsoft.com/downloads/default.asp?URL=/downloads/sample.asp?url=/MSDN-FILES/027/001/829/msdncompositedoc.xml

- Microsoft Data Access Component 2.7. This is available at on the companion CD or on the Web: http://www.microsoft.com/data/download.htm#27RTMinfo

- A Local Area Network and/or Internet connection.

    Note Although the .NET Framework is all that is required for this sample application, the entire .NET Framework SDK is also available on the companion CD.

Install the Web Service File Transfer Utility

The Web Service File Transfer utility is located on the companion CD-ROM in the Web Service File Transfer folder.

To install the Web Service File Transfer utility

1. Install all prerequisite software as described in the "Hardware and Software Requirements" section.

2. Make sure that **IIS Admin Service** and the **World Wide Web Publishing Service** are started.

3. Insert the companion CD into your CD-ROM drive.

4. The Autorun screen should appear. Select **Install Samples**.

5. This will place all the samples on your hard drive in a folder called **.NET Server Solutions for the Enterprise**.

6. Navigate to the **.NET Server Solutions for the Enterprise** folder, and then to the **Web Service File Transfer** folder.

7. Run **Setup.exe** to install the utility on your hard drive.

8. Setup creates a virtual folder in your Web server folder. By default, this is located at:

%systemdrive%\Inetpub\wwwroot\WSFT

9. Setup also creates a folder in **Start**, **Programs**, called **Web Server File Transfer** and the program **Send File Lite**.

For demonstration purposes of the WSFT sample application, two computers must be installed and configured with IIS and the WSFT utility. This enables both computers to act as clients and servers to each other. A WSFT client "uploading" a file to a WSFT server running the WSFT Web service accomplishes file transfer.

Implementation

This section describes the operation of the WSFT utility and how to configure and use it.

Operational Overview

The illustration below shows the basic file transfer process.

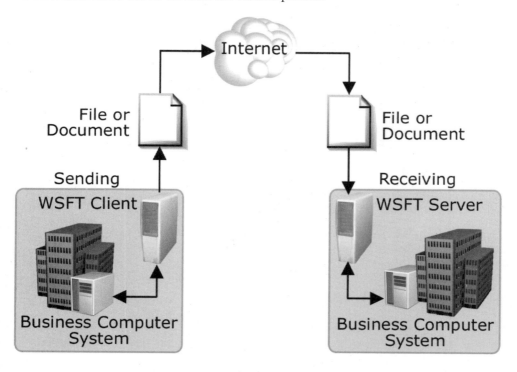

Sending files over the Internet using the WSFT utility

The basic concept of the WSFT utility is to "upload" a file to a receiving Web service. To describe the process in more detail, we start with the sending organization configuring a computer with access to the Internet and the World Wide Web. This computer becomes the WSFT Client. (To keep this illustration as simple as possible, no firewalls are shown.) The WSFT utility is installed and two parameters in the Send File Lite program are configured:

- A file path on the sending (client) side from which the WSFT utility will retrieve the file to be sent.

- An URL to the Web service on the receiving computer.

The receiving organization configures a computer as a Web server also with a connection to the Internet. The WSFT utility is installed and configured as the WSFT Web service to accept files sent to it by a WSFT Client.

This illustration shows a simple file transfer. The utility works just as well between any WSFT client and WSFT Web service on an intranet. As stated above, the WSFT utility uses industry standard SOAP and HTTP protocols resulting in secure and reliable file and data transfer through corporate firewalls.

The next sections will configure the WSFT utility on both the sending (WSFT client) and receiving (WSFT Web service) sides.

Configuring the Sending WSFT Utility

There are two configurable parameters in the WSFT utility on the sending side. They are:

- The location of the file to be sent.

- The URL or Internet address of the receiving WSFT Web service.

To configure the Send File Lite program

1. Go to **Start,** then **Programs**, then **Web Server File Transfer**, and then **Send File Lite**.

   The following screen appears.

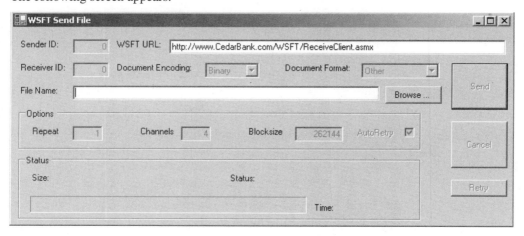

2. The **WSFT URL** field shows the location of the Web service on the receiving system. This should already be configured if the WSFT utility (and Web services) is installed on the same computer running Internet Information Server (IIS). If the WSFT utility were installed on a different computer, this parameter would need to be modified to show the computer where the WSFT Web service files are installed.

3. The **File Name:** entry is the path and name of the file to be sent. You can click **Browse**, and then navigate to the folder and file structure for the file you want to send.

Configuring the Receiving WSFT Web Service

The Web service filename is ReceiveClient.asmx, and is located in the %systemdrive%:\\Inetpub\wwwroot\WSFT folder if you installed the WSFT utility in the default location as described in the install section above. This is the Web service that accepts the file transfer from the WSFT client. This is also the location specified in the Send File Lite program by the **WSFT URL:** field.

> **Note** See step three in the **To configure the Send File Lite program** procedure above.

The WSFT Web service receives the file transfer and places it into a folder on the receiving system. This location is configurable and is a parameter in the Web.config file.

The Web.config file is an XML file located in the %systemdrive%:\\Inetpub\wwwroot\WSFT folder. It can be opened and edited using any text editor such as Notepad.

To configure where the received file will be stored, open the Web.config file and find the `<appSettings></appSettings>` tags. The appearance will be similar to the following:

```
<appSettings>
    <add key="Directory" value="C:\WSFTData\"></add>
    <add key="Extension" value=".txt"></add>
</appSettings>
```

The first line (`<add key="Directory" value="C:\WSFTData\"></add>`) is the directory or folder where the received files will be placed. This folder will be created the first time a file is received.

The second line (`<add key="Extension" value=".txt"></add>`) adds the file name extension ".txt" to every file transferred regardless of the type or format of the file. In addition, the filename is changed to a GUID (Globally Unique Identifier) numeric value.

To send a file

1. Go to **Start,** then **Programs**, then **Web Server File Transfer**, and then **Send File Lite**.

2. Click **Browse** in the **File name:** field, and select the file you want to send.

3. Click **Send**.

4. The file will be sent to the receiving computer and placed in the folder designated by the `<appSettings>` parameters of the Web.config file.

Summary

Web Service File Transfer (WSFT) is a feature-rich sample application that can be used to exchange data between business partners securely, reliably, and with non-repudiation. WSFT features include:

- WSFT is based on industry standards using SOAP with HTTP for data transfer.

- WSFT is built on Microsoft .NET and uses the Web services of .NET.

- Data chunking for easier transmission.

- Data flow control to set a maximum transfer rate.

- Restart transmission to restart the transmission at the point where interruption occurred.

- Secure transmission by requiring authentication and authorization.

- Scalability from small installations through multi-processor systems.

- Performance regardless of document size.

The universal business challenge of transferring data to other businesses reliably and securely over the Internet is met and resolved by the Web Service File Transfer (WSFT) utility.

PART FOUR

Business-to-Consumer Integration

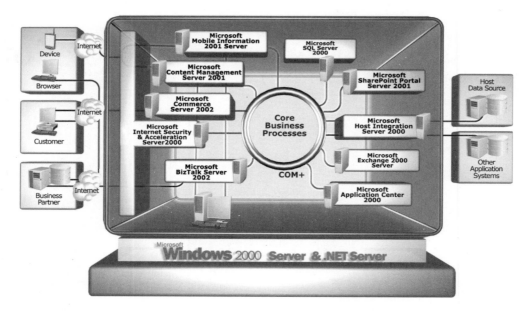

.NET Enterprise Servers

By Jim Christensen

Reaching Consumers Using the Web

On the Internet, before business-to-business (B2B) came business-to-consumer (B2C). Most of the first B2C Web sites provided information for consumers. These Web sites used linked pages of static information, but they were fascinating and even revolutionary because they delivered multi-media information, consisting of text, graphics, sounds, video, and so on. Perhaps even more important, the technology used to build these Web sites, HTML, was relatively easy to learn, enabling many people to enter the high tech industry with little or no formal training.

Before long B2C Web sites became more interactive, allowing users to enter information as well as click links. User interaction combined with security enabled electronic commerce to grow rapidly. Most of us have by now made numerous purchases through Web sites.

From the beginning, building an e-commerce Web site required much more complex technology than building a static HTML Web site of the type seen in the early days of the Web. Maintaining and presenting catalog data, creating the perception of sessions that shopping baskets require using an inherently stateless technology, securely taking orders, and so on, are difficult programming tasks. Programmers and site designers faced a daunting challenge when they attempted to build e-commerce Web sites from scratch and make them perform near flawlessly. Nevertheless, that is exactly what the companies and programmers who pioneered electronic commerce did.

Meanwhile, presenting information over the Web gradually became more challenging. Competition for viewers and customers drove Web sites to more compelling and interesting designs. While the value of an e-commerce Web site can be judged according to the number of products sold and the corresponding revenue, information Web sites tend to compete in terms of site visits (hit count). Companies track the number of people who visit the Web site every day or month, how long they stay at the site, how many pages they view, etc. In general, the greater the number of hits, the better for business. When Web sites charge for advertising, the greater the number of hits, the more they can charge for the advertisements. Conversely, businesses that pay to maintain a Web site that does not get a sufficient number of hits tend to retrench, pulling their content off of the Web. Web content must be interesting, easy to find, and dynamic; i.e., it must change frequently.

Creating and updating an informational Web site gets exponentially more difficult as the site grows in size. Growing a Web site requires more people to coordinate, more content to create, approve, and organize, more links to keep from breaking, more old content to remove or archive, and less time in which to do it. To meet these challenges, successful Web site designers built the required infrastructure themselves, dividing the different types of tasks between specialists.

To date, much of the vast amount of effort expended to build Web sites for dispensing information and selling products over the Web reflects independent efforts to build the same essential functionality over and over. By far, most e-commerce Web sites were built using this approach. Naturally, companies, such as Microsoft, viewed this state of affairs as a business opportunity. In the software business, as in many businesses, whenever the same effort is being duplicated over and over again, it is time to build (and sell) a common infrastructure. Microsoft has been at it for several years now, and some of the products in this space have had several versions released.

The two products that address e-commerce and information Web sites are Microsoft Commerce Server and Microsoft Content Management Server. These servers are the main focus of this section of the book. The remainder of this chapter briefly introduces these two products and reveals their approaches to solving their respective problems. The next two chapters delve deeper into the challenges of building Web sites and managing content, using these two products from Microsoft.

Microsoft Commerce Server

Microsoft Commerce Server provides an infrastructure for building e-commerce Web sites. Underlying this infrastructure, a set of inter-related SQL Server database tables have been defined using a schema that captures the needs of an e-commerce Web site. For example, there are database tables that store product information, and others that store information about the transactions that have been conducted. Other tables store information about online advertising campaigns and product specials that are currently being offered to draw additional business. Additionally, another set of database tables, known as the Data Warehouse, makes it easy to archive and analyze historical data.

Accessing and updating database tables directly, using SQL Server user interfaces or programming interfaces is possible, but unwieldy. The problem with using such interfaces directly is that the data exists as isolated bits and pieces, rather than a representation of information that is conceptually familiar to the business people who are working with it. Commerce Server solves this problem with its other fundamental characteristic: a set of user interfaces and programming interfaces designed specifically to access and manipulate the underlying data in terms that correspond to the concepts and processes of the business, not just e-commerce, but commerce in general.

The set of Commerce Server programming objects represents the first layer of functionality above the raw data. These objects provide access to the data in a controlled fashion that presents logical groups of data together, regardless of how they are stored in the database tables. These programming objects also serve to protect the data, ensuring that the data remains internally consistent when updated by users. A small set of catalog objects store information about the set of products or services that the Web site will offer for sale. There are objects used for storing information about users, called the profile objects. In total, there are several dozen objects that are used to represent the various types of information involved with selling products to customers. The latest version of Commerce Server, Commerce Server 2002, also includes versions of the Commerce Server objects that have been enhanced to work properly in the Microsoft.NET environment.

The Commerce Server objects are used by two different types of clients. One type of client is provided ready-to-use and consists of several different user applications that Commerce Server provides. These user applications extend the Commerce Server objects to convey the needs of the business user into the underlying data. The Commerce Server user applications include Commerce Server Business Desk, Commerce Server Manager, and the Site Packager. The other type of client used by Commerce Server objects consists of the retail Web sites that Commerce Server makes possible.

Commerce Server provides several sophisticated sample Web sites that serve as a reasonable starting point for the development of many Web sites. Other sites might have requirements better served by a different design that must be written from scratch. All of these Web sites use Commerce Server objects to retrieve the data that, when formatted and displayed, constitutes much of the Web site content. Commerc Server's design recognizes that different Web sites need to use different sets of Commerce Server objects, each according to its needs.

Microsoft Content Management Server

Microsoft Content Management Server provides an infrastructure for building Web sites characterized by particularly well-managed content. By this time in the history of the Web, most us have experienced the opposite on many occasions. Who among the readers of this chapter have never clicked a link and received the classic "page not found" error. Indeed, it has happened, and continues to happen, frequently enough that a great many nontechnical people are now familiar with the completely internal error code associated with such failures: 404.

Some of the common problems viewers see on Web sites include out-of-date content, poorly edited content, and content presented inconsistently from page to page. While many of these types of Web site flaws are not critical, they do convey that a Web site was not constructed professionally. While it is clearly difficult to characterize how a tendency toward such mistakes would reflect on a business's bottom line, it does seem safe to assume that it can not possibly help.

How does poorly managed Web site content arise? Once found, broken links are very easy to fix. Most text editing programs include spell checkers, and some even help with proper syntax. It is not difficult to devise a standard layout for pages and tell people to use it. Basically, the problem seems to arise from the high volume of content and rapid rate of change that so many contemporary Web sites experience. Often there are many people changing the content, making it difficult to maintain consistency. Other times, only a few people are assigned to make more changes than they can reasonable make without introducing errors.

Content Management Server addresses these problems through a well architected design. One of the fundamental concepts Content Management Server employs involves the concept of page templates. A page template comprises a basic page that contains a set of common elements that will be exactly the same on all pages based on the template. For those page elements that need to be different from page to page, the elements that make the pages unique, the page template contains "placeholders." There are different kinds of placeholders, which reserve space on the page of a particular type of content. Some placeholders are defined to reserve space for an image, others reserve space for text, and so on.

Content Management Server accommodates people with different skills working together to create a Web site. When someone authors content using Content Management Server, after they have chosen an appropriate template and replaced its placeholders with real content, after they have saved their changes and finished creating the page, the page is automatically submitted to a designated editor who can review the page and either accept it or reject it.

Differentiating user roles is a central theme in Content Management Server, allowing the process of Web site creation to be optimized in a number of different ways that correspond to designing your content in a professional manner. The workflow process, which allows you to submit all new and updated pages automatically to editors for approval, represents one such feature.

A Common Theme: Keeping Separate Jobs Separate

The teams that developed Commerce Server and Content Management Server share the insight that the creation of an enterprise-level Web site, whether focused on e-commerce or on providing information or both, is the result of people with many different skill sets working together effectively. Depending on the context, working together effectively can mean different things. In some contexts, people with different skills need to perform their respective functions, one after the other. In other contexts, people making business decisions need to be able to directly implement those decisions without needlessly relying on technical people to help them.

Commerce Server achieves these objectives by creating different user applications that are each focused on different categories of users. Commerce Server Manager and Site Packager are the tools used by site administrators to manage and deploy Web sites based on Commerce Server. The Commerce Server Business Desk application, intended for use by business managers, allows these business managers to make decisions and put those decisions into effect without relying on site developers to help implement them.

One of the first tasks involved in setting up a Content Management Server installation is assigning the people involved in the effort into different roles. In a typical scenario, the largest group of people will be content authors. Fewer people, presumably with specialized training, will be assigned to the role of editor. Other more technical roles include resource manager, template designer, site programmer, and site administrator. In addition, within a particular role, different people can be assigned responsibility for particular areas of the Web site, and restricted from performing any tasks in other areas. The final piece of the puzzle is the built-in workflow, that will automatically "route" a page from a person in one role to someone in another role, allowing the construction of a page to proceed in a logical order from start to finish.

The next two chapters provide a closer examination of these two B2C products from Microsoft, including how each of them recognizes and accounts for the different roles played by the various people who contribute to the creation and maintenance of enterprise-level Web sites.

By Jim Christensen

Setting Up a Retail Storefront

When the time is right for you to begin selling over the Internet, there are some basic questions you must ask yourself to determine the best way to proceed. If your company is small, or the number of products you sell is small, you should consider a hosted solution such as Microsoft bCentral™ (www.bcentral.com). bCentral provides a complete, hosted Internet solution for small business for a modest monthly or annual fee.

At the other extreme, if you plan to build and operate a serious enterprise-level retail Web site, chances are you want to have the freedom to customize the site to your particular requirements and maintain the control offered by hosting the site in your own data center.

You can hire e-commerce experts to build the site for you, or perhaps you have in-house staff who possess the necessary skills to build such a site. Regardless of who you employ to build the site, starting retail Web site development from scratch makes much less sense today than it did just a few years ago. This chapter explains how Microsoft Commerce Server can be used to significantly reduce the amount of work and risk involved in creating an enterprise-level retail Web site by first taking a careful look at the business problem to be solved from various perspectives, and then by discussing how Commerce Server addresses these problems. The chapter is divided into the following four sections:

- **Scenario**. This section describes the business problem to be solved with respect to enterprise-level retail Web sites.

- **Solution**. This section describes how Microsoft Commerce Server can be used to solve this business problem.

- **Tools and Technology**. This section focuses on the various tools and technologies that can be brought to bear on the business problem.

- **Implementation**. This section drills deeper into select portions of the implementation of the proposed solution, aiming to give the reader a sense of the level of technical expertise required to implement the solution.

This chapter begins with a high-level discussion of the business problem and Microsoft's solution to it, and eventually delves into some coding examples in the Implementation Section, thus, some readers will not want to read to the very end.

Scenario

In order to maximize the chances of success, an enterprise-level retail Web site should be functional, convenient, and smart. The notion of a "functional" Web site covers several aspects of its operation. First, the Web site must possess the basic functionality that qualifies it as a retail Web site: presenting products (or services) for sale, and taking orders for those products. A functional Web site is also available close to 100 percent of the time, runs without encountering errors, and has good response times.

Retail Web sites can be convenient, or not, from several different perspectives. First, and arguably most important, is the customer perspective. Customers must be able to easily find the products of interest, manage their shopping carts, and check out when ready. Another important perspective from which convenience, or ease-of-use, is important concerns the day-to-day maintenance of the Web site. One of the defining features of a Web site is its dynamic nature, and the people tasked with keeping a Web site up-to-date can easily be overwhelmed. The original creation and occasional re-design of Web sites can also be an enormous task for Web site developers, who can benefit from ease-of-use features.

A retail Web site can be "smart" in a number of different ways. There is the artistic, or fashion, sense of smart, wherein the Web site is visually appealing and catchy. Smart can also mean clever. A Web site can be made clever in a number of ways that can enhance the success of the Web site. For example, a Web site can be designed so that it "remembers" a shopper from a prior visit, and learns something about that shopper's tastes. Also, specific advertisements can be shown so as to maximize the likelihood of appealing to the shopper viewing the ad.

In order to thoroughly understand the functionality that a successful retail Web site should strive to provide, let us consider the different experiences that are important to provide to the people in various roles related to the Web site: the shopper, the business manager, the Web site administrator, and the Web site developer.

The Shopper Perspective

Retail Web sites have been around long enough that most of us have a pretty good sense of what we expect as shoppers. Some features are found on virtually every retail Web site, but the elegance of the design varies. Other features are less common, and tend to vary from site to site. These features, broadly defined, are as follows:

- **Navigation**. We expect to be able to browse around the site without having to tell the site who we are. There needs to be an obvious paradigm for moving around the site. Perhaps the most common paradigm involves a navigation pane on the left and a content pane on the right. Sometimes, there is a standardized navigation bar along the top of each page as well. Common activities, such as looking for contact information, what's new, FAQs, or help, should be very uncomplicated to find.

- **Product catalogs**. While browsing, we expect to be able to view products by choosing a category of products, and then perhaps subsequent sub-categories. Sometimes there are products that are naturally related to each other, such as a camera and various accessories for that camera. We expect the accessories to be effortless to find.

  We also expect to be able to search for products using key words or phrases related to the product. Refining the search within a set of search results is also fairly common.

  The information available for particular products should be comprehensive. What is perceived as comprehensive is likely to vary based on the type of product. Almost always the information includes the name of the product, the manufacturer, and the price. Pictures of products are important because Web sites are inherently a visual medium. For hi-tech products, technical specifications should be available. When appropriate, the mechanisms for choosing different sizes and colors of a given product should be uncomplicated and intuitive.

- **Shopping baskets/carts**. We expect to be able to collect our choices in an online shopping basket, and to be able to view and modify the contents of the basket in an intuitive manner. As we find products we want to purchase, we need an trouble-free and obvious way to put them in the basket – the online equivalent of taking a product off the shelf and putting it in a shopping cart – and then continue shopping. We expect to be able to postpone the purchase of the products in the basket, and within reason, to find those products still waiting in our basket when we return at a later time. In a physical store, our ability to postpone the purchase might include running out to the car to retrieve a wallet, but in the online world, longer, but not indefinite, postponement should be possible.

- **Completing the purchase**. If we decide to purchase the products in our basket, we expect the checkout process to be as quick and painless as possible. Some like it when a Web site offers to save personal information, including our credit card information, so that future purchases can be streamlined. It is important that we retain the right to not have that information saved. This is especially true of the credit card information.

  During the checkout process, it is important for the Web site to clearly present the forms into which we enter our information. The best designs often split this entry process over several different pages, and provide pages that offer us a chance to confirm that the information we entered is correct. Associated charges, such as tax, shipping, and handling, must also be summarized clearly, with an obvious way to cancel the transaction in the event that one or more of these charges is not acceptable.

- **Security**. Most shoppers are consciously concerned with security. When entering our credit card information on a Web page, we want to be sure that no unauthorized party can eavesdrop on that exchange. Experienced shoppers may just glance at the URL in the browser's address window to make sure that it begins with "https." Less technically knowledgeable shoppers need to be able to find a plain language assurance of the security measures being employed.

When logging into a Web site, shoppers also expect to be asked to provide a password that assures that the personal information that they provide and which is stored by the Web site is accessible only to them. They expect to be able to change the password whenever they want, and also expect some easy-to-use mechanism for helping them remember passwords that they have forgotten. Reminder phrases created by the shopper, stored by the Web site, and which are retrievable on command by the shopper are a typical way in which password reminders are commonly provided.

Occasionally, articles appear in the press about the credit card numbers stored on a Web site being stolen. In the worst cases, all the thieves need to do is enter the correct URL. Obviously, this frightens shoppers and is not good for Internet commerce. Besides the need to take measures against such security risks, retail Web sites should allow shoppers to choose whether or not the Web site stores the shopper's credit card information in between visits to the site.

There are companies that specialize in the credit card transaction portion of an online purchase, sometimes called payment gateways. The credit card information is provided to, and verified by the gateway, allowing the Web site itself to avoid the hazards associated with accepting and/or storing shoppers' credit card numbers.

If it is determined that the advantages of storing credit card numbers, such as making the shopping experience more convenient, is worth the associated risks, there are ways to let companies that specialize in the appropriate levels of security bear this burden. Electronic wallet services, such as the Microsoft Express Purchase service associated with Microsoft Passport, can be used to store shoppers' information, including sensitive data like credit card numbers. During the purchase process, the retail Web site contacts the wallet service to retrieve the credit card information on behalf of the shopper, freeing the shopper from the need to enter their credit card information for every purchase. Clearly, companies that focus on providing wallet services can dedicate more resources to securing their systems from electronic (and physical) intrusion.

- **Recommendations**. Although much less common, some shoppers come to expect help in making selections. Predictive functionality can be used to make "other people who bought X also bought Y" recommendations. Accessories can be promoted when their associated product is purchased. Fancier models with bigger price tags can be suggested. Smarter searching algorithms can be devised to make recommendations based on less specific criteria. Advertisements and other types of recommendations can be targeted to an individual shopper if enough information can be learned about the likely habits and buying patterns of that shopper (indeed, "targeting" is a common buzz word in the realm of retail Web sites). On the other hand, too much of this proactive selling can annoy shoppers and discourage them from visiting the Web site again.

- **Improvements**. In general, shoppers may expect the retail Web site to be improved over time. Several possible mechanisms exist through which such improvements can be devised. One is a straightforward way for shoppers to provide their suggestions explicitly, and many sites do include links to a feedback page. More sophisticated mechanisms involve an analysis of the ways in which shoppers are using the Web site, without any direct involvement on their part other than just using the Web site in the course of shopping. Such mechanisms require that individual shoppers be tracked as they move from page to page, so that later analysis can revel trends and from which optimizations can be surmised and implemented.

- **Privacy**. Most shoppers are very concerned with privacy. They want to know that any personal information they supply to a Web site is treated as private, and properly protected. It is increasingly common for Web sites to claim strict privacy policies, and prominently post those policies on the Web site. Some shoppers want to know what information is maintained about them, and exactly who has access to that information. There can also be legal issues associated with a retail Web site failing to protect, or intentionally revealing or selling, private information.

- **Different languages and currency**. Increasingly, we expect to be able to view the site in a number of different languages, at least in a few of the more common languages. Related to this, we expect to see the products priced using our normal currency, and in some cases, in more than one currency (for example, Euros and French francs).

- **Miscellaneous features**. There are a multitude of more esoteric features. Some retail Web sites offer auctions, the ability to post reviews of products, or purchase and spend gift certificates. Such new features continue to emerge over time.

The Shopkeeper Perspective

Although the term "shopkeeper" is a bit old-fashioned to apply to retail Web sites, it is used here to capture the variety of different perspectives held by those people tasked with building, maintaining, running, and updating a retail Web site. For the purposes of this discussion, there are three distinct roles associated with a retail Web site:

- **Business Managers**. Business managers are the decision makers for retail Web sites. They decide when a product is going to be sold for a reduced price, or that a new product is going to be offered. They decide when a "free shipping" promotion is going to begin and end. They negotiate ad campaigns with advertisers, and are responsible for making sure that the ads appear on the Web site as called for in the negotiated contracts.

- **Site Administrators**. Site administrators represent a broad category of people that are tasked with keeping the site up and running from day to day. This includes the database administrators who are responsible for maintaining the databases that support the Web site, as well as the system administrators who are responsible for maintaining the servers upon which the Web servers and database servers are running.

- **Site Developers**. Site developers are responsible for creating the Web pages that constitute the retail Web site, and for designing and creating the databases that are used to store the Web site data. Most Web pages in a typical retail Web site do not just contain static HTML. Because much of the data that is presented on the Web pages is actually stored in the associated databases, code in the page must retrieve that data and format it using HTML.

Although there are other roles that can be recognized as unique with respect to retail Web sites, such as suppliers, fulfillment and accounting specialists, and so on, the remainder of this section focuses on the roles identified above. The various expectations of the people in these three roles, at least with respect to the tools and methods available to them for performing their respective tasks related to a retail Web site, are described in separate sub-sections below.

The Business Manager Perspective

Most of the actual unique data on Web pages, such as product prices and descriptions, is stored in databases as different bits of information, and then retrieved and assembled dynamically to create the Web pages viewed by shoppers. Typically, business managers do not access and modify the data stored in those databases directly using the tools supplied with the databases. For the business manager to do so would involve knowing what database tables to modify, and more specifically, which columns within those tables to modify.

One common alternative is for business managers to delegate the technical details of the modifications to site administrators who possess the requisite technical abilities. Another alternative is to create more sophisticated tools. At one level of sophistication, such tools can make the tasks of the site administrators more straightforward and less prone to error. Taken further, such tools can become user-friendly enough for the business managers themselves to modify the relevant data directly. Many business managers see such direct access to the Web site data as a big improvement over having to communicate their decisions to someone else, and then verifying that the changes have been correctly made.

Another important way in which business managers interact with their Web sites has to do with analyzing the activity on the Web site. It is very important for business managers to be able to generate reports, such as sales reports at varying levels of detail. More sophisticated reports can track how users navigate the Web site, or perhaps, fail to navigate the Web site. Such data can be invaluable when considering improvements to the site.

Some Web sites are designed so that different sets of shoppers, or other users, are allowed to access specific subsets of the site. This is an aspect of security that is not directly important to any given user, who may not even know that they are not getting to see the entire Web site. But to the various types of shopkeepers, who have a larger view of the Web site, this type of security is directly important. Business managers are bound to play a role in defining how the Web site is divided in this way, even though they may themselves be limited from accessing the entire site.

The Site Administrator Perspective

If the Web site lacks high-level tools that allow business managers to directly access and modify Web site data, they may call upon the site administrators or site developers to help implement the required changes.

Site administrators are typically tasked with the following types of duties:

- Backup and restore
- Disaster recovery plans
- Hardware replacements and upgrades
- Software installation
- Performance monitoring and tuning
- Security administration and monitoring

Although site administrators are generally accustomed to achieving complex results in these areas with primitive tools, asking them to do so is costly and prone to error. Wherever possible, the best Web site software packages help to automate and simplify the routine tasks in the domain of administrators. This allows fewer site administrators to more successfully manage and grow large-scale retail Web sites.

The Site Developer Perspective

Site developers systematically build whatever infrastructure is requisite to support the functionality required for the retail Web site they are developing. Using good programming principles, they strive for code modularity and re-use. They strive to create a Web site that retains as much flexibility for future modifications as is practical. Where necessary and practical, they develop tools for their own use, the use of Web site administrators, and business managers, although these needs are usually secondary to the creation of the Web site itself.

The vast majority of existing retail Web sites have been created from scratch. When these development efforts began, the e-commerce software packages that are now available were either still under development, or their early versions lacked sufficient functionality to prompt wide adoption. This means that thousands of developers have been duplicating effort over the past several years, building and re-building retail Web site infrastructure that performs essentially the same functions.

Most developers would prefer to use existing, proven infrastructure, and free themselves to work on the functionality that can truly distinguish one retail Web site from another.

Scenario Summary

To be competitive, an enterprise-level retail Web site should be functional, convenient, and smart. Developing such a Web site from scratch, which has been done time and time again, is a huge challenge, and is no longer necessary. Microsoft's current answer to this problem is Microsoft Commerce Server 2000, and will soon be replaced by the even more powerful Microsoft Commerce Server 2002. These products provide a complete infrastructure that can be used to implement a functional, convenient, and smart retail Web site much more quickly than would otherwise be possible. The next section, Conceptual Solution, describes how Commerce Server can satisfy these requirements with a minimum of development effort on your part.

Solution

At the time of this writing in early 2002, Microsoft Commerce Server 2000 has been on the market for over a year, providing an answer to the question of how to quickly build an enterprise-level retail Web site that is functional, convenient, and smart. The follow-up product, Microsoft Commerce Server 2002, due to be released about the time that this book is scheduled to reach store shelves, extends the functionality provided by the earlier version, brings Commerce Server into the world of .NET, and includes even more extensive use of XML. This chapter explains how Commerce Server can be used to satisfy the requirements for, and expectations of retail Web sites from the various perspectives identified in the previous section.

Commerce Server plays the central role in Microsoft's solution for retail Web site creation. Microsoft Windows 2000 and Microsoft SQL Server 2000, as the operating system and database platforms, play important supporting roles respectively, upon which Commerce Server runs.

When using Commerce Server to build a retail Web site, and after you have installed Commerce Server and the associated software upon which it depends, you have several alternatives for how to begin:

- If there isn't a functional, Active Server Page-based (ASP-based) Web site already in existence, and which is going to continue to be used, Web site development can begin with one of the Commerce Server Solution Sites. About the same time that Commerce Server 2000 became available, Microsoft made the Retail and Supplier Solution Sites available for free download (these Solution Sites are available on the Commerce Server 2002 CD). These two Web sites are different configurations of a single code base that can serve as a starting point for developing retail and wholesale Web sites, respectively. They comprise a set of hundreds of ASP routines and the associated infrastructure that, once properly understood, allow customization to be done in a logical, maintainable, and extensible manner.

- The International Retail Site is another type of Solution Site that is supplied in the Software Development Kit (SDK) of Commerce Server 2002, and provides another possible starting point for retail Web site development. It is based on ASP.NET, provides much of its functionality in the form of ASP.NET classes, and uses the managed code version of the Commerce Server objects.

- If the architecture of these various Commerce Server Solution Sites does not meet the needs of a particular retail Web site development effort, Web site development can be started from scratch. An entirely different architecture can be designed and implemented, making use of the Commerce Server COM objects in much the same way that the Solution Sites do. Indeed, the Solution Sites might still serve as a good source of examples for how these objects are intended to be used.

- In those circumstances where there is already an existing, functional, ASP-based Web site in use that is not yet using Commerce Server functionality, it is possible to evolve that Web site into a Commerce Server Web site. Existing areas of functionality can be retrofitted to use the equivalent Commerce Server functionality, either in one large conversion effort, or piecemeal over time. Depending on the existing code base, this is more or less difficult.

Depending on deployment and integration decisions, other Microsoft server products besides Commerce Server, SQL Server, and Windows may have roles to play:

- Microsoft BizTalk Server 2002 can be used to help integrate with business partners and existing enterprise applications. For more information about using Commerce Server in conjunction with business-to-business (B2B) interactions, see Chapter 12 on supplier enablement.

- Microsoft Internet Security and Acceleration Server 2000 (ISA) can be used to provide the firewalls required for proper security.

- Microsoft Application Center Server 2000 can be used to help manage Commerce Server deployments that involve multiple Web servers running in a Web farm.

- Microsoft Content Management Server 2001 can be integrated with Commerce Server to create retail Web sites that incorporate content that is richer and more manageable than that found in most retail Web sites. For more information about integrating Commerce Server and Content Management Server, see Chapter 16 about managing Web content and Content Management Server.

Microsoft Commerce Server Overview

Microsoft Commerce Server can be conceptually divided into three distinct types of functionality, as shown in the following figure:

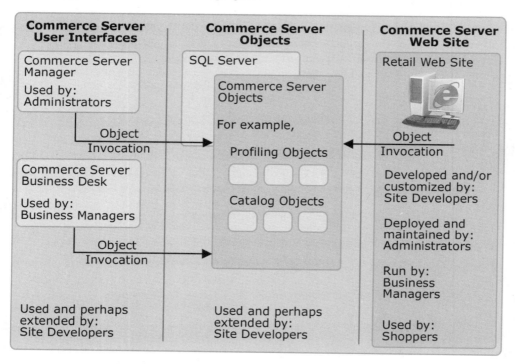

Conceptual division of Commerce Server functionality

The following sections discuss each of these major areas: Commerce Server user interfaces, Commerce Server Web sites, and Commerce Server objects.

Commerce Server User Interfaces

The Commerce Server user interfaces, on the left side of the preceding figure, make it easier for the people who build and manage Commerce Server Web sites to do their jobs. The Commerce Server Manager is a Microsoft Management Console (MMC) snap-in, and provides a user interface for Web site administrators. From this interface, site administrators can manage and configure Commerce Server resources, sites, applications, and Web servers.

When launched to host the Commerce Server Manager, the MMC also hosts several other MMC snap-ins that are useful for Commerce Server administrators, including:

- SQL Enterprise Manager snap-in for managing Commerce Server databases, including the Data Warehouse

- Internet Information Services (IIS) snap-in for managing Web servers

- Windows 2000 Active Directory Users and Computers snap-in for managing Windows 2000 user accounts, computer accounts, and security and distribution groups

The following figure shows the Commerce Server Manager MMC application, with the Profiles global resource node expanded.

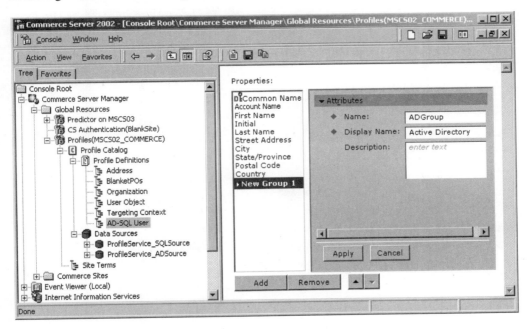

Commerce Server Manager

Commerce Server Business Desk, a Web application, is the other type of Commerce Server user interface. The Business Desk provides a user interface for business managers to perform Web site management. Using this interface, business managers can change the data that drives the Web site, without having to involve an administrator or site developer. For example, if a business manager decides to lower the price of slow-selling product, he or she can be the one to make the change.

The functionality available using Commerce Server Business Desk is presented in the form of different functional modules, grouped into logical categories. For example, the Catalogs category contains the Catalog Definition Designer, Catalog Editor, and Catalog Sets modules; the Orders category contains the Basket Manager, Data Codes, Order Status, Shipping Methods, Tax Rates, and Publish Transactions modules. The following figure shows the Commerce Server Business Desk application, with the Order Status Codes module selected. Callouts show the various parts of the Business Desk screen.

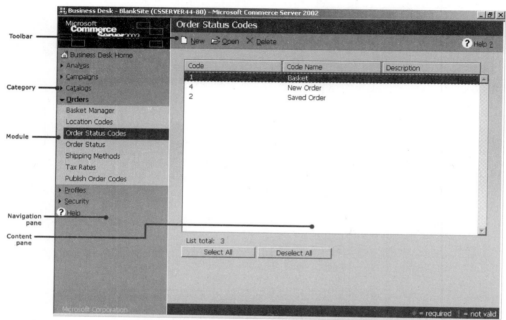

Commerce Server Business Desk

Different Commerce Server user interfaces are of interest to people in the different roles that constitute the shopkeepers. Commerce Server was designed so that business managers can perform their tasks in Commerce Server Business Desk, while site administrators can be more focused on the activities performed in Commerce Server Manager. Site developers, due to the nature of their role, spend some time using both of these interfaces, especially during the initial development of the retail Web site. Site developers may also extend these interfaces to provide additional functionality to site administrators and business managers. Note that some of the skills required in extending these interfaces, and particularly Commerce Server Manager, may exceed the scripting skills common in site developers, and require more advanced, compiled language skills normally associated with software engineers.

Commerce Server Web Site

The Commerce Server Web site, on the right side of the figure at the beginning of this overview, is the retail Web site itself. In general, this Web site uses the Active Server Pages (ASP) technology provided by Microsoft Internet Security and Acceleration (IIS) to create a Web site that runs the bulk of its code on the Web server so that there are fewer dependencies on the browser being used.

Building this Web site so that it is functional, convenient, and smart is the ultimate purpose of using Commerce Server in the first place. This Web site might begin from a number of different sources, as follows:

- Commerce Server 2002 .NET Sample Site, found in the product SDK.

- Commerce Server 2000 Retail Solution Site, which is located on the Commerce Server 2002 CD, and can be downloaded from the Commerce Server Web site at http://www.microsoft.com/commerceserver.

- Written from scratch, using Commerce Server functionality, as appropriate. Setting up such an instance of the Commerce Server Business Desk application is actually done by installing something called the blank site. It provides Business Desk and an empty Web page called default.asp.

- An existing Web site modified to incorporate one or more features of Commerce Server.

In any event, this is where the Web site developers are likely to expend the bulk of their efforts, writing ASP script code to implement the Web site.

As the end result and ultimate purpose of Commerce Server, the Commerce Server retail Web site is of interest to all of the relevant participants, both shoppers and the various types of shopkeepers. Shoppers use the site, site developers create the site, site administrators deploy and maintain the site, and business managers run the site.

Commerce Server Objects

The Commerce Server objects, in the center of the figure at the beginning of this overview, constitute the heart of Commerce Server. These objects are what stand between the Web site data that is stored within SQL Server on the one hand, and the various clients of that data in the Commerce Server user interfaces and a Commerce Server Web site on the other. There is almost never a good reason to go directly to the database tables within SQL Server, and indeed, doing so can render your Commerce Server installation inoperative and unsupportable. Note that there are some configurations of Commerce Server that use both SQL Server and the Active Directory (AD) to store profile data.

Commerce Server objects can be logically grouped according to their function. For example, there is a set of objects used to manage catalogs and catalog data, and there are other objects used for managing different types of profiles, such as user profiles and organization profiles. Rather than being the type of object model that starts with a root object from which all other objects are accessed, Commerce Server objects tend to be much more independent, or related to each other in small groups.

Another way in which the Commerce Server objects and their methods can be categorized is as design-time or run-time. In general, the distinction exists at the method level, but there are some objects that contain all design-time, or all run-time, methods. A design-time method is one that is not used from within the retail Web site, but is used from the Commerce Server user interfaces (Commerce Server Manager and Commerce Server Business Desk) to change values in the databases. For example, the method used to change a product property, such as the list price of that product, is the **SetProductProperties** method of the **Product** object. This method is not called from the Retail Solution Site, but is called from the Commerce Server Business Desk.

Run-time methods (and objects), on the other hand, are called from the retail Web site, whether it is based on the Retail Solution Site or otherwise. This is because most data used for constructing the Web pages in such Web sites is displayed, but not available for modification. In other words, it is read-only. Note that this is not true of all interactions on the retail Web site. Products orders are an obvious example of data provided by the shopper through the Web site that is written to tables in a database using Commerce Server objects. Interestingly, run-time methods are also called from the Commerce Server user interfaces, as these interfaces need to retrieve the data for display as well.

The Commerce Server Manager and the Commerce Server Business Desk both invoke various methods of the Commerce Server objects, both design-time and run-time, to perform their tasks. The Commerce Server retail Web site invokes, by definition, only the run-time methods of the Commerce Server objects to retrieve and occasionally update the data it requires to construct its Web pages.

Another broad distinction to be made among Commerce Server objects is that some objects are not related to the Commerce Server Business Process Pipeline System, and other objects are related to that system. With respect to the latter, these objects are either one of the several different pipeline objects themselves, or one of the numerous pipeline components that can be configured to be executed as part of a pipeline.

Generally speaking, a Commerce Server pipeline is a software infrastructure that defines and links one or more stages of a business process, running them in sequence to complete a specific task. Pipelines divide processing into stages, abstractions that describe a category of work. They also determine the sequence in which each category of work is performed. Each stage of a pipeline contains one or more pipeline components (COM objects) that, again, are run in the defined sequence. A pipeline configuration file (.pcf) defines the sequence of components that are run in the different stages of a pipeline.

Because of their nature as part of a programming platform, the Commerce Server objects are usually exclusively the domain of site developers. The various other types of participants: shoppers, administrators, and business managers, all are users of the objects, but they may not realize it. As with extensions to the Commerce Server interfaces, some of the skills required to extend the set of underlying objects that support Web site operations (though arguably not Commerce Server objects per se) may exceed the site developer's scripting abilities, and require more advanced, compiled language skills normally associated with software engineers.

Feature-by-Feature Solution Summary

This section provides a more detailed look at each of the high-level feature areas and discusses how Commerce Server addresses those needs. The following feature areas of retail Web sites are identified as relevant to shoppers:

- Navigation (other than product catalog navigation)
- Product catalogs
- Shopping baskets/carts
- Completing the purchase
- Security
- Recommendations
- Improvements
- Privacy
- Different languages and currencies
- Miscellaneous features

This section discusses each of these feature areas in terms of how Commerce Server supports their implementation with user interfaces, Web sites, and objects. Any remaining features that are not typically apparent from the shopper's perspective are also discussed.

Navigation

Supporting superior navigation features of various types can obviously contribute to the success of a retail Web site. If shoppers can more easily find the products for sale, other information about those products, and shopping on the site in general, more sales are likely to result. Commerce Server provides a variety of features that support building advanced navigation features into a retail Web site. In addition to some generic routines for generating the URLs that are used when constructing links on Web pages, Commerce Server includes a rich catalog management system that plays a central role in defining a complex set of products that are related to each other in a variety of ways. The Commerce Server Product Catalog System is discussed in more detail in the next section.

By the time it is rendered in the shopper's browser, each page on a retail Web site is just a normal HTML Web page with some content, and some links to other pages. It is useful to categorize these links according to the type of support that Commerce Server provides to the Web site developer for creating different types of links.

- **Product navigation**. This navigation category includes finding products using categories, links to related products, and by a couple of different kinds of searching. This type of navigation is discussed separately in the next section about Product Catalogs.

- **Standardized page navigation**. This navigation category includes the vertical and horizontal navigation bars that are common on most Web pages. By having these navigation bars and their standardized links appear uniformly throughout a Web site, shoppers can quickly learn how to navigate to the pages that present the main set of features on the site.

- **Page sequence navigation**. This navigation category includes those pages that occur in a natural sequence. For example, a checkout process might first present a page that asks the shopper to provide their shipping information. The next page might ask the shopper to provide billing and credit card information. Next, a summary page might show all of the information provided on previous pages, and show a total cost including, tax, shipping, and handling charges. These pages are typically linked using a particularly prominent button labeled "Continue" or something similar.

The next three sub-sections discuss the support provided by Commerce Server for Web site navigation in each of the three types of functionality: user interfaces, Web sites, and objects.

User Interface Support for Non-Catalog Navigation

The only support for managing Web site navigation in the Commerce Server user interfaces concerns the virtual directory location of the Web site that is managed within the Commerce Server Manager, and its interaction with the **GetURL** method of the **AuthManager** object. See the section "Object Support for Navigation" for additional information.

Web Site Support for Non-Catalog Navigation

Much of the infrastructure for presenting these different types of navigation to the shopper must be provided in the code associated with the retail Web site itself. A well-coded Web site isolates the code associated with different aspects of this navigation into routines that can be called to render the presentation of that navigation mechanism on each page in which it occurs.

For example, there should be a routine that creates the HTML that renders a standardized horizontal navigation bar. This HTML may be an HTML table containing a single row, with a number of columns that match the number of links being displayed. It might be designed such that a parameter can be passed that indicates the particular page from which the routine is being called, so that the link to that page can be rendered as text without an associated hot link but with some other type of emphasis to indicate that the shopper is already on that page.

The Commerce Server Retail Solution Site does have such a routine, called **RenderNavbar**. This routine makes several calls to the routine **GenerateURL**, which serves as a front-end to nearly all calls to the **AuthManager** object's method **GetURL**. For more information about the GetURL method, see the next section, "Object Support for Non-Catalog Navigation."

Page sequence navigation is also mostly a matter of the coding of the Web site pages involved in the sequence. The **GetURL** method should be used to generate the URL that is used in the HREF portion of the prominent "Continue" button.

In the ASP.NET-based International Retail Site, included in the Commerce Server 2002 SDK, support for building URLs is provided with the **CommerceApplication** ASP.NET class. This class provides several different versions of a method named **BuildURL**, which ultimately reaches the Commerce Server objects through the Base Class Library (BCL) classes **CommerceContext** and **QueryStringBuilder**. **CommerceContext** has a property called **QueryStringBuilder**, which references the default **QueryStringBuilder** object for the site. The **QueryStringBuilder** BCL class has its own versions of the method **BuildURL**, which in turn invoke one of the following three methods of the **AuthManager** object: **GetURL**, **UrlShopperArgs**, or **UrlArgs**.

Object Support for Non-Catalog Navigation

The **GetURL** method of the **AuthManager** object provides the most common generic navigation support offered by the Commerce Server objects. If the retail Web site is designed to be as browser-independent as possible, it is important that the server-side scripts that are used to create the pages that constitute the Web site include links that have very robust, yet plain, HREF URLs. The **GetURL** method provides a mechanism for generating such URLs for use within a retail Web site. It converts the relative URLs used within the site script, which is important to maintain portability, to absolute URLs. It provides support for authentication and security, appending authentication information to URLs when cookies are disabled. And it allows an arbitrary number of URL query string parameters to be specified, making it possible to create generic pages for displaying dynamic content such as is required for product pages.

Commerce Server 2002 provides some different ways to access the **GetURL** method (and its associated methods **UrlShopperArgs**, or **UrlArgs**) of the **AuthManager** object as .NET managed code. The Commerce Server Primary Interop Assembly (PIA) provides access to the **AuthManager** object using the namespace **Microsoft.CommerceServer.Interop**. The Commerce Server Base Class Libraries (BCL) provides access to the **AuthManager** object through several versions of the **BuildURL** method of the **QueryStringBuilder** class using the namespace **Microsoft.CommerceServer.Runtime**.

Product Catalogs

Commerce Server includes a rich catalog management system that plays a central role in defining a complex set of products that are related to each other in a variety of ways. The catalog system supports hierarchical product catalogs with a configurable schema. Products and product categories can also be defined to have relationships that are outside their hierarchical relationships, which can be useful for associating accessories with a primary product.

There are several catalog objects that provide an extensive API to the Web site developers, allowing them to create Web pages that present these relationships to shoppers in easy-to-use ways. This same API provides design-time support to the Commerce Server Business Desk, allowing the catalog-related modules to be directly accessible to business managers. When the Web pages are properly constructed, business managers can make changes to the relationships between products and categories, both hierarchical and otherwise, which are immediately reflected in the corresponding Web pages.

The following list is a summary of the primary features of the Commerce Server Product Catalog System:

- **Configurable schema**. The Product Catalog System allows the product characteristics maintained for each product to be modified as appropriate for a particular set of products.

- **Hierarchical relationships**. The Product Catalog System provides for products to be organized into a hierarchy of categories and sub-categories.

- **Nonhierarchical relationships**. The Product Catalog System allows non-hierarchical relationships to be defined between products, such as accessories being defined as related to the corresponding primary product.

- **Product variants**. The Product Catalog System allows for different variants of a given product to be defined, such as different sizes or colors of a particular product.

- **Virtual catalogs**. The Product Catalog System allows for new catalogs to be defined that are based on an existing catalog, but differ in a set of specific ways, such as different pricing. Such derivative catalogs are called virtual catalogs.

- **Multilanguage support**. The Product Catalog System allows for a catalog to contain parallel product information in two or more distinct languages and currencies.

The next three sub-sections discuss the support provided by Commerce Server for product catalogs in each of the three types of functionality: user interfaces, Web sites, and objects.

User Interface Support for Product Catalogs

Business managers use several different modules in the Catalogs category in the Commerce Server Business Desk in order to manage their product catalogs:

- **Catalog Designer** (called the Catalog Definition Designer in Commerce Server 2002). The Catalog Designer module is used to make changes to the catalog schema itself, so that different product characteristics can be stored in the Product Catalog System.

- **Catalog Editor**. The Catalog Editor module is used to create catalogs, virtual catalogs, and the categories and products they contain.

- **Catalog Sets**. The Catalog Sets module is used to create and manage named sets of catalogs, which provide a way to organize different sets of catalogs for use by particular groups of users.

Site administrators manage the Product Catalog site resource using the Commerce Server Manager. It is important for making sure that the correct product catalogs are associated with each retail Web site being managed.

Web Site Support for Product Catalogs

In order to use the rich product catalog support provided by Commerce Server, the relevant pages in the retail Web site need to contain a fair amount of code to invoke the Commerce Server catalog objects. See the next section, "Object Support for Product Catalogs" for more information.

The Commerce Server 2000 Retail Solution Site contains extensive support for product catalog usage. There are numerous pages dedicated to pulling information from the Commerce Server catalog objects and formatting it for display to the shopper. For example, the files template\menu.asp, search.asp, srchdept.asp, and stepsrch.asp are all used to support catalog searching, and the files template\menu.asp, default.asp, category.asp, and product.asp are all used to support catalog browsing and product display.

The ASP.NET-based International Retail Site, included in the Commerce Server 2002 SDK, defines both controls and classes that implement catalog functionality for use within the Web site. The controls **CatalogBrowser**, **CatalogNavigationTabs**, **CatalogSearch**, **ProductList**, and **AdvancedSearch** are defined. Each control is implemented in a pair of files of the same name, with HTML for the control defined in a .ascx file and the code for the control defined in a .ascx.vb file. Each control inherits from the class of the same name. For all of these controls except **AdvancedSearch**, an underscore character precedes the control file names.

The namespace **Microsoft.CommerceServer.Site.Catalogs** defines the five classes mentioned above, as well as a number of other supporting classes. These classes access the Commerce Server catalog objects through the Commerce Server Base Class Library (BCL) namespace **Microsoft.CommerceServer.Runtime.Catalog**, which defines more than a dozen classes and several enumerations.

Object Support for Product Catalogs

The Commerce Server Product Catalog System has six different objects, with a combined total of more than 150 properties and methods. These objects provide a structured way to access and extend the underlying database tables used to store the catalog data. The following table lists these objects and describes their main purpose.

Catalog Object	Description
CatalogManager	This object is used to work with the entire Product Catalog System. The methods and properties of this object affect all catalogs contained in the Product Catalog System.
CatalogSets	This object is used to work with catalog sets in the Product Catalog System. Catalog sets allow you to present different collections of catalogs to different users and organizations.
CatalogToVendorAssociation	This object is used in business-to-business scenarios for associating catalogs with their corresponding vendors.
Category	This object is used to work with relationships between categories and products. It can also be used to manipulate parent/child relationships for a category.
Product	This object is used to work with products and variants in a catalog.
ProductCatalog	This object is used to alter catalogs and to modify catalog contents. It is the primary object for working with catalogs in the Product Catalog System.

Several of the catalog objects provided by Commerce Server offer a variety of methods and properties that support searching catalogs and product categories. These methods and properties can be identified by either of the strings "search" or "query" as part of their names.

The **ProductCatalog** object contains a variety of methods related to what Commerce Server calls a "specification search." A specification search is also sometimes called a "step search," and is a search method in which you can perform a progressive drill-down search of products by specifying parameter constraints, such as a category, product, or property. To perform a specification search, you search for properties by progressively reducing the number of products that match your search criteria.

Another type of drill-down search that retail Web sites often provide relies on products being organized into categories and sub-categories. Assuming such an organization, there is support within the Commerce Server catalog objects for creating pages that allow navigation up and down such a hierarchy. The strings that contain "parent," "child," "ancestor," or "descendant" as part of their name can identify the methods and properties that support this functionality.

The Commerce Server Product Catalog System also supports the notion of categories and products that are related to each other in a non-hierarchical manner. A common way for taking advantage of this feature is to provide links on a product page to other related products. The methods and properties that support this functionality can be identified by the strings "relationship" and "related" as part of their name.

The Commerce Server catalog objects possess many more methods and properties than those mentioned here. Refer to the Commerce Server online Help, and specifically to the reference pages for the **CatalogManager**, **CatalogSets**, **CatalogToVendorAssociation**, **Category**, **Product**, and **ProductCatalog** objects for a complete listing.

In Commerce Server 2002, the product catalog functionality can also be accessed using .NET-managed code using either the Commerce Server Base Class Libraries (BCL) or the Commerce Server Primary Interop Assemblies (PIA). In the BCL, the catalog classes have been re-factored a bit to make them easier to use, and are accessed using the namespace **Microsoft.CommerceServer.Runtime.Catalog**. In the PIA, the catalog classes are straightforward wrappers of the classic COM catalog objects, and are accessed using the namespace **Microsoft.CommerceServer.Interop.Catalog**.

Shopping Baskets

Retail Web sites clearly need some way for shoppers to select products and place them into a collection of products chosen for purchase. Such collections are most commonly called a shopping basket or shopping cart. The most common way for a Web site to allow the selection of a product for purchase is to include an "Add to Basket" button on a page in a way that it is clearly associated with a particular product.

The normal shopping paradigm also allows shoppers to easily navigate to a page that displays the contents of their shopping basket. Such pages typically display a table with several columns showing the chosen product, the quantity of the product to be purchased, the unit price, and the total price. It is also common for a remove button to be associated with each row in the table. The product quantity is typically displayed in a editable text box so that the quantity can be easily changed. Depending on whether client-side script is employed to detect when such changes are made, an "Update" button might also be required.

The next three sub-sections discuss the support provided by Commerce Server for shopping baskets in each of the three types of functionality: user interfaces, Web sites, and objects.

User Interface Support for Shopping Baskets

Business managers use several different modules in the Orders category in the Commerce Server Business Desk in order to manage shopping baskets:

- **Basket Manager**. The Basket Manager module is used to manage shopping baskets that are present in the retail Web site. An important periodic task is to search for and delete abandoned shopping baskets.

- **Publish Order Codes**. In this context, the Publish Order Codes module is used to update the retail Web site with any changes made using the Basket Manager module. This module is also used to update the retail Web site with changes made using other modules in the Orders category.

Site administrators manage the Transactions site resource using the Commerce Server Manager. There is not very much to this, but it is important for making sure that basket data is stored in the correct database.

Web Site Support for Shopping Baskets

The implementation of a shopping basket Web page is largely a matter of Web site programming that is beyond the scope of Commerce Server itself, although the Retail Solution Site available on the Commerce Server Web site, and the .NET Retail Sample Site available in the Commerce Server 2002 SDK, provide working versions of such pages.

The Commerce Server 2000 Retail Solution Site contains several pages that correspond directly to the support for shopping baskets:

- **_basket.asp**. This page is used to render the basket page, displaying a table as described above.

- **_additem.asp**. This page performs the processing associated with adding a product to the shopping basket when the user clicks the "Add to Basket" button on the product display page product.asp. This page ends by re-directing to either the basket page or returning to the product page, depending on how the site is configured.

- **_delitem.asp**. This page performs the processing associated with removing a product from the shopping basket, and ends by re-directing back to the basket page.

- **_delall.asp**. This page performs the processing associated with removing all products from the shopping basket, and ends by re-directing back to the basket page.

- **_editqty.asp**. This page performs the processing associated with changing the quantity of a product in the shopping basket, and ends by re-directing back to the basket page.

These pages call Commerce Server objects to load and save shopping baskets from and to the Transactions resource or database. In addition, the page basket.asp uses a Commerce Server pipeline to perform some error checking on the contents of the basket. See the next section, "Object Support for Shopping Baskets" for more information.

The ASP.NET-based International Retail Site, included in the Commerce Server 2002 SDK, defines both controls and classes that implement shopping basket/cart functionality for use within the Web site. This includes the control **Cart**, which is used to render the products currently in the cart. The **Cart** control and all of the other transaction controls are implemented in a pair of files of the same name, with HTML for the control defined in a .ascx file and the code for the control defined in a .ascx.vb file. Each control inherits from the class of the same name.

The namespace **Microsoft.CommerceServer.Site.Transactions** defines the classes corresponding to the transaction controls, as well as an additional supporting class. These classes access the Commerce Server shopping cart objects through the Commerce Server Base Class Library (BCL) namespace **Microsoft.CommerceServer.Runtime.Orders**, which defines more than a dozen classes including the class **Basket** that directly supports the notion of a shopping basket.

Object Support for Shopping Baskets

Object support for shopping baskets can be divided into two broad categories. The first category contains the objects that Commerce Server offers for accessing the Transactions resource (also known as the Transactions database) and for accessing the Product Catalog resource. The following table shows the main objects used for managing shopping baskets in Commerce Server:

Order/Basket Object	Description
OrderGroupManager	This object is used to manage **OrderGroup** objects and their contents without the need to use SQL queries.
OrderGroup	This object is used to store, access, and compute basket and order information. Each **OrderGroup** object contains one or more **OrderForm** objects.
OrderForm	This object is used to store user and purchase information.
Various product catalog objects	Some of the properties and methods provided by the product catalog objects that have already been mentioned are also used in the course of adding products to the shopping basket.

From the shopper's perspective, the products in the shopping basket are associated with the entire **OrderGroup** object, although the implementation can be set up so that the products are divided among different **OrderForm** objects within the **OrderGroup** object according to the vendor associated with that particular product.

The second category consists of the components from the Business Processing Pipeline System. Commerce Server pipelines are used in several different contexts in a typical retail Web site based on Commerce Server, including one that is used to check a basket for errors. In the case of the Commerce Server Retail Solution Site, the pipeline configuration file that defines the pipeline used to check for shopping basket errors is named Basket.pcf and is executed on numerous pages throughout the site.

In Commerce Server 2002, the shopping basket functionality can also be accessed using .NET-managed code using either the Commerce Server Base Class Libraries (BCL) or the Commerce Server Primary Interop Assemblies (PIA). In the BCL, the classes related to shopping baskets and orders have been re-factored a bit to make them easier to use, and are accessed using the namespaces **Microsoft.CommerceServer.Runtime.Orders** and **Microsoft.CommerceServer.Runtime.Pipelines**. In the PIA, the classes used to implement shopping baskets are straightforward wrappers of the classic COM order objects, and are accessed using the namespaces **Microsoft.CommerceServer.Interop** and **Microsoft.CommerceServer.Interop.Orders**.

Completing the Purchase

The shopper's experience of completing a purchase is a natural extension to the shopping basket experience. Once the shopper has placed all products to be purchased in the basket, they click the "Check Out" button to begin the process of providing information about their billing and shipping addresses, credit card information, reviewing the total cost including tax, shipping, and handling, and committing to the purchase. Commerce Server provides a variety of support for this process.

The next three sub-sections discuss the support provided by Commerce Server for purchase completion in each of the three types of functionality: user interfaces, Web sites, and objects.

User Interface Support for Purchase Completion

Business managers use several different modules in the Orders category in the Commerce Server Business Desk in order to manage the shopper process of completing purchases:

- **Location Codes**. The Location Codes module is used to add codes for additional countries/regions and states/provinces. Locations are used by shoppers when entering billing and shipping addresses, and are also used when commuting appropriate taxes on purchases. Commerce Server defines several by default, but depending on the nature and reach of a particular retail Web site, more such codes may need to be added.

- **Shipping Methods**. The Shipping Methods module is used to define and manage the shipping methods that are offered on the retail Web site. Shipping methods can be defined to charge by weight, by quantity, or by subtotal, and can be made available in different languages.

- **Tax Rates**. The Tax Rates module is used to manage tax rates for different combinations of countries/regions and states/provinces. Generally, the tax rate charged is based on the country/region and state/province that the shopper provides with their billing address.

- **Publish Order Codes**. In this context, the Publish Order Codes module is used to update the retail Web site with any changes made using one or more of the other modules discussed above. This module is also used to update the retail Web site with changes made using other modules in the Orders category.

Site administrators manage the Transactions Config site resource using the Commerce Server Manager. It is important for making sure that the various data used during the process of completing a purchase is stored in, and retrieved from, the correct database.

Web Site Support for Purchase Completion

On most retail Web sites, the process of completing a purchase is spread over a sequence of several distinct pages. For example, after clicking the "Check Out" button, the shopper is probably asked for a variety of information such as their billing and shipping addresses and their credit card information. They are also asked to confirm the correctness of the order and approve any ancillary costs such as for tax, shipping, or handling.

The implementation of such a sequence of pages is largely a matter of Web site programming that is beyond the scope of Commerce Server itself, although the Retail Solution Site available on the Commerce Server Web site, and the .NET Retail Sample Site available in the Commerce Server 2002 SDK, provide working versions of such page sequences.

The Commerce Server 2000 Retail Solution Site contains several pages that implement one such sequence of purchase completion pages:

Page(s)	Description
addrform.asp addrbook.asp _setadrs.asp	These pages are used for entering and maintaining addresses for the shopper. The address book feature is more advanced, and allows a shopper to maintain a number of different shipping and/or billing addresses. The page _setadrs.asp is used to process entered addresses, but does not itself present an interface (as indicated by the Solution Sites convention of starting the file name with an underscore character), ending by re-directing the shopper to a different page.
pickship.asp _setship.asp	These pages work together to allow the shopper to choose from the available shipping options.
summary.asp	This page shows the shopper a summary of the order.
crdtcard.asp po.asp	These pages allow the shopper to enter information related to how they are going to pay for the items purchased, using a credit card in the case of the page crdtcard.asp, and using a purchase order in the case of the page po.asp.
confirm.asp	This page allows the shopper one last chance to confirm that the order and all of the related information is correct before submitting it for processing.

These pages call Commerce Server objects to perform their respective tasks using the Transactions and Transactions Config resources (databases). Commerce Server pipelines are used to perform some parts of the purchase completion processing. See the next section, "Object Support for Purchase Completion" for more information.

The ASP.NET-based International Retail Site, included in the Commerce Server 2002 SDK, defines numerous controls and classes related to purchase completion. These include controls categorized as Accounts controls and Transaction controls. As in other areas of functionality, the controls are implemented in a pair of files of the same name, with HTML for the control defined in a .ascx file and the code for the control defined in a .ascx.vb file. Each control inherits from the class of the same name.

The ASP.NET classes related to purchase completion are also found across a number of different classifications and their corresponding namespaces. These include the namespaces **Microsoft.CommerceServer.Site**, **Microsoft.CommerceServer.Site.Accounts**, **Microsoft.CommerceServer.SiteComponents**, **Microsoft.CommerceServer.Site.Transactions**.

These classes access the Commerce Server objects related to purchase completion primarily through the Commerce Server Base Class Library (BCL) namespaces **Microsoft.CommerceServer.Runtime.Orders**, **Microsoft.CommerceServer.Runtime.Profiles**, and **Microsoft.CommerceServer.Runtime.Pipelines**.

Object Support for Purchase Completion

As with object support for shopping baskets, object support for completing the purchase can be divided into two broad categories. The first category contains the objects that Commerce Server offers for accessing a variety of resources including the following:

- **Transactions**. Stores information about shopping baskets and orders.

- **Transactions Config**. Stores information about shipping methods and rates, tax rates, state and region codes, and order status codes.

- **Profiles**. Stores information about the shopper, including name, address(es), billing information, and so on.

- **App Default Config**. Stores information about currency locale and symbols, billing and payment options, privacy options, unit of measure for weight, and so on.

- **Product Catalog**. Stores information about the products being purchased.

The following table shows the main objects used during the completion of a purchase in Commerce Server:

Order Completion Object	Description
AppConfig	This object is used to retrieve a variety of site configuration settings such as the names and codes of various countries and regions.
DataFunctions	This object is used to perform a variety of locale-based formatting, parsing, and value range checking.
EuroDisplay	This object is used to convert and format currency amounts when multiple currencies are displayed.
GlobalConfig SiteConfig SiteConfigReadOnly	These objects are used to access the App Default Config resource.
ProfileObject ProfileService	These objects are used to access the Profiles resource.
Shipping ShippingMethodManager	These objects are used to manage and display shipping information.
Various order-related objects	Some of the properties and methods provided by the **OrderForm** and **OrderGroup** objects that have already been mentioned are also used in the course of completing a purchase.
Various product catalog objects	Some of the properties and methods provided by the product catalog objects that have already been mentioned are also used in the course of completing a purchase.

Clearly, a wide variety of Commerce Server objects are used during the process of completing a purchase.

As with shopping baskets, the second broad category of object support employed during purchase completion involves the use of Commerce Server pipelines. In the Commerce Server Solution Sites, two distinct pipelines are executed during the process of completing the purchase. The order total pipeline, defined by the pipeline configuration file Total.pcf, computes the shipping and handling charges, tax, and the order total The checkout pipeline, defined by the pipeline configuration file Checkout.pcf, receives and accepts payment information and completes the transaction.

In Commerce Server 2002, the purchase completion functionality can also be accessed using .NET-managed code using either the Commerce Server Base Class Libraries (BCL) or the Commerce Server Primary Interop Assemblies (PIA). In the BCL, the classes related to purchase completion have been re-factored a bit to make them easier to use, and are accessed using the namespaces **Microsoft.CommerceServer.Runtime.Orders**, **Microsoft.CommerceServer.Runtime.Profiles**, and **Microsoft.CommerceServer.Runtime.Pipelines**.

In the PIA, the classes used for purchase completion are straightforward wrappers of the classic COM order objects, and are accessed using the namespaces **Microsoft.CommerceServer.Interop**, **Microsoft.CommerceServer.Interop.Orders**, and **Microsoft.CommerceServer.Interop.Profiles**.

Shopper-Centric Security

From the shopper's perspective, there are only a few ways in which security is typically thought. The most visible of these is the password creation when registering on a Web site, and the need to enter a password when returning to that site later.

A less visible security-related feature in retail Web sites concerns the security of private information while it is being transmitted over the Internet. More sophisticated shoppers know by looking at the URLs which ones are secure. URLs beginning with https:// are secure and those beginning with http:// are not. Less experienced users need to be able to find a page with an understandable explanation.

A third security issue that can be of direct concern to shoppers relates to whether their credit card numbers are stored by the Web site in between purchases, and if so, whether or not it is sufficiently secure.

There are other security issues related to retail Web site management that are not of direct concern to shoppers. Generally, this has to do with enforcing the division of the labor related to Web site management into distinct roles, and is discussed later in the chapter.

The next three sub-sections discuss the support provided by Commerce Server for shopper security in each of the three types of functionality: user interfaces, Web sites, and objects.

User Interface Support for Shopper-Centric Security

Business managers use the Users module in the Profiles category to manually reset shopper passwords. One scenario during which this interface is likely to be used is when a retail Web site employs a system in which shoppers are provided a way to report forgotten passwords and in which they are sent a new password in an e-mail message. Even so, a more sophisticated solution could avoid requiring any manual involvement by business managers and automate the entire process using the appropriate Commerce Server objects.

Another scenario in which Web site operators may use a user interface to manage a type of security that is of explicit concern to the shopper is when a Web site administrator directly uses SQL Server interfaces to properly secure the databases in which profile information is stored.

Web Site Support for Shopper-Centric Security

The Commerce Server Retail Solution Site contains a folder named **login** that is dedicated to pages related to user registration and login. It contains the files _guest.asp, login.asp, logout.asp, and newuser.asp.

Many Web sites have a "Forgot your password?" link on their login page. There is no functionality built into the Solution Site to provide shoppers with a mechanism for dealing with forgotten passwords. Rather, this is one of those features that have been left for individual site developers to implement as they see fit for their retail Web site.

Regarding the use of secure HTTP (URLs beginning with https://) for particular pages within the Solution Sites, a mechanism exists through which site developers can easily make any page secure in this regard. It is simple a matter of adding (or removing) a line to the routine **GetSecurePagesDictionary** in the file include\global_siteconfig_lib.asp for each new page that should use secure HTTP (or should not use secure HTTP). In general, due to performance considerations, secure HTTP should only be used where necessary.

In the ASP.NET-based International Retail Site, included in the Commerce Server 2002 SDK, the equivalent functionality for specifying which pages must be accessed using secure HTTP is performed in the configuration file web.config. The **DocumentSecurity** element within the **CommerceServerSite** element contains a list of **Document** elements. Each **Document** element specifies a Web page using the *name* attribute and has a *privacy* attribute that is set to "true" to indicate the requirement for secure HTTP access to the indicated page.

Object Support for Shopper-Centric Security

Object support for security in Commerce Server, at least with respect to that aspect of security that are directly relevant to shoppers, is limited to the use of the **ProfileObject** and **ProfileService** objects. These can be used to programmatically access a shopper's password, either to set it in the first place, or to reset it as appropriate, or to simply retrieve it for login and forgotten password functionality.

In Commerce Server 2002, the profile functionality can also be accessed using .NET-managed code using either the Commerce Server Base Class Libraries (BCL) or the Commerce Server Primary Interop Assemblies (PIA). In the BCL, the profile classes have been re-factored to make them easier to use, and are accessed using the namespace **Microsoft.CommerceServer.Runtime.Profiles**. In the PIA, the profile classes are straightforward wrappers of the classic COM profile objects, and are accessed using the namespace **Microsoft.CommerceServer.Interop.Profiles**.

Recommendations

What might be called "recommendations" from the shopper's perspective is what is broadly known as "marketing" from the shopkeeper's perspective. Shoppers often come to a retail Web site (or a conventional store for that matter) with a particular product in mind, and sometimes even the brand and model. Marketing is the process of getting the shopper interested in products that they did not necessarily already intend to purchase.

Promoting accessories along with their associated products is a form of marketing that is sometimes called cross selling. Getting a shopper to change their mind and buy a model that has more features is a form of marketing that is sometimes called up selling. Offering discounts of various sorts is a form of marketing, and suggests to the shopper that now is a good time to make the purchase.

Advertisements, which we all know are quite common on Web sites, are a less directed form of making recommendations to shoppers, but they certainly qualify as marketing. When information about the shopper is known, such as their age or gender, that knowledge can be used to display advertisements to which they are more likely to respond. This is sometimes called targeted advertising.

Direct mail, often thought of as "junk" mail from the shopper's perspective, must be a statistically effective way to market products, or there wouldn't be so much of it. Most of us are already familiar with the e-mail equivalent of direct mail. This is certainly a marketing technique that is often employed in conjunction with a retail Web site. Notably, the e-mail version of direct mail provides a more convenient way to request removal from the mailing list, usually a link in the e-mail message that you can click; this particular functionality is often called "opt out."

Some popular Web sites use predictive algorithms so that they can make recommendations along the lines of "other people who bought this product were also interested in the following other products." These recommendations are based on relationships that may not have been natural to foresee, but which are based on the actual buying patterns of previous customers. These algorithms are complex and proprietary, and show how the tracking of Web site activity can be exploited to increase future profits.

Commerce Server provides a variety of functionality to support all of these various methods of marketing. They can be used in various customized combinations as additional ways in which to gain an advantage over competitors. These methods are summarized in the following table:

Marketing Method	Description
Cross sells	Recommending related products, such as accessories
Up sells	Recommending upgraded versions of a product

(continued)

Marketing Method	Description *(continued)*
Promotions	Prompting immediate purchase based on discounted or otherwise attractive current prices
Advertisements	Recommending unrelated though potentially targeted products, often receiving revenue in return
Direct Mail	Send potentially targeted e-mail inviting purchases at the Web site
Predictions	Recommending other products based on other customers buying habits

The next three sub-sections discuss the support provided by Commerce Server for recommendations to shoppers, also known as marketing, in each of the three types of functionality: user interfaces, Web sites, and objects.

User Interface Support for Recommendations

Commerce Server offers a wide variety of user interfaces that support the various marketing methods described above. The following table shows the various Commerce Server resources and Business Desk modules that can be used to configure and manage each of these methods:

Marketing Method	Commerce Server Resource(s)	Business Desk Module(s)
Cross sells and Up sells	Product Catalog	All modules in the Catalogs category (see below)
Promotions and Advertising	Campaigns Profiles	All modules in the Campaigns and Users categories (see below)
Direct Mail	Commerce Server Direct Mailer Profiles	Reports List Manager All modules in the Campaigns and Users categories (see below)
Predictions	Predictor Profiles	Segment Viewer Affinity Lists All modules in the Users category (see below)

In the Business Desk, the categories for Catalogs, Campaigns, and Users include the following modules:

Category	Modules
Catalogs	Catalog Definition Designer
	Catalog Editor
	Catalog Sets
Campaigns	Campaign Manager
	List Manager
	Campaign Expressions
	Target Group
	Reference Tables
	Publish Campaigns
Users	Users
	Organizations
	Profile Definition Designer
	Site Terms Editor
	Publish Profiles

These combinations of Commerce Server resources and Business Desk resources comprise a large portion of the Commerce Server functionality, and are too complex to be explained here. However, the Commerce Server online documentation provides extensive information about how the resources are intended to be used to achieve the various types of product marketing being discussed.

Web Site Support for Recommendations

Support for the different recommendations or product marketing in the Web sites varies according to the site in question: the Commerce Server 2000 Retail Solution Site, or the Commerce Server 2002 .NET Sample Site. Information that can be used as a starting point for Commerce Server implementations differs according to individual needs. This section discusses each type of marketing and corresponding support in each of the starter sites.

Cross Sell and Up Sell Web Site Support

The Commerce Server 2000 Retail Solution Site does not include any built-in support for cross sells and up sells. As mentioned earlier, marketing of this type is based on non-hierarchical relationships between products, and without knowing the nature of the products that exist in the catalog; it does not make sense to have code in the product or basket pages to display related products. To add cross sells or up sells to this site, use the Business Desk to establish the appropriate relationships, and then use the relationship oriented methods of the **Product** object on the relevant pages to retrieve and display information about the related products.

For the same reason, the International Retail Site, provided in the Commerce Server 2002 SDK, does not include any built-in support for cross sells and up sells. Adding support for this type of recommendations to the .NET Sample Site would involve the same steps as described for the Retail Solution Site.

Advertising and Promotions Web Site Support

The Commerce Server 2000 Retail Solution Site does include support for advertising and discounts, the latter of which are a form of promotion. In the templates folder, the file layout1.asp defines the layout of most of the pages in the site. This file includes the file banner.inc, also in the template folder. The code in the file banner.inc calls the **GetContent** method of the **ContentSelector** object for those pages that are defined to display advertisements, writing any returned ads to the ASP response stream. The **GetContent** method uses the Content Selection Framework (CSF) and runs the Content Selection Pipeline to determine the ad(s) to be displayed, as configured in the Campaign Manager module in Business Desk.

The Retail Solution Site also contains code to display any discounts configured using the Campaign Manager module in Business Desk. Whenever a shopping basket is displayed, the **CheckBasket** routine is called. This routine runs the basket pipeline, which by default runs the **OrderDiscount** pipeline component. This component checks for any discounts associated with the products in the basket and update the corresponding **OrderForm** objects with any discount information. Subsequent code in the page checks for such information, and if found, displays it.

The International Retail Site, provided in the Commerce Server 2002 SDK, implements advertisements using the ASP.NET class **Ad**, defined in the namespace **Microsoft.CommerceServer.Site.Campaigns**.

Direct Mail Web Site Support

The Commerce Server 2000 Retail Solution Site includes the files ServiceReminder.asp and opt_out.asp. Although these files are not wired into the site by default, they do serve as an example of how to generate personalized e-mail using the Commerce Server Direct Mailer and how to programmatically modify the opt-out list, respectively. The former file shows how shopper information can be retrieved using the **ProfileObject** and **ProfileService** objects and used to construct a personalized e-mail message, and the latter file demonstrates the use of the **ListManager** object.

The International Retail Site, provided in the Commerce Server 2002 SDK, does not include any support for direct mail campaigns.

Predictions Web Site Support

The Commerce Server 2000 Retail Solution Site includes support for displaying predictions on the basket page. Assuming that the basket is not empty, up to five predictions can be displayed under the heading of "Recommendations" after the checkout button is used. The **PredictorClient** object is used to retrieve these predictions, if available.

The International Retail Site, provided in the Commerce Server 2002 SDK, does not include any prediction functionality.

Object Support for Recommendations

Commerce Server provides a wide variety for object support for the various types of recommendations that can be built into a retail Web site. Each of the previously categorized types of recommendations are addressed in turn.

Object Support for Cross Sells and Up Sells

Adding cross sells and/or up sells to a retail Web site consists of defining the appropriate relationships between products, or categories of products, and then adding code to the appropriate Web pages so that they can make recommendations regarding the related products.

Both the **Category** and **Product** objects in Commerce Server 2000 have **RelatedCategories** and **RelatedProducts** properties that can be used to retrieve the relevant information for inclusion on the corresponding product pages of a retail Web site.

In Commerce Server 2002, the related category and product functionality can also be accessed using .NET managed code using either the Commerce Server Base Class Libraries (BCL) or the Commerce Server Primary Interop Assemblies (PIA). In the BCL, the **Category** and **Product** classes can be used to retrieve information about related categories and products, respectively, and are accessed using the namespace **Microsoft.CommerceServer.Runtime.Catalogs**. In the PIA, the **Category** and **Product** classes are straightforward wrappers of the classic COM **Category** and **Product** objects, and are accessed using the namespace **Microsoft.CommerceServer.Interop.Catalog**.

Object Support for Advertising and Promotions

Commerce Server supports targeted advertising and promotions using the Content Selection Framework (CSF). For pages in a retail Web site, selecting content using the CSF consists of calling the **GetContent** method of the **ContentSelector** object, and passing a **Dictionary** object that specifies a variety of information about the content to be selected. To support the much more complicated process of configuring the various advertising and promotion campaigns using the modules of the Campaigns category in Commerce Server Business Desk, there are a wide variety of additional objects, including **ContentList**, **ContentListFactory**, **ContentListSchema**, **ExpressionEval**, **ExpressionStore**, **ExprEvalContext**, and **ExprFltrQueryBldr**.

In Commerce Server 2002, the advertising and promotions functionality can also be accessed using .NET managed code using either the Commerce Server Base Class Libraries (BCL) or the Commerce Server Primary Interop Assemblies (PIA). In the BCL, this functionality can be accessed using the namespace **Microsoft.CommerceServer.Runtime.Targeting**. In the PIA, the classes used for advertising and promotions are straightforward wrappers of the corresponding classic COM objects, and are accessed using the namespace **Microsoft.CommerceServer.Interop.Targeting**.

Object Support for Direct Mail

The main Commerce Server object used to support direct mail is the **ListManager** object, and is available in both the 2000 and 2002 versions of Commerce Server. In the 2002 version, it is available as a classic COM object, and as a wrapper class in the Primary Interop Assembly (PIA) using the namespace **Microsoft.CommerceServer.Interop.Targeting**. When programmatically constructing e-mail messages, the **ProfileObject** and **ProfileService** objects can be used to access addressing information as well as other information to personalize the message. The functionality provided by these profile objects is available using the COM objects, their PIA equivalents using the namespace **Microsoft.CommerceServer.Interop.Profiles**, or using their BCL equivalents using the namespace **Microsoft.CommerceServer.Runtime.Profiles**.

Object Support for Predictions

The **PredictorClient** object is used when accessing the Commerce Server prediction functionality in a retail Web site. Three additional objects, **PredictorService**, **PredictorServiceAdmin**, and **PredModelBuilder** are used by the user interfaces for managing the prediction functionality.

In Commerce Server 2002, the **PredictorClient** object is available in the Commerce Server Primary Interop Assembly (PIA) using the namespace **Microsoft.CommerceServer.Interop.Targeting**; the other three prediction objects are not available in the PIA and must be accessed using traditional COM programming. None of the prediction objects are available using the Commerce Server Base Class Libraries (BCL).

Improvements

The effectiveness of improvements to a retail Web site over time is judged somewhat differently depending on one's perspective. Shoppers appreciate improvements that make it easier to find the products that interest them, and once found, improvements that make it easier for them to make an informed decision about whether to buy the product in question. Other types of improvements may streamline processes for the shopper.

Shopkeepers are more likely to judge improvements based on the bottom line – have the improvements lead to increased sales? Of course it may be difficult to determine the degree of contribution for a particular improvement. Improvements to business processes might make the Web site staff more effective, which theoretically, over the long run, could be tracked and watched for improvements.

In the course of devising improvements to a retail Web site, most ideas remain in the realm of inspiration and subjective human judgments, perhaps inspired by suggestions from the shoppers themselves. However, there is a particular area of Commerce Server functionality that can provide some degree of objectivity when determining how the Web site should be improved. Commerce Server calls this process "closing the loop" and it consists of using the Business Analytics System to collect and analyze data about how the retail Web site is being used. This, of course, includes an analysis of which products are selling well, which shoppers typically complete purchases, and so on. Perhaps less obviously, Web site improvements can also include much more subtle analyses, such as how shoppers most commonly browse the site. Commerce Server includes a data warehouse designed specifically for storing data related to retail Web site use. It is an ongoing task for site administrators to make sure that the various types of data collected are periodically imported into the data warehouse so that the reports analyzed by business managers reflect current data.

The next three sub-sections discuss the support provided by Commerce Server for Web site improvements in each of the three types of functionality: user interfaces, Web sites, and objects.

User Interface Support for Improvements

Commerce Server provides several user interfaces that are used in the course of analyzing Web site activity in order to devise improvements to the site. The Analysis category in Business Desk contains two modules related to reporting, and a viewer.

- **Reports**. The Reports module is used to initiate running a report. There are two types of reports, static and dynamic. Static reports run in the background, and when complete, appear in the Completed Reports module. Dynamic reports are displayed in a browser window and have advanced interactive capabilities.

- **Completed Reports**. The Completed Reports module is used to view static reports that have concluded.

- **Segment Viewer**. The Segment Viewer module is used to view different groups of users who share particular characteristics or behavior such as usage trends. Such analysis can be used to make marketing decisions based upon similarities among users.

Commerce Server 2002 includes more than 30 pre-defined reports, most of which are dynamic. Because dynamic reports allow the business manager viewing the report to choose many different ways to examine the available data, each dynamic report can be seen as many different reports all rolled into one. Combined with the ability to customize existing reports define entirely new reports, and export report data in a format compatible with Microsoft Excel, Commerce Server offers a very rich reporting environment.

Commerce Server categorizes reports into the following types:

Report Category	Reports
Product Sales Reports	Buyer Browse to Purchase, Customer Sales, Order Events, Product Sales, Shopping Basket Events
Web Usage Reports	Activity by Browser, Directories, Entry Path Analysis, Top Referring Domains by Requests, Top Requested Pages, Usage Summary by Day of Week, Usage Summary by Hour of Day, Usage Summary by Week of Year, Usage Trends
Advertising Reports	Ad Reach and Frequency by Date, Ad Reach and Frequency per Advertiser, Campaign Event Summary, Campaign Item Summary
User Reports	Distinct Users by Time, New Registered Users, Registered User Properties, Registered Users by Date Registered, User Days to Register, User Registration Rate, User Trends
Visit Reports	Entry Pages, Exit Pages, General Activity Statistics, User Visit Trends
Diagnostic Reports	Bandwidth Summary, Bandwidth Trends, Hits by HTTP Status, Hits by Win32 Status
Query String Reports	Query Strings (multi-value), Query Strings (single value)

In order for the business managers to be able to run the available reports and analyze the trends they expose, the site administrators must make sure that the corresponding data is routinely imported into the data warehouse from which the reports are derived. The data warehouse is maintained in Microsoft SQL Server, and many of the tasks involved in populating and maintaining the data warehouse are performed using the user interfaces provided by SQL Server. For this reason, the Microsoft SQL Servers node is included in the Microsoft Management Console (MMC) interface that constitutes Commerce Server Manager. Site administrators configure the data warehouse using the Data Warehouse global resource in the Commerce Server Manager node, and import data using the Microsoft SQL Servers node. Data is imported using several SQL Server Data Transformation Services (DTS) tasks designed specifically for importing various types of Commerce Server data.

Web Site Support for Improvements

Because improvements to the retail Web site almost always involve changes to the Web site itself, it is only possible to make a very general statement about how support for improvements is or is not designed into a particular implementation. Web site implementations that are modular and well-designed, as are the Commerce Server 2000 Retail Solution Site and the Commerce Server 2002 .NET Sample Site, are generally be less difficult to improve than Web site implementations that are not as modular or well-designed.

For example, the Retail Solution Site code includes a folder called "template" that contains a number of ASP files that are used to define the layout of the pages in the site. If an envisioned improvement concerned page layout, the design of this site is such that it is quite straightforward to change the layout of the pages in the site, or some subset of those pages.

The International Retail Site, available in the Commerce Server 2002 SDK, is designed in a modular way using ASP.NET controls and classes, providing an environment that should be trouble-free to modify and extend as improvements are devised and implemented.

Object Support for Improvements

Commerce Server provides two objects that are directly related to Analysis reports:

- **AsyncRpt**. This object is used to asynchronously render (display) or export a static report.
- **ReportRenderer**. This object is used to synchronously render (display) or export a static report.

Neither of these objects have a Primary Interop Assembly (PIA) equivalent in Commerce Server 2002, and therefore can only be accessed through classic COM mechanisms.

The **CreateFromDWCalc** method of the **ListManager** object can be used to create a list from an Analysis report.

Commerce Server 2002 does not provide a managed code version of either the **AsyncRpt** or **ReportRenderer** object, although it does provide PIA access to the **ListManager** object using the namespace **Microsoft.CommerceServer.Interop.Targeting**.

Privacy

Internet users are increasingly aware of privacy issues. They want to know how the information that they provide to the Web site is used, and in particular, whether that information is shared with any other businesses.

When browsing a retail Web site, a shopper should be able to effortlessly find the site's privacy policy statement, and be able to understand it. It is common for every page on a site to contain a link to a page that explains the site's policy regarding privacy.

Different Languages and Currency

One of the ways in which Commerce Server 2002 represents a significant improvement over Commerce Server 2000 concerns support for multiple languages and currencies. The Product Catalog System has been enhanced to support descriptive and pricing information in different languages, driven by a language choice that is tracked for each user. The Content Selection Framework (CSF) has likewise been improved to allow language choice to be one of the criterion upon which advertisements and discounts are chosen for display for a particular user.

The International Retail Site, available in the Commerce Server 2002 SDK, is specifically designed to demonstrate the improved support for multiple languages and currency in Commerce Server 2002.

Miscellaneous Shopper Features

Various retail Web sites offer additional features that are not generally considered to be part of the core features that retail Web sites must provide. Such additional features include:

- **Auctions**. While some Web sites might use auctions as their main selling paradigm, other retail Web sites might use auctions, perhaps only occasionally, to draw additional attention to their site, or to accelerate the sale of otherwise poorly selling products.

- **Product reviews**. Allowing shoppers to post reviews of products that are available for purchase on the site can be an effective sales tool. Shoppers tend to trust the opinions of other shoppers, presuming that they have less to gain from making positive remarks about a product. Note, however, that whenever a Web site allows its users to post information, care must be taken to monitor that information for obscenities and so on. One effective way for this to be done is to provide a link through which other users can lodge complaints about particular postings.

- **Gift certificates**. Many retail Web sites can benefit by offering a mechanism for their shoppers to purchase gift certificates. The recipient of the gift certificate, generally notified by e-mail, is invited to visit the site and apply the value of the gift certificate to a purchase of their choice.

In general, Commerce Server does not provide out-of-the-box solutions for the types of specialized features mentioned here. Auction functionality is a partial exception. The Commerce Server 2002 SDK includes an **Auction** object and code that demonstrates its use. There are too many possibilities, with new such features being conceived and implemented constantly. Instead, Commerce Server provides a framework through which the various aspects of a new feature can be implemented.

For example, consider the case of gift certificates. To properly integrate gift certificate functionality into a retail Web site that uses Commerce Server, several different implementation tasks are required, as follows:

- **Data**. In order to offer a gift certificate, certain data needs to be gathered and stored. In addition to the normal shopper information such as name, e-mail address, billing address, credit card number, and so on, information about the gift certificate recipient, the amount of the gift certificate, and a unique code through which the gift certificate can be spent need to be stored. Business managers and developers need to work together to define a database schema to represent this information, and then developers need to create the corresponding database tables, and so on. The tools provided with the database, most likely SQL Server in this case, should be used for this work.

- **Objects**. One of the main reasons for developing custom objects for new functionality is to hide the internal details of the database schema, and to create an interface that is more intuitive with respect to the functionality being added. If a **GiftCertificate** object is developed, it might have properties such as, for example, **RecipientName**, **RecipientEmail**, **OriginalGiftAmount**, and **RemainingGiftAmount**, and methods such as **Spend** and **SendReminder**.

- **User interfaces**. One of the ways in which new features can be more or less integrated into a Commerce Server site concerns the degree to which new, compatible user interfaces are developed to support the new features. Gift certificate functionality must include some way for business managers to manage outstanding gift certificates. Because business managers are likely to be familiar with the Business Desk, the best approach is to create a new Business Desk module specifically designed for working with gift certificates.

The initial page of the new module would probably display a list of outstanding gift certificates, and provide a way to sort and search within those certificates. For example, a business manager should be able to search for all gift certificates older than a specified date (perhaps so that a reminder e-mail can be sent to the recipient). Choosing a particular gift certificate and displaying all of the information about it is another likely behavior that mirrors how the existing Business Desk modules are designed. This would allow business managers to, for example, track down information about a particular gift certificate when the recipient makes an inquiry about it (such as when they have lost the gift certificate ID).

With respect to site administrators and the user interfaces that they use, the gift certificate database should be added to the Commerce Server site as a custom resource. This would allow it to be managed through the Commerce Server Manager and deployed using the Commerce Server Site Packager.

Commerce Server includes extensive documentation that describes how to add new Business Desk modules and custom resources to a site.

- **Web site**. Most new Web site features involve developing new pages for the Web site, though in some circumstances the new features might be integrated into existing pages. Regardless of the architecture of the retail Web site, whether it is based on the Commerce Server 2000 Retail Solution Site, the Commerce Server 2002 International Retail Site, or some other architecture, it makes sense to gain a thorough understanding of that architecture so that new pages can be added in a complimentary manner.

Shopkeeper-Specific Features

Although most retail Web site features map directly to some aspect of the shopper's experience with the site, several Commerce Server features do not. For example, some aspects of security do not directly impact the shopper's experience. A new feature in Commerce Server 2002 is an enhanced security model for the Business Desk, providing the ability to control an individual business manager's access to particular modules, or even to particular tasks within a given module.

Another area of functionality that is not necessarily very visible to shoppers concerns the activities that occur in the course of fulfilling the order after it has been made. There are several Business Desk modules that are used in this context, as follows:

- **Order Status Codes**. The Order Status Codes module is used to manage the codes associated with the different phases of an order. Often, the default order status codes (New Order, Saved Order, and Basket) are not be sufficient to adequately track the order fulfillment process. In this case, the appropriate new order status codes can be defined using this module.

- **Order Status**. The Order Status module is used to manage outstanding orders that are present in the retail Web site. Managing orders includes changing the order status as the order progresses through the fulfillment process and deleting cancelled or inadvertently created duplicate orders.

- **Publish Order Codes**. In this context, the Publish Order Codes module is used to update the retail Web site with any changes made using one or more of the other modules discussed above. This module is also used to update the retail Web site with changes made using other modules in the Orders category.

Tools and Technologies

To implement a retail Web site using the Microsoft technology described in this chapter, the following .NET Enterprise Server products are required:

- Microsoft Commerce Server
- Microsoft SQL Server
- Microsoft Windows 2000 Server

If the Web site is to be integrated with Microsoft Content Management Server in order to provide more user-friendly content authoring and content management workflow, the Content Connector for Commerce Server add-on to Content Management Server and Content Management Server is required. For more information about this integration possibility, see Chapter 16 for information about solutions using Content Management Server.

Note the lack of version/year numbers in the list above. As this book is going to press, new versions of several of these products are soon to be released. By the time you are reading this, Commerce Server 2002 should already be available, or will be shortly. Content Management Server 2002 is scheduled for release shortly thereafter. If and when Content Connector will be revised to support these new versions is not known at this time. Interested suppliers should refer directly to the Microsoft Web site for more precise information about release dates, software requirements, and version compatibility.

Companies that want to develop a Web site that incorporates the functionality of both Commerce Server and Content Management Server might want to consider acquiring the Microsoft Solution for Internet Business (MSIB), and especially if they are considering making use of Microsoft or one of its certified partners to help with the implementation. The MSIB bundles the required servers and implementation assistance into a single package.

Site programmers working with Commerce Server, either in conjunction with Content Management Server or by itself, are likely to want Microsoft Visual Studio. This is especially true if the 2002 version of Commerce Server is being used. As with all of the .NET architecture, Visual Studio.NET is not required to create Web applications that use the .NET Framework. On the other hand, it is hard to envision why a site programmer would prefer to use any other tool. If the .NET features of Commerce Server 2002 are going to be used, also using Visual Studio.NET will almost certainly provide a significant productivity boost.

Finally, depending on the deployment scenario and the firewall requirements of the Web site, Microsoft Internet Security and Acceleration Server (ISA) could have a role to play.

Implementation

Clearly, anything close to a comprehensive discussion of the implementation of a retail Web site based on Commerce Server is far beyond the scope of this chapter. Instead, the final section of this chapter provides a taste of Commerce Server programming by comparing the code used for product catalog keyword searching in the Commerce Server 2000 Retail Solution Site and the equivalent functionality in the Commerce Server 2002 International Retail Site, which is included in the Commerce Server 2002 SDK. To be clear, product catalog keyword searching, also known as "free text" searching, maps to a SQL full-text search of the catalog databases. As mentioned earlier, the International Retail Site is based on ASP.NET, and thus differs significantly in its implementation approach. An overview, including annotated code excerpts from the Retail Solution Site, is presented first. Then, a similar tour of the approach used in the International Retail Site is presented.

Throughout the code excerpts used in the following subsections, italic text is used for annotations added here for clarity. Also, linefeeds have been added to the code in some places to avoid the reading difficulties associated with automatically wrapped lines of code. In an attempt to further enhance readability, the description of each routine also begins with a heading that contains the name of the routine.

Keyword Searches in the Retail Solution Site

The keyword search functionality in Commerce Server 2000 Retail Solution Site begins in the page search.asp. Following the standard flow of execution in this solution site, the include file setupenv.asp ends by calling the routine **Main**, which is the first routine in the page. This function assigns the HTML for the content area of the page to the variable **htmPageContent.** The include file layout1.asp inserts the contents of this variable into the table cell that corresponds to the content area of the page. For more information about these details of page execution, see the topic "Page Execution Model" in the Solution Sites documentation.

Main

The code for the routine Main, annotated for easier comprehension, is:

```
Sub Main()
    Dim sPhrase, sCacheKey, sCatalogSetID
    Dim sSearchPhrase
    Dim rsSearchResults, iRecordCount
```

*The following constant, **MIN_SEARCHRESULTS**, is actually used as the starting record, not the minimum number of search results to return. If more than 50 records are returned by the search, the Retail Solution Site, as released, cannot show the matches beyond the 50th one. To do so, the page would need to be enhanced so that it could be called again with an additional query string parameter that indicates the appropriate starting record. Then, "next page" and "previous page" links could be conditionally added, and the search page could call itself with different starting record values.*

```
    Const MIN_SEARCHRESULTS = 1
    Const MAX_SEARCHRESULTS = 50

    Call EnsureAccess()
    sPageTitle = mscsMessageManager.GetMessage("L_Search_HTMLTitle", sLanguage)

    ' Initialize
    sPhrase = ""
    sSearchPhrase = ""
```

*The keyword(s) to be searched for are passed to this page as the value of the query string parameter "keyword." The routine **GetRequestString** is used to retrieve the keyword(s) from the query string.*

```
' Get search phrase
sPhrase = LCase(GetRequestString("keyword", Null))
If IsNull(sPhrase) Then
    sSearchPhrase = ""
Else
    sSearchPhrase = sPhrase
End If
```

*The site caches the results of keyword searches and checks it using the routine **bFullTextResultsAreCached**. If the same keyword has been used before, the previous results are immediately assigned to the variable **htmPageContent** and the routine **Main** is done (note that the body of the if condition is empty). If the search result for this particular search is not found in the cache, the site routine **rsFreeTextSearch** is called to perform the requested search. The **RecordSet** object resulting from the search is then passed to the routine **htmRenderFullTextSearchResults** for conversion to HTML and assignment to the variable **htmPageContent**.*

```
' If results are cached, the query doesn't need to be run
If bFullTextResultsAreCached(sSearchPhrase, htmPageContent, sCacheKey) Then
    '
Else
    Set rsSearchResults = rsFreeTextSearch(sSearchPhrase, _
                                           MIN_SEARCHRESULTS, _
                                           MAX_SEARCHRESULTS, _
                                           iRecordCount)

    htmPageContent = htmRenderFullTextSearchResults(sSearchPhrase, _
                                                    rsSearchResults, _
                                                    sCacheKey, _
                                                    iRecordCount)

End If
' The result to display is now in htmPageContent.
End Sub
```

rsFreeTextSearch

The annotated version of the routine **rsFreeTextSearch**, found in the include file catalog.asp, follows:

```
Function rsFreeTextSearch(ByVal sPhrase, _
                          ByVal iStartingRecord, _
                          ByVal iRecordsToRetrieve, _
                          ByRef iRecordCount)
```

```
Dim sPropertiesToReturn, sPropertiesToSortOn, _
    rsResult, iClassType, sCatalogsToSearch
```

The properties to be returned in the record set, and their sort order, are hardwired in the next two string assignments.

```
' "name" and "description" are required product
' properties and cannot have null values.
sPropertiesToReturn = PRODUCT_NAME_PROPERTY_NAME & "," & _
                      PRODUCT_DESCRIPTION_PROPERTY_NAME & "," & _
                      CATALOG_NAME_PROPERTY_NAME & "," & _
                      CATEGORY_NAME_PROPERTY_NAME & "," & _
                      CATALOG_PRODUCTID_PROPERTY_NAME & "," & _
                      CATALOG_VARIANTID_PROPERTY_NAME & "," & _
                      DEFINITION_TYPE_PROPERTY_NAME

' "name" is a required product property and cannot have null value.
sPropertiesToSortOn = CATEGORY_NAME_PROPERTY_NAME & "," & _
                      PRODUCT_NAME_PROPERTY_NAME
```

*The values used in the following assignment are from the **CatalogClassTypeEnum** enumeration, which defines the enumeration values as powers of two so that they can be combined into a bit field.*

```
' iClassType determines the type of entities to search.
' (See FreeTextSearch documentation)
iClassType = cscProductFamilyForVariantsClass Or _
             cscProductClass Or _
             cscCategoryClass
```

*The routine **sUserCatalogsAsString** is in the include file catalog.asp and returns a string that contains a comma-separated list of the catalogs associated with the current user.*

```
sCatalogsToSearch = sUserCatalogsAsString()
```

*The routine ends by calling the **FreeTextSearch** method of the global **CatalogManager** object, passing a combination of the parameters passed to this routine and the parameters initialized within the routine. The **RecordSet** object returned by the method **FreeTextSearch** returned by this routine to its caller.*

```
Set rsFreeTextSearch = _
        MSCSCatalogManager.FreeTextSearch(sPhrase, _
                                          sCatalogsToSearch, _
                                          iClassType, _
                                          sPropertiesToReturn, _
```

```
                                        sPropertiesToSortOn, _
                                        True, _
                                        iStartingRecord, _
                                        iRecordsToRetrieve, _
                                        iRecordCount)


End Function
```

htmRenderFullTextSearchResults

The annotated version of the routine **htmRenderFullTextSearchResults,** found in the page search.asp, follows:

```
Function htmRenderFullTextSearchResults(ByRef sPhrase, ByRef rsResultSet, _
                                        sCacheKey, iRecordCount)
    Dim htmTitle, htmContent
```

The following assignment of the return value of the routine ***RenderText*** *is simply used to retrieve a heading for the lines of search results for the current language being used.*

```
    htmTitle = RenderText( _
            mscsMessageManager.GetMessage("L_FREETEXT_SEARCH_RESULT_TEXT", _
                                        sLanguage), _
            MSCSSiteStyle.Title) & CRLF
```

The real work of formatting the results in the ***RecordSet*** *object as HTML is performed in the routine* ***RentderSearchResults****, which is found in the include file catalog.asp.*

```
    htmContent = RenderSearchResults(sPhrase, rsResultSet, _
                                    iRecordCount, MSCSSiteStyle.Body)
```

The title and content are combined and returned as the result of this routine.

```
    htmRenderFullTextSearchResults = htmTitle & htmContent
```

Before returning, the formatted results of the current search are cached in the special cache used only for the results of full text searches.

```
    Call CacheFragment("FTSearchPageCache", sCacheKey, htmRenderFullTextSearchResults)

End Function
```

RenderSearchResults and RenderSearchResultRow

The routines **RenderSearchResults** and **RenderSearchResultRow** are found in the include file catalog.asp. The former routine either returns a string indicating that no matches were found, or builds up a string consisting of:

- A line reporting the number of matches found.

- An HTML formatted line with one of the search results for each record in the passed **RecordSet** object. This is accomplished by calling the routine **RenderSearchResultRow**, which formats the line appropriating for the type of search result (product, category, and so on), including a link to the corresponding product or category page.

As released, these routines do not format the results using the HTML **TABLE** element, though it is possible to change these routines to do so.

Keyword Searches in the International Solution Site

The keyword search functionality in the Commerce Server 2002 International Retail Site takes an entirely different approach, using ASP.NET classes and the Commerce Server Base Class Libraries (BCL). Our examination begins with the page SearchResults.aspx and its associated codebehind file SearchResults.aspx.vb. The layout of the search result page is specified by the HTML in the file SearchResults.aspx, and consists of a form with several embedded tables. Near the bottom of the page, and ASP.NET **DataGrid** control is defined to display the results of the search and is given the ID "searchResults". This control has the search results bound to it at the end of the routine **PerformSearch**.

Search_Click

The routine **Search_Click** is defined in the class **CatalogBase**, which is inherited by many of the classes that support pages through the International Retail Site. This routine ends up being executed when the catalog search button is clicked on any of these pages. The annotated version of the routine **Search_Click**, found in the file CatalogBase.vb, follows:

```
Private Sub Search_Click(ByVal Sender As Object, _
                    ByVal e As System.EventArgs) _
          Handles catalogSearchCtl.SearchBtn_Click
```

*The catalog(s) to be searched for the keyword(s) specified in the search control are recorded in their respective properties in the **CatalogBase** class, and are retrieved in the next routine shown, **Page_Load**.*

```
searchCatalogVal = catalogSearchCtl.Catalog
searchKeywordsVal = catalogSearchCtl.Keywords
```

The query string parameter "callingPage=CatalogBase" is established and control is transferred to the page SearchResults.aspx.

```
Dim paramNames(0) As String
Dim paramValues(0) As String
paramNames(0) = URLQueryParameterNames.callingPage
paramValues(0) = "CatalogBase"

CommerceApplication.ServerTransfer("SearchResults.aspx", paramNames, paramValues)
```

```
End Sub
```

Page_Load

The annotated version of the routine **Page_Load**, found in the file SearchResults.aspx.vb and called when the page is requested, follows:

```
Private Sub Page_Load(ByVal sender As System.Object, _
                      ByVal e As System.EventArgs) Handles MyBase.Load

   If (Not Page.IsPostBack) Then
      catalogNavTabsCtl.SetTabs()
      catalogBrowserCtl.RenderList()
```

Because the passed query string parameter is "callingPage=CatalogBase", the variable **catalogBasePage** *is initialized for the subsequent retrieval of the catalog(s), keyword(s), and count of the number of matching results to display.*

```
      If Request.Params(URLQueryParameterNames.callingPage) = "CatalogBase" Then
         Dim catalogBasePage As CatalogBase
         catalogBasePage = CType(Context.Handler, CatalogBase)
```

The catalog(s), keyword(s), and count of the number of matching results to display are retrieved from their respective properties in the appropriate **CatalogBase** *object, and then passed to the routine* **PerformSearch**.

```
         Dim searchCatalog As String = catalogBasePage.SearchCatalog
         Dim searchKeywords As String = catalogBasePage.SearchKeywords
         Dim displayNo As Integer = catalogBasePage.DisplayNo
         PerformSearch(searchCatalog, searchKeywords, displayNo)
      End If
   End If
End Sub
```

PerformSearch

The annotated version of the routine **PerformSearch**, found in the file SearchResults.aspx.vb, follows:

```
Protected Sub PerformSearch(ByVal searchCatalog As String, _
                            ByVal searchKeywords As String, _
                            Optional ByVal displayNo As Integer = -1)
```

*Define objects of class **DataSet**, class **CatalogSearch**, and class **CatalogSearchOptions** (the latter two classes are in the Commerce Server 2002 Base Class Library (BCL) for catalogs, accessed using the namespace **Microsoft.CommerceServer.Runtime.Catalog**.*

```
Dim data As DataSet
Dim displaySearchResults As Boolean = True
Dim catalogSearch As Microsoft.CommerceServer.Runtime.Catalog.CatalogSearch = _
        New Microsoft.CommerceServer.Runtime.Catalog.CatalogSearch()
Dim searchOptions As CatalogSearchOptions = New CatalogSearchOptions()
```

*Set the ClassTypes property of the CatalogSearchOptions object to include contain the indicated search targets using the **CatalogClassTypes** enumeration, available using the namespace **Microsoft.CommerceServer.Runtime.Catalog**.*

```
' Set the class type to get Products, Families and Families for variants
searchOptions.ClassTypes = CatalogClassTypes.ProductClass Or _
                           CatalogClassTypes.ProductFamilyClass Or _
                           CatalogClassTypes.ProductFamilyForVariantsClass
```

*Assign the passed keywords and **SearchOptions** object to the corresponding properties in the CatalogSearch object, and set the record count in the **SearchOptions** object to the passed value.*

```
catalogSearch.FreeTextSearchPhrase = searchKeywords
catalogSearch.SearchOptions = searchOptions
catalogSearch.SearchOptions.RecordsToRetrieve = displayNo

Try
    ' if "all catalogs" is selected
    If searchCatalog = CommerceApplication.ResourceString(ResID.allCatalogs) Then
```

*If the search request is for all catalogs, retrieve a string collection of all catalogs and assign it to the **CatalogNamesCollection** property of the **CatalogSearch** object. Also set the properties to be returned as established in the constant **SEARCH_RETURNPROPERTIES**. This constant contains a string that specifies four required catalog properties to be returned. Otherwise, an error could occur when the different catalogs have different properties defined.*

```
        Dim catalogCollection As ReadOnlyStringCollection
        catalogCollection = GetCatalogs()

        If (Not catalogCollection Is Nothing) _
```

```
        AndAlso (catalogCollection.Count > 0) Then

    catalogSearch.CatalogNamesCollection = catalogCollection
    searchOptions.PropertiesToReturn = SEARCH_RETURNPROPERTIES
```

*Perform the actual search using the **Search** method of the **CatalogSearch** object.*

```
        data = catalogSearch.Search()
    End If

  Else
```

*Instead of using the **CatalogNamesCollection** property of the **CatalogSearch** object to specify which catalogs are to be searched, use the **CatalogNames** property, assigning the passed catalog name to it (although the CatalogNames property can handle multiple catalogs using a comma-separated list of catalog names, the user interface of the International Retail Site only permits a choice between all catalogs and a particular, single catalog). Note that it could improve performance if this search was also set up to only return the properties specified in the constant **SEARCH_RETURNPROPERTIES**, since those are the only properties displayed. This optimization is left as an exercise for the reader.*

```
    catalogSearch.CatalogNames = searchCatalog
```

*Perform the actual search using the **Search** method of the **CatalogSearch** object.*

```
        data = catalogSearch.Search()
    End If
```

Check for exceptions thrown during the search.

```
  Catch Ex As Exception
    data = Nothing
  End Try
```

*If no results are returned, record that no results should be displayed using the **displaySearchResults** variable.*

```
  'If the Dataset returned by Search is empty
  ' then do not display search results
  If data Is Nothing OrElse data.Tables(0).Rows.Count = 0 Then
    displaySearchResults = False
  End If
```

*Turn the visibility of different controls on or off using the value of the **displaySearchResults** variable.*

```
' Set the visibility of the controls depending on search results
productHeader.Visible = displaySearchResults
typeHeader.Visible = displaySearchResults
searchResults.Visible = displaySearchResults
noSearchResults.Visible = Not displaySearchResults
```

If there are not any results to display, retrieve either an error string or a string indicating that no matches were found.

```
If displaySearchResults = False Then

    ' If data  is Nothing means that search has failed
    If data Is Nothing Then
        ' Need to add a better message for this case
        noSearchResults.Text = _
            CommerceApplication.ResourceString(ResID.searchFailed)

    Else
        noSearchResults.Text = _
            CommerceApplication.ResourceString(ResID.noSearchResults)
    End If
```

*Otherwise, set the text for the two header controls and bind the search data to the **DataGrid** control defined in the file SearchResults.aspx (ID = "searchResults").*

```
Else

    ' Bind the data set to the searchResults control
    productHeader.Text = CommerceApplication.ResourceString(ResID.product)
    typeHeader.Text = CommerceApplication.ResourceString(ResID.type)
    searchResults.DataSource = New DataView(data.Tables(0))
    searchResults.DataBind()
End If

End Sub
```

By binding the search results to the **DataGrid** control using the **DataView** object, the page renders the results within the grid control.

The author trusts that this short implementation section has provided a sense of the Web site programming advances that are possible when using ASP.NET and the .NET Framework. There is definitely a learning curve involved, but the better programming structure made possible by the class inheritance, separation of HTML and code, and so on, which is possible when using ASP.NET is well worth the effort.

By Jim Christensen

Managing Web Content

Some Web sites on the Internet are much more focused on content than other sites, both in terms of volume of content and the timeliness of that content. Newspaper and periodical Web sites are perhaps the most extreme example of such content-intensive sites, often with new content being posted throughout the course of each day. Such sites often require highly specialized solutions. Short of such extremes, there are numerous other types of content-oriented Web sites out there, ranging from corporate Web sites to governmental information sites to entertainment sites to internal company sites. This chapter will focus on one of Microsoft's best solutions for this type of site: Microsoft Content Management Server. The chapter is divided into the following sections:

- **Scenario**. This section further describes the business problem to be solved.

- **Solution**. This section describes how Content Management Server can be used to solve this business problem.

- **Tools and Technology**. This section focuses on the various tools and technologies involved in solving the business problem.

- **Implementation**. This section drills deeper into select portions of the proposed solution to give the reader a sense of the level of technical expertise required in implementing the solution.

This chapter progresses from a high-level discussion of the business problem and Microsoft's solution to it to a more granular discussion of some coding examples in the "Implementation" section. If you are looking for more of an overview, you may want to skip the last section.

Scenario

One of the most powerful aspects of using a Web site to present information is the ability to publish frequent updates. Unlike more traditional media, such as print, a Web site can be updated on a continuous basis, limited only by the Web site staff's ability to generate the updates. As anyone who has ever participated in Web site management knows, the amount of such work should not be underestimated. The work can be divided into two broad categories:

- **Web site navigation**. Web site navigation concerns a user's ability to move from page to page within a site, using the links that are displayed on the current page. As pages are removed from the site, the links to those pages must also be removed or they will break. As pages are moved within the site, the links to those pages must be changed or they will break. As new pages are added to the site, links to those pages must be added or they will never be found.

  Most Web sites employ some sort of standardized navigation scheme that is used on most, if not all, pages in the site. Often, the left and/or top of each page is used to display frequently used links and links that relate to the content of the current page. The effort required to keep the navigation working properly as the site is updated depends on the infrastructure used to create the navigation scheme. This effort often requires specialized technical skills, and must be performed by someone other than the person or people making the decisions about what updates should be made.

- **Page content**. At a basic level, the purpose of a page in a Web site is to display content to a user. Creating even relatively simple pages that contain only images and text requires a number of different tasks. Images must be created, text must be written and edited, the layout of images, text, and navigation must be designed and implemented in Hypertext Markup Language (HTML), the final result must be tested and approved, the lifespan of the content must be determined and managed, and so on. Looking beyond the content of any one page or small set of related pages, the combined content of the entire Web site at any given point in time also requires planning and careful management. These tasks require disparate skills, and are often performed by different people working together to produce the set of pages that constitute the Web site.

A common theme in both categories is that there are different roles, filled by people with different skills, who must work together to make updates to the Web site happen as smoothly as possible. Generally speaking, the following roles contribute to Web site creation and management:

- Content managers

- Writers

- Graphic artists

- Editors

- Developers

- Administrators (of various sorts: Web site, database, and so on)

Creating and managing a Web site in a way that enables the people in these different roles to work well together, and that eliminates or minimizes any bottlenecks that would otherwise occur, is a significant business problem and is the focus of this chapter. The next section discusses how Content Management Server can be used to solve this business problem.

Solution

Microsoft Content Management Server is a new Microsoft product that optimizes the process of creating and updating Web sites by recognizing that a variety of people with different skill sets contribute to this process. Content Management Server recognizes a number of different roles, and provides user interfaces and an architecture that solve many of the traditional interaction difficulties between the people in various roles.

These interaction solutions take various forms. In some cases, the best solution is to isolate the tasks performed by the various roles, effectively minimizing the amount of interaction required. For example, the Content Management Server architecture provides templates that page designers use to perform page layout abstractly. A set of these templates is made available to content authors. The content authors simply drag the content they've created into the appropriate template.

In other cases, the best solution to role interaction difficulty is to create user interfaces that provide a workflow between the different roles. For example, after a content author has created a new page by dragging their content into the appropriate template, they use the user interface to submit their new page to the appropriate editor for approval. The editor is provided with a user interface through which they can see the pages awaiting their approval, and through which they can perform their review and either accept or reject the page. Accepted pages proceed to the next step in the publication process, and rejected pages are returned to the content author for the appropriate revisions.

This section of the chapter explains how the role-centric architecture of Content Management Server provides a good solution to many of the problems inherent in the process of creating and updating Web site content.

- **The Basic Idea**. At the core, the basic idea behind Content Management Server is simple: use the Web site as its own work environment. The people who produce the Web site content are given privileged access that allows them to create and edit their content in their browsers by selectively placing the Web site in authoring mode. This section further describes this experience from a user's point of view, and introduces the Web site infrastructure that makes this possible.

- **Concepts and Terminology**. Content Management Server has a unique architecture that is designed to address the optimization of role interactions. This architecture introduces a number of new concepts and terms that are somewhat different than more traditional Web site architecture. Gaining sufficient understanding of these new concepts and the associated terminology is necessary to understanding the various roles defined by Content Management Server.

- **Roles and Rights**. Dividing the tasks associated with creating and updating Web sites into different roles and different areas of responsibility is central to the design of Content Management Server, and is touched upon in the section "The Basic Idea." This section discusses these roles in greater detail and discusses how people in different roles contribute to the process of creating and updating a Web site. Understanding these roles is crucial to understanding the functionality provided by Content Management Server.

- **Creating a Content Management Server Web Site**. Given a basic understanding of the Content Management Server architecture and roles, this section summarizes the steps, performed by people in different roles, involved in using Content Management Server to create a Web site.

- **Content Management Server 2002**. Microsoft released Content Management Server 2001 in the summer of 2001. Work is currently underway on the 2002 version, but it will not be released until several months after this book has been published. This section discusses the ways in which the 2002 version will be different than the 2001 version.

The Basic Idea

The basic idea behind Content Management Server is simple: create a Web site within a Web site, where each page has an alter ego that, when displayed, shows controls that allows different types of content to be altered. What was text in the "normal" view of a Web page becomes an edit control in the alternate view. What was a picture in the "normal" view of a Web page becomes an image chooser control in the alternate view. Taken together, these alternate views comprise an authoring mode for the Web site, built right into the Web site itself.

Generally speaking, in order for a Web site to be successful, its largest group of users needs to be the general public, or whatever broad class of users for whom the Web site was created. In Content Management Server terminology, such users are called "subscribers." They subscribe to the Web site. In cases where subscriptions are free, there are no sign-up procedures, and the Web site is on the Internet, the Web site is allowing everyone to be a subscriber.

Again speaking generally, the next largest group of Web site users is the set of people who create content for the Web site. Now, it could be argued that these people are not users of the Web site, but rather creators of the Web site. On the other hand, it could be argued that they are also users of the Web site, just a privileged class of users who are authorized to change the content as well as look at it. And with respect to Content Management Server, which provides the unique Web site architecture that makes the dual-mode Web site possible, such people are clearly users of Content Management Server. In Content Management Server, this set of people is broken down further according to a more refined division of work responsibilities: there are authors and editors and, to a lesser extent, moderators (more on this last point later).

These different types of content contributors are the primary set of users to whom Content Management Server is targeted. There are other roles, such as site administrators and site programmers, but they will typically be fewer in number and, if the Web site is well-designed and thought through, have less frequent interactions with the Web site.

Using Content Management Server, when a content author wants to create a new page in the Web site, they perform the following steps:

1. Log in to the Web site using credentials authorized to author content in the Web site.

2. Browse to the location in the Web site where the new page is meant to reside.

3. Click the **Switch to Edit Site** link. This changes the Web site from Live mode to Edit mode, and re-renders the page with a menu of editing commands.

4. Click the **Create New Page** link in the edit menu. This re-renders the page so that it is effectively read/write rather than read-only. A Web control is displayed in those positions on the page where the author is expected to provide content, and can be initialized to describe the type of content expected.

5. The author uses the Web controls to provide the type of content expected, such as by dragging an image into an image control, or typing text into an edit control.

6. Click the **Save and Exit** link in the (reduced) edit menu. This saves the new page and starts the workflow process through which the page will eventually appear in the Web site in Live mode. This workflow is basically an approval process, and includes tasks such as editing of the text and checking that the images and so on are appropriate.

The process of modifying an existing page is not much different. Instead of clicking **Create New Page** in the edit menu, click **Edit** to modify the current page. The page is re-rendered with the existing content shown within the corresponding controls, ready to be modified as appropriate. When **Save and Exit** is clicked, the page re-enters the approval workflow.

In Content Management Server, this basic process of process of putting the Web site into authoring mode to make changes is what comprises the Web Author application. If you think about it, this application is unique in that its user interface continually changes to mirror the very result of its operation. The Web Author application is used to produce a Web site, and the structure of the Web site itself provides the navigation paradigm for the application. There is an ease to the way this design eliminates the need for a mental abstraction to picture the Web site structure in different terms, such as a tree control.

The actual process of creating and updating pages in Content Management Server has a number of options, such as the ability to set start and end dates for a given Web page, that have not been mentioned here. Content Management Server also provides several other tools in addition to the Web Author application. These tools are generally used by people in roles that are more technical than the content contributor roles, such as site administrators and site developers, and generally involve a more involved set of concepts and terminology than has been revealed thus far. These topics and more will be discussed in the remainder of the chapter.

Concepts and Terminology

Understanding the unique architecture of Content Management Server requires an understanding of a number of new concepts and the associated terminology. This section provides an overview of these concepts and introduces the terminology used to describe them. The discussion starts with the more basic, fundamental concepts and then moves to more advanced concepts. However, because the concepts are interrelated, it is difficult to talk about them in isolation from each other. Some terminology is used in the explanation of one concept, before its corresponding concept has been explained. Such terminology appears in italics to indicate that its explanation is forthcoming.

This section describes concepts and terminology that relates to both the 2001 and 2002 versions of Content Management Server, and points out differences where appropriate.

Maintained in a Database

The various entities that together constitute a page in a Content Management Server Web site are kept in a Microsoft SQL Server database. Of course, data-driven Web sites are nothing new. Many Web sites contain pages with script that retrieves data from a database and then formats the data as HTML. The difference with Content Management Server is that more of the page elements are kept in the database. In Content Management Server, a page is comprised of a page template and a set of resources and content associated with the placeholders in that template. All of these elements, the template, the resources, and the content, are kept in the database.

Note that in Content Management Server 2002, some of the entities that are kept in the database in the 2001 version will be moved to the file system, which is more like how other Web sites are maintained. Better source control is one of the advantages that will be gained by making this change. For more information about these forthcoming changes, see the section on Content Management Server 2002 later in this chapter.

Framed vs. Frameless Sites

In typical usage, Content Management Server assumes that Web pages will be designed with distinct areas for navigation and content. Most of us are quite familiar with this classic Web interface paradigm: navigation area(s) on the left and/or top portion of the page, with a content area to the right and/or below the navigation area(s). The navigation area(s) contains links to other pages in the site, and the content area contains the specific content associated with the current page. While some parts of the navigation area(s) might change based on the current page being shown, it is common for at least some aspects of the navigation to remain the same for all pages. This navigation strategy seems to work well, enabling users browsing the Web site to easily find their way between the major areas of the site.

One of the most basic decisions to be made when designing a Content Management Server Web site concerns how the pages will be divided into these different areas. In Content Management Server, two basic types of Web sites are possible:

- **Framed sites**. A framed site uses the **FRAMESET** and **FRAME** tags to divide Web pages into distinct areas.

- **Frameless sites**. A frameless site uses **TABLE**, **DIV**, or **SPAN** tags (or some combination) to divide Web pages into distinct areas.

The decision between a framed and a frameless site is a fundamental choice and has major implications for how both *navigation templates* and *page templates* must be constructed. The *MSCMS Site Programmer Guide* contains much more detailed information on this topic than can be covered here.

Templates

The use of predefined page templates for authoring Web content is one of the key defining features of Content Management Server. Page template designers create various page templates, using a combination of HTML and script to define the overall layout of different types of pages. Content authors then choose the appropriate page template from a *template gallery* for the content they are creating, and drag their specific content into the *placeholders* in the template, without needing to do any HTML tagging.

Content Management Server 2001 uses another type of template, known as a navigation template, to control the navigation choices displayed for a given channel. In framed sites, navigation templates are used to control the navigation content displayed in the navigation frame. In frameless sites, navigation templates are used to control the content displayed when the current URL specifies a *channel* rather than a *posting*.

The previous discussion about framed versus frameless sites stated that the choice between a framed site and a frameless site has significant consequences for how navigation and page templates must be constructed. The names of these different types of templates originated when framed sites were more popular. This is apparent because in a framed site, a given Web page has a navigation template associated with the navigation frame and a page template associated with the content frame. Content authors only need to determine the appropriate page template for the content they are producing, with the choice of navigation template being something determined behind the scenes by the site programmer.

In a frameless site, two distinct approaches are possible. In one approach, the differences between a navigation template and a page template begin to break down. Both types of templates contain similar (or perhaps identical) code for dividing the page into distinct areas by using one or more **TABLE**, **DIV**, or **SPAN** tags. Both types of templates must contain the code required to create the navigation area for the page. And both types of templates must contain the code and/or HTML to create the content to be displayed in the content area.

The largest difference between the two types of templates is that it is still just page templates, and not navigation templates, that contain *placeholders* to be filled in by content authors. When the URL specifies a *channel*, a navigation template is used to display the page (this is similar to a URL that specifies a directory in a file-based Web site). When the URL specifies a *posting*, a page template is used to display the page (this is similar to a URL that specifies a file in a file-based Web site). A problem arises with this approach for many Web site designs because the lack of *placeholders* in navigation templates prevents standard authoring techniques from being used.

In the second approach, the navigation templates associated with channel URLs are designed to redirect to an appropriate default posting. Sometimes, the default posting is just the one named "default" or "index," or it can be the first posting in the channel. Another alternative is to define a custom property for the channel and use that property to store the name of the default posting for the channel. Note that in Content Management Server 2002, a new property called **DefaultPostingName** has been added to the **Channel** object. This strategy must account for the possibility that the channel will not have any postings in it and must be prepared to display something appropriate.

Placeholders

When page template designers creates a page template, one of their main tasks is to define placeholders for the template. Placeholders reserve areas on the page into which content authors will add their specific content. Placeholders are defined as a particular type, which controls the type of content that can replace the placeholder when the template is used to create a page.

For example, a placeholder might be defined to contain an image, and the page template designer might put a temporary image into the placeholder. It is considered good practice to make the temporary image contain text such as "Place your photograph here," so that the author knows what type of image to put into that placeholder, and so that it will be easy for an editor to notice if the image is not replaced. Note that if the default Content Management Server image is left in the placeholder, it will never be shown on the live site, but it will also not serve to tell the author what type of image is supposed to be used.

Or a placeholder might be defined to contain unformatted text, and the page template designer might put the text, "Place the title of the article here," and then surround the placeholder with HTML formatting tags.

Pages and Postings

Pages and postings are closely related. Indeed, from the perspective of content contributors using the *Web Author* application, the difference is not apparent. When they switch to the mode in which they can edit the site, they are presented with commands like **Create New Page** and **Create Connected Page**. In this process, both pages and postings are created, but from the author's perspective, it is just a new page.

When a content author using Content Management Server 2001 uses the *Site Builder* application to create new pages, the differences between pages and postings will be more apparent. (Note that the Site Builder application is not even available in Content Management Server 2002; it has been renamed Site Manager, and has been re-factored as a tool for site administrators only.) In the Site Builder application, content authors begin by creating pages in the folder hierarchy, choosing the appropriate page template upon which to base the page. The author then adds content to each of the placeholders in the page template, such as by dragging or copying and pasting, text from another application such as Microsoft Word. The author can also set *page properties*, including *custom properties*, to establish the page as having certain characteristics. Eventually, the author submits the page that he or she has created to be approved by an editor.

At some point, a posting must be created for the new page. In the *Site Builder* application, the author might create the posting prior to submitting the page to an editor for approval, or the author might let the editor create the posting for the page during the approval process. In any event, a page cannot appear on the Web site unless it has been posted. In the Web Author application, the page and the corresponding posting are created at the same time.

A posting is a page that has been assigned to a *channel*, which specifies the location within the Web site where the page will appear. Postings have some other *properties* that serve to extend the properties associated with the corresponding page. For example, postings are assigned lifetime properties, such as the date at which they should first become available on the Web site, and the date or duration after which they should no longer be available. Other properties can be used to mark a posting as important, hidden, and subject or not to crawling and indexing by Web robots.

Note that in Content Management Server 2002, there will be no distinction made between pages and postings. Essentially, what are "pages" in the 2001 version will now move behind the scenes in the 2002 version, and what are "postings" in the 2001 version will be called "pages" in the 2002 version.

Folders and Channels

Folders and channels correspond to pages and postings, respectively. Folders are containers that are used to organize pages, and can be created in a hierarchical fashion. Besides the obvious benefit of organizing pages according to their purpose so that they are easier to find in the future, folders also allow access to different sets of pages to be controlled. Users in different roles, such as authors and editors, can be granted the right to access some folders but not others, which provides a way to enforce the division of responsibility for different portions of a Web site.

Channels are containers that are used to organize postings, effectively determining the organization of a Web site from the perspective of someone browsing the Web site. Using the default URL scheme for a Content Management Server Web site, the channels are visible as the components of the URL after the domain name. For example, the underlined portion of the URL "http://www.microsoft.com/cmserver/default.htm" is the channel portion of the URL. In effect, channels mirror the folder structure of a file-based Web site, a structure that is not inherently present in a Content Management Server Web site due to the fact that the entire site is maintained in a database.

Like folders, access to channels can be controlled using *rights groups*. This provides a mechanism through which access to the Web site can be restricted in different ways for different users.

The Content Management Server documentation recommends that the folder hierarchy created to organize pages be set up to mirror the channel hierarchy created to organize postings. Real-life experience has shown that it is much easier to administer the Web site when this recommendation is followed.

If the Web Author application is used to create and update content for the Web site, the site administrator needs to enable Web authoring in the channel's **Properties** dialog box. One of the required settings is that the corresponding folder must be defined, so that when new postings are created in the Web Author application, the pages will be created in the correct folder. Of course, from the perspective of the content author creating the posting/page, the distinction between the two is not apparent.

Note that in Content Management Server 2002, folders will move behind the scenes. The Site Manager application, formerly the Site Builder application, will not have a folder hierarchy.

Properties

Various entities within Content Management Server, such as pages, postings, and channels, have properties associated with them. Some properties are built-in, and defining custom properties can extend the properties associated with some entities.

Properties can be read and written using the appropriate user interface(s) or using the Content Management Server *Publishing Application Programming Interface (API)*. The script code within both navigation templates and page templates is often written so that it examines various properties of current postings and channels in order to create the appropriate content for the current page. For example, within a given channel, postings for which the **IsImportant** property is set to **True** might be displayed more prominently than postings for which the **IsImportant** property is set to **False**.

Resources

Resources are defined by Content Management Server as any content stored in a *resource gallery*, although they tend to be multimedia enhancements to Web pages. In most Web sites, the most common type of resource is an image. Other common types of resources include sound and video clips. Any other types of content can be stored as a resource, but will usually be shown on Web pages as downloadable links rather than embedded within the Web page itself. A common example is fiscal year-end statistics in a Word or PDF document.

The purpose of resources in Content Management Server is to provide a mechanism for maintaining a centralized location for preapproved images, videos, and so on, generally for use on multiple Web pages. Because access to *galleries*, including resource galleries, can be controlled using rights groups, control over who can access which resources can easily be implemented.

Galleries

Galleries are the type of organizational container used for templates and for resources. Template designers create navigation and page templates and store them in template galleries. Resource managers store the various site resources, presumably gathered from a variety of sources, such as graphic artists, in resource galleries.

Like folders and channels, galleries can be created and arranged hierarchically, allowing whatever organization best suits the needs of a given Web site. Also, like folders and channels, access to galleries can be controlled using rights groups, enabling a site administrator to enforce policies about which resources are allowed to appear in different portions of the Web site.

Roles

As mentioned earlier, one of the most powerful and fundamental aspects of Content Management Server is its built-in recognition of the different skill sets that contribute to the process of creating and updating a Web site. Web sites are a result of ongoing collaboration between people in different roles, including site administrators, site developers (who are responsible for template design in Content Management Server), content authors, and editors. There is an entire section dedicated to these different roles, and how rights can be granted within roles, later in this chapter.

Even the users who are the intended audience of the Web site are assigned to a role. Such users are said to be "subscribers," and subscriber access to the Web site can be controlled just like access for other roles, by using rights groups.

Rights Groups

Rights groups are the mechanism used to control access of various types to different users within Content Management Server. Different types of rights groups correspond to different job functions. Authors need rights that control the pages they can create, editors need rights that control the pages they can approve, and moderators need rights that control the areas of the Web site for which they are responsible. Subscriber rights control the areas of the Web site to which they have access. Rights for template designers and resource managers are used to control their access to template and resource galleries, respectively. Administrators can step in to do any task, and they also have rights allowing them to create channels and to establish rights groups for others.

The different types of rights also correspond roughly to different types of containers, such as channels, folders, and galleries. For example, author and editor rights groups are used to control access to folders, moderator and subscriber rights groups are used to control access to channels, and template designer and resource manager rights groups are used to control access to template and resource galleries, respectively.

The first step is to create one or more rights groups for a particular role. Second, users are assigned to different rights groups. Third, rights groups are assigned to different containers. For a user to have the right to work in a particular container, acting in a particular role, they must belong to at least one of the rights groups for that role for that container.

Web Author

Web Author is a set of client-side and server-side scripts that are used in conjunction with the pages (postings) in a Web site, allowing the pages to be viewed in several different modes. This effectively allows content authoring and approval to be performed within the context of the Web site itself. In Live mode, the pages are seen as subscribers are meant to see them, with actual content in the page template upon which the page is based. If the subscriber is also acting in another role, such as author or editor, the page includes the link **Switch to Edit Site**, which re-renders the page in a mode that allows editing. The following figure illustrates a page in Live mode in the Method Systems sample site that comes with Content Connector.

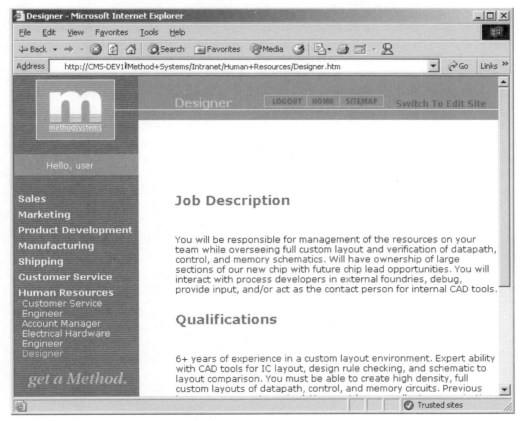

In Edit mode, the page is rendered such that the link that previously said, **Switch to Edit Site** now says, **Switch to Live Site**. More important, it is now rendered with a special editing menu of more than a dozen commands, as shown in the following figure.

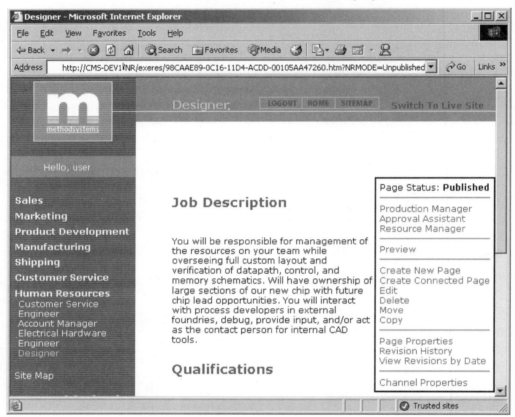

The **Edit** command can be used to change the content on the page, causing the page to be re-rendered such that the text that can be changed, the text in the placeholders, is rendered within special HTML editing controls. The special editing menu is still present, but has a reduced set of commands available, as shown in the following figure.

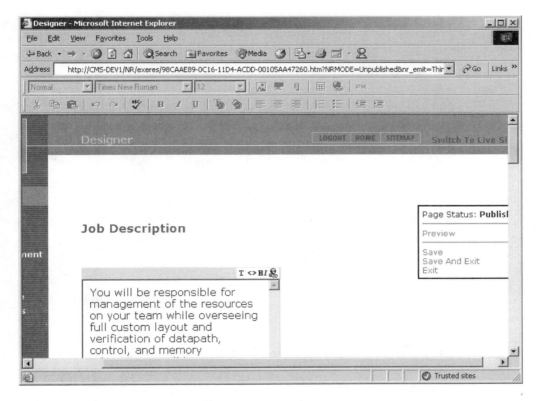

After the page content has been modified, the **Save and Exit** command can be used to return to the previous mode.

It is also important to note that in Content Management Server 2002, the Web Author application is being updated so that it will be much more extensible by site developers.

Site Builder

The Site Builder application is the main Microsoft® Win32® application in Content Management Server 2001. Users in different roles can use the Site Builder application to complete the tasks associated with their role:

- Site administrators use the Site Builder application to create the various container hierarchies to be used by people in the other roles, and to manage user roles and their associated rights groups.

- Template designers use the Site Builder application to add, move, delete, and otherwise manage the navigation and page templates for which they are responsible.

- Resource managers use the Site Builder application to add, move, or delete the resources under their management.

- Authors, editors, and moderators can use the Site Builder application for their respective tasks, although it is more common for these users to work in the Web Author application than in the Site Builder application.

The following figure shows the Site Builder application with the folder hierarchy partially expanded. Depending on a user's role, they may not see all of the types of containers in the left pane.

In Content Management Server 2002, the Site Builder application will be renamed Site Manager, and have its authoring functionality removed. This formalizes and finalizes the trend for authors, editors, and moderators to do their work exclusively within the Web Author application.

Connected Pages

Connected pages provide a way to share content between different pages. When looking at a particular page in Edit mode in the Web Author application, one of the available commands is **Create Connected Page**. If this command is chosen, the author is led through a series of pages to select a destination channel, a template gallery, and then a template within that gallery. If any of the placeholders in the chosen template are named the same as the placeholders in the template used by the original page, they will automatically adopt the same content. (If none of the placeholders have the same name, it is not particularly useful to create the connected page in the first place.) Placeholders with unique names must be given their own content.

This means that template designers must be involved in the process of creating Web sites that use connected pages. The template designers need to create families of similar templates that contain placeholders designed to hold the same content, and importantly, that have the same names. Presumably, other things about the templates are different, such as other placeholders being present or absent, and formatting.

Content Connector

Content Connector for Microsoft Commerce Server 2000 is an optional feature of Content Management Server 2001. It allows Content Management Server to be used in conjunction with Commerce Server to take advantage of the unique strengths of each product in a single Web site. There are two main integration points provided by Content Connector. First, Content Connector can be used to provide more extensive personalization functionality than is possible using Content Management Server's subscriber rights groups alone. Second, Content Connector can be used to provide product catalog pages based on products in the Commerce Server Product Catalog System, but that are managed within the context of Content Management Server.

For more information about Content Connector for Commerce Server 2000, see the section on Content Connector later in this chapter.

Publishing API

Content Management Server 2001 has an extensive application programming interface (API), known as the Publishing API (PAPI). One of the main purposes of the PAPI is to be used by template designers when writing the script code within navigation and page templates. PAPI gives them programmatic access to the entire hierarchy of channels and postings, and the various properties of those entities. The PAPI also provides access to resource and template galleries, to templates themselves, to the placeholders within the templates, and to information about users.

For more information about the PAPI, see the section "Programming with Content Management Server" later in this chapter.

URL Generation

When template designers use the publishing API in template script to generate navigation links, they use several properties of the **Channel** and **Posting** objects related to URL generation. Regardless of the URL mode in use (hierarchy-based, the default, or GUID-based), the dynamic nature of this URL generation means that channels and postings can be moved around within the Web site without breaking any of the associated links. This, of course, is a huge advantage over traditional, file-based Web sites. Another advantage when using hierarchy-based URLs is that the URLs used in Live mode are quite readable, and do not end with the long, obscure query strings that tend to break many search engines.

Roles and Rights

Microsoft Content Management Server defines distinct roles that participate in the process of creating and updating Web sites. For the most part, these roles correspond directly to the natural roles that apply to Web sites, though in a few cases, the names have been changed to correspond to terminology used for various concepts in the Content Management Server architecture.

Content Management Server also employs the notion of rights groups, which can be established to limit various types of access to particular users. Rights groups are created and associated with different types of containers, such as folders, channels, and galleries, with different types of rights groups being associated with different types of containers. When a user is put into a rights group associated with a particular container, that user will be allowed to work on the entities in that container. For example, if there is a folder named PressReleases that is used to contain press release pages for the Web site, and it has a single rights group named PressRelAuthors associated with it, only those content authors in that rights group will be allowed to create or update pages in the folder PressReleases.

The following table lists the roles in Content Management Server, their descriptions, and the rights groups to which they belong.

Role	Description
Subscriber	The subscriber role is used to define the set of people allowed to view the Web site using a browser. While many Web sites allow anyone to access their content without logging in, other Web sites require users to log in, sometimes charging a fee, in order to view particular portions of the site. Users who have identified themselves by logging in are subscribers, while users who have not identified themselves are considered to be a special type of subscriber called a guest.

(continued)

Role	Description *(continued)*
Subscriber *(continued)*	The subscriber role is used to define the set of people allowed to view the Web site using a browser. While many Web sites allow anyone to access their content without logging in, other Web sites require users to log in, sometimes charging a fee, in order to view particular portions of the site. Users who have identified themselves by logging in are subscribers, while users who have not identified themselves are considered to be a special type of subscriber called a guest.
Author	The author role is used to define the set of people allowed to create pages and post those pages to the Web site.
	Author rights groups are associated with channels, folders, and galleries, providing a mechanism to control, which authors can create and update different types of pages, including the templates, and resources that are used to create those pages. Note that authors are not allowed to add or remove resources or templates, and may be limited to using particular ones. By defining different author rights groups, different groups of authors can be restricted to creating pages for particular subsets of the Web site.
Editor	The editor role is used to define the set of people allowed to review the content of the pages created by authors and either approve them or decline them. By definition, editors can do everything an author can do, and they can approve or decline pages for publication.
	Editor rights groups are also associated with channels, folders, and galleries, similar to the author rights groups. In addition to the activities permitted to authors, editors are allowed to approve or decline pages. Like authors, editors are prohibited from adding or removing both resources and templates. By defining different editor rights groups, different groups of editors can be limited to editing content for only a subset of the Web site.
Moderator	The moderator role is used to define the set of people allowed to review the proposed posting location (the channel) of the pages created by authors, and the duration for which they will be available for viewing on the Web site. Moderators can approve or reject these aspects of a posting, or directly modify them before approving the posting. Note that moderators do not re-approve a posting unless the posting properties themselves are modified. In other words, content changes do not require a second approval by a moderator to be seen on the Live site.
	Moderator rights groups are associated with channels, providing a mechanism for controlling which moderators control postings to which channels. By defining different moderator rights groups, different moderators can be assigned to control postings on different subsets of the Web site.

(continued)

Role	Description *(continued)*
Moderator *(continued)*	Note that due to customer feedback about how Content Management Server is actually used, the role of moderator may not be carried forward in future versions of Content Management Server, including the 2002 version.
Resource manager	The resource manager role is used to define the set of people allowed to add or remove the resources used in the pages in the Web site. Resources are the items that can be added to a page or template other than basic HTML. For example, images, sounds and video clips, are all resources.
	Resource manager rights groups are associated with resource galleries, providing a mechanism for controlling which resource managers are in charge of which resource galleries. By defining different resource manager rights groups, different resource managers can be limited to managing resources for only a subset of the Web site.
	In order for resource managers to be able to create resource galleries themselves, they must be added to the administrators rights group, as only administrators are allowed to create containers such as galleries. Every company will need to decide for itself whether the convenience associated with enlarging the group of administrators is worth the risks.
Template designer	The template designer role is used to define the set of people allowed to create templates for the Web site. Although there are two distinct types of templates, page templates and navigation templates, both types are controlled using this one role. People in this role are also referred to as site developers.
	Template designer rights groups are associated with template galleries, providing a mechanism for controlling which template designers are in charge of creating and updating templates in different galleries. By defining different template designer rights groups, different template designers can be limited to creating templates for only a subset of the Web site.
	In order for template designers to be able to create template galleries themselves, they must be added to the administrators rights group, as only administrators are allowed to create containers, such as galleries. Every company will need to decide for itself whether the convenience associated with enlarging the group of administrators is worth the risks.

(continued)

Role	Description *(continued)*
Administrator	The administrator role is used to define a set of people who have unlimited access to the Web site and the Content Management Server tools used to develop the Web site. This includes the responsibility for creating the various types of Content Management Server containers in the Web site infrastructure, such as folders, channels, and galleries.
	There is only one administrators rights group, and it is created when Content Management Server is installed. Any user added to this rights group will have permission to perform any action within Content Management Server. This includes the ability to create containers of various types (folders, channels, and galleries) and for establishing the rights groups associated with the other roles.
	It is likely that in the 2002 version of Content Management Server, multiple administrator rights groups will be possible, creating the possibility of site administrators that are allowed to perform administration tasks for only a particular subset of a Web site.

Creating a Web Site

Having gained an understanding of the concepts and terminology used by Content Management Server, and an understanding of the different roles played by the people involved in developing a Web site, let's review the basic development steps with respect to the different roles and tasks, and the order in which those tasks are performed:

1. The Web site is designed on paper, taking the Content Management Server architecture into account.

2. The site administrator(s) uses the Site Builder application to create the containers of various types (folders, channels, galleries, and so on), according to the Web site design.

3. The template designer(s) and resource manager(s) use the Site Builder application to prepare templates for authoring, according to the Web site design (some templates require resources).

   In Content Management Server 2002, Microsoft Visual Studio .NET will provide the best environment for template design and creation.

4. The resource manager(s) creates or otherwise acquires resources required by the Web site design and use the Site Builder application to upload the resources. The authors will use these resources in their content.

5. Authors log into the Web site, find the appropriate place in the site to add a new page, then switch to editing mode. They choose to create a new page, pick a template, then drag content into place and insert resources. Then they save and submit the page for approval.

6. Editors log into the Web site and check for pages awaiting their approval. They review and edit the pages, and approve or decline them as required.

7. Moderators log into the Web site and check for pages awaiting their approval. They review the page location, lifetime, and so on, and approve or decline them as required.

8. Subscribers visit the Web site, log into it if required, and see the new page.

Content Connector for Commerce Server 2000

Content Connector for Commerce Server 2000 is an optional set of features within Content Management Server 2001. It provides mechanisms for creating Content Management Server Web sites that incorporate Commerce Server functionality in the following areas:

- **Product catalog**. Content Connector introduces the concepts of simple product pages and rich product pages.

- **Targeting**. Content Connector introduces the concept of personalized content objects (PCOs), which provide a mechanism through which content managed by Content Management Server can be targeted to particular users, positions on a page, and so on, using the extensible content selection pipeline mechanisms provided by Commerce Server.

The product catalog and targeting functionality provided by Content Connector both depend on a new type of profile defined within the Commerce Server Profiling System, known as a page profile. When Content Connector is installed, a new profile called "MSCMS Page Profile" is added and visible in the Profile Designer module (Users category) in Commerce Server Business Desk. Like other profiles in Commerce Server, such as user and organization profiles, content profiles can be extended with new properties as required.

Simple and Rich Product Pages

A simple product page is essentially like the page product.asp in the Commerce Server 2000 Solution Sites. It is a single page (posting) that displays information about the product that is specified by the query string parameters **catalog name**, **category name**, and **product key**.

Rich product pages are Content Management Server pages that are created for individual products, and which are based on a page template with placeholders to be filled as appropriate, such as product reviews or specifications. Rich product pages go through the normal Content Management Server page approval and publication process.

When a Web site that uses Content Connector is installed, such as the Method Systems sample site that comes with Content Connector, a new site resource is added. This site resource is called Content Connector, and it is accessible through Commerce Server Manager. The following table shows the four properties that can be set for the Content Connector site resource, all of which are related to simple and rich product pages.

Content Connector site resource property	Description
Catalog Root Channel	This property specifies the root channel for the product catalog for which simple and/or rich product pages are going to be displayed.
Default Rich Product Template	This property specifies the default page template or template gallery to be used when converting a simple product page into a rich product page. If a template gallery is specified, the user will be prompted to select a template in that gallery when converting a simple product page into a rich product page.
Default Simple Product Posting	This property specifies the default posting associated with catalog products for which no rich product page has (yet) been created.
Display Rich Products Only	This Boolean property controls whether products for which rich product pages have not (yet) been created are shown in the live Web site. It allows sites to not require all products to have rich product pages, showing the simple product page instead. For sites that do require rich product pages for all products, this property is useful during the initial creation of rich product pages, and when new products are added.

Personalized Content Objects

Content Connector contains personalized content objects (PCO), which are the mechanisms for controlling what content is going to appear, where it is going to appear, and to which users it is going to appear. PCOs can be used to link articles and other information to the products for which they are relevant, and to link product pages to additional content about those products.

PCOs are an extension of the Commerce Server Content Selection Framework, and are processed using a Commerce Server pipeline. PCOs are created and managed by business managers and allow content to be selected to appear in a posting based on a number of different factors, such as the current user, the context of the posting within the Web site, and the position on the page in which the content will appear.

The details of PCOs are too complex to be described here, but the following two separate Content Connector documents provide good descriptions of how to use PCOs to target content in a Content Connector Web site:

- **MSCMS Content Connector Tutorial.pdf**. This document provides a tutorial on the unique features of Content Connector, including page profiling, page personalization, and product pages.

- **MSCMS Business Desk Users Guide.pdf**. This document provides information about using the Business Desk modules that are installed when a Content Management Server Web site is unpacked. There are seven such modules, in two new categories, all of which are described in more detail in the following section.

Business Desk Extensions

Content Connector adds two new categories to Commerce Server Business Desk: Content and Targeting. The Content category contains two modules that are used to create and manage Web site content. These modules are shown in the following table.

Module	Description
Page Profiles	The Page Profiles module is used to manage page profiles, which are used for simple and rich product pages and for content targeting using PCOs. Note that the Web Author application is accessed from this module to create, edit, and approve pages.
Product Pages	The Product Pages module is used to view product catalogs, determine whether a particular product uses a rich or simple product page, and create rich product pages.

The Targeting category contains five modules that are used to create and manage PCOs. These modules are shown in the following table.

Module	Description
Personalized Content Objects	The Personalized Content Objects module is used to create and manage PCOs.
Content Groups	The Content Groups module is used to create combinations of content expressions, allowing more complex possibilities for content delivery.
Content Expressions	The Content Expressions module is used to create expressions to determine whether particular content meets a specific criterion.
Page Positions	The Page Positions module is used to associate particular content with specific locations on a page, allowing an additional basis for filtering of personalized content.
Publish PCOs	The Publish PCOs module is used to put changes made to PCOs in other modules into effect, and is also used to refresh or delete a PCO cache.

User Authorization

Broadly speaking, users in a Content Connector Web site are divided into guest users and privileged users. In order to see the Web site, even guest users must be given subscriber rights in Content Management Server. Guest users themselves can be divided into non-registered and registered guest users. Registered guest users are those users that have provided some registration information. This information is stored in a Commerce Server user profile. By providing this information, registered guest users can participate in the personalized content made possible with PCOs.

Privileged users can also be divided into different groups with different privileges. In the Method Systems sample site that comes with Content Connector, there are three types of privileged users: partners, content contributors, and administrators. Partners are further divided into three groups: education, OEM, and government. Partner users are subscribers with respect to Content Management Server roles, but are each allowed to see content that is specifically tailored for them.

Content contributors are privileged users that have been assigned to the Content Management Server roles of author or editor, and as such, can see the links that allow them to enter the Web site in editing mode. Administrators, as usual, are the ultimate privileged user and can see all content and work with the Web site in all modes.

Programming with Content Connector

Content Connector also provides the means to write programs that interact with the Content Connector functionality that is manipulated using the Commerce Server Manager, the Commerce Server Business Desk, and the Content Management Server Site Builder applications. The name of this collection of programming objects is the Content Connector for Commerce Server 2000 Framework API. More information about this API is available in the next section, "Programming with Content Management Server."

Microsoft Solution for Internet Business

In the same way that the Microsoft Solution for Supplier Enablement (MSSE) is a complete package for implementing solutions based on Microsoft BizTalk Accelerator for Suppliers (AFS), the Microsoft Solution for Internet Business (MSIB) is a complete package for implementing solutions based on Content Connector.

Each of these packaged solutions includes the necessary related products, which in the case of MSIB are Content Management Server, Commerce Server, and SQL Server. The MSIB also includes an operational Web site that serves as a starting point for Web development, extensive additional documentation, and additional assistance in designing the solution.

Depending on individual circumstances, such as the size of existing IT staff, the MSIB might be the most cost-effective way to pursue a solution that combines Content Management Server and Commerce Server using Content Connector.

Programming with Content Management Server

Content Management Server 2001 has an extensive API, known as the Publishing API (PAPI). PAPI uses an object model that contains objects that correspond to the various user interface elements manipulated by using the Site Builder application, such as channels, postings, and placeholders. Many of the objects are collections of a particular type of object (**Channels/Channel**, **Postings/Posting**, and so on).

Content Connector for Commerce Server 2000 also provides an API, known as the Content Connector Framework API. Objects in this API begin with the letters "NRCS" (for legacy reasons), such as the **NRCSSession** object and the **NRCSCatalog** object. These objects provide programmatic access to the object extensions used to store much of the Content Connector–specific data, as well as to the remaining few miscellaneous objects in the API.

Object-level descriptions of these APIs are provided in the following sub-sections.

Publishing API

One of the main purposes of the PAPI is to be used by template designers when writing the script code within navigation and page templates. The PAPI gives template designers programmatic access to the entire hierarchy of channels and postings, and the various properties of those entities. Access to resource and template galleries, to templates themselves, to the placeholders within the templates, and to information about users, is also provided.

The following table lists the objects available in the 2001 version of the Publishing API and provides a brief description of each object.

Object	Description
AllowedValues	The **AllowedValues** object is a collection of allowed value strings and is returned by the **AllowedValues** property of the **CustomProperty** object.
Autosession	The **Autosession** object is the root object of the Content Management Server object model and is automatically available in all templates that include the file Authenticate.inc, which creates an instance of this object called **Autosession**. The methods and properties of this object provide a wide variety of functionality, including: • User authentication • Information about the current mode • Access to the root containers of hierarchies

(continued)

Object	Description *(continued)*
Autosession *(continued)*	<ul><li>Information about the current user's system-wide rights</li><li>Database commitment</li><li>Creation of new **Searches** objects</li></ul>
Channel	The **Channel** object stores the information required to store, organize, and manage access to postings, including information about the channel hierarchy.
Channels	The **Channels** object is a collection of **Channel** objects and contains several sorting methods.
ChannelsAndPostings	The **ChannelsAndPostings** object is a mixed collection of **Channel** and **Posting** objects and contains several sorting methods. This object is included in Content Management Server 2001 for backward compatibility only and will not be included in future versions.
CustomProperties	The **CustomProperties** object is a collection of **CustomProperty** objects and is returned by the **CustomProperties** property of the **Channel** and **Posting** objects.
CustomProperty	The **CustomProperty** object is used to access any custom properties used to extend certain objects. A **CustomProperty** object consists of a name/value pair and a list of allowed values.
Error	The **Error** object stores information about the last error that occurred in Content Management Server.
Placeholder	The **Placeholder** object is used to store an item of formatted content for a page. The properties of a **Placeholder** object determine the types of media they can store and the level of formatting allowed to content authors.
Placeholders	The **Placeholders** object is a collection of **Placeholder** objects.
Posting	The **Posting** object represents a posting stored in a channel and is a collection of references to the parts (the page template, resources, and placeholders) that make up an HTML page in Content Management Server. Note that the properties of the **Posting** object are a combination (union) of the properties of the posting and the properties of the page upon which the posting is based. In other words, the publishing API does not have a **Page** object, but page properties (visible in the Site Builder and Web Author user interfaces) are accessible programmatically through the **Posting** object.
Postings	The **Postings** object is a collection of **Posting** objects and provides several sorting methods.
Resource	The **Resource** object represents an item, such as an image or other multimedia file, stored in a Content Management Server resource gallery.

(continued)

Object	Description *(continued)*
ResourceGalleries	The **ResourceGalleries** object is a collection of **ResourceGallery** objects and provides several sorting methods.
ResourceGallery	The **ResourceGallery** object stores the information required to retrieve resources from a resource gallery, including information about the resource gallery hierarchy.
Resources	The **Resources** object is a collection of **Resource** objects and provides several sorting and filtering methods.
Searches	The **Searches** object allows you to search for **Channel**, **Posting**, **Template**, **TemplateGallery**, **Resource**, and **ResourceGallery** objects that match specific criteria. Some searches will return a single object, while others will return a collection object.
SessionSettings	The **SessionSettings** object encapsulates adjustable settings of the **Autosession** object, such as settings to turn on or off certain automatic filters applied to collections.
Template	The **Template** object represents a page template stored in a Content Management Server template gallery.
TemplateGalleries	The **TemplateGalleries** object is a collection of **TemplateGallery** objects and provides several sorting methods.
TemplateGallery	The **TemplateGallery** object stores the information required to store, organize, and manage page templates and is used when navigating through the template gallery hierarchy.
Templates	The **Templates** object is a collection of **Template** objects and provides several sorting methods. Only page templates are available using this object; a template gallery containing both navigation and page templates will appear to contain only page templates.
User	The **User** object is used to represent Microsoft Windows NT and Lightweight Directory Access Protocol (LDAP) accounts and can access both the full and shortened names of a user. The properties of many other objects, such as the **CreatedBy**, **OwnedBy**, and **LastModifiedBy** properties, contain a **User** object rather than a string, allowing a site programmer more flexibility in choosing how to display user information.
Users	The **Users** object is a collection of **User** objects and is contained by the **Approvers** property of the **Posting** object.

Content Connector Framework API

The following table lists the objects available in the Content Connector Framework API and provides a brief description of each object.

Object	Description
NRCSSession	The **NRCSSession** object is the root object of the Content Connector Framework object model and is automatically available in all templates that include the file ConnectorApp_include.asp, which creates an instance of this object called **pNRCSSession**.

This object's **SelectContent** method is the normal way in which content is selected for display in a Content Management Server Web site. |
NRCSPosting	The **NRCSPosting** object extends the functionality of the associated Content Management Server **Posting** object where the posting represents a non-profiled, non-product page.
NRCSProfiledPosting	The **NRCSProfiledPosting** object extends the functionality of the associated Content Management Server **Posting** object, where the posting represents a profiled, non-product page.
NRCSSimpleProductPosting	The **NRCSSimpleProductPosting** object extends the functionality of the associated Content Management Server **Posting** object, where the posting represents a simple product page. Although such postings do not have a profile, they do have access to the current product (through the query string in the URL) and to all of the catalog, category, and property information for that product.
NRCSRichProductPosting	The **NRCSRichProductPosting** object extends the functionality of the associated Content Management Server **Posting** object, where the posting represents a rich product page. Rich product pages have a page profile, and can therefore participate in PCOs. They also have access to the current product (through the query product and profile mapping) and to all of the catalog, category, and property information for that product.

(continued)

Object	Description *(continued)*
NRCSProductContainerRoot	The **NRCSProductContainerRoot** object provides access to all of the catalogs in a site, as well as to an initialized Commerce Server **CatalogManager** object.
NRCSCatalog	The **NRCSCatalog** object extends the functionality of the associated Commerce Server **ProductCatalog** object.
NRCSCategory	The **NRCSCategory** object extends the functionality of the associated Commerce Server **Category** object.
NRCSFactory	The **NRCSFactory** object is used to create and transform Content Connector framework objects and Commerce Server objects.
NRCSPersonalizedContentObjectSelector	The **NRCSPersonalizedContentObjectSelector** object provides more control (sort order and filtering of results) over the execution of a PCO pipeline than is provided by the more common call to the **SelectContent** method of the **NRCSSession** object.

Deploying Content Management Server

Content Management Server provides two tools that can be used to help manage real-life deployment scenarios: Site Deployment Manager and Site Stager. Usually, content is developed and tested on one computer or set of computers, and then deployed to different computers that host the live Web site. Site Deployment Manager consists of sophisticated export and import functionality that can be used to easily duplicate a particular Content Management Server configuration from one computer to another.

Even if the dynamic construction of Web pages from page elements stored in a Content Management Server database will not work for all Web sites, such as when the live site is not hosted on Windows-based servers, the workflow features in Content Management Server that are related to role separation can still be employed. The Site Stager application can be used to create a static HTML (or ASP) version of the Content Management Server Web site.

Each of these tools is described in additional detail in the following sub-sections.

Site Deployment Manager

Site Deployment Manager is a conceptually distinct tool that is accessed through the Site Builder application. Only Content Management Server administrators are permitted to perform the export and import operations that constitute the Site Deployment Manager.

On computers serving as the deployment source (the development or staging computers), the **Site Deployment Export** dialog box is used to initiate the export process, resulting in a .rop file. This export process continues in the background, regardless of whether the Site Builder application is closed.

On computers serving as the deployment destination (the production computers), the **Site Deployment Import** dialog box is used to initiate the import process, extracting the state of various objects from a .rop file. Like the export process, the import process is performed in the background, and the Site Builder application can be closed without interfering with it.

The basic steps involved in deploying Content Management Server are:

1. Export one or more objects to a package on the source computer, stored in a .rop file.

2. Copy (or otherwise access) the .rop file to the destination computer.

3. Import the object(s) in the .rop file into the destination computer.

As suggested by step 1, the export/import operations available in Site Deployment Manager can be performed in an incremental fashion. In other words, not all object types need to be exported, nor do all of the objects of a particular type need to be exported together. For example, just one portion of a Web site can be exported, such as a particular branch of channels or postings. Further, there are options for choosing whether to preserve the existing container hierarchy on the destination computer, or change it to correspond to a new hierarchy represented in the .rop file.

The following types of Content Management Server objects can be deployed to another computer by exporting their state into a .rop file:

- Folders and pages

- Channels and postings

- Resource galleries and resources

- Template galleries and templates

- Rights groups and rights groups members

Site Deployment Manager is sophisticated enough to understand the various dependencies that can exist between these types of objects, such as pages being dependent on page templates and resources. Whenever an object is included in an export operation, Site Deployment Manager will also automatically export any other objects upon which the former objects depend.

What cannot be deployed using Site Deployment Manager are any file-based elements of the Web site, such as include files or other ASP files. Another deployment mechanism must be employed for such files, ranging from manual copying to a fully automated solution using a product like Microsoft Application Center.

Site Stager

Some Web sites might really benefit from the explicit role separation and workflow features of Content Management Server, yet are unable to deploy Content Management Server in a production environment, such as when the hosting computers are not Windows-based. The Site Stager application that comes with Content Management Server provides a solution to this dilemma. Site Stager can be used to make a functional copy of a Content Management Server site for which the dynamic construction of pages has been done in advance, resulting in a static HTML Web site that can be hosted using a wide variety of Web servers.

Depending on the nature of the Content Management Server Web site, the Web site created by Site Stager might be pure static HTML or it might include some ASP script, or perhaps a combination of both. If the resulting Web site includes ASP script, it will obviously have to be hosted on a server that can process ASP.

Sites are staged according to characteristics established in a Site Stager profile. A Site Stager profile consists of a profile name and description, information about the source and destination of the staging, and the settings of several staging options. Staging source information includes the URL of the site to be staged and the user (called the "stage as user") from whose perspective the site will be examined. This user must have subscription rights to the site, and may not be entitled to see the entire Web site.

Staging destination information includes the destination directory (in which the staged site will be built) and the name of the default file for the site, such as index.htm. It is recommended that distinct profiles should always specify distinct destination directories, so that Site Stager jobs working at the same time will never overwrite one another.

Staging options include an indication of whether the staged site should use the same names as the source site, or whether auto-generated channel and posting names should be used. Staging options also include the ability to set non-incremental staging, or two different types of incremental staging (Synchronized or Passive), and a means through which a standardized file extension can be provided, such as ".htm".

Site Stager can be configured to run automatically, based on a schedule, or it can be run manually, initiated using a **Stage Now** button. In order for Site Stager to be executed automatically, the Windows Task Scheduler service must be installed and started. Site Stager produces log files that record exactly what has been done, which is especially important when Site Stager is configured to run late at night, when no one is around.

In order for Site Stager to work flawlessly, site programmers need to take a number of special considerations into account, such as the following:

- Site programmers need to use the Publishing API method **ResolveURL** for all explicitly coded links in navigation and page templates.

- If a coding technique called template switching is used, the browser detection code must be performed in client-side scripting rather than server-side scripting.

- Conditional code that tests the **IsModePublished** property of the **Autosession** object must be changed to also check the **IsModeStaged** property.

Refer directly to the Content Management Server documentation, and in particular to the *Site Administrator's Guide* and the *Site Programmer's Guide*, for all such considerations.

Content Management Server 2002

At the time that this book was published, the release of Content Management Server 2002 was still several months away – long enough that it was still difficult to have complete confidence in the exact feature set, and long enough that it still made sense to discuss the 2001 version in much of this chapter. Wherever possible, Content Management Server functionality was discussed in a generic way so that the concepts mastered could be applied to either version. This section of the chapter will highlight the ways in which the 2002 version, as planned, will be different than the 2001 version.

The various changes that distinguish the 2001 and 2002 versions of Content Management Server are described according to how they affect the people in the various roles, such as site programmers, site administrators, authors, and editors. Changes that do not fit neatly into any of these categories are addressed at the end of the section. It is important to note that because this product is still being developed, the changes discussed here are not guaranteed to be present in Content Management Server 2002.

Site Programming Changes

The arena of site programming is where the most significant changes to Content Management Server will be made for the 2002 version. Like many of the other Microsoft .NET Enterprise Servers, Content Management Server is being re-worked to fit into the .NET programming paradigm.

The following list highlights the major differences:

- Allowing Content Management Server Web sites to be built using ASP.NET will enhance the development experience.

- Visual Studio .NET will become the required tool for developing ASP.NET Web sites based on Content Management Server. This is due to the degree of integration between Visual Studio .NET and Content Management Server 2002, as many of the remaining items in this list will make apparent.

- Templates will no longer be maintained within SQL Server. They will be maintained on the file system as normal .NET-based Web pages. Among other benefits, this will provide many more options for source control.

- Content Management Server will not change templates. In other words, there will not be any behind-the-scenes modifications made to templates, as was done in the 2001 version. This means that the template that site programmers see during a debugging session will be exactly the same template that they wrote, helping to alleviate a source of confusion in the 2001 version.

- To support backward compatibility, templates can be written to work with either ASP or ASP.NET.

- Content Management Server will behave in a more standard way with respect to being an Internet Information Services (IIS) application, and will use either the global.asa or global.asax file, as appropriate, for application initialization.

- The concept of page definitions will be made explicit rather than implicit, and will contain placeholder definitions, including their type and configuration, and revision information. Page definitions will be stored with the templates that use them, and can be shared across multiple templates. In fact, connected pages will be required to share a page definition.

- The Publishing API (PAPI) will be extended in two orthogonal ways. Some of the objects in the COM version will get some new properties and methods, and this new version of the object model will be wrapped up as a managed code version for use in .NET-based implementations.

- Content Management Server 2002 allows users to store XML content in placeholders and to access that content through the PAPI. Returned XML will support XSD validation and data binding to supported server controls.

- Content Management Server will extend the framework of Visual Studio .NET to provide direct developer access to the Content Management Server objects and data structures, as well as providing a seamless debugging environment that is aware of Content Management Server.

- Integration with Visual Studio .NET will provide an extensible palette of placeholder server controls that can be dragged and dropped into template code.

- Integration with Visual Studio .NET will be extensible with respect to integrating custom Content Management Server components.

- Integration with Visual Studio .NET will allow the creation of Content Management Server projects that allow templates to be written in Microsoft Visual Basic® .NET, Microsoft Visual C#™, or any other language that supports the common language runtime. When a Content Management Server project is open, the Visual Studio .NET menus will be extended to support actions such as starting the Site Manager application (formerly the Site Builder application) and the Web Author application.

- Integration with Visual Studio .NET will provide tool windows and chooser dialog boxes to create, edit, and delete template galleries and templates, placeholder definitions, custom properties for templates, and code segments that employ a multiple selection clipboard.

- Content Management Server 2002 uses ASP.NET server controls for several different purposes, and although people in a variety of roles will use these controls, they significantly change the way site programming is performed. These controls can be dragged into templates from within Visual Studio .NET. The following table explains these server controls.

Server control	Description
Console	The Console server control is visible to users other than simple subscribers and allows a variety of actions to be performed, such as: • Switch between the Live mode and Editing mode of the Web site • Author pages • Approve pages • Determine the approval state of various pages • Change channel and page properties The Console server control can also be extended to provide actions customized to particular business needs.
HTML Placeholder	The HTML Placeholder server control allows HTML content to be authored within a rich edit control. It is a server control version of the ASP placeholder used in the 2001 version of the Web Author application. In Live mode, this control emits the stored HTML for display to a subscriber. When template designers are creating templates, this control works within and extends the Visual Studio .NET property browser.
Single Image Placeholder	The Single Image Placeholder server control allows authors to select an image from a resource gallery or upload an image to the Content Management Server database. In Live mode, this control emits the necessary HTML to display the stored image. There is also design-time support for configuring this placeholder in Visual Studio .NET.
Single Attachment Placeholder	The Single Attachment Placeholder server control allows authors to upload an attachment, such as Microsoft Word or Excel documents, to the Content Management Server database. In Live mode, this control emits the necessary HTML to display a link to the stored attachment. There is also design-time support for configuring this placeholder in Visual Studio .NET.

Content Management Server 2002 is meant to be extended with new ASP.NET server controls. One area in which such extensions can be created concerns custom navigation controls. Content Management Server will provide programmatic access to an XML representation of the channel/page hierarchy so that site programmers can build their own navigation controls, such as a tree control, that bind to this representation.

It is also expected that third-party developers will create new placeholder server controls based on the .NET Framework. They will be able to begin by deriving a new server control from either a standard .NET-based server control or one of the out-of-the-box Content Management Server controls, and then extending its functionality to suite their purposes.

- A new API for site deployment functionality will be exposed in Content Management Server. It will be called the Site Deployment API (SDAPI).

- ASP.NET caching will be used to improve the performance of dynamic sites, including the caching of relatively static fragments of otherwise dynamic pages. Caching controls allow independent caching of template fragments that are reused in many templates, such as banners, global navigation or common placeholders. Note that caching needs to consider the role of the user, so that, for example, simple subscribers do not see the links provided to authors and editors for switching to Edit mode.

- Site programmers will have access to the various authentication mechanisms supported by ASP.NET, such as Windows authentication (including basic, digest, and Kerberos variants), Forms authentication, and Default (anonymous) authentication. This means that subscribers can have a single sign-on with all IIS-compatible applications. The authentication mechanisms now available in the 2001 version of Content Management Server will still be available. Site programmers will also be able to devise authentication mechanisms of their own design and map them into the Content Management Server authentication model.

Administration Changes

Site administrators will be directly affected by the following changes that are planned for the 2002 version of Content Management Server:

- The Site Builder application is being renamed Site Manager. It will have its authoring and editing functionality stripped, and will no longer be a tool shared by so many different roles (authoring and editing will be handled exclusively within the Web Author application).

- Content Management Server 2002 will have better integration with Microsoft Application Center, allowing easier deployment of file-based Web site assets.

- Site migration tools will be provided to help ease the burden of upgrading Web sites from the 2001 version to the 2002 version.

- A new role, called channel manager, will be introduced in Content Management Server 2002. Some Web sites based on the roles defined for the 2001 version found that the site administrator could end up being a bottleneck with respect to container creation. Assigning additional people to the role of channel manager, with authorization to create new channels in a particular area of the site, should help ease the reliance on site administrators without the need to grant full site administrator privileges to too many people.

Authoring and Editing Changes

There are two big changes slated for Content Management Server authors and editors. First, no authoring or editing will be performed in the Site Builder application. Indeed the name of that application is being changed to Site Manager, presumably to suggest its more limited, administrative role going forward. The Web Author application is being ported to the .NET-based environment, and will serve as the primary user interface through which authors and editors will perform their functions in the 2002 version.

Because authors and editors will not be working within the Site Builder application in Content Management Server 2002, the distinction between pages and postings will not be very apparent to them. This trend was begun in earlier versions of the Web Author application, where to the extent that an author or editor used the Web Author application rather than the Site Builder application to perform their tasks, the distinction was already diminished. In general, the types of users who are aware of the somewhat subtle distinctions between pages and postings, and between folders and channels, will be substantially reduced in the 2002 version. Because these distinctions have lead to confusion in the past, this should be viewed as a step in the right direction.

Content Management Server 2002 also introduces the Office Connector for Microsoft Word. The Office Connector will allow content contributors to author and edit their content in Microsoft Word XP, use the Office Connector to preview their content, and then publish their content directly into the workflow of a Content Management Server Web site. The published content might be an entire Word document or just a portion of it. Depending on the configuration of Word-enabled placeholders in a particular Content Management Server template, it may be possible to upload attachments, in-line graphics, and links from Word documents as well.

Miscellaneous Changes

Content Management Server 2002 will have improved accessibility features, and will also be re-worked so that it works better in an international setting. It will very likely be translated into a couple of different languages as well.

Tools and Technologies

To implement a Web site with managed content using the Microsoft technology described in this chapter, the following .NET Enterprise Server products are required:

- Microsoft Content Management Server

- Microsoft SQL Server

And if the Web site is going to be integrated with Microsoft Commerce Server in order to provide additional features, the Content Connector for Commerce Server add-on to Content Management Server, and Commerce Server itself, is required.

Note the lack of version/year numbers in the previous list. As this book is going to press, new versions of several of these products are soon to be released. Commerce Server 2002 is due to be released in early spring of 2002, and Content Management Server 2002 will be released shortly thereafter. If and when Content Connector will be revised to support these new versions is not known at this time. Interested suppliers should refer directly to the Microsoft Web site (www.microsoft.com) for more precise information about software requirements and version compatibility.

Companies that want to develop a Web site that incorporates the functionality of both Content Management Server and Commerce Server might want to consider acquiring the Microsoft Solution for Internet Business (MSIB), and especially if they are considering hiring Microsoft or one of its certified partners to help with the implementation. The MSIB bundles the required servers and implementation assistance into a single package.

Site programmers working with Content Management Server, either in conjunction with Commerce Server or by itself, might want Microsoft Visual Studio to make developing solutions easier. This is especially true if the 2002 version of Content Management Server is being used. As with all of the .NET-based architecture, Visual Studio .NET is not required to create Web applications that use the .NET FrameworkHowever, the degree of integration expected between Content Management Server 2002 and Visual Studio .NET is extensive, and will almost certainly provide a significant productivity boost.

For Web site assets that are maintained on the file system, and this set will grow with Content Management Server 2002, Microsoft Application Center can be used to simplify the deployment of a Content Management Server Web site onto multiple servers in a Web farm.

Finally, depending on the deployment scenario and the firewall requirements of the Web site, Microsoft Internet Security and Acceleration Server (ISA) might be another product to consider.

Implementation

During initial development, programming tasks comprise much of the work involved in getting a Content Management Server Web site up and running. Some sample code is included with Content Management Server, but almost all Web site development projects will significantly modify this code, so you could start from scratch to produce the customized functionality that is typically required.

A comprehensive demonstration of the types of coding that are common is far beyond the scope of this chapter. Rather, this final section of the chapter will provide detailed explanations of a routine called **BuildTopNavTable**, implemented in two different ways. First, the routine as it might be coded for a Content Management Server 2001 implementation, using the COM-based Publishing API from Microsoft Visual Basic Scripting Edition (VBScript), will be shown. Second, the routine will be shown as it might be coded for a Content Management Server 2002 implementation, using the .NET-based Publishing API, the .NET Framework, and Visual C#.

Note that unlike the implementation sections in some other chapters, the code in this chapter was not borrowed from an existing product sample. It was devised specifically for this chapter, and has been commented exclusively with annotations in italic font that should not be considered part of the code itself.

The functionality of the routine **BuildTopNavTable** is the same in both implementations, although some of the details are different. For example, in the COM-based VBScript version, the result is returned as a string that contains the HTML that will display the constructed table. In the .NET Visual C# version, the result is returned as an object of class **Table** from the namespace **System.Web.UI.WebControls**, which can then be added to the controls on the page.

The routine is called **BuildTopNavTable** because it builds a horizontally oriented list of hyperlinks to the top-level channels in a Content Management Server Web site. These hyperlinks are implemented as an HTML table with the following characteristics:

- The table contains a single row.

- The single row contains one cell for each sub-channel of the root channel in the site.

- The text in each of the channel cells is the display name of the channel.

- The channel cells are ordered alphabetically according to their names (as opposed to their display names).

- The channel within which the current channel is contained is shown in bold font, and is not a link to that channel.

- All other channels are shown in regular font, and are constructed as links.

COM Version of BuildTopNavTable

The implementation of the routine **BuildTopNavTable** in this section is coded in VBScript and was tested within a page template using Content Management Server 2001.

```
Function BuildTopNavTable()
```

All of the variables are declared up front, and should be self-explanatory from their names, mostly.

```
Dim ReturnString
Dim SpacerCell
Dim ChannelCell
Dim RootSubChannel
Dim SubChannelsOfRoot
Dim CurChannelMatriarch    ' Sub-channel of the root
                           ' containing the current channel.
```

Begin building the return string, providing an ID and class, and adding a spacer as the first cell.

```
ReturnString = "<TABLE ID=""TopNavTable"" Class=""TopNav""><TR>"
```

Find the current channel's matriarch channel, defined here to be the channel directly under the root channel that is an ancestor of the current channel.

```
Set CurChannelMatriarch = AutoSession.ThisChannel
While Not CurChannelMatriarch.Parent.IsRoot
    Set CurChannelMatriarch = CurChannelMatriarch.Parent
WEnd
```

Retrieve a collection of the sub-channels of the root channel and sort them alphabetically according to their Name property.

```
Set SubChannelsOfRoot = AutoSession.RootChannel.Channels

SubChannelsOfRoot.SortByName()
```

Run through the collection of the root channel's sub-channels, filling in the rest of the table's row.

```
For Each RootSubChannel In SubChannelsOfRoot
```

Use the channel GUID property to test whether the matriarch channel has been found in this iteration. If so, build the channel cell as a bold font, non-linked display name. If not, build the channel cell as regular font, linked display name.

```
If ( RootSubChannel.GUID = CurChannelMatriarch.GUID ) Then
    ChannelCell = "<TD><B>" + RootSubChannel.DisplayName + "</B></TD>"
```

```
    Else
        ChannelCell = "<TD><A HREF=""" + _
                        RootSubChannel.URL + _
                        """>" + _
                        RootSubChannel.DisplayName + _
                        "</A></TD>"
    End If
```

Append the channel cell and another spacer cell to the return string.

```
        ' Add the sub-channel link
        ReturnString = ReturnString + ChannelCell
```

Do it again until all of the sub-channels of the root channel have been processed.

```
    Next    ' end of For Each loop
```

Append the end of the row and the end of the table to the return string, and return it.

```
    ReturnString = ReturnString + "</TR></TABLE>"

    BuildTopNavTable = ReturnString

End Function
```

At the position in the page template where the table should be displayed, the following line of code could be used to send the resulting HTML back to the browser for display:

```
<%= BuildTopNavTable() %>
```

.NET-Based Version of BuildTopNavTable

The implementation of the routine **BuildTopNavTable** in this section is coded in Visual C# and was tested within a page template using Content Management Server 2002.

Classes in these two namespaces are used.

```
using Microsoft.Web.UI.WebControls;
using Microsoft.ContentManagement.Publishing;
```

*The function returns a **Table** object from the Microsoft.Web.UI.WebControls namespace.*

```
private Table BuildTopNavTable() {
```

Most of the variables are declared up front, and should be self-explanatory from their names, mostly. The UI-related variables are declared first, then the variables related to Content Management Server objects.

```
TableRow    Row;
TableCell   Cell;
Table       TopNavTable;
HtmlAnchor NavLink;

Channels SubChannelsOfRoot;
Channel  CurChannelMatriarch;  // sub-channel of the root
                               // containing the current channel.
```

Get the current Content Management Server context and create the single row object to be filled in.

```
CmsHttpContext CMSContext = CmsHttpContext.Current;

Row = new TableRow();
```

Find the current channel's matriarch channel, defined here to be the channel directly under the root channel that is an ancestor of the current channel.

```
CurChannelMatriarch = CMSContext.Channel;
while ( CurChannelMatriarch.Parent != CMSContext.RootChannel ) {
    CurChannelMatriarch = CurChannelMatriarch.Parent;
}
```

Retrieve a collection of the sub-channels of the root channel and sort them alphabetically according to their Name property.

```
SubChannelsOfRoot = CMSContext.RootChannel.Channels;

SubChannelsOfRoot.SortByName();
```

Run through the collection of the root channel's sub-channels, filling in the rest of the table's row object.

```
foreach ( Channel RootSubChannel in SubChannelsOfRoot ) {
```

Create a table cell object for this iteration and do any initialization that does not depend on the upcoming test.

```
Cell = new TableCell();
Cell.Wrap = false;
```

Test whether the matriarch channel has been found in this iteration (note that the channel GUID property is not required in the test in this version). If so, build the channel cell object to display a non-linked display name using bold font. If not, build the channel cell object to display a linked display name using regular font.

```
if ( RootSubChannel == CurChannelMatriarch ) {
    Cell.Text = RootSubChannel.DisplayName;
    Cell.Font.Bold = true;
}
```

```
    else {
        NavLink = new HtmlAnchor();
        NavLink.InnerHtml = RootSubChannel.DisplayName;
        NavLink.ID = "NavLink_" + RootSubChannel.GUID;
        NavLink.Title = "NavLink_Channel_" + RootSubChannel.DisplayName;
        NavLink.HRef = RootSubChannel.url;

        Cell.Controls.Add(NavLink);
    }
```

Add the channel cell object to the row.

```
        Row.Cells.Add(Cell);
```

Do it again until all of the sub-channels of the root channel have been processed.

```
    }  // end of foreach loop
```

Create and initialize the table object to be returned, including an ID.

```
    TopNavTable = new Table();

    TopNavTable.ID = "TopNavTable";
```

Add the row object to the table object and return the table object.

```
    TopNavTable.Rows.Add(Row);

    return(TopNavTable);

} // end of BuildTopNavTable()
```

The returned table object can be added to the page's controls collection from which the corresponding HTML will eventually be sent to the browser for display:

```
Controls.Add(BuildTopNavTable());
```

PART FIVE

Wireless Integration

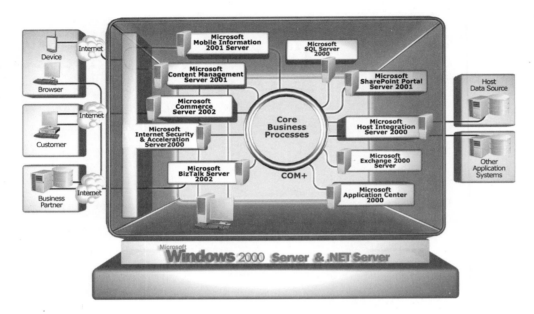

.NET Enterprise Servers

Integrating Location-Based Mobile Services

Introduction

The three chapters in this part ("Integrating Location-Based Mobile Services," "Location-Based Mobile Service Architectures," and "Delivering Location-Based Mobile Services") address the specialized task of building back office servers capable of supporting location-aware applications on mobile terminals such as mobile telephones, personal digital assistants (PDAs), and in-car systems. Location-based mobile services (LBMS) are defined as those mobile services that depend on the location of a user's mobile terminal in order to target the information delivered to meet location- and time-dependent user needs. A typical example is the delivery of emergency or breakdown response to a motorist where the person's phone or in-car device can determine location. The location is sent to a server over a wireless link along with a services request, which could be as simple as "send help!" In-car navigation and telematics systems that calculate routes and guide the user to a chosen destination or guidance of two or more mobile users to a single rendezvous point is a sub-part of LBMS.

These chapters highlight how several .NET Enterprise Servers and technologies can help enterprises integrate wireless applications with existing line of business applications. The scenarios in these chapters use Windows 2000 Server, Mobile Information Server, Internet Information Server, Internet Security and Acceleration Server, Exchange Server, MSMQ, XML and SOAP. Host Integration Server can also be used as an option.

Location-Based Mobile Services Delivery

An LBMS delivery system can direct information, advertising, and safety warnings to mobile devices at specific locations (and times). Maps or three-dimensional displays of a person's surroundings can be delivered to support independent local travel or to provide context for more detailed guidance. Many wireless carriers, automobile manufacturers, and map data companies see LBMS as a broad new market opportunity comparable in size to voice telephone services in potential size.

In the last two years, efforts to standardize the delivery of the core geographic content and computations via XML and SOAP have moved to the point of demonstrated usability for commercial mass-market applications.

Some characteristics of LBMS are common across delivery platforms. The .NET Framework and compatible delivery architectures allow the corresponding low-level core geographic computations ("navigation services") to be provided by dedicated service providers. This ability to specialize is very important in creating an economically viable means to collect the necessary information about the world, make it internally consistent and deliver it in the right form to wireless operators and other mobile services providers with end-user applications. At the same time, much of the complexity in designing and building delivery systems comes from the diverse technical approaches to both locating the geographic position of the mobile terminal–the "location" part of LBMS and this is compounded by the patchwork of technical means that are used to implement wireless data communications. Microsoft Mobile Information Server abstracts the latter and provides a single platform with easy adaptation to individual wireless carriers. So far there are few if any equivalent server products that can act as a platform for delivering the core geographic services. There are several characteristics of the location side of location-based mobile services that require a basic understanding before beginning the design of a delivery system using the Microsoft .NET Framework and associated server products.

Geographic data collection and integration are often very expensive and it is a great advantage to be able to leverage an investment in a geographic database and corresponding computational algorithms across the broadest possible range of location-aware mobile applications. Some applications require delivery via transports with a native capability to support asynchronous messaging and to pass through corporate firewalls without either security risk or the need for special handling. Other applications are able to operate within the synchronous model of standard web services via HTTP on TCP port 80.

This chapter considers these common characteristics and the development of a solution architecture for the navigation service provider based on a particular .NET compatible delivery model—the MAGIC Services Protocol. Most of the content applies in general to delivery of core geographic services to mobile applications via XML and SOAP. The back-end must be scalable from a low-load or prototyping configuration to a load-balanced high availability system capable of reliably supporting high loading without failing to meet time-sensitive delivery requirements. A Visual Studio .NET solution with a sample application capable of fully exercising a .NET MSP 2.0 server is included.

The focus is on setting up a generic location-aware mobile service that provides end-user services via a Mobile Location-based Service Provider (MSP). Location-based mobile services benefit both end-user and service provider. They allow users to find services when and where they are needed. They provide guidance to these services and, in the case of breakdown and emergency services, may provide guidance for the service to reach the mobile user. Users benefits from the increased feeling of security and access to information about their surroundings. The service provider gains additional revenue through revenue sharing with services, advertising, the increased use of wireless air-time, the ability to charge more for enhanced service packages, and the reduction in the rate of switching ("churn") as users move from one wireless provider to another. These services may be delivered worldwide or to a narrowly focused geographic area.

One of the big challenges in building a LBMS delivery system in today's environment is the fragmented nature of the wireless data communications and location technologies in use. A successful delivery architecture can hide much of the complexity by encapsulating a mix of low-level technologies in a standardized wrapper. Microsoft's .NET Framework and suite of enterprise server products provide a set of building blocks for implementing robust and scalable delivery platforms using the Internet standard XML and SOAP, over HTTP, SMTP, and TCP/IP transports.

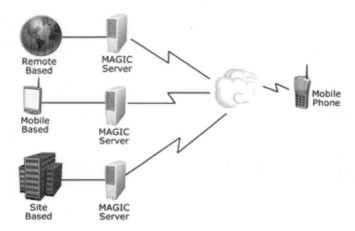

Mobile activities span scales from global to a single building

The Mobile Service Provider, MSP, integrates information from a number of sources, including locale and regional geographic services, traffic and weather services, points of interest, and bricks and mortar services that a traveler may discover through proximity with or without advertising. The MSP relies on a back-end service, a Navigation Service Provider (NSP), for core geographic content and services. These back-end navigation services may be passed through the MSP transparently or the MSP may take on a client or server role. The MAGIC Services Protocol (see http://www.MAGICServicesForum.org) is the emerging public standard for .NET-compatible delivery of core geographic services such as map creation, route determination, route guidance, and the interconversion of addresses and geographic positions. This chapter is based on the use of the MAGIC Services Protocol version 2.0 (MSP 2.0) although any .NET compatible core geographic service could be used interchangeably.

There are four basic scenarios for the delivery of mobile services:

- Unidirectional communication from server to client (geocasting): information is delivered to all receivers in a region via satellite broadcast, FM sub carrier, or similar low-cost high volume distribution channel.

- Bidirectional communication between client and server over wireless network: Services delivered to the mobile user are usually (but not always) delivered to the mobile terminal over a wireless data link. While there are specialized data networks for commercial applications, this scenario delivers LBMS to the mass-market, which implies a wireless operator.

- Bidirectional communication between navigation service provider (NSP) and MSP.

- Bidirectional communication between mobile devices (peer-to-peer) where the client and server roles may change dynamically.

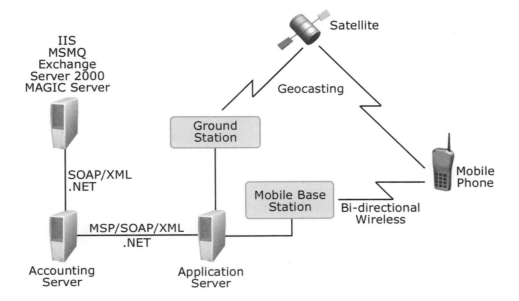

IIS
MSMQ
Exchange
Server 2000
MAGIC Server

Satellite

Geocasting

Ground
Station

SOAP/XML
.NET

Mobile Base
Station

Mobile
Phone

Bi-directional
Wireless

MSP/SOAP/XML
.NET

Accounting
Server

Application
Server

Basic elements for delivery of mobile services

The following list suggests some of the major features that a NSP should offer to the MSP, as well as the contributing services and administrative features.

- **Easy integration with content suppliers**. Location defined by address or geographic coordinates (latitude, longitude, and altitude) represents the common key that allows information from different content suppliers to be integrated into a single coherent model for service delivery. If individual content suppliers are able to deliver their specialized information to the NSP without the need for manual intervention, then the costs can be much lower and the information much fresher.

- **High performance**. LBMS is a mass-market product. As such it demands the same level of performance and reliability as telephone or electrical services. A NSP is part of the infrastructure and must be able to adapt to varying load conditions and offer a very high level of availability.

- **Strong security**. Location information is one of the most sensitive kinds of personal data that might be accessible in a networked world. The power of LBMS comes from the use of location information to tailor services to the situation of the mobile person. It is essential that whatever model the end-user has for the possible uses and accesses of this position information is guarded by a credible and auditable level of security.

- **User transaction logging**. There are many billing models in place now. No single provider has yet promoted a standard way to charge for LBMS. A common theme involves tracking certain units of work – transactions – and billing based on the number of transactions of various types. While other models may ultimately prevail (flat rate, in particular), in today's market providers must track usage in several different ways to meet the contractual requirements of data suppliers.

- **Content usage logging**. Some services involve the delivery of content for which there are royalties or revenue shares to be paid. In some cases, navigation may involve a mixture of information from several suppliers and the royalties for use of each may be computed on a pro rata basis. It is inconceivable to operate a comprehensive mass-market NSP business without the need to use non-owned content. Thus the ability to track content usage is also a requirement for an enterprise-scale NSP delivery system.

- **Ability to access the service from multiple client device types**. One of the key functions of a delivery platform is to insulate both the content management side of the operation and application developers from as much of the detailed characteristics of the target mobile terminals as possible. Unfortunately there is an extremely wide range of terminal device capabilities. An NSP delivery system must manage some of the different computing, memory, and connectivity capabilities of the terminal devices. Some clients will be enterprise servers at a MSP with gigabytes of memory available for caching and working storage. Other devices may have less than 1 kilobyte free for working memory. This requires some level of adaptation via flexible caching and compression techniques in order to allow a single platform to serve a broad range of consuming devices.

- **Manageability**. A successful NSP solution needs a corresponding monitoring and management capability. Critical resource allocations and utilization levels of those resources must be accessible and controllable. Wizards or other tools with the ability to reduce the possibility of making bad allocations are essential. It is also important to have the ability to provide managers with precise information about faults and unusual conditions along with the capability to respond to those notifications.

The main concerns in designing a location-based service are the nature of the application as seen by the end-user and the corresponding content that must be integrated and geo-referenced. Geo-referencing is the process of locating the real-world target of the information either in absolute geographic coordinates or with respect to a place, road, or other geographic entity. A solution based on Microsoft products and the .NET Framework can meet almost any conceivable set of requirements.

Building .NET Location-Based Mobile Services Solutions

Developing the NSP infrastructure for a LBMS application requires an understanding of the location technology, means of accessing the location of the mobile terminal, the bandwidth and other characteristics of the connection between client and server, and the memory and other computational resources of the target class of mobile terminal devices. Due to the limitations of the mobile Internet, these will be the limiting factors in establishing the operating characteristics of the delivery system. Among other things, you need to understand the relative amount of time that the mobile device may need to operate autonomously when a connection is not possible.

Mobile Internet Technology and Market Forces

There are several distinguishing characteristics of the mobile Internet. In this chapter, the focus is on both packet-switched public networks (i.e. the fixed Internet extended to mobile devices through data transports that support IP, the Internet Protocol) and connection-based air interfaces that can transport XML-based messaging (e.g. GSM, GPRS and third-generation wireless technologies). In particular, there are severe limitations to the availability of a connection, high and unpredictable round-trip time for requests and responses (latency), and limited bandwidth.

What makes the mobile Internet so interesting? The position of the mobile terminal can be used in many ways to personalize and adapt the behavior of an application to meet the needs and expectations of the user in a very direct way. Technologies to determine the position of a terminal are evolving rapidly. Handset manufacturers and wireless operators in North America and Western Europe face increasingly stringent government requirements to provide the location of the mobile terminal to emergency service providers in the case of calls made to emergency numbers such as 911 and 112.

The LBMS View of Mobile Networks

There is a simple high-level view of the environment in which LBMS are delivered and consumed. A mobile terminal (phone, PDA, or in-car device) is able to communicate wirelessly with other network nodes. It is also able to determine its physical location on the earth's surface. The connectivity enables interaction with a mobile or navigation service provider and most of the navigation services are controlled in some way by the position of the mobile terminal.

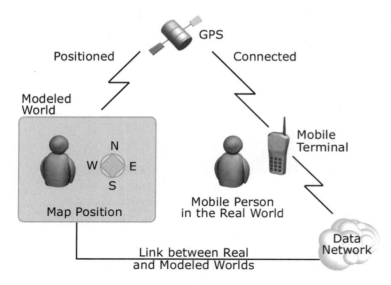

Coherence between the modeled world and the real (physical) world

The essential capability needed to deliver useful and accurate location-based services is to link the location of the person in the real world to a position within a model of the real world, which is used to compute responses to requests for information about mobility in the real world. Computing happens on the model. The person carries out the activity in the real world. Positioning via some locations technology allows the person and the computation to be coordinated or to be *coherent*. Coherence is the hallmark of location-based services that seem natural, useful, and correct to mobile users. Let's take a look at the components and see how world-model coherence can be achieved with technology in the field today.

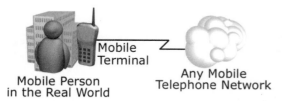

Simple model: Mobile person with connected device

First, what part of the population of mobile devices has the potential to participate in LBMS? Let's look at the overall population of connected mobile devices such as phones, pagers, PDAs, and in-car systems. There are now more than ten million in-car navigation and telematics systems worldwide. More than half are in Japan and the bulk of the remainder is in Western Europe. There are a similar number of wirelessly connected PDAs and two-way pagers, with a more even distribution around the world. There are about a billion mobile phones, and these are also distributed more evenly geographically.

Only phones have reached the mass-market. And because the number of phones is so much larger than the combined total of other connected mobile devices, there is little reason to consider PDAs and two-way pagers except as delivery points for a few niche and high-value applications. In-car systems are even more specialized and expensive, although there are around 600 million personal vehicles in the world and almost 60 million new (replacement) vehicles produced worldwide each year. Many analysts believe that phones will absorb the PDA and two-way pager market, as costs come down and miniaturization combined with economies of scale make specialized devices ever less attractive.

Many car manufacturers are building at least rudimentary connectivity into all new car models, and it is likely that at least half of the personal vehicle population will be connected in the next ten years. In short, there are two large populations of connected mobile devices – about a billion mobile telephone handsets and a few hundred million connected automobiles in the near future.

Mobile Terminal

Mobile Person
in the Real World

Data Capable
Network: GSM,
GPRS, CDPD, 3G

LBMS requires a data communications capability

Connectivity is not enough, however. You also need a data communications capability. Ideally, this should be a packet-switched networking capability identical with, or at least similar to, the IP networking possible on the Internet. A shorthand way to express this requirement is to use the term "wireless Internet," although there are other kinds of data capable networks that meet the needs of LBMS. Today there is a patchwork of different incompatible technologies for data communications between the fixed Internet and the mobile terminal. Hopefully, standard networking and internetworking will evolve just as in the case with the fixed IP-based Internet, but today different environments exist in the major markets: Japan, North America, and Western Europe.

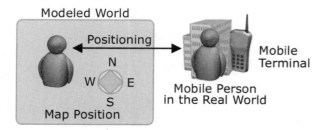

Modeled World / Positioning / N / W E / S / Map Position / Mobile Terminal / Mobile Person in the Real World

LBMS requires positioning capability

Location Technology and LBMS

The second requirement is some kind of location technology to determine the position of the mobile terminal. The location in the physical world (measured by the location technology) is communicated via the data communications channel to establish a link with a model of the world, operated by a navigation service provider. As noted, this link and the data communications are fundamental requirements for delivering services conditioned on the location and mobility of the mobile person.

Unfortunately the range of location technologies is at least as broad as the range of data communications technologies. While products such as Microsoft Mobile Information Server exist to shield the service provider from some of the details of the different technologies used for data communications, the navigation service provider must be prepared to deploy a solution to manage the complexity of the underlying location technology. This may be deployed as an identified Position Proxy Server subsystem or as functionality within the NSP's navigation service delivery system. Over the next few years it is likely that standards will evolve, driven by the wireless industry, to make the request for the position of a mobile terminal easy, while protecting the privacy interests of the mobile user.

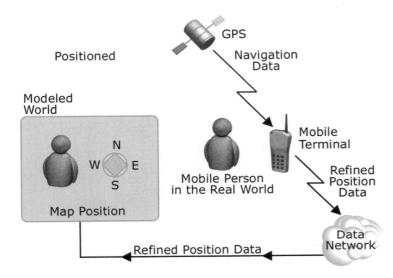

Unassisted Global Positioning System (GPS) location

There are three categories of location technology:

1. Device-borne

2. Network

3. Observational

Device-borne positioning depends on systems that transmit time signals or time-difference signals from precisely known orbits (GPS) or fixed locations (LORAN) and use an on-board computation capability to determine the location. These technologies can be easily retrofitted to mobile terminals but at significant cost in terms of parts, weight, and battery consumption. In this case the device "owns" the location.

Network positioning uses the fixed base stations of a communications network to determine the position of mobile terminals in communication range. Several techniques are used, but the net result is that the network operator gets the benefit of economies of scale and the per-mobile terminal cost may be quite low compared to device-borne location technologies. A network operator is very well positioned to use or sell location information because the operator will know the identity and perhaps other information about the terminal and its user in the course of normal business. Network positioning allows the wireless operator to "own" the location.

Observational techniques make use of radio or other observations of mobile terminals to determine their location. This approach may achieve economies of scale, but it lacks a direct business relationship with the mobile users. Also, this approach makes it difficult to identify terminals and match them to their users. The operators of observational location systems "own" the locations.

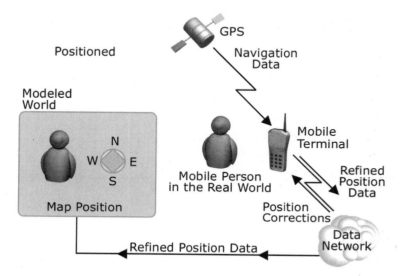

Assisted GPS positioning can improve precision by a factor of ten

Device-borne location can be made more precise if additional information on system errors is available to allow the onboard system to refine the position information. With current technology, raw GPS positions are available only with good signals from four or more satellites. This is usually only possible outdoors and away from large blocking structures, such as office buildings. Using the data communications capability to access additional computational capability and/or better information on system parameters and systematic errors can improve both the availability and accuracy of GPS locations.

With current technology unassisted GPS positioning using mass-market devices has a precision of ten or twenty meters under good conditions. With differential GPS (DGPS) and other techniques the precision can be improved to perhaps two meters under ideal conditions.

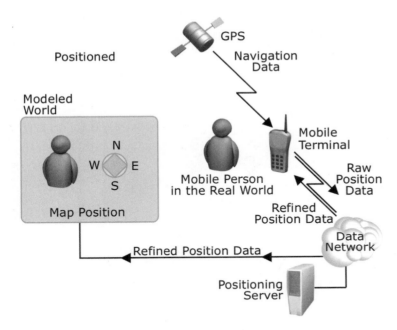

Assisted GPS moves signal processing to the server

It is possible to split the computational effort of GPS location determination between a device and a remote server. In such assisted GPS configurations the essential information is the signal as received by the mobile terminal from each of the visible GPS satellites. The signal contains information that allows estimation of the time the message was transmitted from the satellite. Knowing the time that the signal is received by the mobile terminal allows estimation of the travel time of the message and hence the distance from each satellite to the mobile terminal. If the signal processing needed to recover the message from the received signal can be moved to the server, then much greater computational power and other techniques can be used to obtain a location that is much more precise than that possible by a device on its own. Precisions of less than a meter are possible as well as operation in signal conditions that would prevent an autonomous system from functioning at all.

Assisted GPS is the first case we have considered where the device does not "own" and control the location information. There are a number of techniques that use the time of travel of signals from the base stations of the mobile service provider (or from the device to those base stations), sometimes in combination with knowledge of the relative signal strength as measured by different antennas at a single ground location or multiple ground locations.

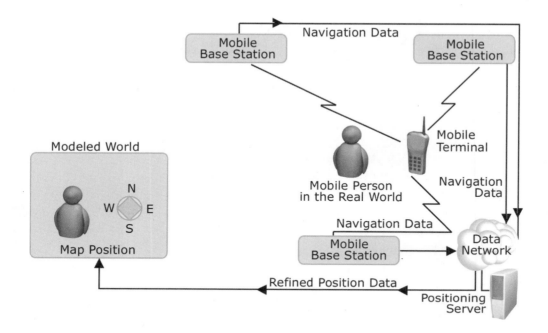

Network location determination gives location to the wireless operator

A network operator can monitor the location of many thousands of mobile terminals simultaneously. Since the location information can be aggregated by the operator across a whole network, the operator can provide access to the location of mobile terminals through a Positioning Proxy Server (PPS). A PPS can hide the underlying location technology and allows use of map-matching, blunder removal, filtering, and predictive techniques enabling the operator to offer a high quality positioning service to LBMS providers and others. Unfortunately, today's implementations are quite imprecise in comparison with GPS technology, typically 100 meters to 1 km or greater. This precision seriously limits the usefulness of network locations. This is a point that implementers of navigation service systems must take into account. Positioning Proxy servers seem to be needed to support buddy-finding and many other interesting mobile applications. Building a PPS into a delivery system has many advantages.

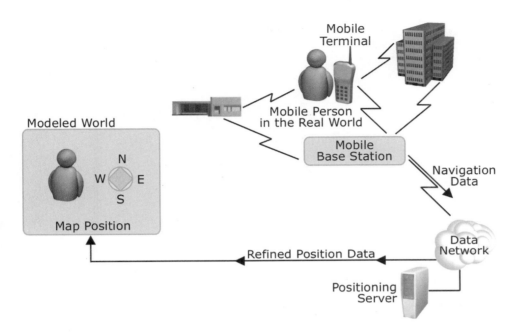

Observational location technology lacks consumer relationship

Observational approaches to location allow the operator to control access to location information, but they lack the link to the identity of the mobile terminal. Even worse, they do not routinely carry data communications with the mobile terminals. The result is that the usability of the location information is limited to aggregated properties of the motion of anonymous mobile terminals. This provides information on travel rates, for example the speed of traffic on roads or pedestrian traffic in a shopping area. It is not particularly useful for delivering generic location based services.

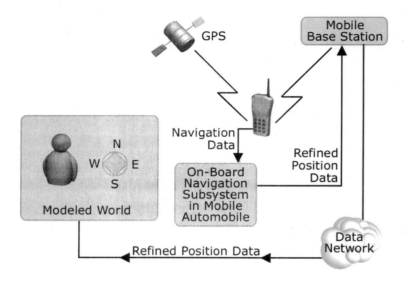

Automobiles have good positioning

Earlier we identified mobile phones and in-car systems as the two important mass-markets for location-based mobile services. In-car devices often have an advantage over phones and other less computationally capable devices because they typically have a combination of GPS sensor data, on-board inertial sensors such as accelerometers, gyroscopes, and speed sensors that allow the determination of very accurate positions at a very high repetition rate (tens of measurements per second). This enables an in-car system to operate in almost any environment.

Of course, one of the reasons cars are outfitted with this extra (expensive) equipment is because the navigational task is more difficult in a car moving at up to 60 meters per second. The consequences of error are potentially more disastrous than providing personal navigation services to a walking person.

There is already a market for the position information from cars, and functional elements corresponding to a PPS are often included in commercial systems. The primary use of the location information is to estimate current traffic speeds based on recent or historical observations of vehicle motion.

LBMS User Scenarios

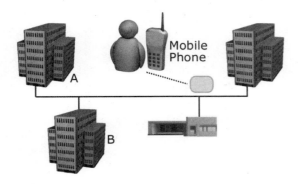

The prototypical LBMS is navigation from A to B

The capabilities of a navigation service delivery architecture are typically focused on mobility—planning and executing travel in the real world. The prototypical location-based mobile service is guidance along a route that takes the user from a starting location to a selected destination. The core components are data communications between a model of the world where guidance is computed, and the ability of the mobile device to be located in the real world. The guidance reflects the current situation of the traveler.

The first systems were autonomous. All functionality resided in the mobile terminal, typically a rather large and expensive box in a car. Data communication was simple, reliable, and high bandwidth because it happened inside the on-board memory of the device. Reaching the mass-market means reaching less capable terminals. This means moving the model of the world and the computations partially or wholly to a remote server, accessible via a network connection with uncertain availability and latency, and low bandwidth.

Much of the functionality of a mobile or navigation service provider's delivery system provides simple and standard service interfaces that hide the complex implementations needed to meet the commercial requirements of a mass-market location-based application.

Market Segmentation

It should be clear from the previous discussion that technology and market forces tend to divide the LBMS market into three segments, characterized by the target mobile terminal:

- Huge numbers of thin clients on data-capable mobile phones positioned by the network or other means

- Large numbers of thick clients in cars, positioned by on-board GPS and other navigation sensors

- Small numbers of relatively capable PDA clients that may have high value applications

Connectivity and Synchronization Requirements

Connectivity between client and navigation service provider has three dimensions:

- **Availability**. Availability measures how much of the time a connection is actually available. Availability can be quantified by the average, minimum, and maximum wait times between the initiation of a connection by an application and the minimum, average, and maximum time before unexpected loss of connection. High availability implies low wait time and long connection time.

- **Bandwidth**. Bandwidth is the net bit rate of useful messages between client and server during a connection. Mobile devices operating over wireless connections may be forced to operate with effective bandwidths under 9.6 KBps!

- **Latency**. Latency measures the delay between a client request and a server response. Latency may involve more than simple network characteristics if the server's time to serve the request is significant. Latency is an issue especially in synchronous, stateless operations where client, server, and the mobile user's motion through the real world must be in harmony for an application to be useful and safe.

In comparison with other networks, mobile delivery has poor availability, low bandwidth, and unpredictable latency. Since many applications require better performance, these characteristics should improve over time. If we look at today's situation however, the uncertainties of availability and latency encourage a strategy of caching and synchronization. The main driving factor in determining how extensively they must be pursued is the timing requirements of the application itself. Pedestrian navigation support or panic button services cannot benefit much from caching. In-car navigation systems on the other hand cannot function without autonomous real-time capabilities, based on cached local information and periodic updates.

LBMS Protocol Standards

The Standards Landscape

Many groups, including the International Standards Organization (ISO), the OpenGIS Consortium, WAP Forum, Location Interoperability Forum (LIF), OpenLS, OASIS, and others have worked on various pieces of LBMS delivery standardization. The field is too new for de facto standards to be available, so there has been a lot of confusion. In the last year or two, the rise of XML and SOAP encoding as an XML-based over-the-wire format has achieved critical mass in technical mindshare. Microsoft's .NET Framework is a direct expression of this convergence on a single network service model.

MAGIC Services Protocol

In 2000, Microsoft, Bosch, Panasonic, Hitachi, Alpine, Increment-P (Pioneer), Telcontar, MobileGIS, Navigation Technologies, VDO Siemens, and Tele Atlas formed the MAGIC Services Initiative. The MAGIC Services Initiative is the first major effort to develop a common API, architecture, and XML-based service delivery protocol for the full range of LBMS. Version 1.0 of the MAGIC Services Specification was published early in 2001 and an update, Version 2.0 was approved in early 2002. The main difference between 1.0 and 2.0 is the adoption of XML-encoded request and response message units to carry information between client and server. Simple Object Access Protocol (SOAP) was selected as an over-the-wire packaging structure. A wide range of transports is possible including HTTP, SMTP, and TCP/IP. MAGIC Services Protocol Version 2.0 (MSP 2.0) is fully compatible with the Microsoft .NET Framework. It is possible to build applications very quickly with Microsoft Visual Studio .NET, using the development environment and automated proxy code generation via web references to the MAGIC Services definitions in WSDL at http://www.MAGICServicesForum.org/Registry/Interfaces/.

The Eight MAGIC Services

The MAGIC Services are organized functionally as shown in the following table:

Service Name	Service Description
Session	Connect to and disconnect from a MAGIC Service provider.
	Negotiate service conditions and parameters that persist for a complete session.
Context	Set or get user and service provider preferences and defaults.
	Set or get service conditions and parameters that change occasionally during a session.
Query	Select and retrieve modeled elements based on spatial, temporal, and mobility relationships.
	Select geometry corresponding to addresses and other place and route descriptions (geocoding) and the reverse operation (reverse geocoding).

(continued)

Service Name	Service Description *(continued)*
Mobility	Plan travel.
	Review route, travel time, cost, sensitivity of planned travel.
	Receive real-time guidance during travel.
Positioning	Control determination of, access to, and delivery of position, track, velocity and other motion data.
	Get motion data for this or other mobile terminals.
Rendering	Submit a plan for a rendered depiction of a place, region, or route.
	Create a graphic (2- or 3-dimensional), text, voice, or other depiction based on a submitted plan.
Update	Send information about the real world back to a service provider in order to augment or correct the underlying navigable model of the real world.

This functionality is exposed at the API level via sixteen functions. Each function has two parameters, each of which is an XML document described by a schema in the MAGIC Services Registry at http://www.MAGICServicesForum.org/Registry/Schemas/.

Full details are available on the MAGIC Services Forum Web site at http://www.MAGICServicesForum.org/.

The key point is that the MAGIC Services are directly accessible as Microsoft .NET services, which can be connected to a Windows client application via automated proxy generation using a Visual Studio .Net Web reference. One practical note: since Visual Studio .NET creates a proxy with a fixed target URL, it may be useful to manually edit the automatically generated proxy code. Assuming the proxy was generated for the Session service by making a web reference to the official WSDL definition at http://www.MAGICServicesForum.org/Registry/Interfaces/Session.wsdl/, the following changes can be made to allow the proxy to be pointed at any URL using an ISAPI extension DLL named MSP2_Session.dll, by replacing the generated code with a static binding.

For example:

```
CMSP2_SessionServiceT(ISAXXMLReader *pReader = NULL)
    :Tclient(_T("http://localhost/MSP_Session/MSP2_Session.dll?Handler=Default"))
```

with code calling a function that returns the service provider URL dynamically as in the following code snippet:

```
CMSP2_SessionServiceT(ISAXXMLReader *pReader = NULL)
    :Tclient(SessionServerInfo.GetSessionServerURL())
```

It is important to note that explicit knowledge of a number of implementation techniques and conventions is completely encapsulated within the Visual Studio .NET IDE and the .NET Framework at one level. The conventions of MSP 2.0 completely encapsulate the specialized knowledge that is otherwise needed to develop navigation services for LBMS. Together, .NET and MSP 2.0 provide complete infrastructure for rapid development of enterprise-level location-based mobile services and applications.

Solution Architectures

Because the service infrastructure is provided, development of a mobile services delivery system really focuses on the server components needed to host the infrastructure. Additionally, you need to focus on a few details that are connected with the specific nature of the services to be provided, along with the characteristics of the target mobile terminals.

Operating System and Enterprise Server Components

A good low risk strategy is to start with a small service capacity and establish a plan for scaling up: adding servers, disk storage, and moving from single servers to clusters with network load balancing. Such a scale-up can usually be accomplished with no code changes and conceptually simple physical and operating systems upgrades or changes. Once a family of interoperable building blocks has been selected, the main design, implementation, support, and maintenance benefits are derived from reconfiguring them as needed to adapt to changing service delivery volumes. The most capable configurations will group functionality with different usage characteristic on dedicated servers or clusters. This allows the service level to be precisely tuned to the actual usage.

In these three chapters we examine deployment configurations for a navigation service provider supporting the full range of MAGIC Services with configurations ranging from a single server (the Small Space Server or the Position Proxy Server) to a fully disaggregated collection of dedicated function servers.

Importance of the Lab

Our experience in building complex service delivery systems shows that a lab is essential early in the design cycle. It is impossible to use product information or even experience with the individual operating system, networking, and server components to establish a workable design that meets project or product specifications. It is critical to actually build and refine an initial schematic design with real equipment and software components. The information gained in early prototyping will make all the difference in building and deploying a successful system.

Deployment Options

There are three basic deployment options: the synchronous and stateless model, the stateful server model, and the sync-and-go model.

Option 1: The Synchronous and Stateless Model

The smallest and simplest configuration is a single server operating in a stateless mode. Although state is implied in many MAGIC Services operations, the state need not be maintained on the server but can be held on the client and forwarded as needed in the SOAP header. Peer-to-peer implementations most often follow the synchronous and stateless model. Synchronous operation also avoids the complexity associated with asynchronous communications between client and server, which introduce additional state requirements on both client and server, as well as extra complexity in implementing the trigger mechanisms on the server side.

A starting configuration can be a single server running Windows 2000 (or even Windows CE) and IIS, MSMQ, SQL Server 2000, and ISA Server. The firewall could be a third party hardware solution or else another server with ISA server. In these chapters, we will assume ISA server running on a single computer (Standard Edition) or running in an array across several computers for load balancing and redundancy (Enterprise Edition)

Most of the technology involved in this option is also used in the other options as well. Therefore, this option works well if you want to start off small, and then scale up to a more enterprise-level configuration, as described in our next solution.

In the synchronous solution, the server computer can be stateless. The client computer implementation is responsible for selecting those addition parameters needed to convey proper context to the server. This information is placed in the SOAP header and the server computer extracts that information before processing the request in the SOAP body. This solution allows maximum server scalability and minimum complexity because no state information must be maintained. Complicated timeout protocols are also avoided. The Synchronous solution is a good choice when the network node in the server role is inherently not very powerful as in peer-to-peer configurations.

This model provides the least scalability, availablity, and redundancy. It is the simplest to implement and administer.

Option 2: The Stateful Server Model

A stateful server can minimize traffic over the network link. It is also necessary if asynchronous notifications are to be delivered to the client. Although the server resource requirements are higher, the stateful server model is normally the right one. One of the benefits of the client-server architecture is that system complexity and client resource requirements can be reduced by making the server do more of the processing and a larger share of the processing.

This model offers increased security, load balancing, and the best possible performance. More processing power is available through clustering computers together, and support for advanced processor hardware configurations in Windows operating system versions.

Option 3: Sync-and-Go Model

The third model is an extension of the second with additional complexity in the client computer. With sync-and-go the client is capable of autonomous operation for some amount of time or over some geographic region. The server computer delivers the needed information to support the operation in a "sync" operation after which the client can "go" autonomously until the limits of that content are reached. Normally the client and server are able to "sync" again prior to the client reaching this limit and the client is therefore able to "go" continuously. This model is applicable mostly to mosre capable clients such as in-car systems. These systems have access to tens of megabytes of volatile memory and sometimes carry tens of gigabytes of read-write disk.

Tools and Technologies

Operating Environment and Scalability

In developing any commercial system, it is essential to develop a scaled roadmap that allows validation of the service architecture in a lab or prototype phase, with a simple way to scale up to an initial commercial presence. Once this model is running, you can gradually meet increasing service loads, by separating functionality across computers, almost without limit. The following two-server configuration is quite capable of prototyping all of the functionality described here. A commercial deployment would separate functionality as described in a later chapter.

Hardware	Installed Software
Gateway Server	Windows 2000 with latest service pack
• Single-Processor 1+ GHz	Internet Security and Acceleration (ISA) Server
• 500 MB RAM	
• 40 GB mirrored IDE (RAID 0) hard drive	
Small Space Server	Windows 2000 Server SP2
• Dual-Processor 2 GHz	Internet Information Systems (IIS) 5.0
• 4 GB RAM	MSMQ
• 100 GB mirrored IDE (RAID 0) hard drive	SQL Server 2000
	Exchange Server 2000 (if SMTP supported)

A full capability configuration can be built from the following components:

Hardware	Installed Software
Gateway Server Array (1-16 servers)	Windows 2000 Server SP2
	ISA Server – Enterprise Edition
• Single-Processor 500 MHz	Host Integration Server (opt)
• 500 MB RAM	
• 40 GB RAID 0 SCSI disk	
Transport Conversion Server Cluster (2-16 servers)	Windows 2000 Advanced Server
	.NET Framework
• Dual-Processor 2 GHz	IIS 5.0
• 4 GB RAM	MSMQ
• 100 GB RAIS 5 SCSI array	Exchange Server 2000
Accounting Server (2-4 servers)	Windows 2000 Advanced Server
• Dual-Processor 2 GHz	SQL Server 2000
• 4 GB RAM	.NET Framework
• 100 GB RAID 5 SCSI array	Commerce Server 2000 (opt)

(continued)

Hardware	Installed Software *(continued)*
Core Navigation Server (2-16 servers) • Quad-Processor 700 MHz • 1 gig RAM • 200 GB RAID 5 SCSI array	Windows 2000 with latest service pack IIS 5.0 .NET Framework Host Integration Server (opt)

General Considerations

Host Integration Server can be included if it is necessary to establish client-server connectivity with a mainframe system at the Gateway or for content integration at the Core Navigation server. These options are discussed in more detail in the next chapter.

Hardware

In general, it is a good idea to use identical components in each kind of server. This enhances both maintainability and compatibility.

Software

The latest patches and service packs should always be applied to server computers under the control of a reliable scheduling mechanism. Virus checking is very important at least through to the Transport Unpacking server because raw content from outside the Gateway reaches this point without prior examination. Migration from Windows 2000 Server to Advanced Server and on to DataCenter Server requires more administration but is otherwise relatively trouble free. The main transition is from single servers to server clusters and the configuration of network load balancing. Since some of the services require state information, the design has to allow for the possibility that the server or even cluster providing core navigation services may not itself hold the state information for the user session. Different approaches are possible, including a separate server function to manage sessions and state. Another workable alternative is to have the accounting server manage the session and attach any needed context and pass it on to stateless navigation servers.

As usual, all unneeded Windows services, users, and groups should be removed from each server in order to reduce complexity, increase performance, and eliminate potential security problems.

Gateway Server

The Gateway Server computer is the main contact point that customers and business partners have with the mobile service. The Gateway server manages access to transport-specific, accounting, and back-end server computers where the requests are satisfied and results returned in response messages. However, because this server is exposed to the Internet, you should not keep any sort of customer, corporate, or sensitive data on it. Instead, you should keep that information on the back-end SQL Server.

Transport Unpacking Server

The Transport Unpacking or Conversion server takes SOAP envelopes delivered via different transports such as HTTP, SMTP, and TCP/IP and validates the content, eliminates extraneous information, performs virus checking and sends request messages toward the back-end for processing. It also performs the reverse operations in order to package response messages for delivery to the client.

Accounting Server

The database server computer holds sensitive data for the mobile service, such as customer profiles, marketing lists, and payment information. Because the database server is behind a firewall that allows only SQL protocols to get through, you reduce the risk of compromising your data. Instead, the server is able to talk to the computers running Commerce and BizTalk Server without opening either to the Internet.

Core Navigation Server

The core navigation server does the low-level geographic calculations to produce the route, map or other core result requested by the application.

Implementation

When implementing ConsolidatedRetail.com, make sure to perform the following steps:

Implementing ConsolidatedRetail.com

1. Install the .NET Server products on your systems.

2. Install the B2B software solutions on your systems.

3. Verify that you have installed B2B software solutions properly.

4. Deploy the solution to your site.

Installing Microsoft Software

Install the following software with the following configurations on following computers in the order listed:

Gateway Server

1. Windows 2000 Server
2. ISA Server (Standard for single server or Enterprise for array)
3. Configuration settings:
   - Open inbound ports include 25 (SMTP), 80 (HTTP) and 443 (SSL)
   - Open outbound ports include 25 (SMTP), 80 (HTTP) and 443 (SSL)

Accounting Server

1. Windows 2000 Server or Advanced Server SP2
2. SQL Server 2000

Transport Unpacking Server

1. Windows 2000 Server or Advanced Server SP2
2. IIS 5.0
3. Exchange Server 2000
4. MSMQ

Core Navigation Server

1. Windows 2000 Server or Advanced Server SP2
2. IIS 5.0
3. MSMQ
4. Data and software components to implement core geographic services

Deployment Checklist

- Remove all unwanted services in all servers, including the following:
  - Terminal Services
  - Registry
  - RunAs
  - RAS

- NNTP

- Messenger

- IIS Admin

- Close all unnecessary ports in the servers. You can do this by commenting out the respective ports on the services file.

- Connect the external NIC of External ISA servers to the Internet gateway router. Make sure the external NIC IP address is the same as the allocated Internet IP address.

- Configure the Internet DNS server computer hosting the Fully Qualified Domain Name (FQDN) to point to your Internet IP address.

- Test from an entirely different network to try connecting to FQDN using the Sample Application.

Security Checklist

Before you connect your LBS delivery system to the public Internet, you should take the following steps to ensure the safety of your network.

- Apply the latest service pack to Windows 2000.

- Apply all known critical updates from http://www.microsoft.com/windowsupdate.

- Apply all known hotfixes from http://www.microsoft.com/security.

- Apply the IIS lockdown tools.

- Make sure you have not published the entire Web site or the IP address on the ISA server. Instead, always use a destination to publish the site.

- Enable packet filtering on the ISA server with intrusion detection. Enabling this detection will ensure that no one will make an unsolicited TCP connection to your ISA server.

- Change the names of your administrators.

- Remove any sample and administration sites.

- In the IIS/Application mappings, remove everything but .wsdl.

- In /Network Connections/Advanced settings, disable the bindings for "file and printer sharing for Microsoft Networks" and "Client for Microsoft Networks" in the NIC connected to the public network.

Additional Information

The following links contains the installation documents used to deploy the solution in the lab.

- Step-by-Step Guide to Installing Cluster Service

  http://www.microsoft.com/windows2000/techinfo/planning/server/clustersteps.asp

- Introduction to Network Load Balancing

  http://www.microsoft.com/WINDOWS2000/en/datacenter/help/introduction.htm

- Q259267 - Microsoft Cluster Service Installation Resources

  http://support.microsoft.com/support/kb/articles/Q259/2/67.ASP?LN=EN-US&SD=gn&FR=0&qry=howto%20SQL%20cluster&rnk=10&src=DHCS_MSPSS_gn_SRCH&SPR=MSALL

- Q243218 - INF: Installation Order for SQL Server 2000 Enterprise Edition on Microsoft Cluster Server

  http://support.microsoft.com/support/kb/articles/Q243/2/18.ASP?LN=EN-US&SD=gn&FR=0&qry=WLBS%20MSMQ&rnk=2&src=DHCS_MSPSS_gn_SRCH&SPR=MSALL

By Carl Stephen Smyth

Location-Based Mobile Services Architecture

Scenario

This chapter looks in more detail at the design of a scalable navigation services platform for location-based mobile services (LBMS). The goal is to first understand the functional components that handle services access, transport conversion and message extraction, authentication, billing, session management, and the actual computation of the low level core navigation services that support mobile service providers' applications, which guide mobile users in the real world. These functions can be implemented by scalable combinations of Microsoft's operating system and .NET Enterprise Server products. They can be packaged as single servers for space publishing applications, medium-size multi-server systems for corporate internal use, or in large multi-cluster DataCenter installations for commercial delivery of core navigation services to multiple mobile service providers.

Solution

In this section we cover some of the complex issues enterprises face in creating an architecture for Location-based Mobile Services (LBMS). First, we discuss some key design considerations, including MSP 2.0 protocol, transport considerations, Navigation Service Provider (NSP) architecture, and service delivery targets. We describe three options for caching, and wrap up this section with a brief summary.

Key Design Considerations

Certain characteristics of the target mobile device population are the primary influences on server configuration for the navigation service provider. These include the peak level of service requests, the average level of service requests, the size of the geographic area served, and whether or not peer-to-peer service is possible.

The following table illustrates four possibilities:

Type of Mobile Terminal	Peak Service Level	Average Service Level	Geographic Area	Peer-to-Peer	Type of Solution
Phone	10 000 000/ day	4 000 000/ day	Large country	No.	Clustered and redundant multiple processor with disaggregated functionality
Car	50 000/day	20 000/day	Large country	Yes	Large single servers with disaggregated functionality
Any	2 000/day	500/day	Parking garage	No	Single Space Publishing Server
Any	200 000/day	180 000/day	Region	Yes	Position Proxy Server

Delivery to automobiles and hand held mobile phones are the two most prevalent mass-market models. While most industry planning, design, and implementation is focused on a small number of location-based services (e.g., personal navigation, driving directions, store finders, and map generation), core navigation services need to become ubiquitous and offer a standard platform before the full range of applications will appear.

At present the technical difficulties of building an in-house solution represent a large barrier to developers of location-based services. Typically these have been high-cost and low volume. The emergence of Internet standards for distributed computing enabled progress toward lower development costs and new business models that allow the provider role (NSP) to be separated from the consumer role (MSP). Ultimately the combination of specialization and interoperability will expand the market for all participants.

MSP, NSPs and Other Content Providers

In addition to the target mobile terminal, the relationship between navigation service provider and mobile service provider is an important factor. You will recall that a navigation service provider computes the response to a request for service by taking the location of the mobile terminal into account. The navigation service provider uses a computationally accessible model of the world to derive information about mobility in the real world. The mobile service provider has the direct customer relationship and hosts applications that depend on the capabilities of the navigation service provider and which also integrate information from a number of independent specialized content providers. From the mobile service provider's point of view, the navigation service provider is just one of many content providers. It is, of course, highly desirable for these content providers to use a common mechanism for delivering the content. The rise of XML as a data representation language and SOAP as a remoting protocol over the last few years has led to some convergence toward a common way to deliver content.

The .NET Framework and its support by the MAGIC Services Protocol fit well with this trend. One of the surprising consequences is that both the providers and consumers of navigation services for location-based mobile services can maintain architectural relationships that mirror their business relationships.

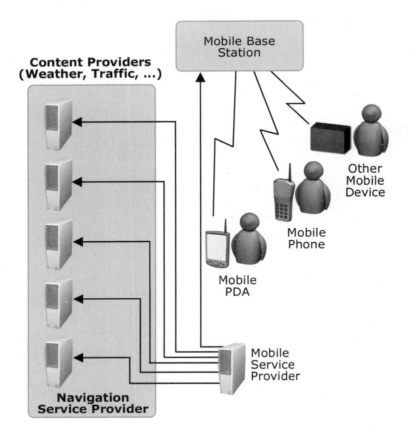

Navigation Service Provider is one of many content suppliers

The MSP's customers, the end users, want to be able to carry a single device that can adapt to their surroundings as they move geographically and change modes of transportation. Applications built to rely on a standard navigation services platform such as MSP 2.0 will eventually allow geographic roaming and a choice of service providers the same way that is now possible with voice telephony. As is also happening in voice services, location-based services will eventually become transparently portable across geographic and carrier (or MSP) service boundaries.

Ultimately this locational transparency is essential to develop a mass market in location-based (and all non-voice) mobile services, if consumers are to perceive high value, ease of use, and lack of confusion in accessing the services.

Two other aspects of perceived value are also enhanced by developing interoperable delivery platforms. First, many improvements in the existing capabilities of a mobile device can be derived from personalizing and customizing the locality in which the device is used. Such customization is not an application in itself.

It is just a degree of location-awareness that can condition the operation of other services, such as voice and text messaging services, to the location of one or more users and the mobility characteristics of a geographic area.

For example, a network operator could provide a buddy-finder service for a group of people that have a business or social reason to meet. Some requirements to consider are individual location, time of day, urgency of the meeting, and other factors. Second, the cost of location-awareness is driven by data and development costs. Both can be reduced by ubiquitous location-aware mobile devices that can connect to service providers via network standard protocols and encodings and make industry standard navigation service requests via MSP 2.0.

NSP, MSPs, and Other Customers

The navigation service provider, on the other hand, normally serves a variety of customer types, mobile service providers among them. NSPs prefer to use the same delivery mechanisms for each customer type. This allows the navigation service provider to offer quality services to a range of customers, large and small, and at a competitive price, since all of the customers present themselves the same way.

One of the distinguishing characteristics of Internet standards such as XML and SOAP is that these standards enable new economies of scale and reduce the cost of individual transactions. The additional benefits of simplified application development and deployment further encourage market development.

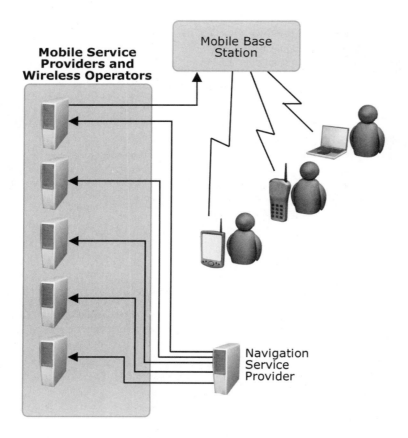

Each mobile service provider is just another customer

The greatest benefit is a reduced need to customize technical details of service delivery to meet special requirements of individual customers. It is hard to overstate the importance of the role of the Internet, TCP/IP, HTTP and SMTP, XML and SOAP in enabling the flexible and efficient distribution of labor and reward in mobile services.

MSP 2.0 in the Protocol Stack

The MAGIC Services Protocol Version 2.0 lies at the top of the application level of a protocol stack on the client and server network nodes. MSP 2.0 encodes navigation service requests and responses in XML, according to the definitions of XML schemas written in XML Schema Language and available for reference in the MSP 2.0 Registry at http://www.MAGICServicesForum.org/Registry/Schemas/.

These request and response messages can be carried over any available transport, including HTTP, HTTPS, SMTP, and TCP/IP. The SOAP rules completely define the packaging and delivery of the requests and responses, and the XML schemas completely define the internal structure of the request and response documents.

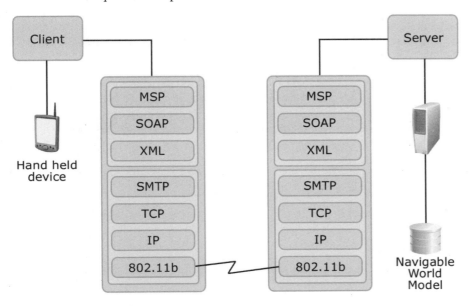

MSP 2.0 sits on top of XML and SOAP in the protocol stack

In this example, the transport is SMTP carried by TCP/IP over a short-range wireless link. The entire lower part of either protocol stack could be replaced by any combination capable of reliably delivering the MSP 2.0 SOAP envelopes. The fact that the client and server roles can be ignorant of the underlying transport allows different technologies to be used for network communications in support of the "free roaming" capability.

Transport Considerations

There are some specific characteristics of certain popular transports that are worth noting. These include the ubiquitous protocol of the web, HTTP, as well as SMTP and "raw" TCP/IP. Other common protocols such as FTP are also quite usable in certain situations.

HTTP

Choosing which transport to use is not easy. HTTP and HTTPS are almost universally available. Corporate firewalls are normally open to HTTP traffic, though some do look at the payload and distinguish between normal web browsing and serving and distributed computation of the sort supported by SOAP. Server software supporting HTTP, such as Microsoft IIS or Apache, is highly developed and extremely reliable. Many development tools and SDKs are available to decrease the development effort.

On the negative side, the request/response model of HTTP does not support asynchronous notification very well. Some applications depend on the client being notified when certain conditions are met, such as changes in traffic or road conditions. If HTTP is used in such cases, the application of HTTP imposes some extra burdens on both client and server. There is little practical experience with the current crop of asynchronous add-ons in the connection-hostile mobile world.

SMTP

SMTP is another highly developed and widely used Internet protocol. SMTP is even more mature than HTTP and widely and robustly delivers email messages in very high volume everywhere in the Internet. SMTP has the distinct advantage for asynchronous response delivery, since the messaging paradigm of email is naturally one-way.

Disadvantages of SMTP include the poor support for development of non-email applications and the sometimes quirky treatment of mail that is misdirected. SMTP is also subject to abuse in the form of high volume unsolicited message traffic (SPAM) and mechanisms for the transfer of viruses and worms. There is little that can be done about SPAM within the context of location-based services. Dealing with malicious content is quite feasible. The transport unpacking function has no need to allow or enable any mechanism for execution of any part of the service request messages or other information in the SOAP envelope. In some cases it may be useful to scan these elements for viruses and that is certainly true if there is any possibility of using the underlying mail system as a relay point.

TCP/IP

It is possible to use lower-level transports such as TCP/IP to deliver requests and responses at the TCP socket level. This may be a good approach in tightly couple client-server applications but foregoes much of the built-in robustness of HTTP or SMTP.

Other Transports

As noted, there is no restriction on the transport selected except that it reliably carry the SOAP envelopes containing the service request and responses. From a practical point of view, high volume server delivery of navigation services can be done with the least technology risk and the lowest development cost when built on top of either or both HTTP and SMTP. HTTP has the advantage of direct support by the .NET Framework and Visual Studio .NET. The hooks are already in the generated proxy code, so it might be feasible to manually modify a proxy generated from an HTTP web reference to also support SMTP.

Navigation Service Provider Architecture

Scalability and reliability are enhanced by separation or disaggregation of functionality into groups that respond in a similar way to specific aspects of the imposed request loading. For example, moving core navigational computations into a subsystem allows tight coupling with the world model used in those computations and enables the computational resources required to meet the needs of the end user applications to be adjusted to precisely meet the peak and average load. The following sections show how to divide NSP functionality into four subsystems. Each can be implemented on separately scalable servers or server clusters depending on the scale of the operation. It is also possible to combine adjacent subsystems in a single server in small systems. The case where all subsystems are co-located on a single server is distinguished as the "Space Publishing Server." The Space Publishing Server is typically delivered by a system integrator to the owner of a parking structure, office building, airport or other small space as an aid to people moving within that structure. In that case the NSP functions are a means of "publishing" the mobile space in a way that network applications may access directly for travel planning, guidance, and display purposes.

Back-End – Front-End Division

The first level of subdivision is made by separating the secure low-level computations from the components that concern themselves with network access, security, authentication, billing, accounting, and high-level protocols.

Back-End

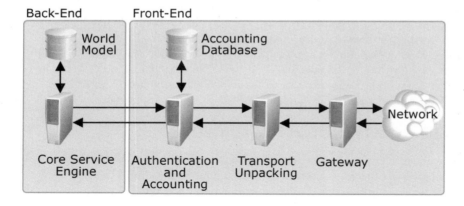

The Navigation Service Pipeline split into front-end and back-end

The back-end computations are typically very difficult. The normal way to compute a response to requests for information about travel from point A to point B is to perform a search through a state space of all possible travel to discover a feasible (though not necessarily precisely optimal) way to move through the navigable world model from a representation of point A to a representation of point B. The results are reported back as though they referred to travel in the real world.

For example, the request might be to continuously update the travel time from a car's current position to a rental car return location at an airport. On the NSP side, this would involve periodically noting the current position of the car in the real world, finding a corresponding data reference in the navigable world model, finding a representation of the car return location in the model, searching through all of the possible drivable road network for a short or simple or fast path between the current location and the return location (taking current traffic, weather, road condition, road construction, and time-dependent restrictions on travel and turns into account). Once the path is found (or it is determined that no path can be found), then the travel time on the path is computed and returned to the end-user. These calculations can easily involve millions of database accesses and storage of large search trees in memory. In most cases, the ability to perform the back-end calculations will determine the overall throughput capability of a NSP.

Computer architectures, such as the compatible family of Windows operating systems and .NET Enterprise Server products, makes adaptation of a system to actual usage loads a relatively predictable process. The further subdivision of functionality into components that manage the rapidly changing location of mobile objects in a "positioning store" and integration of new information about mobility in the real world (traffic, weather, etc) may be necessary in the largest systems.

Sometimes the main function of the NSP is simply to track the location of mobile devices and serve up information about their location on request. This functionality can be implemented on a special-purpose version of a NSP back-end called a "Position Proxy Server."

Back-End

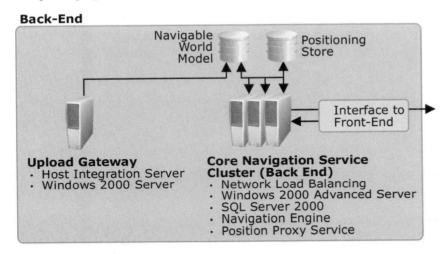

Upload Gateway
- Host Integration Server
- Windows 2000 Server

Core Navigation Service Cluster (Back End)
- Network Load Balancing
- Windows 2000 Advanced Server
- SQL Server 2000
- Navigation Engine
- Position Proxy Service

Core Functions of the NSP back-end

The core navigation service hosts the navigation engine and the position proxy service. Together these two components serve responses to MSP 2.0 requests. The host for these services will normally be in a cluster running Windows 2000 Advanced Server and use NLB to distribute incoming requests. SQL Server 2000 manages the navigable world model and the position information used by the position proxy service.

To upload information from external data suppliers requires provider-specific protocols and methods. Windows access to mainframe computers can be simplified by using Host Integration Server 2000.

Front-End

The front-end connects with the Internet or in some cases with a wireless network operated by a single wireless company. The latter situation will almost certainly not persist more than a few years into the future as IP connectivity reaches all parts of a combined fixed and wireless Internet.

The gateway server is at the front of the front-end. It performs the normal firewall functions of restricting access to just those TCP ports used by legitimate MSP 2.0 accesses. It is the point of contact for establishing a network connection between client and server. The gateway may be the access point for connections to wireless devices. In that case Mobile Information Server can be used to hide most of the complexity and simplify administration. It may be possible to use the built-in capabilities of Mobile Information Server directly when HTTP or SMTP are used for SOAP envelope transport. In other cases custom adapters may have to be written to interface with the back-end processes.

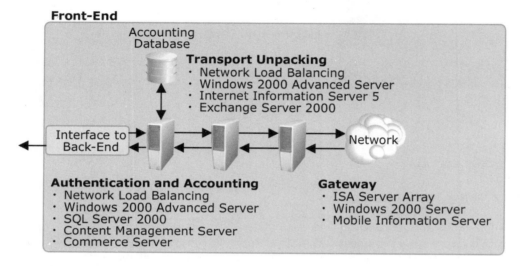

NSP front-end

The transport unpacking server takes incoming SOAP envelopes in SMTP, HTTP, or other transports, unpacks the content, validates it, and forwards the content to the authentication and accounting server, if the content is valid. The transport unpacking server is the logical endpoint providing the MSP 2.0 services from the external point of view. If SMTP is supported, then Exchange Server can run on this server as a robust SMTP and message storage system, buffering SMTP traffic to and from the NSP. While Exchange Server functionality is not precisely designed for this kind of application, it is well integrated with the other components in a Windows environment. In some cases it may be possible to use the SMTP service of IIS and MSMQ but this normally requires more custom coding.

Authentication and accounting are necessary for each MSP 2.0 request. One reason is that content providers often charge fees based on per-transaction usage and fine-grained accounting is needed to meet contractual requirements. The second is to make certain that session state information exists for each incoming request.

State information arrives in three ways.

- It may be created on initial connection to the NSP.

- It may be a consequence of a previous request.

- It may be extracted from the SOAP header in stateless server configurations.

SQL Server 2000 manages the accounting information. Related online business transactions are handled by Commerce Server.

Successful authentication during the initial connection produces a session ID token that is used in subsequent requests to allow rapid authentication.

Space Publishing Server

Combining the front-end and back-end NSP components into a single server provides a way for the owners of public facilities such as sports stadiums, airports, central city cores, parking structures, office buildings, and corporate campuses to make their property accessible to mobile applications. MSP 2.0 provides a standard way to request information about mobility in and around structures including travel within buildings. It also makes it possible for an upstream service provider to offer very accurate and detailed guidance at the beginning or destination phase of personal travel.

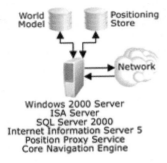

Space publishing server combines all NSP components

A space publishing server is normally built using a single server computer running Windows 2000 Server with SQL Server 2000, IIS and the low-level core navigation and position proxy services. In general, it is better to integrate with a large volume NSP over the Internet and make the connection through the NSP gateway, rather than a special interface point. This allows a large and varying number of SPSs to be associated with a NSP. The NSP may use UDDI or other directory services to find SPSs, or the SPS owner may have an explicit relationship with the NSP.

Typically an SPS owner makes money or saves on expenses by publishing. Access to the SPS is usually free to the user.

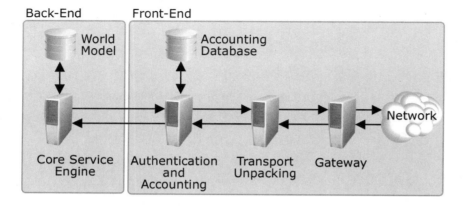

Integrating SPS with a NSP

Service Delivery Targets

The nature of the target mobile terminal or MSP determines the overall characteristics of the service load seen by a NSP. Almost all of the customization of functionality is done through implementation of the client. MSP 2.0 has a language-independent specification of an API for application development. This specification is in the OMG Unified Modeling Language (UML) and can be found in the MAGIC Services Registry at http://www.MAGICServicesForum.org/Registry/Interfaces/. Tools exist to generate skeleton code from a UML model. The Rational Rose product from Rational Software is one such tool. UML models may be viewed and manipulated in Microsoft Visio and Microsoft Visual Modeler.

Five Targets

NSP clients can be grouped into three classes:

- In-car systems and Personal Digital Assistants (PDAs) - delivery via wireless link

- Mobile phones - delivery via wireless link

- Mobile Service Providers - delivery via Internet

Each is characterized by onboard computing capability, positioning technology, and onboard read/write storage. Additionally, the

- Space Publishing Server

  often has one or more larger navigation service providers as clients; and the

- Position Proxy Server

  may have a wide range of clients on both the fixed and mobile Internet.

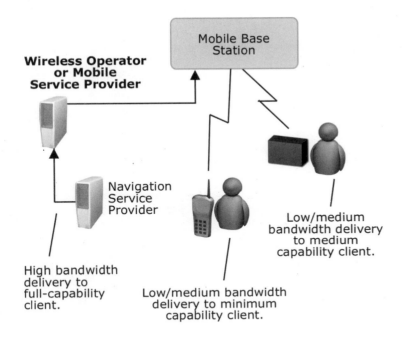

Three classes of mobile terminals

A closer look at the first three targets shows that the mobile targets both have modest network connectivity and differ in terms of the computational capability of the mobile terminal themselves. While the minimum capability clients may require the most server capacity, the medium capability clients (PDAs and in-car systems) are the most difficult to deploy because they may have different amounts of on-board data and processing capability. In-car systems may have a complete multi-gigabyte static dataset that allows much of the core navigation functionality to be served on-board, relying on a remote NSP only for services that depend on other or dynamically varying information. The trend to lower cost of components and transfer of in-car functions from specialized components to general-purpose onboard systems makes for a confused picture.

Delivery to Mobile Phones

Delivery of the full range of MSP 2.0 supported services to a mobile phone using uncompressed XML with possible variations in the underlying schema is not practical with today's devices. There is often only a few kilobytes (KB) of RAM available and some form of compression is almost certain to be required. In addition, many of today's technologies do not directly support IP and delivery across the wireless link will be circuit-switched along with the voice service. That means even in the case where an application on the phone can interact directly via MSP 2.0 functionality, it will not communicate via MSP 2.0 natively and protocol conversion will take place at a gateway in the MSP. Mobile Information Server can be a good solution to organize the delivery of information from the NSP gateway to the MSP gateway.

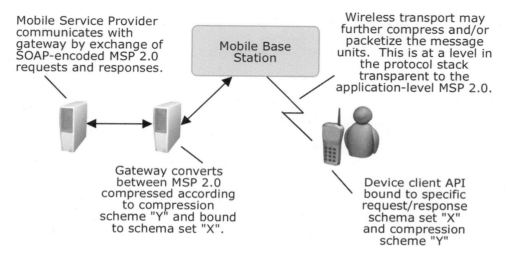

Mobile Service Provider communicates with gateway by exchange of SOAP-encoded MSP 2.0 requests and responses.

Mobile Base Station

Wireless transport may further compress and/or packetize the message units. This is at a level in the protocol stack transparent to the application-level MSP 2.0.

Gateway converts between MSP 2.0 compressed according to compression scheme "Y" and bound to schema set "X".

Device client API bound to specific request/response schema set "X" and compression scheme "Y"

NSP Delivery to mobile phone

The MSP 2.0 Framework specification allows for registered compression and encoding schemes. This allows a NSP to deliver information to a mobile phone via an MSP either as native character-encoded XML or under a specific (registered) compression scheme. Because a compression scheme usually takes advantage of the known structure of the information being compressed, it is usually necessary to identify both the scheme and the assumed structure. MSP 2.0 allows the negotiation of schema used to describe the structure of request and response packets so this is especially relevant if the compression is intrinsically schema independent. In such a case the schema must be known in order to recover the information sent across the link.

Mobile devices that operate with compressed MSP 2.0 normally use the compressed form directly so that no decompression is required on the client.

Delivery to In-Car Systems

In-car systems share the connectivity limitations of mobile phones and the same compression schemes are likely to be used in an automotive environment. Compressed MSP 2.0 using compression scheme X with schema set Y is called CMSP 2.0/X-Y.

One of the defining characteristics of in-car systems and some smart phones and PDAs is the availability of significant onboard computing power, RAM, and read-write non-volatile storage. This allows a number of strategies that minimize data communications including onboard caching and the sync-and-go mode of operation. In sync-and-go, the client requests that the server determine the information resources required forn the device to travel autonomously. In the sync phase this information is packaged by the server and delivered to the client. Once delivered, the client then goes ahead with the travel, connecting to the service provider on when traveling beyond the scope of the onboard information.

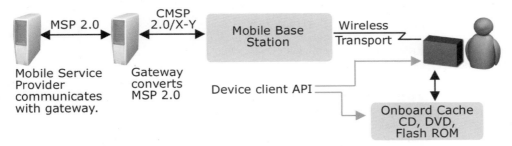

NSP delivery to in-car system

The onboard application contains all of the code needed to perform the entire application and client-server interactions focus on information transfer and planning rather than direct computation. In order to reduce the cost of in-car systems, the client capabilities have to be scaled back. This can be done with a lot of flexibility when the application is build on top of the MSP 2.0 API. This allows the system developer to make choices about whether the functionality is implemented in the client itself or remoted to the NSP. Technology and market trends are moving in the direction of reducing parts and parts cost in the car as in-car systems become more common. Several manufacturers have stated the goal of equipping all of their models with basic onboard equipment – positioning and data communications – within the next two years.

There is another consideration that has produced a different trend, however. One of the problems with building state-of-the-art devices into cars is that the automotive design cycle is very long (several years) and testing requirements quite strict. This means that relatively old designs show up in new cars and it is not feasible to make mass-market retro-fits. In addition to the long development cycle, car manufacturers are expected or required to provide support and parts for as long as ten years after their cars are sold. The result is that manufacturers are often in the position of supporting components in cars that are a human generation old. As a result, some manufacturers are exploring ways that small devices, mobile phones, PDAs, or special-purpose electronics, can be "docked" in a car in such a way that they connect with some onboard systems but are otherwise easily removable and accompany the user rather than the vehicle.

Both of these trends make development on a service platform that can be implemented in different ways a very attractive strategy.

Delivery to a Mobile Service Provider

In many cases the MSP builds location-based applications where most of the application resides in the MSP and only a small part communicates with the mobile terminal. Obviously such applications are not capable of directly using a platform like MSP 2.0. In this case, the MSP takes the client role. Communication between MSP and NSP is likely to be very high bandwidth and with minimum compression. Quite often the NSP will co-locate the NSP servers with the MSP. This enhances connectivity, security, and maintainability at some cost of increased maintenance difficulty for the NSP.

NSP Delivery to Mobile Service Provider

A single MSP may work with several NSPs in order to obtain full geographic coverage. As previously noted, an NSP is just one of many suppliers to an MSP. A single service model and protocol across all NSPs is highly desirable for both technical and business reasons. The standardization brings a degree of commoditization to the NSP offerings and gives the MSP added leverage to obtain the services on good terms.

Information Update

MSP 2.0 also provides a reverse path for information low from client to server. This allows a mobile application to deliver updated information about the real world to the NSP. The basic principle of computing navigation services is to use a detailed model of the things in the real world, such as roads, towns, lakes, signs, hotels, and other elements in computations that answer questions about or provide guidance for mobile activities in the real world. The matching or coherence between the modeled and real world largely determines the perceived quality of the services. The capability to enhance coherence through feedback from the real world is extremely valuable.

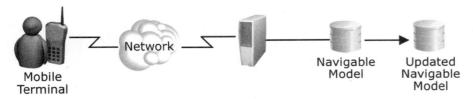

Information update

One of the persistent difficulties in supplying meaningful and useful updates has been the lack of a common underlying conceptual model on which such communications could be based. The details of a common model are not very important as long as the meaning of the elements is well understood by clients and servers alike.

Solution Parameters

Developing a mobile service delivery system starts with consideration of the key parameters. The nature of the target device and the communications link are key factors. It is also important to understand the level of responsibility the NSP has for positioning mobile terminals. In many situations, the NSP has absolutely no responsibility for answering requests for the position of mobile devices. In some, such as with a position proxy server, that is the primary kind of request to be expected.

Wireless Connectivity

If the NSP must manage connection to mobile devices then Mobile Information Server should be built into the gateway server. If not, then precise requirements on the need to support specific compression schemes and alternative MSP 2.0 schemas should be obtained from the MSP.

Identifying Service Requirements

If the NSP is building a vertical system, then there is a lot of flexibility to make tradeoffs between client capabilities and server capabilities. Information can be staged to capable clients in time for its use by location-aware asynchronous delivery. If, for example, the application is shuttle scheduling and monitoring on a corporate campus, dynamic conditions such as measured recent travel time on specific links within the campus road network can be delivered on a communications-available basis. When a new building goes online or a road is opened or closed, the information can be scheduled for delivery to each shuttle before the new information would have any bearing on travel.

Peak, average, and other measures of request volume are needed in order to scale the services. A typical core navigation server can handle a few transactions per second with latency (round trip delay) of a few seconds. Relaxing the peak performance requirements can significantly reduce system cost. Unfortunately system behavior is often judged by its worst-case (i.e. peak load) performance.

Caching Options

In the case where the system designed has control over both client and server roles, caching can be a powerful tool to improve real-time performance and decrease the influence of the "not-quite-there-yet" state of data communications in many environments. Since bandwidth and reliability are likely to increase considerably over time, convergence to a small number of stereotypical design patterns should evolve. Unfortunately that is the future.

Option 1: No-Caching Solution

The first option is to use no caching whatsoever. This may be the only choice if the wireless operator or MSP is not involved in the system and the target mobile terminal is not very capable.

Option 2: Modest (80/20) Caching

This is the usual choice and follows the 80/20 rule. Most data communications probably involve a small fraction of the total range of information traveling over the link. Recognizing when the same information is about to be re-sent and relying on the receiving end to assume that the information is the same when not transmitted can often produce a much improved utilization of the communications link.

Option 3: Sync-and-Go Solution

A common strategy with more capable clients such as PDAs and in-car systems is to let the server determine the relevant portion of the world model needed to support mobile activities over a few minutes to a few hours. The portion of the model is uploaded to the device, which can then operate autonomously until the limits of the model information are reached. In some cases, the core navigational code may also be uploaded. This is a powerful technique in dynamically delivering a data-software combination that looks like a simple service to the onboard application on the other side of the client API.

Solution Summary

Here is a brief recap of the highlights for each type of solution: mobile phones, in-car systems, mobile service providers, space publishing servers, and position proxy servers.

Mobile Phone

Phones have limited memory and processor. Phones are well-connected for wireless devices. Caching is important. A stateless server may be needed. Proprietary or specialized compression schemes may be needed. Use Mobile Information Server if connection to phone is required.

In-Car

In-car systems are capable and can trade off onboard data for data communications reliability. Cars almost always have positioning devices and may require position proxy service. Proprietary or specialized compression schemes may be needed.

Mobile Service Provider

A mobile service provider will have high bandwidth and expect a common delivery standard across NSPs. It may be necessary to co-locate server computers with the MSP. The full range of services, protocols, and compression schemes must be supported.

Space Publishing Server

Space publishing usually includes construction of a computer representation of the space (building, parking structure, stadium). The model and its maintenance may dominate the development and operating cost. The server is a turnkey system operated by the owner of the published space. Many NSPs may access a SPS. SPS operators usually provide access for free.

Position Proxy Server

Position proxy server usually requires high performance and availability. Privacy and security are very important and users must agree to terms of service. Authentication is likewise a critical function.

Tools and Technologies

Here is a brief summary of the tools and technologies needed to work with the products and servers already covered in the Solution section.

- Generate API skeleton code using UML generating tools such as Rational Rose.

- View UML with Microsoft Visual Modeler.

- Use WSDL to describe service delivery point compatible with .NET.

- Deliver code in CLR-compatible form to sync-and-go clients.

Implementation

Use the following steps as a guide to implement a NSP delivery system:

Implementing an NSP Delivery System

1. Analyze requirements to determine which of the five models applies.

2. Determine how to distribute functionality from gateway to core navigation across physical servers or server clusters.

3. Build your configuration in a lab with all server components and core navigation engine.

4. Measure performance and functionality.

5. Refine design if requirements not met and go back to step 3.

6. Deploy the solution to your site.

Installing Microsoft Software

Install the following software with the following configurations on following machines in the order listed:

Gateway Server

1. Windows 2000 Server

2. IIS 5.0

3. ISA Server (Standard or Enterprise depending on scale)

4. Mobile Information Server (if end-to-end connection to mobile terminal required)

5. Set packet filtering for selected transports.

Transport Unpacking Server

1. Windows 2000 Server or Advanced Server

2. IIS 5.0

3. Exchange Server 2000 (if SMTP used)

Authentication and Accounting Server

1. Windows 2000 Server or Advanced Server

2. SQL Server 2000

3. IIS 5.0

4. Commerce Server 2000 (if mobile commerce support required)

Core Navigation Server

1. Windows 2000 Server or Advanced Server

2. SQL Server 2000

3. Navigation Engine

Space Publishing Server

1. ISA Server (Standard)

2. Windows 2000 Server

3. SQL Server 2000

4. IIS 5.0

5. Exchange Server 2000 (if SMTP used)

6. Navigation Engine

Position Proxy Server

1. ISA Server (Standard)

2. Windows 2000 Server

3. SQL Server 2000

4. IIS 5.0

5. Exchange Server 2000 (if SMTP used)

Additional Information

The following links contain specifications and other resources needed to design a NSP solution.

http://www.magicservicesforum.org/

http://www.omg.org/

http://www.opengis.org/

http://www.msdn.microsoft.com/

By Carl Stephen Smyth

Delivering Location-Based Mobile Services

Introduction

This chapter looks at the need to meet the specific requirements of in-car systems, hand-held mobile devices such as mobile phones and PDAs, space publishing, and position proxy services. User scenarios and corresponding delivery solutions are described within the Microsoft .NET and MAGIC Services Protocol Version 2.0 (MSP 2.0) frameworks. The underlying concepts apply in general to implementations using a request-response model, encoding parameters in XML documents, and the use of SOAP to carry the requests and responses between client and server.

MSP 2.0 enables clients to access servers that model navigable spaces of any size. For large spaces, from regions as large as the entire planet down to a single country or perhaps a region of a large country, the navigable model is likely to be built and services delivered to a large, mass-market service provider. Examples include large Internet portals and service providers, mobile service providers such as wireless network operators and telematics service providers, and large geodata suppliers. From consumers' point of view, MSP 2.0 enables their application to connect to a server that can supply expert information and navigational guidance for a room, a building, a parking garage, a city, a national road network, or the whole planet. Since the connection and information transfer are based on standards and are widely implemented, the user community will grow to expect these services to be as widely available as voice telephony is now.

Some geographic information is needed as a framework to reference travelers' locations as well as their intended travel destinations. Typically the framework data consists of geometry and attributes that define administrative regions such as countries, provinces, cities, and towns as well as roadways and other elements of the fixed transportation infrastructure. Large data suppliers are becoming increasingly aware that "real-time" distribution of framework geographic information will be the norm in the near future. Although connectivity constraints and the lack of standardized application-ready delivery formats have limited direct network distribution in the past, it is rapidly becoming both possible and desirable for large data vendors to deliver this data or information derived from it on an as-needed basis. MSP 2.0 provides a complete service-based model for a framework data distribution channel.

MSP 2.0 Basics

The MAGIC Services Protocol Version 2.0 (MSP 2.0) consists of eight service categories. Each service has one or more functions. Each function has two parameters. Each is an XML document described in an officially recognized schema written in XML Schema Language and available for reference on the http://www.MAGICServicesForum.org/Registry/ site. The first parameter is a request document and the second is a response document.

In addition to an internal set of base schemas accepted by the MAGIC Services Initiative, there are additional external schemas developed by other groups active in LBMS delivery and the positioning of mobile devices. Each service provider must support the MSP 2.0 base schemas. Optionally each service provider may support some, none, or all external schemas, and also may support private schemas.

Each service is described by a WSDL file located in the MSP 2.0 Registry at http://www.MAGICServicesForum.org/Registry/Interfaces/.

Session Service

The Session service enables an application to make contact with a potential service provider or to disconnect from a service provider.

The Session service has two functions:

Function	Description	Parameter Schema Location
Connect	The Connect function enables a client (usually the network node where the application resides) to make an initial connection to a service provider, establishing identity and authority to consume specific services. Many aspects of the client-server interaction may be negotiated.	http://www.MAGICServicesForum.org/ Registry/Schemas/Connect_Request_t/B ase.xsd/
	The response of the server is returned. On a successful request, a SessionID_t identifier is returned as an attribute to be used to authenticate requests during the remainder of a client session.	http://www.MAGICServicesForum.org/ Registry/Schemas/Connect_Response_t/ Base.xsd/
Disconnect	The Disconnect function enables a client to end a session gracefully.	http://www.MAGICServicesForum.org/ Registry/Schemas/Disconnect_Request_t /Base.xsd/
	The service provider response may provide accounting or other session summary information in response.	http://www.MAGICServicesForum.org/ Registry/Schemas/Disconnect_Request_t /Base.xsd/

Context Service

The MAGIC Services client (and possibly the server) holds information that characterizes the session, activity, application, locale, and modeling capabilities of the service provider, rendering requirements of the device, traveler, vehicle, and other characteristics that influence the services to be delivered. This information can be examined or modified by the client via the Context interface. The Context interface may also be used to discover the schema used by a service provider.

The Context service has a single function:

Function	Description	Parameter Schema Location
Context	Schema defines either information that should be stored by, or retrieved from, the server regarding one or more of the context information categories (activity, application, rendering capabilities, positioning method, etc). This information changes slowly (usually constant for one entire use of an application) but within a session. There may be an option for the server to store the context permanently.	http://www.MAGICServicesForum.org/ Registry/Schemas/Context_Request_t/B ase.xsd/
	Response schema defines the form of the returned response with the requested information.	http://www.MAGICServicesForum.org/ Registry/Schemas/Context_Response_t/ Base.xsd/

Semantics Service

The Semantics interface is used to transform the language, script, encoding, or classification of a name expression, to convert unstructured address expressions into a computationally useful form (parse), or to generate a natural address expression from a structured computational form (generate).

The Semantics service has three functions:

Function	Description	Parameter Schema Location
Parse	Schema requests conversion of unstructured text describing addresses or other location information that is defined relative to elements modeling geographical entities such as roads, buildings, or other points of interest.	http://www.MAGICServicesForum.org/ Registry/Schemas/Parse_Request_t/Base .xsd/
	Schema defines the form of the returned response with the requested information.	http://www.MAGICServicesForum.org/ Registry/Schemas/Parse_Response_t/Ba se.xsd/

(continued)

Function	Description	Parameter Schema Location *(continued)*
Generate	Schema requests conversion of structured Location based on addresses or other location information that is defined relative to elements modeling geographical entities such as roads, buildings, or other points of interest.	http://www.MAGICServicesForum.org/ Registry/Schemas/Generate_Request_t/ Base.xsd/
	Schema defines the form of the returned response with the requested information.	http://www.MAGICServicesForum.org/ Registry/Schemas/Generate_Response_t /Base.xsd/
Transform	Schema requests the conversion from one human language, script, encoding, or classification of a name expression to another corresponding language, script, encoding or category.	http://www.MAGICServicesForum.org/ Registry/Schemas/Transform_Request_t /Base.xsd/
	Schema defines the form of the returned response with the requested information	http://www.MAGICServicesForum.org/ Registry/Schemas/Transform_Response _t/Base.xsd/

Query Service

The query interface supports queries across space, time, and the four modeling realms: linguistic, entity, functional, and physical. The process is broken into two parts: Select – validate a Query Request and return a token (Query Plan) for use by Retrieve – request delivery of selected elements by element index.

The query specification may be in a specialized language specifically designed for MAGIC Services or a standard language (or subset) such as Structured Query Language (SQL). It is assumed that the results returned for each language are the same: a mathematical set.

Automobiles move at up to about 60 m/sec on road surfaces. There is no possibility to provide network-based real-time guidance in in-car navigation with the network communications and positioning capabilities available now or in the near future. In-car systems often employ a positioning subsystem (with navigation sensors such as GPS, rate gyros, accelerometers, speed sensors, and connections to an on-vehicle bus), which requires high-speed access to the road data used for navigation. This access is used to improve the agreement between the data modeling the road and the path of the vehicle as observed by the positioning sensors. This requirement is supported by a specific kind of Selection that returns a simple Node (ID, Position) Link (ID, start end, end end, Node IDs, shape points, road class, and form of way). This query, or any other query service, can have the condition that the data is available on the device (in cache or local storage) to prevent unwanted network data transfers.

The Query service has two functions:

Function	Description	Parameter Schema Location
Select	The request schema defines a collection of data items that could be retrieved. The definition of what should be retrieved and filters to restrict the selection to certain kinds of items is contained within the structure of the schema. These items include road network datasets, geocoding (selection of geometry by location), and reverse geocoding (selection of a location by geometry). Note that Context may filter the items returned (e.g. a boating application may not find road information relevant and therefore will filter out road information).	http://www.MAGICServicesForum.org/ Registry/Schemas/Select_Request_t/Bas e.xsd/
	The response schema includes an identifier (a Query Plan) that the server can recognize later in providing Retrieve responses. Different servers may have different capabilities and some may return a fault on a Select request that is too difficult.	http://www.MAGICServicesForum.org/ Registry/Schemas/Select_Response_t/B ase.xsd/
Retrieve	Schema defines either properties (count, data size, etc) of the collection of items that correspond to a Query Plan or the collection of items itself. Items may be retrieved as complete data structures or as identifiers that can be used to retrieve complete data structures in a later query. The schema provides a way for portions of the data to be retrieved with control over the size (and order) of the results. Required orders are sorted according to a collating sequence, proximity, matching significance, sequence of characters (e.g., send 10 names at a time with 1st character "E" and second "I").	http://www.MAGICServicesForum.org/ Registry/Schemas/Retrieve_Request_t/B ase.xsd/
	Schema defines the form of the returned requested information. Since it is possible to Select very large data sets, the response may provide information on the amount of data already retrieved, the amount in the current retrieval, and the amount remaining to be retrieved.	http://www.MAGICServicesForum.org/ Registry/Schemas/Retrieve_Response_t/ Base.xsd/

Mobility Service

The Mobility service has three functions. The Plan function validates a specification for travel (Travel Request) and returns a token (Travel Plan) for use in other functions. The Review function requests information on characteristics of the travel represented by a Travel Plan such as route geometry, fuel consumption, directions, or travel time. The Guide function provides information and instructions to guide the maneuver to a destination.

The following table shows the function, description, and parameter schema location.

Function	Description	Parameter Schema Location
Plan	The request schema defines the requirements of travel. This includes initial direction of travel, starting, intermediate, and destination points as well as mode of transport, cost and time restrictions, and specific requests such as to use a particular road. Different servers may have different capabilities and some may return a fault on a Select request that is too difficult.	http://www.MAGICServicesForum.org/ Registry/Schemas/Travel_Plan_Request _t/Base.xsd/
	The response schema includes an identifier (Travel Plan) that can later be recognized by the server in Review and Guide requests.	http://www.MAGICServicesForum.org/ Registry/Schemas/Travel_Plan_Respons e_t/Base.xsd/
Review	The request schema defines a request for the characteristics of travel corresponding to a Travel. These characteristics include travel time, fuel use, sensitivity of travel to delays, and static travel directions.	http://www.MAGICServicesForum.org/ Registry/Schemas/Review_Request_t/B ase.xsd/
	Schema defines the form of the returned requested information.	http://www.MAGICServicesForum.org/ Registry/Schemas/Review_Response_t/ Base.xsd/
Guide	The request schema defines a request for either synchronous (one response per request) or asynchronous (responses as needed sent without an additional request) delivery of maneuver information (commands, geometry, or landmark information) in the form of a schedule giving the predicted time and position where the information should be presented via the UI.	http://www.MAGICServicesForum.org/ Registry/Schemas/Guide_Request_t/Bas e.xsd/
	The response schema defines the form of the maneuver schedule.	http://www.MAGICServicesForum.org/ Registry/Schemas/Guide_Response_t/B ase.xsd/

Positioning Service

The Positioning interface Position function allows the client device to obtain the location, velocity or track of the device. This may be implemented on the device or via a network service provider. The Location function allows the use of addresses and other location information that is defined relative to geographical entities such as roads or buildings.

The Positioning service has two functions:

Function	Description	Parameter Schema Location
Position	The request schema defines requests for geographic position, velocity or track of the device. This may be implemented on the device or via a network service provider.	http://www.MAGICServicesForum.org/ Registry/Schemas/Position_Request_t/B ase.xsd/
	The response schema defines the form of the returned requested information.	http://www.MAGICServicesForum.org/ Registry/Schemas/Position_Response_t/ Base.xsd/
Location	The request schema defines the structure of location information that is defined relative to elements modeling geographical entities such as roads, buildings, or other points of interest.	http://www.MAGICServicesForum.org/ Registry/Schemas/Location_Request_t/ Base.xsd/
	The response schema defines the form of the returned requested information.	http://www.MAGICServicesForum.org/ Registry/Schemas/Location_Response_t /Base.xsd/

Rendering Service

The rendering interface allows the client to Plan – validate a Rendering Request and receive a token (Rendering Plan) for use in other methods. Render – obtain a graphic rendering corresponding to a Rendering Plan, and Interact – obtain interpretations of gestures made at the user interface (such as pointing at a specific pixel in a rendered bitmap).

The Rendering service has three functions:

Function	Description	Parameter Schema Location
Plan	The request schema defines the requirements of rendering. This includes what is to be rendered, how it should be rendered, and in what form the results should be delivered.	http://www.MAGICServicesForum.org/Registry/Schemas/Render_Plan_Request_t/Base.xsd/
	The response schema includes an identifier (Rendering Plan) that the server can later recognize in Render or Interact requests.	http://www.MAGICServicesForum.org/Registry/Schemas/Render_Plan_Response_t/Base.xsd/
Render	The request schema provides a structure including a Rendering Plan and any other parameters necessary to make a specific rendering according to the requirements of the Rendering Plan.	http://www.MAGICServicesForum.org/Registry/Schemas/Render_Request_t/Base.xsd/
	The response schema defines the form or the returned requested information.	http://www.MAGICServicesForum.org/Registry/Schemas/Render_Response_t/Base.xsd/
Interact	The request schema defines structure for point, line drawing, area drawing and other user interface interactions with a rendering. The structure includes the Rendering Plan and implicitly refers to the most recent rendering made according to that plan.	http://www.MAGICServicesForum.org/Registry/Schemas/Interact_Request_t/Base.xsd/
	The response schema defines the form of the returned requested information.	http://www.MAGICServicesForum.org/Registry/Schemas/Interact_Response_t/Base.xsd/

Update Service

The Update interface allows the client to report information back to the underlying service provider. This may most commonly be the current location or track of the mobile terminal, but in principle it could encompass a wide range of information. Four types of updates are **Delete** – an indication that those elements corresponding to a Query Plan should be deleted, **Insert** – a set of new elements that should not duplicate existing information, **Modify** (geometry or attributes) – a set of changes to apply to each element retrieved by a Query Plan, and **Assert** – an expression of a belief in the truth of some expression describing the world (as when guided to a non-existed hotel). These are indicated within the request and response schemas. There is a possibility of private or public updates. The governing principle is trust.

The Update service has a single function:

Function	Description	Parameter Schema Location
Update	The request schema defines a structure for describing the nature of the update (delete, insert new, modify, assert) as well as the content.	http://www.MAGICServicesForum.org/ Registry/Schemas/Update_Request_t/Ba se.xsd/
	The response schema defines an acknowledgement of the update and may contain a request for a further update of a specific nature.	http://www.MAGICServicesForum.org/ Registry/Schemas/Update_Response_t/ Base.xsd/

The Registry

Service providers deliver MAGIC Services via MSP 2.0 interactions with their servers. Each service provider may register offered servers and their supported Service Modes via a registration and service discovery facility. The offered services may be defined by a corresponding WSDL document available via the registration and service discovery mechanism. The guiding principle is that all structural information (message syntax) is defined in XML (WSDL or XML Schema Language). This information is accessible online to clients and other agents seeking information about MAGIC Services.

Compression/Decompression (CODEC) schemes as well as the capabilities of protocol conversion bridges (SMTP->HTTP, for example) are also registered. This allows a client to establish communications via an efficient compressed channel if the chosen server agrees to operate in that mode. MAGIC Services do not prescribe any specific CODEC or bridge details, but they do require that CODECs and bridges offered for use be registered in a consistent way so that connection and Service Mode negotiations can be completely automated.

The Registry can be found at http://www.MAGICServicesForum.org/Registry/ and at other locations published from time to time by MAGIC Services Forum. Beneath the Registry root, the directory structure is as shown in the accompanying diagram. Each leaf folder contains at least one XML Schema language file named Base.xsd with the base schema for the parameter of the same name as the folder. The leaf folder may contain additional registered XML schemas with names ending in .xsd. Documentation for each non-base schema is contained in a file with the same name as the corresponding schema file but with the extension .xml. For example, a schema defined by the file MySchema.xsd would be documented in a file MySchema.html. In addition, a sample XML document conforming to the schema may exist under the corresponding name with extension .xml. In the example above, this would be MySchema.xml.

Schema Evolution and Versioning

A client may have different interactions with the server depending on the version of the specification supported by the server. Client-server negotiation of the service definition is part of the connection sequence. In Version 1.0, we assumed a simple refusal on the part of the server whenever the client proposes a service model that the server does not wish to provide. In version 2.0, the interface structure is fixed, but the type of request-response parameters is defined by XML schemas and new schemas may be added to the MAGIC Services Registry.

The API

MAGIC Services are delivered to an endpoint in a client or peer device. The functionality is accessed through a client component–the MAGIC Services Client. The client may expose a standard programming language interface (API) in one or more programming languages. These programming language bindings are each derived from a UML specification of the interfaces.

The defining form of the UML specification of the interfaces is the UML model stored in the Interfaces folder in the Registry at http://www.magicservicesforum.org/Registry/Interfaces/MSP20.mdl/

The individual functions correspond to the sixteen definitions given above. For examples in specific programming languages, see the Session example below or refer to the complete MSP 2.0 specification.

Simple Methods + (Complex) XML Parameters

Version 1.0 of the MAGIC Services Specification had fixed API methods defined by C++ header files. This approach has a number of disadvantages, including inflexibility and complexity. Early design decisions had to be taken without the benefit of implementation and operation experience. Changing a method definition (function signature) is a significant task. Validating an XML document against a standard set of XML schemas in a registry is not.

As a result, the design for Version 2.0 has moved significantly in the direction of streamlined and generic methods, organized along functional lines, with highly structured parameters. This allows interfaces to remain fixed, while the structure of the information flowing across these interfaces evolves according to experience and the changing needs of the mobile information services market.

Caching Transparency

An implementer of the MAGIC Services API has complete freedom to use or not use the MAGIC Services Protocol to remote some or all of the computations. With a very thin client and adequate connectivity, a client may remote all computations. A thicker client with uncertain connectivity may adopt a "sync-and-go" strategy where results and other information are cached on the client.

Schema Delegation

Most of the parameters for most of the methods are defined as XML documents. XML Schemas defining the structure of these documents are published in a central Registry. The separation between the rather rigid structure of the method parameters and the ease of extensibility and evolution made possible though registered schema publication allows the MAGIC Services API interfaces to remain fixed from a programming language perspective, while evolving rapidly to meet market and technical requirements. The separation of the slowly varying part of the specification (programming language methods and parameter types) from the rapidly evolving part (defined by registered XML schemas) is called "Schema Delegation."

Session Service Example

The Session Service is the most important MSP2.0 service. It serves as a good example to illustrate how each of the services enables an application developer to submit a request and receive a response through the MSP2.0 API.

Session Service

The Session Service allows an application to make contact with a potential service provider. The interface has two methods: Connect and Disconnect. Connect allows a client (usually in a mobile device) to make an initial connection to a service provider, establishing identity and authority to consume specific services. Many aspects of the client-server interaction may be negotiated via the Connect_Request_t type message structure. The response of the server is returned as a Connect_Response_t structure. On a successful request, a SessionID_t identifier is returned as an attribute to be used later as a shortcut to identify a client session.

The request schema allows for specification of a number of service parameters, including:

Contract Name - the name of the company, person, or other entity contracting for services.

Authority - the specific contractual details authorizing use of services under specific conditions.

Authentication - the information allowing the server to establish the identity of the requester. A password or X.509 certificate are examples.

Respond-to IP Address - when delivering to a MSP this is a list of IP addresses that may make requests.

User ID - when delivering through an MSP this is a unique identifier for the end user that has a private association with the mobile terminal or its owner.

Timeout - the requested length of a session in minutes. The server may respond with a smaller value.

QoS (Quality of Service) - an integer between 0 and 5 indicating the maximum MAGIC Services level of service requested. This may be changed to another value by the server. The level of service is roughly connected with the level of detail available in the services. Level 0 implies global services with most populated places, major roads, and other geographic features larger than a few hundred meters.

Priority - an integer between 0 and 7 indicating the maximum MAGIC Services priority of service requested. The lowest value is 0 and the highest value (most important) is 7. This may be changed to another value by the server. The server will attempt to order priority according to the priority value but this is not guaranteed.

Compression Method - a sequence of keys indicating requested compression methods in order of decreasing preference. Compression happens ahead of encryption.

Encryption Method - a sequence of keys indicating requested encryption methods in order of decreasing preference.

Private - information exchanged with service provider as a string in a format subject only to agreement between client and server.

Server Capabilities - this describes requested capabilities. If the list is empty then the response gives the full capabilities of the service provider. If this element is not present then the response also has no Server Capabilities element. The capabilities are described by giving the name of a service and function with the URI for each of the schemas accepted by the functions. For example:

```
Session.Connect(http://www.magicservicesforum.org/Registry/Schemas/Connect_Request_t/Base.
xsd/ , http://www.magicservicesforum.org/Registry/Schemas/Connect_Response_t/Base.xsd/)
```

indicates that the service provider supports the standard session connect functionality.

The application developer would create the XML request document and call a function of the form:

```
Result_Code_t
Connect (Connect_Request_t Request, Connect_Response_t Response)
```

where the Connect_Request_t and Connect_Response_t types are some kind of string or memory reference in most computing environments. The structure of these types is defined by the corresponding XML schemas.

The function call delivers the request to the service provider. If it is a synchronous function, the client blocks until the response document has been returned and unpacked by the proxy code. Asynchronous requests return immediately.

The result of computation returns in the response document, which follows the same general form as the request schema. All schemas can be found in the MAGIC Services Registry at http://www.MAGICServicesForum.org/Registry.

In the .NET proxy code generated by Visual Studio .NET, the connection would be through a pre-established web reference or a dynamic connection mechanism based on discovery of service providers through UDDI and examination of published WSDL files. The services for all MSP 2.0 providers are identical, using the document-style SOAP binding.

Space Publishing

As the size of an area becomes smaller and more detailed, several forces work together to discourage large providers from developing and maintaining navigable models (databases) that describe an area and the possibilities for mobility within the area. First, the work required to survey and validate a high-resolution model is very high. At the same time, the market is likely to be much smaller than for a global or national model. Finally, smaller features tend to change more often than large features so that the maintenance effort increases as the resolution of a model becomes more detailed, because it goes out of date more quickly than a large area. As a consequence, the party that is most financially motivated to maintain and offer a detailed model of a small space is the owner or administrator of the space. MSP 2.0 enables providers to publish information about a room, a building, a parking garage, or a city core in a way that allows interested travelers a standard access method for travel planning and guidance.

A space publishing server (SPS) combines all of the NSP functionality into a single low-cost server.

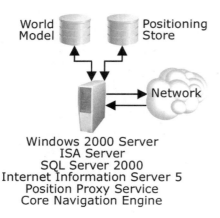

Space publishing

Scenarios

A typical space publishing scenario is to bring a model of parking facilities under control of a single owner or authority into the Internet. This allows applications to plan and guide travelers at the ends of their car trips from and to parking places. This planning and guidance normally happens as part of an application that makes use of a large-scale NSP to navigate public roads. The NSP usually connects to the SPS rather than the end user application. This allows the NSP, for example, to determine whether any parking space is available before routing a car to a specific parking location.

The guidance to parking scenario is explored in more detail in the Delivery to the Automobile section.

Design

The design is based on the aggregated NSP architecture where all components are put on a single server running Windows 2000 Server. ISA Server is used to provide firewall services and in conjunction with RRAS to control access. A SPS may have access restricted to certain NSPs or MSPs. This is usually a turnkey system provided by a systems integrator.

Delivery to the Automobile

Automotive applications are characterized by good positioning, large amounts of on-board storage and computing power, high-speeds that impose real-time constraints on service delivery, and serious product liability exposure. There are approximately ten million in-car navigation systems installed world-wide in 2002, perhaps 75% in Japan, 20% in Europe, and the remainder in North America and Australia. Perhaps two million additional location-aware emergency service units are installed world-wide. The section outlines the deployment of a "sync-and-go" model that works well in the automotive environment.

Scenarios

The typical scenario is turn-by-turn navigation from origin to destination. A slightly more complex application happens when the destination that the person wishes to visit includes the need to park the car and then complete travel on foot to a precise location within a nearby building. In many cases this final transition may be the most difficult and stressful part of a trip so the consumer perceives great value in complete guidance to the final destination.

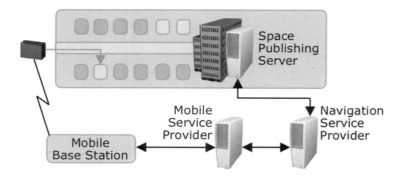

Guidance to parking

One of the problems with parking is that a given structure may not always be available. There may be time limits on operation of high demand may use up all of the parking spaces. A space publishing server can be invaluable in travel planning since it can predict availability and even estimate waiting time for a space to open up if the facility is full when the car arrives.

Design

The full-function NSP contains a list of SPS representing parking facilities. The NSP make operate its own SPS to fill in information for parking that is not directly represented by a SPS. The SPS and NSP agree on access terms and billing arrangements. Normally the SPS is offered at no cost to the consuming NSP.

The NSP core navigation extends its planning functions by requesting sub-plans from the SPS, which are then incorporated into the search for the travel solution offered to the end-user application. The end user application is not aware of the existence of the SPS in this approach. This allows all planning functionality to be handled by the NSP and the client application to be as small and simple as possible.

Delivery to the Mobile Phone

Here we consider very thin clients, such as today's mobile telephone handsets. Data capable mobile phones already number in the hundreds of millions and will reach a billion in the next few years. Because of emergency service requirements in the US and Western Europe, most of these phones will be position aware by 2004. This large population of connected and location-aware devices is a very attractive target but the delivery of location-based services is not an easy task.

Scenarios

The emergency call is a standard scenario used to illustrate the delivery of high-value location based services to a mobile phone user. Suppose a person with a mobile phone is injured when their car slides off an icy road into a ditch at night. This scenario reflects the essence of systems that are standard equipment on millions of new cars in North America.

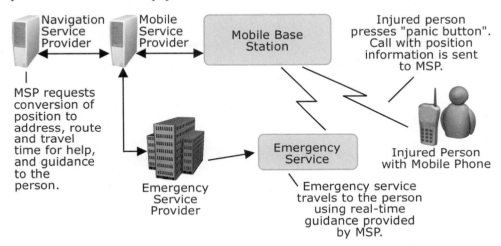

Panic button

The injured person presses a "panic button". This sends a special message to a special kind of MSP: an Emergency Service Provider. (In many places this is the Public Service Answering, or Access Point or PSAP.) The Emergency Service Provider uses an NSP to locate the injured person and direct help toward that location.

A second common scenario is when a mobile person wants to rendezvous with one or more "buddies" who may also be mobile at the same time. The task is to first determine network and geographic presence–determine which of the buddies are nearby and connected – and then guide them to a single location.

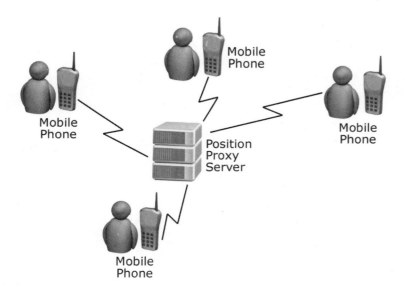

Buddy finding

Finally, mobile people with mobile phones are a huge resource for improving the navigable models maintained by the NSPs. In many cases the NSP can ask a simple application on the mobile phone to provide simple updates to attributes of real-world entities such as streets and buildings.

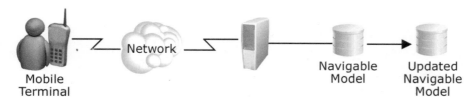

Updating the navigable world model

Design

Delivery to mobile phones requires the greatest offloading of computation and storage onto the NSP. Since the market potential is huge, the corresponding investment is easily justified. The completely disaggregated design is the best choice. A position proxy service may be shared by several wireless operators.

Delivery to MSP

In many cases the NSP has absolutely no connection with the mobile consumer of the navigation services. A MSP offers end user applications that communicate with the mobile terminal in a proprietary fashion. The MSP must have access to either a world model (geographic data content) or a service provider delivering navigation services computed on a world model. A standardized, high capacity delivery pipeline allows the MSP to outsource both the data and the navigation engine (or at least drive the responsibility back to the data supplier).

Scenarios

There is really only one scenario: the NSP provides a full range of MSP 2.0 services at whatever QoS levels are commercially feasible. QoS must vary widely with geographic market, since high quality geographic data is very expensive and only available in a few areas. Data capable of supporting in-car navigation is available in Western Europe, North America, and Japan. Only in Japan does it seem to have reached a state where data providers actually earn significant profits. The key factors in developing a sustainable business globally are the rationalization of the data supplier business and the expansion of the end-user market to data capable mobile phones.

Delivering to a mobile service provider

The wireless operators are passing through a painful transition phase where the new spectrum, technology, and infrastructure needed to broaden the end-user market are themselves very expensive in comparison with the end user revenues then generate. Most operators agree that there is no choice but to move forward; however, the pace may be slower than pure technical factors would dictate.

The ability of a NSP to easily scale services delivered through a simple mechanism such as .NET and MSP 2.0 is a strong recommendation for the use of a compatible set of operating systems, enterprise server components, and Internet standard service delivery architectures.

Design

If the user base is small, use a space publishing server. If the application is access to location information for a community of mobile devices, use a position proxy server. Otherwise use a fully disaggregated NSP architecture with the number of servers scaled to meet expected load. There is no easy way to get realistic server capacities except to build prototype systems in a lab.

Position Proxy Service

The position proxy server (PPS) is a specialized system that focuses on the MSP 2.0 Positioning service.

Scenarios

A PPS delivers its services to applications running on a group of related mobile terminals. Privacy, security, and the regularization of a mixture of location technologies are all important aspects of PPS operation. The primary scenario is to provide standardized access to location information for the group.

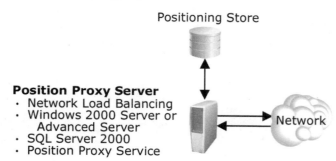

Position Proxy Server

PPS functionality to meet this limited requirement can be provided without a specialized navigation engine. Regulatory and legal requirements may impose greater responsibility for authorizing access, authenticating users, protecting information, archiving and retrieval in the case of criminal or other investigations.

Design

A large load requires all of the components of a fully disaggregated NSP, with the possible exception of a core navigation engine. An upload server is not likely to be necessary but additional storage capacity and offline storage capabilities required to meet security and regulatory requirements.

Summary

Five different delivery models cover most of the location-based services delivery infrastructure needs as we understand them in these early days of the wireless Internet. The delineation of a few standard models based on scalable computing platforms and universally accepted Internet standards such as HTTP, SMTP, TCP/IP, SOAP, and XML provide a reasonably clear starting point for the development of navigation service delivery systems for the location-based services that are anticipated by many in the wireless carrier and mobile applications community.

Additional Information

For more information on MSP 2.0, including protocol and API specifications as well as sample client code, please visit the MAGIC Services Forum at http://www.magicservicesforum.org/.

The Future

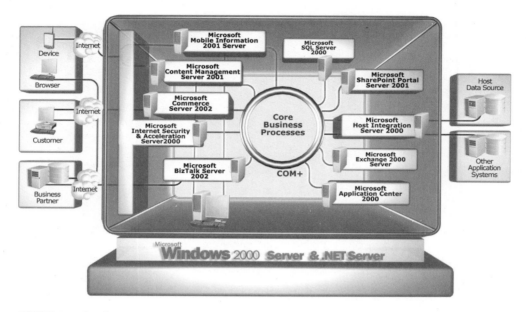

.NET Enterprise Servers

By James Wilson and William Harding

A Vision for the Future

This book would not be complete without a high level overview of how the .NET E-Business Servers are evolving into a powerful set of tools and technologies. The future vision for Microsoft's .NET E-Business Servers is "better together." This strategy addresses a broad set of processes and services necessary to establish a trading network, business portal, customer relationship management and profiling, product management, content management, and integration with existing line of business applications. In this chapter we provide a quick review of .NET E-Business Servers along with solutions available today, and an overview of e-business processes and services that Microsoft's vision for the future will address.

.NET E-Business Servers Today

The preceding chapters show the applications you can build today using Microsoft's e-business server products. The current suite of e-business servers addresses both intra and inter enterprise deployment scenarios. The figure below shows a conceptual overview of the current e-business servers and how they fit into the framework of solutions and portal services available in the e-business suite today. Chapter 3, "Overview of .NET Enterprise Servers," provides a broad overview of each server. Here, we provide a brief recap of the highlights to show how these servers are evolving into the vision for tomorrow.

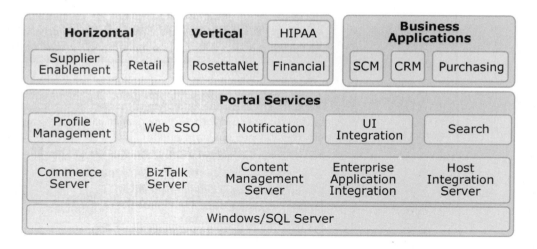

.NET E-Business servers today

E-Business Servers Today

The current suite of e-business Servers offers enterprise customers a broad array of products and features on which to build solutions. Commerce Server enables you to build a retail Web site, comprising a broad set of features to address profiling systems, targeting systems, catalog systems, order processing systems, business analytics, business desk and solution sites. BizTalk Server enables you to conduct electronic business transactions with your partners over the Internet. Major features include business process orchestration, message routing, trading relationship management, and a tracking system. Content Management Server provides business users with an easy way to manage their Web site content, using a content repository, integration with Microsoft Office, revision tracking, workflow publishing, and content syndication and aggregation. Enterprise Application Integration and Host Integration Server provide adapters to integrate BizTalk Server with legacy applications, along with a suite of tools for host system integration and protocol support.

Solutions

Solutions can take many forms. Solutions focus on specific business scenarios, providing a clear, targeted value proposition. Whitepapers target specific scenarios, describing solutions to performance problems, configuration and so forth. Microsoft partner-led offerings represent another type of solution. Accelerator products give customers a jump-start to help get e-business applications up and running quickly. Out-of-the-box solutions bundle products, technologies and consulting services to provide turnkey operations for enterprise customers.

The framework of portal services and e-business servers provides the foundation on which to build out-of-box solutions for horizontal and vertical markets. All of these solutions allow enterprise customers to solve business problems, lower costs, and achieve faster time to market. Currently, Microsoft has several solutions and accelerators shipping or under development.

HIPAA - Health Care Accelerator

Microsoft® BizTalk™ Accelerator for HIPAA streamlines the development and deployment of integration solutions for data exchange that is consistent with the standard regulations of the Health Insurance Portability and Accountability Act of 1996 (HIPAA). HIPAA was enacted primarily to improve the portability and continuity of individual and group health insurance coverage in the United States. HIPAA mandates that health care organizations comply with HIPAA guidelines when they transmit information electronically. The goal of HIPAA is to reduce health care costs without impacting. After HIPAA is instituted (currently slated for October 16, 2003), there will be one content set and one format that all must accept.

BizTalk Accelerator for HIPAA enables organizations in the health care industry to exchange, monitor, and control HIPAA-specific transactions. Built as an add-on to Microsoft BizTalk Server 2002, BizTalk Accelerator for HIPAA provides the necessary document specifications and components that enable customers to develop BizTalk Server 2002-based solutions that are HIPAA-specific. BizTalk Accelerator for HIPAA includes all the document specifications and components that you need to rapidly develop and deploy applications for processing the full range of HIPAA-specific transactions using Microsoft BizTalk Server 2002. All HIPAA transaction set schemas represented as annotated XML-Data Reduced (XDR) document specifications in BizTalk Server.

BizTalk Accelerator for HIPAA also takes advantage of the BizTalk Server 2002 platform for converting other document formats into Extensible Markup Language (XML), data mapping and transformation, application integration, and electronic data interchange (EDI). In addition to handling data transfer and application integration, BizTalk Server 2002 includes a suite of tools, which provide several interfaces for creating and transforming XML files and for control of business processes. BizTalk Server 2002 is a member of the Microsoft® .NET Enterprise Servers family of products.

This accelerator helps the health care insurance industry build standards-based technology solutions and reduce the amount of time and money that organizations need to spend to comply with HIPAA regulations. Health care and allied organizations affected by HIPAA can use the integration capabilities of BizTalk Server 2002 to automate business processes and quickly build integration solutions. This helps them to comply with federal law while leveraging existing IT investments. The interoperability of BizTalk Server 2002 with health care and allied organizations' legacy systems, combined with the BizTalk HIPAA schemas, provides the industry with the tools to meet the HIPAA mandate.

RosettaNet

Microsoft® BizTalk™ Accelerator for RosettaNet streamlines the development and deployment of RosettaNet standards-based supply chain integration solutions. BizTalk Accelerator for RosettaNet supports the RosettaNet Implementation Framework (RNIF) version 1.1, which is an open network application framework that enables RosettaNet Partners to collaboratively execute RosettaNet Partner Interface Processes (PIPs). Using the PIP patterns included with Accelerator for RosettaNet, users can develop any existing PIP.

BizTalk™ Accelerator for RosettaNet includes several applications that enable you to develop, administer, and test RosettaNet standards-compliant PIP implementation XLANG schedules. There are two additional applications for schema management and messaging configuration. This solution provides the application adapters and server platform necessary to build RosettaNet-based solutions that will integrate applications, connect trading partners in supply chains, and enable the orchestration of complex, collaborative business processes.

Built as an add-on to Microsoft BizTalk™ Server 2002, Accelerator for RosettaNet provides the necessary applications to rapidly develop BizTalk Server 2002-based solutions that are compliant with the RosettaNet Framework. These solutions enable users to automate their e-business processes, such as order management and inventory management. Accelerator for RosettaNet also uses BizTalk Server 2002 to take advantage of its platform for managing Extensible Markup Language (XML), electronic data interchange (EDI), and flat-file data processing among businesses.

In addition to a server element for handling data transfers, BizTalk Server 2002 includes a suite of tools, which provide several interfaces for creating and transforming XML files and for collaborative creation of business processes. The applications contained in BizTalk Accelerator for RosettaNet, combined with BizTalk Server 2002, enable users to streamline supply chain practices and to collaborate with trading partners and suppliers using the RosettaNet standard. BizTalk Server 2002 is a member of the Microsoft® .NET Enterprise Servers family of products.

By using Microsoft BizTalk Server 2002 and BizTalk Accelerator for RosettaNet, businesses of all sizes can integrate diverse information systems and orchestrate the flow of information within their companies and with trading partners. RosettaNet and BizTalk Accelerator for RosettaNet are complementary efforts. RosettaNet is focused on standardizing supply chain processes and BizTalk Server enables you to build RosettaNet-compliant processes.

Accelerator for Suppliers (AFS)

Microsoft BizTalk Accelerator for Suppliers (AFS) integrates Microsoft Commerce Server 2000, BizTalk Server 2000, and SQL Server 2000 to enable suppliers to trade interactively through multiple electronic sales channels (such as procurement applications, marketplaces, and directly over the Web). These interactions include the exchange of electronic product catalogs and purchase orders between trading partners. It also enables functionality (known as remote shopping) that empowers the supplier and enhances the online shopping experience by allowing a buyer to directly access a supplier Web site while making purchases through a trading partner e-procurement application or a marketplace buyer application.

Microsoft Solution for Internet Business (MSIB)

MSIB enables organizations to quickly build a dynamic, personalized Internet presence that manages relationships with customers and partners more effectively, provides rich retail capabilities, and allows them to compete more effectively in the global Internet economy.

Enterprise E-Business Processes and Services

The figure below shows an overview of the various functions and relationships required to conduct e-business transactions in a fast paced environment. The agile enterprise must be able to perform content, product and customer relationship management in a secure environment.

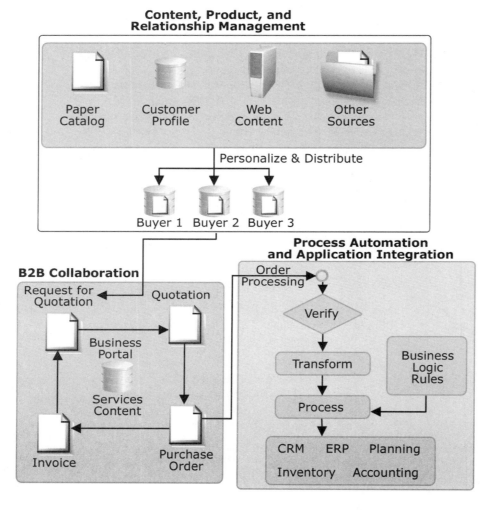

E-Business processes and services

The agile enterprise needs to collaborate with business partners to facilitate processing orders, invoices, and other business documents across traditional organizational boundaries. Process automation and application integration with legacy systems, where much of the corporate databases reside, represent critical functions as well.

Future Solutions and Accelerators

As described in the previous section, several solutions are available currently and more are under development. For example, at the time of this writing, BizOffice and Financial Services Accelerator are being developed and will soon be available.

BizOffice

BizOffice represents the integration of Microsoft Office XP and BizTalk Server 2002. This will enable Microsoft Office users to seamlessly and securely interact with their business partners directly from their Office applications, manage document flows as part of a wider business process workflow, and do both in a safe recoverable environment.

BizOffice brings considerable additional value to BizTalk Server by providing a B2B digital dashboard, which gives non-technical users access to all of the sophisticated capabilities of BizTalk Server; an Office (Excel, Word and (later) XDocs) client; and a wider range of customers for BizTalk services. BizOffice brings significant value to Office by providing B2B capability directly to the desktop (B2D); a platform for Internet, inter-enterprise Office solutions; and an automated workflow and document flow in a safe, recoverable environment.

From the perspective of the BizOffice customer, BizOffice appears as a Microsoft SharePoint Team Services (STS) application, which can be used as or can host end-user applications. Inside, BizOffice consists of a platform application, which uses STS, SQL Server and BizTalk Server together with one or more BizOffice Solutions, which implement specific scenarios. BizOffice solutions are end-user applications which use the BizOffice Platform to provide consistent document process and application management across all solutions; provide specific document maps appropriate to the application; and orchestrate STS to a specific application purpose.

Financial Services Accelerator

Microsoft BizTalk Financial Services Accelerator (FSA) provides customers, partners and System Integrators with a foundation of support for core financial services application infrastructure and business processes. Financial Services is segmented into 3 primary sectors: Securities, Banking and Insurance. Within each of these sectors, there exist protocols for business data interchange. Some protocols overlap. Additionally, there are defined business processes that cross sector boundaries and include the use of the various sector protocols. Some protocols overlap sectors as well in an attempt to ease the burden of implementing the business process.

The Financial Services Accelerator will ship on BizTalk Server 2002 and have identical requirements.

.NET E-Business Servers Tomorrow

Microsoft's vision for the future will empower enterprises to bring their business offerings and services to their customers through automation of business documents, integration of business partners, and integration of line of business and enterprise resource planning applications. In addition, the information you or your business need will be available wherever you are, using whatever computing device, platform, or application you have. This vision for the future will increase the agility of enterprises by improved interaction with customers and suppliers, faster response to changes in the business environment, increased profitability through improved relationship management with customers, partners, and employees.

Solving the problems associated with this vision is the key challenge for the next generation of computing and the Internet. At the heart of solving these problems is eXtensible Markup Language, or XML. Just as the Web revolutionized how users talk to applications, XML transforms how applications talk to each other.

With the help of XML-based technologies such as SOAP, a new type of software is being created that uses XML to provide Web-based services. Because XML Web services break down the distinctions between the Internet, standalone applications and computing devices of every kind, they enable businesses to collaborate to offer an unprecedented range of integrated and customized solutions. These solutions enable their customers to act on information any time, any place, and on any device.

As XML Web services gain momentum among developers as the next generation of Internet-based computing, providing a platform that makes it simpler to build these solutions and provide a reliable framework for integration and interoperability is vital. Such a platform must be based on open standards and combine all the power of personal computers, smart devices, legacy systems, and the richness of the Internet.

Microsoft's platform for building, deploying, operating and integrating XML Web services is .NET. As we have shown in this book, the .NET e-business servers are a vital part of Microsoft .NET, and can be used today to solve real business computing problems. In the future, many new features will be added to the current suite of e-business servers.

The e-business vision and Microsoft .NET will enable enterprises (small, medium and large) to bring products and services to market securely through the Internet, improving responsiveness and cost efficiency. Enterprises will be able to streamline operations by automating business processes within the enterprise and with external business partners. Enterprises will be able to provide one-stop access to information and services as well. Prepackaged solutions and accelerators will bring everything together to jump-start your e-business ventures.

With this anthology of e-business scenarios, we attempted to give enterprise customers a broad overview of these exciting new technologies with some details for implementing Microsoft's e-business products and services. Today, you can enable enterprise-scale e-business applications using current offerings. Tomorrow, the "better together" vision will augment Microsoft's powerful .NET platform, providing better, faster, more cost efficient ways to conduct business over the Internet. This is only the beginning.

Sample Applications

This appendix describes the various sample applications that are available on the companion CD-ROM disc. A short explanation of each application is provided. For complete information about each application, see the appropriate chapter where the specific application is discussed.

Sample Host-to-Web Applications

These sample applications simulate a fictitious bank (Cedar Bank). They demonstrate the major features of the .NET Framework and COMTI by retrieving customer account information using mainframe COBOL transactions by way of CICS or IMS. They also show you how to call a COMTI Automation server from Web-based or other COM-based client applications. These sample applications require a live connection to a mainframe host environment and Microsoft Host Integration Server 2000 to be installed. They use the COMTI typelib and COBOL programs installed with Host Integration Server 2000 and are located in the CedarBank tutorials folder. See Chapter 7, "Integrating Host Data to the Web," for complete information. The following folders on the CD contain all the files you need to run that sample application.

ASP.NET VB Host Program Access

This sample program is written in Visual Basic .NET. It is an early bind to the Remote Environment component object and demonstrates the use of single data values and recordsets. This program uses the COMTI typelib and COBOL program for CICS MSLINK in the CedarBank tutorials folder associated with the Host Integration Server 2000 program files. This sample application requires that IIS, ASP.NET and Host Integration Server 2000 be installed and running on the same computer.

VB.NET Early Bound Host Program Access

This client, written in Visual Basic .NET, is an early bind to the Remote Environment component object and demonstrates the use of single data values and recordsets. This means that the remote environment is selected and bound into the executable during compile time. Generally the early bind is more efficient than the late bind version. This program uses the COMTI typelib and COBOL program for CICS MSLINK in the CedarBank tutorials folder associated with the Host Integration Server 2000 program files. This sample application requires that IIS, VB.NET and Host Integration Server 2000 be installed and running on the same computer.

C# Early Bound Host Program Access

This client, written in C#, is an early bind to the Remote Environment component object and demonstrates the use of single data values and recordsets. This means that the remote environment is selected and bound into the executable during compile time. Generally the early bind is more efficient than the late bind version. This program uses the COMTI typelib and COBOL program for CICS MSLINK in the CedarBank tutorials folder associated with the Host Integration Server 2000 program files. This sample application requires that IIS, C#, and Host Integration Server 2000 be installed and running on the same computer.

VB.NET Host Program Access as Web Service

This sample program is written in Visual Basic .NET. It is an early bind to the Remote Environment component object and demonstrates the use of single data values and recordsets returned through a Web Service. This program uses the COMTI typelib and COBOL program for CICS MSLINK in the CedarBank tutorials folder associated with the Host Integration Server 2000 program files. This sample application requires that IIS, ASP.NET and Host Integration Server 2000 be installed and running on the same computer.

VB.NET Host Program Access Web Service Web Client

This sample program, written in Visual Basic .NET, demonstrates a Web client application accessing the Web service. This program requires that the VB.NET Host Program Access as Web Service be setup and running.

VB.NET Host Program Access Web Service Windows Forms Client

This sample program, written in Visual Basic .NET, demonstrates a Windows forms client application accessing the Web service. This program requires that the VB.NET Host Program Access as Web Service be setup and running.

SQL Server to DB2 Data Transfer–VB.NET

This sample program written in Visual Basic .NET, uses the SQL Server 2000 Data Transformation Services (DTS). This program creates the Northwind database on an IBM OS/390 DB2 system and copies the data from SQL Server 2000 to the DB2 database. This sample requires SQL Server 2000 SP2.

SQL Server to DB2 Data Transfer–Visual Basic 6.0

This sample program written in Visual Basic 6.0 SP 5, uses the SQL Server 2000 Data Transformation Services (DTS). This program creates the Northwind database on an IBM OS/390 DB2 system and copies the data from SQL Server 2000 to the DB2 database.

Customer Order Entry Application

This sample program is written in Visual Basic.NET and uses the ADO.NET provider for SQL Server 2000. This program demonstrates how to query the Northwind SQL Server demonstration database and enter a new order.

Customer Order Display Application

This sample program is written in Visual Basic .NET and uses the ADO.NET provider for SQL Server 2000. This program demonstrates loading the Customers and Orders tables from the Northwind SQL Server demonstration database and browse the records.

VB.NET OLE DB Query Processor

This sample program written in Visual Basic .NET can access an OLE DB provider and allow the user to run SQL queries against the provider database. In addition, you can save the results as an XML data file and create a matching XML schema (XSD) file.

Connection String Manager

This utility will automatically produce the database connection string, which can be copied and pasted into your program. For example, you can select the OLE DB provider for SQL Server from a drop down list, complete the property page displayed, and the result is the connection string code that can then be copied to your program.

Web Service File Transfer

This sample application can be used be exchange data between business partners securely, reliable, and with non-repudiation. It is similar to FTP but uses Web Services and HTTP and SOAP protocols. See Chapter 13, "Using Web Services to Transfer Files," for complete information.

Automating Electronic Procurement

This sample application shows how BizTalk Server can be used with XML Web services, and how managed code written in Visual Studio .NET can be used to access and extend BizTalk Server. The scenario used in this sample demonstrates how to automate the exchange of documents between trading partners in a business transaction. See Chapter 11, "Automating Electronic Procurement," for complete information.

Glossary

-A-

Active Directory

The directory service for Windows NT 4.0 and Windows 2000 Server. Active Directory stores information about objects on the network and makes this information available for authorized system administrators and users. It gives network users access to permitted resources anywhere on the network using a single logon process. It also provides system administrators with an intuitive hierarchical view of the network and a single point of administration for all network objects.

Active Directory Service Interfaces (ADSI)

A Component Object Model-based (COM-based) directory service model that allows ADSI-compliant client applications to access a wide variety of distinct directory protocols, including Windows Directory Services, Lightweight Directory Access Protocol (LDAP), and Novell Directory Services (NDS), while using a single, standard set of interfaces. ADSI shields the client application from the implementation and operational details of the underlying data store or protocol.

Active Server Pages (ASP)

A server-side scripting environment used to create dynamic Web pages or to build Web applications. ASP pages are files that contain HTML tags, text, and script commands. ASP pages can call Component Object Model (COM) components to perform tasks, such as connecting to a database or performing a business calculation. With ASP, you can add interactive content to Web pages or build entire Web applications that use HTML pages as the interface to your customers.

ActiveX Data Objects (ADO)

A high-level, language-independent set of object-based data access interfaces optimized for data application. ADO enables client applications to access and manipulate data from a database server through an OLE DB provider.

ActiveX Data Objects (Multidimensional) (ADO MD)

A high-level, language-independent set of object-based data access interfaces optimized for multidimensional data application. Visual Basic and other automation languages use ADO MD as the data access interface to multidimensional data storage. ADO MD is a part of ADO version 2.0 and later.

ANSI X12

EDI standards set by Accredited Standards Committee X12, whose work is approved by the American National Standards Institute.

application integration component (AIC)

A COM object that the BizTalk Server state engine calls to deliver data to an application. If a messaging port is configured in BizTalk Server 2002 to include the use of an AIC for application integration, this component is automatically instantiated and passed the requisite data. The component then determines how to handle communicating this data back to the application. This can be done using private API calls, invoking other COM objects, using database writes, and so on.

Application Programming Interface (API)

In the same way that most applications will have a user interface (often a graphical one), many applications will also present an Application Programming Interface (API) with which other applications can interact. The API consists of the functions, messages, data structures, data types, and statements that programmers can use in creating applications that run under Windows 2000.

ASCII

American Standard Code for Information Interchange.

asynchronous communication

An interaction between two or more processes in which one process communicates with another and can continue processing independently from the other process.

attribute

A characteristic of a record or field. An attribute can contain several properties.

auditing

Tracking the activities of users by recording selected types of events in the security log of a server or workstation.

authenticated access

A user access option that you can set at the Default Web Site or Application levels in IIS. As opposed to anonymous access, authenticated access requires a user to have a valid account and password to access the site. The three types of authenticated access are Basic authentication, Digest authentication, and Integrated Windows authentication.

authorization

A process that verifies that a user has the correct permissions to access a resource such as a Web page or database, or has the correct privileges to perform a task such as performing backups. Authorization is typically set up by a system administrator, or site developer, and checked and cleared by the computer. The user provides some type of identification, such as a code number or a password, which the computer verifies against its internal records.

-B-

BizTalk Accelerator for HIPAA

An add-on product to Microsoft BizTalk Server 2002 that allows organizations to quickly and easily build HIPAA solutions. BizTalk Accelerator for HIPAA includes several applications that enable health care providers, payers, and clearinghouses (acting on behalf of providers or payers) to exchange, monitor, and control HIPAA-specific transactions. BizTalk Accelerator for HIPAA provides the necessary document specifications, applications, and components to rapidly develop BizTalk Server 2002-based solutions that are HIPAA specific.

BizTalk Accelerator for RosettaNet

An add-on product to Microsoft BizTalk Server 2002 that allows organizations to quickly and easily build RosettaNet solutions. BizTalk Server Accelerator for RosettaNet includes several applications that enable users to develop, administer, and test RosettaNet standards-compliant Partner Interface Processes (PIPs) implemented as BizTalk Server 2002 XLANG schedules.

BizTalk Accelerator for Suppliers (AFS)

An add-on product to Microsoft BizTalk Server 2002 that enables suppliers to connect to both B2B trading partners and line-of-business applications through multiple online channels.

BizTalk Document Tracking

A Web-based user interface (UI) that is used to access all BizTalk Messaging Services tracking information. It can also track XLANG schedule status for BizTalk Orchestration Services.

BizTalk Editor

A tool with which you can create, edit, and manage specifications. With BizTalk Editor you can create a specification based on a specification template, an existing schema, certain types of document instances, or a blank specification.

BizTalk Framework

A platform-neutral e-commerce framework that is based on Extensible Markup Language (XML) schemas and industry standards. The framework enables integration across industries and between business systems, regardless of platform, operating system, or underlying technology. Specifically, it is composed of three things: schema, products, and services.

BizTalk Mapper

A tool with which you can create maps that define the correspondence between the records and fields in one specification and the records and fields in another specification. A map contains an Extensible Stylesheet Language (XSL) style sheet that is used by BizTalk Server to perform the transformation described in the map.

BizTalk Messaging Management database

A Microsoft SQL Server database that stores the information related to all server configurations, including group and server settings, receive functions, and all messaging configuration information for the objects that are created by using BizTalk Messaging Manager, or by accessing the BizTalk Messaging Configuration object model.

BizTalk Messaging Manager

A graphical user interface (UI) that can be used to configure BizTalk Messaging Services to exchange documents between trading partners and applications of the home organization.

BizTalk Messaging Services

Services that include sending, receiving, parsing, and tracking documents; receipt generation and correlation; and data mapping, integrity, and security.

BizTalk Orchestration Designer

A design tool used to create drawings that describe long-running, loosely coupled, executable business processes. The XLANG schedule drawing is compiled into an XLANG schedule that is used to execute the automated business process.

BizTalk Orchestration Services

Services that include designing, compiling, and running XLANG schedules. Additional services include the ability to create custom COM+ applications to host dedicated XLANG schedule instances, and the persistence of XLANG schedules.

BizTalk Server Administration

A Microsoft Management Console (MMC) interface that is used to administer the BizTalk Server 2002 group of servers and their properties, to monitor receive functions, and to monitor work items in the Microsoft SQL Server queues that are used by the server group.

-C-

CICS or CICS/VS

Acronym for Customer Information Control System or Customer Information Control System/Virtual Storage. An IBM transaction processing program that provides an environment on IBM mainframes in which applications can communicate with terminals or other applications.

Component Object Model (COM)

The object-oriented programming model that defines how objects interact within a single application or between applications. In COM, client software accesses an object through a pointer to an interface, which is a related set of properties and methods.

Component Object Model (COM) component

A binary file containing code for one or more class factories, COM classes, registry-entry mechanisms, loading code, and so on.

COMTI

COM Transaction Integrator (COMTI) is the synchronous COM application integration solution in Microsoft Host Integration Server 2000. COMTI enables integration between mainframe-based transaction programs (TPs) and component-based .NET Enterprise Servers applications. This is necessary when a synchronous or transactional solution is needed while both systems are running at all times.

cookie

Information about a user, such as an identification number, a password, click history, or number of times the user visited a site, stored in a file. A cookie can also store ticket data. Commerce Server supports both persistent and non-persistent cookies. Persistent cookies are stored on the computers of the users. Non-persistent cookies are used to track the activity of authenticated users who visit your site. When the session ends, the non-persistent cookie is deleted.

-D-

data translation

A process that converts data from one format to another format. Data translation occurs within BizTalk Server at run time. The rules that are specified in a map are used to convert data from a source specification format to a destination specification format, as well as to perform any operations or calculations that are required on the data.

delimited flat file

A file that contains one or more records that are represented as a group of fields separated by a delimiter character. The records themselves are also separated by delimiter characters.

destination

The name of the organization for the channel through which a document is processed. The destination is defined in BizTalk Messaging Services.

destination application

A home-organization application that has been designated in a messaging port as the destination for documents.

destination organization

A trading partner organization that has been designated in a messaging port as the destination for documents.

destination specification

The specification in a map that represents the outgoing document. BizTalk Mapper maps from a source specification to a destination specification.

document definition

A set of properties that represents a specific document. Document definition properties include a pointer to a document specification and can include global tracking fields and selection criteria.

document instance

A representation of the actual data that is sent to BizTalk Server. A document instance differs from a specification in that the specification defines the structure of the data, while a document instance is a representation of the specific data contained in a structure.

document standard

The structure that defines a transaction set, such as an X12 850 standard. An implementation guideline can be created from a document standard.

document type

A designation for the type of document on which a specification is based. For example, if a specification is based on 850Schema.xml from the X12 standard, when that specification is opened in BizTalk Editor, 850 appears in the document type field on the Reference tab for the root node.

document type definition (DTD)

A standard definition that specifies which elements and attributes might be present in other elements and attributes and that specifies any constraints on their ordering, frequency, and content.

DRDA

Distributed Relational Data Architecture. A connection protocol for distributed relational database processing that is used by IBM relational database products. The DRDA protocol comprises protocols for communication between an application and a remote database, and communication between databases. The DRDA protocol provides the connections for remote and distributed processing. The DRDA protocol is built on the Distributed Data Management Architecture.

-E-

EDIFACT

Electronic Data Interchange For Administration, Commerce, and Transport. The international EDI standard as developed through the United Nations. This standard is commonly used in Europe, as well as Japan and other Asian countries/regions. Also known as UN/EDIFACT.

Electronic Data Interchange (EDI)

A set of standards used to control the transfer of documents, such as purchase orders and invoices, between computers.

The transfer of data between different companies using networks, such as the Internet.

Ethernet

An IEEE 802.3 standard for contention networks. Ethernet uses a bus or star topology and relies on the form of access known as Carrier Sense Multiple Access with Collision Detection (CSMA/CD) to regulate communication line traffic. Network nodes are linked by coaxial cable, by fiber-optic cable, or by twisted-pair wiring. Data is transmitted in variable-length frames containing delivery and control information and up to 1,500 bytes of data. The Ethernet standard provides for baseband transmission at 10 megabits per second.

Extensible (XML) Structure Definitions (XSD)

A schema language. The XSD language is the one most recently recommended by the World Wide Web Consortium (W3C) for defining Extensible Markup Language (XML) structures.

Extensible Markup Language (XML)

A specification developed by the World Wide Web Consortium (W3C) that enables designers to create customized tags beyond the capabilities of standard HTML. While HTML uses only predefined tags to describe elements within the page, XML enables tags to be defined by the developer of the page. Tags for virtually any data item, such as a product or an amount due, can be used for specific applications. This enables Web pages to function as database records.

Extensible Stylesheet Language (XSL)

A style sheet format for Extensible Markup Language (XML) documents. XSL is used to define the display of XML in the same way that cascading style sheets (CSS) are used to define the display of Hypertext Markup Language (HTML). BizTalk Server uses XSL as the translation language between two specifications.

extranet

An extension of a corporate intranet using World Wide Web technology to facilitate communication with the suppliers and customers of a corporation. An extranet allows customers and suppliers to gain limited access to the intranet of a company in order to enhance the speed of communications and the efficiency of business relationships.

-F-

file transfer

The process of sending and receiving data files to and from computers.

firewall

A security checkpoint that separates an intranet from the Internet (or Internet groups). Only specific data may pass through a firewall.

-G-

globally unique identifier (GUID)

A 128-bit number that is guaranteed to be globally unique. Traditionally, GUIDs are created by running the Guidgen.exe command line program. The Guidgen.exe program never produces the same number twice, no matter how many times it is run or how many different computers it runs on. In Commerce Server, the GenID object can be used to generate GUIDs.

-H-

Hypertext Transfer Protocol (HTTP)

The client/server protocol used to transmit and receive all data over the World Wide Web. When you type a URL into your browser, you are actually sending an HTTP request to a Web server for a page of information.

-I-

IEEE

Institute of Electrical and Electronics Engineers. An organization that maintains the standards for the 802.x protocols used in communications on local area networks.

Internet domain name

The name used for hosting a site on the Internet. An Internet domain name is a combination of a second-level domain name (such as "Microsoft") and a top-level domain name (such as "com" or "net"), separated by a period. Before establishing a commerce site on the Internet, a business must first apply for and register a second-level domain name with an authorized Domain Name System (DNS) registration authority. This name must meet the requirements for external DNS naming, and must not already be registered or in use. To register the name, a business must obtain (or have an Internet Service Provider (ISP) obtain on its behalf) at least one Internet Protocol (IP) address valid for use on the Internet and the IP addresses of at least two currently active DNS servers on the Internet. Also called an Internet address, domain name, and URL.

Internet Service Provider (ISP)

A public provider of remote connections to the Internet. An ISP is a company that enables remote users to access the Internet by providing dial-up connections or installing leased lines. An ISP may host commerce sites for client companies, hosting several sites on a single server or server cluster. The ISP may provide the infrastructure and perform administration tasks common to all sites, while allowing clients to perform some site administration tasks from their remote computers.

intranet

A network designed for information processing within a company or organization. Its uses include such services as document distribution, software distribution, access to databases, and training. An intranet is so called because it usually employs applications associated with the Internet, such as Web pages, Web browsers, File Transfer Protocol (FTP) sites, e-mail, newsgroups, and mailing lists, in this case accessible only to those within the company or organization.

-L-

LAN

Local area network. A high-speed communication system consisting of hardware (computers and peripherals) and software (programs and data files) that are interconnected by cable in a way that allows these resources to be shared. The connected devices are located within a limited geographic area such as a building or campus.

-M-

MAC address

Media access control address. A 12-digit hexadecimal address used by the media access control layer of an 802.2 connection. The MAC address corresponds to the VTAM MACADDR= parameter and to the Remote Network Address parameter for an 802.2 connection with Host Integration Server 2000.

Meta data

Data used to describe other data. For example, data type is a piece of meta data that further describes a property.

Message-Oriented Middleware (MOM)

Message-Oriented Middleware is a set of products that connects applications running on different systems by sending and receiving application data as messages. Examples are RPC, CPI-C and message queuing. The Microsoft solution is MSMQ.

Microsoft Operations Manager (MOM)

An open, highly scalable, enterprise operations management and monitoring application in Microsoft Windows 2000 that enables centralized, dynamic monitoring and automated problem resolution of the events generated by users, application software, servers, and desktops.

MOM uses rules to monitor and generate a response to various events. This response can range from a user notification to an automated resolution of the problem.

Multipurpose Internet Mail Extensions (MIME)

A standard that extends the Simple Mail Transfer Protocol (SMTP) to permit data, such as video, sound, and binary files to be transmitted by Internet e-mail without having to be translated into ASCII format first.

-P-

pipeline

A software infrastructure that defines and links together one or more stages of a business process, running them in sequence to complete a specific task. Each stage of a pipeline contains one or more pipeline components (COM objects) that can be configured to work with the unique requirements of the site.

pipeline component

The Component Object Model (COM) server object that implements the required pipeline component interfaces. Each component performs operations on some part of an OrderForm object or Dictionary object before sending it to the next component or stage in the pipeline.

proxy server

A firewall component that manages Internet traffic to and from a local area network (LAN) and can provide other features, such as document caching and access control. A proxy server can improve performance by caching and directly supplying frequently requested data, such as a popular Web page, and can filter and discard requests that the owner does not consider appropriate, such as requests for unauthorized access to proprietary files.

-S-

selection criteria

A name-value pair designated in a document definition. The name-value pairs are used to uniquely identify a document definition for inbound EDI interchanges, based on values found in the functional group header, and to insert values in the functional group header for outbound EDI interchanges.

service

A program, routine, or process that performs a specific system function to support other programs, particularly at a low (close to the hardware) level. When services are provided over a network, they can be published in Active Directory, facilitating service-centric administration and usage. Services have a set of common administrative functions. For example, a service can be started, stopped, paused, or resumed; its start parameters can be modified; and it can be administered using command line utilities and scripts. Commerce Server includes the following resources that are also services: Direct Mailer, Predictor, and List Manager.

SNA

Acronym for Systems Network Architecture. A widely used communications framework developed by IBM to define network functions and establish standards for enabling computers to exchange and process data.

source application

A home-organization application that has been designated in a channel as the source of documents.

source organization

A trading partner organization that has been designated in a channel as the source of documents.

-T-

TCP/IP

Transmission Control Protocol/Internet Protocol. The transport protocol in use by many academic, defense, scientific, and commercial organizations to provide communication across wide area networks (WANs). TCP/IP provides communication across interconnected networks that include a variety of different operating systems.

three-tier architecture

An architecture that divides a networked application into three logical areas: the user interface layer (also called the top tier), the business logic layer (also called the middle tier), and the database layer (also called the bottom tier or back end). Layers can have one or more components. For example, there can be one or more user interfaces in the top tier. Also, each user interface can communicate with multiple applications in the middle tier at the same time, and the applications in the middle tier can use multiple databases at a time. Components in a tier can run on a computer that is separate from the other tiers, communicating with the other components over a network.

TP

Transaction program. An application program that uses Advanced Program-to-Program Communications (APPC) to exchange data with another TP on a peer-to-peer basis.

trace file

A file containing detailed records of internal activities on the SNA network, including calls made to APIs, the activities of APIs, and the activities of communication links and internal flows.

For a computer running Host Integration Server 2000 or Windows 2000 or Windows NT-based client, trace files are created when SNA tracing is turned on with the Host Integration Server 2000 Trace Options (snatrace) utility.

tracing

The action of tracking the activities of APIs, communication links, and internal flows, including the calls made to APIs. Tracing stores a history of activity in trace files.

trading partner

An external organization with which your home organization exchanges electronic data. The exchange of data among trading partners is governed by the agreements, pipelines, and distribution lists that are created between your organization and the trading partners.

transaction

A discrete activity within a computer system, such as an entry of a customer order or an update of an inventory item, that consists of a group of operations that succeed or fail collectively. That is, if one operation fails, the entire transaction is rolled back, and the effects of any operations that took place before the failure are undone. Transactions are usually associated with database management, order-entry, and other online systems. In BizTalk Orchestration Designer, transactions are represented as a collection of actions that are grouped within a Transaction shape.

-U-

Uniform Resource Identifier (URI)

Identifies points of content on the Internet. The content can be a page of text, a video or sound clip, an image, or a program. The most common form of URI is the Web page address, also known as the Uniform Resource Locator (URL). A URI usually includes the file name for the resource, the name of the computer the resource resides on, and the protocol used to access it. For example, http://www.microsoft.com/sql/techinfo/security/password.htm.

Uniform Resource Locator (URL)

The address of a file (resource) accessible on the Internet. The type of resource depends on the Internet application protocol. For example, for the Hypertext Transfer Protocol (HTTP) used on the World Wide Web, the resource can be an HTML page, an image file, a program such as a Common Gateway Interface (CGI) application or Java applet, or any other file supported by HTTP. The URL contains the name of the protocol required to access the resource, a domain name that identifies a specific computer on the Internet, and a hierarchical description of a file location on the computer.

-W-

WAN

Wide area network. A high-speed communication system, consisting of hardware (computers and peripherals) and software (programs and files), that provides communications services and allows resources to be shared over a larger geographic area than that served by a LAN. Contrast with LAN.

Web server

In general use, a computer equipped with the server software that uses Internet protocols such as HTTP to respond to Web client requests on a Transmission Control Protocol/Internet Protocol (TCP/IP) network.

In Commerce Server, a Web server is a physical server computer running Internet Information Services (IIS) 5.0; it inherits properties from the IIS Web Site. A Web server appears under an application in the Commerce Server Manager console. One commerce application can use multiple Web servers that serve different types of content for the application.

Web site

In general use, a collection of files and applications accessed through a Web address, covering a specific theme or subject, and managed by a particular person or organization. A Web site resides on servers connected to the Web network and provides content that is available to worldwide users 24 hours a day, seven days a week. Web sites typically use HTML to format and present information and to provide navigational facilities that enable users to move within the site and around the Web. From an Internet Information Services (IIS) 5.0 administration standpoint, Web Site specifically means a virtual server (such as the Default Web Site). A virtual server is a virtual computer that resides on an HTTP server but appears to the user as a separate HTTP server. Several virtual servers can reside on one computer, each one capable of running its own programs and each one with individualized access to input and peripheral devices. Each virtual server has its own Internet domain name and Internet Protocol (IP) address

-X-

X.25

The CCITT standard used for communication over a packet-switching network. X.25 uses the protocol called Qualified Logical Link Control (QLLC).

XLANG language

A language that describes the logical sequencing of business processes, as well as the implementation of the business process by using various implementation technologies. The XLANG language is expressed in XML.

XML schema

The definition of the structure of an XML file. A schema contains property information as it pertains to the records and fields within the structure.

Index

A

ABAP/4 (Advanced Business Application Programming) 121
Accelerator for HIPAA 485
Accelerator for RosettaNet 486
Accelerator for Suppliers (AFS)
    catalog publishing architecture 255–256
    catalog publishing solutions 250–256
    catalog publishing tasks 251–254
    cXML 264–265
    document formats supported 251, 257, 263–266
    .NET E-Business Servers 487
    overview 240, 248
    purchase order reception architecture 259–262
    purchase order reception solutions 256–262
    purchase order reception tasks 258–259
    remote shopping architecture 269–271
    remote shopping solutions 262–271
    remote shopping tasks 267–269
Accounting servers 430–431, 457
Adapter for SAP *See* BizTalk Adapter for SAP
Adapter for SAP Manager *See* BizTalk Adapter for SAP Manager
Adapter Manager
    associating filters with R/3 destinations 170
    configuring 166–172
    creating new filters 169–170
    creating Routing Keys 171
    filtering IDocs 169
    generating BizTalk Server specifications 170, 177
    overview 160
    selecting Message queues 168–169
    selecting R/3 destinations 167–168
Advanced Business Application Programming (ABAP/4) 121
advertising 336, 339–341
AFS *See* Accelerator for Suppliers (AFS)
AFS Solution Site 283–290
AIC (application integration components) 161, 226–228
Application Center 2000 24–26
application integration components (AIC) 161, 226–228
application integration into enterprises *See* Enterprise Application Integration (EAI)
application integration with SAP *See* integrating applications with SAP

architecture
    catalog publishing in AFS 255–256
    COMTI 139–140
    navigation service provider (NSP) 443–447
    purchase order reception in AFS 259–262
    remote shopping in AFS 269–271
ASP.NET 18–19, 22
auctions 345
audience 4–5
Authentication servers 457
authorization 383
automating e-procurement *See* e-procurement

B

B2B *See* business-to-business
B2C *See* business-to-consumer
BAPI *See* Business Application Programming Interface
BAPI Browser 123
BAPI Explorer 123–125
basic supplier purchasing model 244
basket rendering routines 273–283
basket.asp 273–276
baskets 309, 327–330
bCentral 307
BizOffice 489
BizTalk Accelerator for HIPAA 485
BizTalk Accelerator for RosettaNet 486
BizTalk Accelerator for Suppliers *See* Accelerator for Suppliers (AFS)
BizTalk Adapter for SAP
    Adapter Manager *See* BizTalk Adapter for SAP Manager
    application integration components (AIC) 161
    application integration solutions 130
    business example 158–159
    components 160–161
    hardware requirements 159–160
    IDoc Handler 161
    installing 162
    installing prerequisite software 162
    MSMQ *See* Microsoft Message Queuing
    overview 157
    software requirements 159–160, 162
BizTalk Adapter for SAP Manager
    associating filters with R/3 destinations 170
    configuring 166–172
    creating new filters 169–170
    creating Routing Keys 171
    filtering IDocs 169
    generating BizTalk Server specifications 170, 177
    overview 160
    selecting Message queues 168–169
    selecting R/3 destinations 167–168
BizTalk Framework Initiative 194

BizTalk Messaging Manager 172–174, 205–206
BizTalk Messaging Port 161
BizTalk Messaging Services 232–233
BizTalk Server
    See also e-procurement
    additional resources 28, 182, 237
    application integration solutions 130
    configuring 172–175, 205–206, 208
    converting documents to C# classes 224–226
    e-commerce 194–195
    generating specifications 170, 176–177
    global assembly cache (GAC) 229
    hardware requirements 201
    hub system document flow 213–214, 216–217
    integrating with EDI *See* integrating BizTalk with EDI
    integrating with SAP *See* integrating BizTalk with SAP
    overview 26–27, 200
    selling through trading partners 248
    sending IDocs 177–179
    software requirements 201
    supplier system document flow 215, 218–219
    XLANG schedule activation 219
    XLANG schedule correlation 221–222
BOR (Business Object Repository) 123
BuildTopNavTable 397–401
Business Application Programming Interface (BAPI)
    application integration solutions 127–130
    challenges 123–125
    overview 121–123
Business Desk 317–318, 347, 382
business exchanges 192
Business Object Repository (BOR) 123
business-to-business
    See also e-commerce
    direct automated business transactions 192
    electronic integration 190–192
    marketplaces and exchanges 191–192
    overview 185
    point-to-point automated business transactions 192
    value-added networks (VANs) 190
business-to-consumer
    Commerce Server *See* Commerce Server
    Content Management Server *See* Content Management Server
    managing Web content *See* managing Web content
    overview 301–305
    retail Web site setup *See* retail Web site setup
buyer applications 249–250

C

C#
    converting BizTalk documents to classes 224–226
    overview 16

C++ 17
caching 454–455, 469
catalogs 250–256, 309, 324–327
channels 174, 368
class libraries 14–15
COBOL programs 149
coherence 412
COM for ABAP service 134, 164–166
COM Transaction Integration (COMTI)
   architecture 139–140
   direct client to 142
   .NET Runtime 141
   overview 138
Commerce Extensible Markup Language (cXML) 247, 264–265
Commerce Server
   See also retail Web site setup
   additional resources 30–31
   advertising 336, 339–341
   auctions 345
   baskets 327–330
   Business Desk 317–318, 347, 382
   business-to-consumer overview 302–303
   catalogs 324–327
   Content Connector 375, 380–383
   Content Selection Framework 381
   cross selling 336, 338–340
   currency 345
   direct mail 336, 339, 341
   gift certificates 345–346
   htmRenderFullTextSearchResults 352
   improvements 341–344
   International Solution Site 353–357
   keyword searches 349–357
   languages 345
   marketing 336–341
   navigation features 321–323
   objects 319–321
   Order Status 347
   Order Status Codes 347
   overview 29–30, 307, 314–316
   Page_Load 354
   PerformSearch 355–357
   personalized content objects (PCOs) 381–382
   predictions 336, 340–341
   privacy 344
   product catalogs 324–327
   product reviews 345
   promoting products 336, 339–341
   Publish Order Codes 347
   purchasing 330–334
   recommendations 336–341
   RenderSearchResultRow 353
   RenderSearchResults 353

Commerce Server *(continued)*
    Retail Solution Site 349–353
    rsFreeTextSearch 350–352
    Search_Click 353–354
    security 334–335
    selling through trading partners 248
    shopping baskets 327–330
    simple product pages 380–381
    solutions summary 321
    targeted advertising 336
    up selling 336, 338–340
    user interfaces 316–318
    Web site 319
Commerce Server Manager 316–318
common language runtime 13–14
Common Programming Interface for Communications (CPI-C) 121
COMTI (COM Transaction Integration)
    architecture 139–140
    direct client to 142
    .NET Runtime 141
    overview 138
configuring
    Adapter Manager 166–172
    BizTalk Adapter for SAP Manager 166–172
    BizTalk Server 172–175, 205–206, 208
    COM for ABAP service 164–166
    data links for OLE DB Provider for DB2 80–90
    data sources for OLE DB Provider for DB2 79
    DCOM Connector 163–164
    GENTRAN 204–205, 207
    Host Integration Server 78–79
    MSMQ 166
    SAP DCOM Connector 163–164
    SAP R/3 systems 163
    SQL Server 93–94
    SQL Server DTS packages 94–102
    Web Service File Transfer (WSFT) 295–297
connected pages 375
Connection String Manager sample applications 495
ConsolidatedRetail.com 430
Content Connector 375, 380–383
Content Connector Framework API 387–388
Content Management Server
    See also managing Web content
    additional resources 32–33
    BuildTopNavTable 397–401
    business-to-consumer overview 303–304
    channels 368
    concepts overview 364
    connected pages 375
    Content Connector 375, 380–383
    creating Web sites 379

Content Management Server *(continued)*
    deploying 388–391
    folders 368
    framed vs. frameless sites 365–366
    future version functionality 391–395
    galleries 369
    navigation templates 365
    overview 32, 361–364
    page templates 365–366
    pages 367–368
    placeholders 366–367
    postings 367–368
    programming 384–388
    properties 369
    Publishing API (PAPI) 375, 384–386
    resources 369
    rich product pages 380–381
    rights 376–379
    rights groups 370
    roles 370, 376–379
    Site Builder 373–374
    Site Deployment Manager 389–390
    Site Manager 374
    Site Stager 390–391
    SQL Server databases 364
    templates 365–366
    terminology overview 364
    URL generation 376
    Web Author 371–373
Content Selection Framework 381
Context service 461–462
Conversion servers 430
core navigation servers 430–431, 457
CPI-C (Common Programming Interface for Communications) 121
cross selling 336, 338–340
currencies 311, 345
customer order display sample applications 495
customer order entry sample applications 495
cXML (Commerce Extensible Markup Language) 247, 264–265

D

Data Transformation Services (DTS)
    See also integrating SQL Server with DB2
    configuring DTS packages 94–102
    data integration 111
    DTS Run Utility for Windows 104
    DTSRun application 105
    Enterprise Manager and DTS packages 102–103
    managing 102
    sample applications 107–110, 495
    scheduling DTS packages for execution 105–106
DB2 *See* integrating SQL Server with DB2

DCOM Connector
    COM for ABAP service 134, 164–166
    configuring 163–164
    Object Builder 129, 134–135
delivering location-based mobile services (LBMS)
    See also MAGIC Services Protocol Version 2.0 (MSP 2.0)
    additional resources 479
    API 469–470
    Context service 461–462
    delivery to in-car systems 473–474
    delivery to mobile phones 474–477
    delivery to mobile service provider (MSP) 477–478
    Mobility service 465
    overview 406–410, 459–460
    position proxy server (PPS) 478–479
    Positioning service 466
    Query service 463–464
    Registry 468–469
    Rendering service 466–467
    Semantics service 462–463
    Session service 460–461, 470–472
    space publishing server (SPS) 472–473
    summary 479
    Update service 467–468
deploying
    Content Management Server 388–391
    location-based mobile services (LBMS) 426–427, 431
device-borne positioning 415
direct automated business transactions 192
direct mail 336, 339, 341
document definitions, creating 172–173
dot net *See* .NET
DTS *See* Data Transformation Services (DTS)
DTS Import/Export Wizard 94–101
DTS Run Utility for Windows 104
DTSRun application 105
dtsrunui.exe 104

E

EAI (Enterprise Application Integration)
    API based integration 56–57
    approaches 54–58
    business case 53–54
    business logic based integration 57–58
    challenges 50–52
    data source based integration 55–56
    implementing 58–61
    integrating host data to the Web 137
    integrating SQL Server with DB2 *See* integrating SQL Server with DB2
    market 61
    overview 49
    user interface based integration 54–55
E-Business Servers *See* .NET E-Business Servers

e-commerce
    BizTalk Server 194–195
    business-to-business integration 190–192
    challenges 188–195
    Electronic Data Interchange (EDI) 193
    exchanging data 193–195
    middleware 189, 193–194
    overview 185–187
    types of purchases 187–188
    XML 193–195
EDI (Electronic Data Interchange)
    business-to-business e-commerce 193
    characteristics 193
    integrating BizTalk *See* integrating BizTalk with EDI
electronic commerce
    BizTalk Server 194–195
    business-to-business integration 190–192
    challenges 188–195
    Electronic Data Interchange (EDI) 193
    exchanging data 193–195
    middleware 189, 193–194
    overview 185–187
    types of purchases 187–188
    XML 193–195
Electronic Data Interchange (EDI)
    business-to-business e-commerce 193
    characteristics 193
    integrating BizTalk *See* integrating BizTalk with EDI
electronic document standards 247
electronic procurement *See* e-procurement
Enterprise Application Integration (EAI)
    API based integration 56–57
    approaches 54–58
    business case 53–54
    business logic based integration 57–58
    challenges 50–52
    data source based integration 55–56
    implementing 58–61
    integrating host data to the Web 137
    integrating SQL Server with DB2 *See* integrating SQL Server with DB2
    market 61
    overview 49
    user interface based integration 54–55
Enterprise Manager 102–103
enterprise-level retail Web site *See* retail Web site setup
envelopes, creating 172–173
e-procurement
    See also BizTalk Server
    additional resources 237
    application integration components (AIC) 226–228
    BizTalk Messaging Services 232–233
    converting BizTalk documents to C# classes 224–226
    global assembly cache (GAC) 229
    hardware requirements 222

e-procurement *(continued)*
    hub system document flow 213–214, 216–217
    implementation overview 229
    sample applications overview 496
    sample applications preliminary setup 229–233
    sample applications, running 233–235
    sample applications, uninstalling 236–237
    scenario 211–212
    software requirements 222
    solutions 212–222
    SQL Server 229–231
    supplier system document flow 215, 218–219
    tools and technologies 222–228
    Visual Studio .NET 223–228
    XLANG schedule activation 219
    XLANG schedule correlation 221–222
    XML Web services 223–228, 233–235
Exchange 2000 Server 33–35
exchanges, business 192
Extensible Markup Language *See* XML

F

filtering IDocs 169
Financial Services Accelerator (FSA) 489
folders 368
framed vs. frameless sites 365–366
FSA (Financial Services Accelerator) 489

G

GAC (global assembly cache) 229
galleries 369
Gateway servers 430–431, 457
GENTRAN
    configuring 204–205, 207
    integrating BizTalk with EDI *See* integrating BizTalk with EDI
    overview 197, 201
GETACCTS COBOL transaction program 142
getaccts method 142, 149
GETBAL COBOL transaction program 142
getbal method 142, 149
gift certificates 345–346
global assembly cache (GAC) 229
GotDotNet 22

H

hardware requirements
    BizTalk Server 201
    e-procurement 222
    integrating BizTalk with EDI 199–203
    integrating BizTalk with SAP 159–160
    integrating host data to the Web 144–149

hardware requirements
    location-based mobile services (LBMS) 429
    Web Service File Transfer (WSFT) 293
Health Insurance Portability and Accountability Act (HIPAA) 485
Host Integration Server
    additional resources 37
    configuring 78–79
    overview 35–36
    software requirements 144–145
host-to-Web integration *See* integrating host data to the Web
htmRenderFullTextSearchResults 352
HTTP 442
hub system document flow 213–214, 216–217

I

IDoc Handler 161
IDocs
    application integration solutions 130
    filtering 169
    overview 121–123
    sending to BizTalk Server 177–179
    sending to SAP R/3 systems 179–181
implementing
    ConsolidatedRetail.com 430
    Enterprise Application Integration (EAI) 58–61
    e-procurement 229
    integrating applications with SAP 132–136
    integrating BizTalk with EDI 203–209
    integrating BizTalk with SAP 161
    integrating host data to the Web 150–156
    integrating SQL Server with DB2 73
    location-based mobile services (LBMS) 430–432, 456–458
    managing Web content 397–401
    navigation service provider (NSP) delivery systems 456–458
    selling through trading partners 272–273
    Web Service File Transfer (WSFT) 294–297
improvements to retail Web sites 311, 341–344
InspectBasket.asp 276–283
installing
    BizTalk Adapter for SAP 162
    Microsoft software 431–432, 457–458
    SQL Server 93–94
    Web Service File Transfer (WSFT) 293–294
integrating applications into enterprises *See* Enterprise Application Integration (EAI)
integrating applications with SAP
    accessing SAP R/3 from external applications 121
    APIs 120–125
    BAPI *See* Business Application Programming Interface
    challenges 123–125
    IDocs *See* IDocs
    implementing 132–136
    message body formats 133–134
    Microsoft Message Queuing (MSMQ) 133–134

integrating applications with SAP *(continued)*
    middleware 132–133
    Object Builder 129, 134–135
    overview 113–115
    processes 119–120
    Remote Function Call *See* Remote Function Call (RFC)
    SAP application connector software 134–136
    SAP DCOM Connector 129, 134–135
    scenario 116–119
    solutions 126–130
    summary 136
    tools and technologies 131
integrating BizTalk with EDI
    configuring BizTalk Server 205–206, 208
    configuring for Internet transmission 204–206
    configuring for routing received documents to MSMQ 207–208
    configuring GENTRAN 204–205, 207
    e-business software solutions 200–201
    file transfers 200
    file transport methods 202
    hardware requirements 199–203
    implementing 203–209
    planning for growth and scalability 209
    scenario 197
    software requirements 199–203
    solutions 198–199
    tools and technologies 199–203
    trading partner interfaces 201–203
integrating BizTalk with SAP
    BizTalk Messaging Manager 172–174
    configuring BizTalk Adapter for SAP Manager 166–172
    configuring BizTalk Server 172–175
    configuring COM for ABAP service 164–166
    configuring components overview 162
    configuring MSMQ 166
    configuring SAP DCOM Connector 163–164
    configuring SAP R/3 systems 163
    creating channels 174
    creating document definitions 172–173
    creating envelopes 172–173
    creating organizations 173
    creating ports 173–174
    creating receive functions 174–175
    generating BizTalk Server specifications 170, 176–177
    hardware requirements 159–160
    implementation overview 161
    installing BizTalk Adapter for SAP 162
    installing prerequisite software 162
    scenario 157
    sending IDocs to BizTalk Server 177–179
    sending IDocs to SAP R/3 systems 179–181
    software requirements 159–160, 162
    solutions 157–159

integrating BizTalk with SAP *(continued)*
    tools and technologies 159–161
    tracing 172
integrating business partners into enterprises
    BizTalk Server 194–195
    business-to-business electronic integration 190–192
    e-commerce challenges 188–195
    Electronic Data Interchange (EDI) 193
    exchanging data 193–195
    middleware 189, 193–194
    overview 185–187
    types of e-commerce purchases 187–188
    XML 193–195
integrating host data to the Web
    browser to .NET Web Service connections 143
    COBOL programs 149
    COMTI architecture 139–140
    COMTI overview 138
    direct client to COMTI connections 142
    hardware requirements 144–149
    Host Integration Server 144–145
    implementing 150–156
    .NET Runtime COMTI integration 141
    sample applications 140–143, 493–494
    scenario 137
    software requirements 144–149
    solutions 138–143
    tools and technologies 144–149
    Visual Studio .NET 145
integrating SQL Server with DB2
    See also Data Transformation Services (DTS)
    configuring data links for OLE DB Provider for DB2 80–90
    configuring data sources for OLE DB Provider for DB2 79
    configuring Host Integration Server 78–79
    configuring software overview 78
    configuring SQL Server 93–94
    configuring SQL Server DTS packages 94–102
    creating data links for OLE DB Provider for DB2 80
    data integration using DTS 111
    DTS Import/Export Wizard 94–101
    DTS package management 102
    DTS Run Utility for Windows 104
    DTSRun application 105
    Enterprise Manager 102–103
    implementation overview 73
    installing software overview 78
    installing SQL Server 93–94
    overview 63–64
    preparing DB2 tables on AS/400 90–93
    sample applications 107–110, 495
    scenario 65–68
    scheduling DTS packages for execution 105–106
    solutions 69–70, 74–77

integrating SQL Server with DB2 *(continued)*
    tools and technologies 71–73
    Windows 2000 server 77
Intermediate Documents *See* IDocs
International Solution Site 353–357
Internet Security and Acceleration (ISA) Server 2000 38–39
introduction 3–10
ISA Server 38–39

J

JScript .NET 17–18

K

keyword searches 349–357

L

languages 311, 345
LBMS *See* location-based mobile services
location technology 414–420
location-based mobile services (LBMS)
    Accounting servers 430–431
    additional resources 433
    architecture *See* location-based mobile services (LBMS) architecture
    building .NET solutions 411
    coherence 412
    connectivity 422
    ConsolidatedRetail.com 430
    Conversion servers 430
    core navigation servers 430–431
    delivering *See* delivering location-based mobile services (LBMS)
    deployment checklists 431
    deployment options 426–427
    device-borne positioning 415
    enterprise server components 425
    Gateway servers 430–431
    hardware requirements 429
    implementing 430–432
    lab prototyping 426
    location technology 414–420
    MAGIC Services 423–425
    MAGIC Services Protocol Version 2.0 *See* MAGIC Services Protocol Version 2.0 (MSP 2.0)
    market segmentation 421
    mobile Internet technology 411
    mobile networks 411–414
    mobile service provider *See* mobile service provider (MSP)
    navigation service provider *See* navigation service provider (NSP)
    network positioning 415
    observational positioning 416
    operating environment 427–429
    operating systems 425
    overview 405
    protocol standards 422–423

location-based mobile services (LBMS) *(continued)*
    scalability 427–429
    security checklists 432
    software requirements 429, 431
    stateful server model 427
    sync-and-go model 427, 455
    synchronization requirements 422
    synchronous and stateless model 426–427
    tools and technologies 427–430
    Transport Unpacking servers 430–431
    user scenarios 421
location-based mobile services (LBMS) architecture
    Accounting servers 457
    additional resources 458
    Authentication servers 457
    caching options 454–455
    content provider relationships 437–439
    core navigation servers 457
    customers 439–440
    delivery to in-car systems 451–452
    delivery to mobile phones 450
    delivery to mobile service provider (MSP) 452
    Gateway servers 457
    HTTP 442
    identifying service requirements 454
    implementing 456–458
    implementing navigation service provider (NSP) delivery systems 456–458
    in-car systems 451–452, 455
    information updates 453
    key design considerations 435–441
    MAGIC Services Protocol Version 2.0 *See* MAGIC Services Protocol Version 2.0 (MSP 2.0)
    mobile phones 450, 455
    mobile service provider (MSP) and other content providers 437–439
    mobile service provider (MSP) and other customers 439–440
    mobile service provider (MSP) overview 455
    navigation service provider (NSP) and other content providers 437–439
    navigation service provider (NSP) and other customers 439–440
    navigation service provider (NSP) architecture 443–447
    overview 425, 435
    position proxy server (PPS) 456, 458
    service delivery targets 448–452
    SMTP 442
    software requirements 457–458
    solution overview 435
    solution parameters 453–454
    solution summary 455–456
    space publishing server (SPS) 458
    TCP/IP 442
    tools and technologies 456
    transport considerations 441–443
    Transport Unpacking servers 457
    wireless connectivity 453

M

MAGIC Services 423–425
MAGIC Services Protocol Version 2.0 (MSP 2.0)
    API 469–470
    caching 469
    Context service 461–462
    information updates 453
    Mobility service 465
    overview 408, 423, 460
    Positioning service 466
    protocol stacks 440–441
    Query service 463–464
    Registry 468–469
    Rendering service 466–467
    schema delegation 470
    schema evolution 469
    Semantics service 462–463
    Session service 460–461, 470–472
    space publishing server (SPS) 472–473
    Update service 467–468
    versioning 469
managing Web content
    See also Content Management Server
    BuildTopNavTable 397–401
    Business Desk extensions 382
    Content Connector 380–383
    Content Selection Framework 381
    creating Web sites 379
    deploying Content Management Server 388–391
    implementing 397–401
    Microsoft Solution for Internet Business (MSIB) 383
    overview 359
    personalized content objects (PCOs) 381–382
    rich product pages 380–381
    scenario 360–361
    simple product pages 380–381
    solutions overview 361–362
    tools and technologies 396
    user authorization 383
market segmentation 421
marketing 336–341
message body formats 133–134
message broker 189
Messaging Manager 172–174, 205–206
methods
    getaccts 142, 149
    getbal 142, 149
Microsoft .NET Alerts 21
Microsoft .NET Enterprise Servers 6, 19–20, 23, 46
Microsoft .NET Framework *See* .NET Framework
Microsoft .NET global assembly cache (GAC) 229
Microsoft .NET My Services 20–22

Microsoft .NET Passport 21–22
Microsoft Application Center 2000 24–26
Microsoft ASP.NET 18–19, 22
Microsoft bCentral 307
Microsoft BizTalk Accelerator for HIPAA 485
Microsoft BizTalk Accelerator for RosettaNet 486
Microsoft BizTalk Accelerator for Suppliers *See* Accelerator for Suppliers (AFS)
Microsoft BizTalk Adapter for SAP *See* BizTalk Adapter for SAP
Microsoft BizTalk Adapter for SAP Manager *See* BizTalk Adapter for SAP Manager
Microsoft BizTalk Server *See* BizTalk Server
Microsoft Commerce Server *See* Commerce Server
Microsoft Content Management Server *See* Content Management Server
Microsoft Exchange 2000 Server 33–35
Microsoft Host Integration Server
    additional resources 37
    configuring 78–79
    overview 35–36
    software requirements 144–145
Microsoft Internet Security and Acceleration (ISA) Server 2000 38–39
Microsoft Message Queuing (MSMQ)
    additional resources 182, 237
    configuring 166
    message body formats 133–134
    overview 161
Microsoft Mobile Information 2001 Server 43–44
Microsoft SharePoint Portal Server 2001 45–46
Microsoft Solution for Internet Business (MSIB) 383, 487
Microsoft SQL Server
    additional resources 42, 182
    configuring 93–94
    Content Management Server 364
    Data Transformation Services *See* Data Transformation Services (DTS)
    editions 77
    e-procurement 229–231
    installing 93–94
    integrating with DB2 *See* integrating SQL Server with DB2
    overview 40–41
    sample applications 107–110, 495
    selling through trading partners 248
Microsoft Visual Basic .NET 16–17, 495
Microsoft Visual C# .NET
    converting BizTalk documents to classes 224–226
    overview 16
Microsoft Visual C++ .NET 17
Microsoft Visual Studio .NET *See* Visual Studio .NET
middleware 132–133, 189, 193–194
Mobile Information 2001 Server 43–44
mobile Internet technology 411
mobile service provider (MSP)
    customers 439–440
    navigation service provider (NSP) delivery to 452, 477–478
    overview 407–410, 455
    relationship with content providers 437–439
mobile services *See* location-based mobile services (LBMS)

Mobility service 465
MSIB (Microsoft Solution for Internet Business) 383, 487
MSMQ (Microsoft Message Queuing)
    additional resources 182, 237
    configuring 166
    message body formats 133–134
    overview 161
MSP *See* mobile service provider
MSP 2.0 *See* MAGIC Services Protocol Version 2.0
My Services 20–22

N

navigation of retail Web sites 308, 321–323
navigation service provider (NSP)
    architecture 443–447
    back-end functionality 444–445
    client grouping into classes 448–449
    customers 439–440
    delivery to in-car systems 451–452
    delivery to mobile phones 450
    delivery to mobile service provider (MSP) 452, 477–478
    front-end functionality 445–447
    implementing delivery systems 456–458
    overview 408–410
    relationship with content providers 437–439
    space publishing server (SPS) 447, 455, 472–473
navigation templates 365
.NET
    additional resources 21–22
    building LBMS solutions 411
    overview 11–12
    server platform overview 19–20
.NET Alerts 21
.NET E-Business Servers
    Accelerator for HIPAA 485
    Accelerator for RosettaNet 486
    Accelerator for Suppliers (AFS) 487
    BizOffice 489
    current status 483–489
    enterprise e-business processes and services 487–488
    Financial Services Accelerator (FSA) 489
    future solutions and accelerators 489
    future status 490–491
    Health Insurance Portability and Accountability Act (HIPAA) 485
    Microsoft Solution for Internet Business (MSIB) 487
    overview 483
    Partner Interface Processes (PIPs) 486
    RosettaNet 486
    RosettaNet Implementation Framework (RNIF) 486
    solutions 484–487
.NET Enterprise Servers 6, 19–20, 22, 23, 46
.NET Framework
    ASP.NET 18–19

.NET Framework *(continued)*
    class libraries 14–15
    common language runtime 13–14
    JScript .NET 17–18
    overview 12
    programming languages 15–18
    Visual Basic .NET 16–17
    Visual C# .NET 16
    Visual C++ .NET 17
    Visual Studio .NET 12–13
.NET My Services 20–22
.NET Passport 21–22
.NET Runtime 141–143
.NET Web Service 143
network positioning 415
NSP *See* navigation service provider

O

Object Builder 129, 134–135
observational positioning 416
OCI documents 266
OLE DB Provider for DB2
    configuring data links 80–90
    configuring data sources 79
    creating data links 80
Order Status 347
Order Status Codes 347
organizations, creating 173
overview 3–10

P

page templates 365–366
Page_Load 354
pages 367–368, 375
PAPI (Publishing API) 375, 384–386
Partner Interface Processes (PIPs) 486
PCOs (personalized content objects) 381–382
PerformSearch 355–357
personalized content objects (PCOs) 381–382
PIPs (Partner Interface Processes) 486
placeholders 366–367
point-to-point automated business transactions 192
ports, creating 173–174
position proxy server (PPS) 456, 458, 478–479
Positioning service 466
postings 367–368
PPS (position proxy server) 456, 458, 478–479
predictions 336, 340–341
privacy 311, 344
product catalogs 250–256, 309, 324–327
product reviews 345
programming languages 15–18
promoting products 336, 339–341

properties, Content Management Server 369
protocol stacks 440–441
Publish Order Codes 347
Publishing API (PAPI) 375, 384–386
purchasing from retail Web sites 309, 330–334
purchasing models 243–246

Q

Query service 463–464
queued RFC 129

R

receive functions, creating 174–175
ReceiveClient.asmx 296
recommendations 310, 336–341
Registry 468–469
Remote Function Call (RFC)
    challenges 123–125
    overview 121–123
    queued RFC 129
    synchronous RFC 129
    transactional RFC 129
RemoteBasket.asp 273–283
Rendering service 466–467
RenderSearchResultRow 353
RenderSearchResults 353
resources, Content Management Server 369
Retail Solution Site 349–353
retail Web site purchasing model 243
retail Web site setup
    See also Commerce Server
    advertising 336, 339–341
    auctions 345
    baskets 309, 327–330
    business manager perspective 312
    catalogs 309, 324–327
    cross selling 336, 338–340
    currencies 311, 345
    direct mail 336, 339, 341
    gift certificates 345–346
    implementation overview 348–349
    improvements 311, 341–344
    International Solution Site 353–357
    keyword searches 349–357
    languages 311, 345
    marketing 336–341
    navigation 308, 321–323
    overview 307
    predictions 336, 340–341
    privacy 311, 344
    product catalogs 309, 324–327
    product reviews 345
    promoting products 336, 339–341

retail Web site setup *(continued)*
    purchasing 309, 330–334
    recommendations 310, 336–341
    Retail Solution Site 349–353
    scenario 308–314
    security 309–310, 334–335
    shopkeeper perspective 311–312
    shopper perspective 308–311
    shopping baskets 309, 327–330
    site administrator perspective 313
    site developer perspective 313
    solutions overview 314–315
    targeted advertising 336
    tools and technologies 347–348
    up selling 336, 338–340
RFC *See* Remote Function Call
rich product pages 380–381
rights 376–379
rights groups 370
RNIF (RosettaNet Implementation Framework) 486
roles 370, 376–379
RosettaNet 486
RosettaNet Implementation Framework (RNIF) 486
Routing Keys, creating 171
rsFreeTextSearch 350–352

S

sample applications
    Connection String Manager 495
    customer order display 495
    customer order entry 495
    e-procurement 229–237, 496
    integrating host data to the Web 140–143, 493–494
    overview 493
    SQL Server to DB2 data transfer 107–110, 495
    Visual Basic .NET OLE DB query processor 495
    WSFT *See* Web Service File Transfer
SAP Business Object Repository (BOR) 123
SAP DCOM Connector
    COM for ABAP service 134, 164–166
    configuring 163–164
    Object Builder 129, 134–135
SAP R/3 systems
    additional resources 182
    application connector software 134–136
    BAPI *See* Business Application Programming Interface
    challenges 123–125
    Common Programming Interface for Communications (CPI-C) 121
    configuring 163
    IDocs *See* IDocs
    integrating applications *See* integrating applications with SAP
    integrating BizTalk *See* integrating BizTalk with SAP
    overview 157

SAP R/3 systems *(continued)*
    Remote Function Call *See* Remote Function Call (RFC)
scheduling DTS packages for execution 105–106
schema
    delegation 470
    evolution 469
Search_Click 353–354
security
    location-based mobile services (LBMS) 432
    retail Web sites 309–310, 334–335
selling through trading partners
    Accelerator for Suppliers (AFS) *See* Accelerator for Suppliers (AFS)
    AFS Solution Site 283–290
    basic supplier purchasing model 244
    basket rendering routines 273–283
    basket.asp 273–276
    BizTalk Server 248
    buyer applications 249–250
    catalog publishing solutions 250–256
    Commerce Server 248
    cXML 247, 264–265
    electronic document standards 247
    implementation overview 272–273
    InspectBasket.asp 276–283
    OCI documents 266
    overview 239–240
    purchase order reception solutions 256–262
    purchasing models 243–246
    remote shopping solutions 262–271
    RemoteBasket.asp 273–283
    retail Web site purchasing model 243
    scenario 241–247
    solutions overview 248
    supplier purchasing model using remote shopping 244–245
    tools and technologies 272
    xCBL 247
Semantics service 462–463
Send File Lite 296–297
Session service 460–461, 470–472
SharePoint Portal Server 2001 45–46
shopping baskets 309, 327–330
Simple Object Access Protocol (SOAP) 22
simple product pages 380–381
Site Builder 373–374
Site Deployment Manager 389–390
Site Manager 374
Site Stager 390–391
SMTP 442
SOAP (Simple Object Access Protocol) 22
software requirements
    BizTalk Server 201
    e-procurement 222
    integrating BizTalk with EDI 199–203
    integrating BizTalk with SAP 159–160, 162

software requirements *(continued)*
    integrating host data to the Web 144–149
    location-based mobile services (LBMS) 429, 431, 457–458
    Web Service File Transfer (WSFT) 293
Solution Sites
    AFS 283–290
    International 353–357
    Retail 349–353
space publishing server (SPS) 447, 455, 458, 472–473
SQL Server
    additional resources 42, 182, 237
    configuring 93–94
    Content Management Server 364
    Data Transformation Services *See* Data Transformation Services (DTS)
    editions 77
    e-procurement 229–231
    installing 93–94
    integrating with DB2 *See* integrating SQL Server with DB2
    overview 40–41
    sample applications 107–110, 495
    selling through trading partners 248
stateful server model 427
Sterling Commerce GENTRAN *See* GENTRAN
supplier purchasing model using remote shopping 244–245
supplier system document flow 215, 218–219
sync-and-go model 427, 455
synchronous and stateless LBMS model 426–427
synchronous RFC 129

T

targeted advertising 336
TCP/IP 442
templates 365–366
tools
    e-procurement 222–228
    integrating applications with SAP 131
    integrating BizTalk with EDI 199–203
    integrating BizTalk with SAP 159–161
    integrating host data to the Web 144–149
    integrating SQL Server with DB2 71–73
    location-based mobile services (LBMS) 427–430, 456
    managing Web content 396
    retail Web site setup 347–348
    selling through trading partners 272
    Web Service File Transfer (WSFT) 293–294
tracing 172
trading partners *See* selling through trading partners
transaction programs
    GETACCTS COBOL 142
    GETBAL COBOL 142
transactional RFC 129
Transport Unpacking servers 430–431, 457

troubleshooting tracing overview 172
turnkey communications lines 190

U

up selling 336, 338–340
Update service 467–468
URL generation 376
user authorization 383

V

value-added networks (VANs) 190
Visual Basic .NET 16–17, 495
Visual C# .NET
    converting BizTalk documents to classes 224–226
    overview 16
Visual C++ .NET 17
Visual Studio .NET
    additional resources 22
    application integration components (AIC) 226–228
    converting BizTalk documents to C# classes 224–226
    e-procurement 223–228
    hardware requirements 145
    integrating host data to the Web 145
    overview 12–13
    software requirements 145
    XML Web services 223–228, 233–235

W

Web Author 371–373
Web content, managing *See* managing Web content
Web Service File Transfer (WSFT)
    configuring 295–297
    hardware requirements 293
    implementing 294–297
    installing 293–294
    operational overview 294–295
    sample application overview 291, 496
    scenario 291
    software requirements 293
    solutions 291–292
    summary 297–298
    tools and technologies 293–294
Web sites, creating 379
Windows 2000 Server 77
WSFT (Web Service File Transfer)
    configuring 295–297
    hardware requirements 293
    implementing 294–297
    installing 293–294
    operational overview 294–295
    sample application overview 291, 496
    scenario 291
    software requirements 293

WSFT (Web Service File Transfer) *(continued)*
    solutions 291–292
    summary 297–298
    tools and technologies 293–294
WSFT Web service 296–297

X

xCBL (XML Common Business Library) 247
XLANG schedules
    activation 219
    correlation 221–222
XML
    additional resources 22
    business-to-business e-commerce 193–195
    e-procurement 223–228, 233–235
    Web services 194–195, 223–228, 233–235
XML Common Business Library (xCBL) 247

Author Biographies

James Wilson

James Wilson has been with Microsoft for over six years. Jim is the Documentation Manager for .NET Integration Server and is responsible for all user and SDK documentation for Host Integration Server 2000 and the earlier SNA Server products. Jim has also managed SDK documentation for Office 2000 Tools. His first assignment at Microsoft was in the Technical Services group. Prior to joining Microsoft, Jim worked for 14 years as Project Manager and Systems Analyst for large enterprises leading the design and development of three-tier client/server business applications.

William J. Harding

William Harding has been with Microsoft four years as the lead writer on several Microsoft products. Prior to Microsoft, William worked eight years at Novell, Inc. as a program manager, and principle technical writer and editor on a variety of NetWare products and independent technical books and journals. Prior to Novell, William was an assistant professor at Utah State University and served as an officer in the U.S. Air Force working on Space Operations and Space Defense systems. William has more than 20 years experience working in the computer industry, consulting, teaching, writing and editing.

Steven Baker

Steven Baker has been with Microsoft for more than five years, first as a vendor/consultant, and most recently as a programmer/writer. He has 30 years experience in the software field as a developer, technical writer, magazine editor, and book author. In addition to consulting at Microsoft, Steven was the editor-in-chief of *Programmer's Journal* magazine for six years and a contributing editor at *UNIX Review* magazine for 10 years. He has authored several hundred articles on various aspects of computer programming published in a large number of trade magazines including *Dr. Dobb's Journal*, *Microsoft Systems Journal*, *Software Development*, *Windows NT Systems*, *Computer Language*, *LAN Magazine*, *Byte*, *UNIX Review*, and *Performance Computing*.

Jim Christensen

Jim Christensen has been with Microsoft for over five years and is the lead programmer/writer for Commerce Server, BizTalk Accelerator for Suppliers, and more recently, Content Management Server. Prior to joining Microsoft, Jim worked for a variety of startups in Silicon Valley for over a dozen years, primarily as a software engineer. Jim has BA degrees in Computer Science and Philosophy from the University of California at Santa Cruz.

Scot Vidican

Scot Vidican has been with Microsoft for more than five years and is the lead programmer/writer for the BizTalk Server SDK. Scot has also worked on several technologies in the Internet Explorer and DirectX Media groups. Prior to Microsoft, Scot worked for 5 years as a software engineer at GrayMatter Software in Seattle. Scot has a BA degree in Business Administration and Computer Science from Western Washington University.

Carl Stephen Smyth

Carl Stephen Smyth is Chief Scientist at MobileGIS Ltd., a supplier of mapping and other core geographic services to location-based mobile service providers. Mr. Smyth joined MobileGIS in 2001 after nine years with the Microsoft Corporation, where he was Program Manager for Navigation in the Automotive Business Unit. Previously he was a co-founder of Microsoft's Geography Business Unit. Prior to joining Microsoft in the early 90's, he was an architect for BBN Advanced Simulation Divisions' SIMNET project. Before that, he was V.P. of R&D at GeoSystems Software, Director of Database Technology at Landmark/Zycor. Steve began his career in geosciences and computing as a manager of numerical modeling of the ocean and atmosphere for the US National Oceanic and Atmospheric Administration's Pacific Marine Environmental Laboratory in Seattle. He received BS degrees in Geology and Oceanography from the University of Washington, Seattle. He is now completing a PhD in Geography at University College, Cork, Ireland.

Prybar

The human arm is ingeniously contrived, but its strength is extremely limited. However, team it up with a lever, and it's a different story. Long before Archimedes said he could move the world if he had a lever that was long enough, people were aware of the added strength a lever could give. With a bar supported on a fulcrum, there is almost no limit to what pure muscle power can move. Put a claw on the end of a **prybar** and it can extract nails that fingers alone could never grasp. Prybars are also great for lifting, prying, pulling, and scraping materials such as flooring, siding, molding, sheeting, trim, and shingles.*

At Microsoft Press, we use tools to illustrate our books for software developers and IT professionals. Tools are an elegant symbol of human inventiveness and a powerful metaphor for how people can extend their capabilities, precision, and reach. From basic calipers and pliers to digital micrometers and lasers, our stylized illustrations of tools give each book a visual identity and each book series a personality. With tools and knowledge, there are no limits to creativity and innovation. Our tag line says it all: *The tools you need to put technology to work*.

*From THE GREAT TOOL EMPORIUM by David X. Manners (published by E.P. Dutton/Times Mirror Magazines, Inc., 1979)

Microsoft Press® Resource Kits

powerhouse

resources to minimize costs while maximizing performance

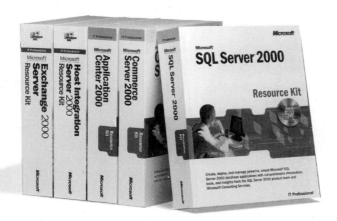

Deploy and support your enterprise business systems using the expertise and tools of those who know the technology best—the Microsoft product groups. Each RESOURCE KIT packs precise technical reference, installation and rollout tactics, planning guides, upgrade strategies, and essential utilities on CD-ROM. They're everything you need to help maximize system performance as you reduce ownership and support costs!

Microsoft® Windows® 2000 Server Resource Kit
ISBN 1-57231-805-8
U.S.A. $299.99 Canada $460.99

Microsoft Windows 2000 Professional Resource Kit
ISBN 1-57231-808-2
U.S.A. $69.99 Canada $107.99

Microsoft Office XP Resource Kit
ISBN 0-7356-1403-2
U.S.A. $69.99 Canada $99.99

Microsoft Small Business Server 2000 Resource Kit
ISBN 0-7356-1252-8
U.S.A. $69.99 Canada $99.99

Microsoft SQL Server™ 2000 Resource Kit
ISBN 0-7356-1266-8
U.S.A. $69.99 Canada $99.99

Microsoft Exchange 2000 Server Resource Kit
ISBN 0-7356-1017-7
U.S.A. $69.99 Canada $99.99

Microsoft Application Center 2000 Resource Kit
ISBN 0-7356-1023-1
U.S.A. $69.99 Canada $99.99

Microsoft Commerce Server 2000 Resource Kit
ISBN 0-7356-1128-9
U.S.A. $69.99 Canada $99.99

Microsoft Host Integration Server 2000 Resource Kit
ISBN 0-7356-1182-3
U.S.A. $69.99 Canada $99.99

Microsoft Press® products are available worldwide wherever quality computer books are sold. For more information, contact your book or computer retailer, software reseller, or local Microsoft® Sales Office, or visit our Web site at mspress.microsoft.com. To locate your nearest source for Microsoft Press products, or to order directly, call 1-800-MSPRESS in the United States (in Canada, call 1-800-268-2222).

Prices and availability dates are subject to change.

***Microsoft*®**

mspress.microsoft.com

MICROSOFT LICENSE AGREEMENT
Book Companion CD

IMPORTANT—READ CAREFULLY: This Microsoft End-User License Agreement ("EULA") is a legal agreement between you (either an individual or an entity) and Microsoft Corporation for the Microsoft product identified above, which includes computer software and may include associated media, printed materials, and "online" or electronic documentation ("SOFTWARE PRODUCT"). Any component included within the SOFTWARE PRODUCT that is accompanied by a separate End-User License Agreement shall be governed by such agreement and not the terms set forth below. By installing, copying, or otherwise using the SOFTWARE PRODUCT, you agree to be bound by the terms of this EULA. If you do not agree to the terms of this EULA, you are not authorized to install, copy, or otherwise use the SOFTWARE PRODUCT; you may, however, return the SOFTWARE PRODUCT, along with all printed materials and other items that form a part of the Microsoft product that includes the SOFTWARE PRODUCT, to the place you obtained them for a full refund.

SOFTWARE PRODUCT LICENSE

The SOFTWARE PRODUCT is protected by United States copyright laws and international copyright treaties, as well as other intellectual property laws and treaties. The SOFTWARE PRODUCT is licensed, not sold.

1. **GRANT OF LICENSE.** This EULA grants you the following rights:

   a. **Software Product.** You may install and use one copy of the SOFTWARE PRODUCT on a single computer. The primary user of the computer on which the SOFTWARE PRODUCT is installed may make a second copy for his or her exclusive use on a portable computer.

   b. **Storage/Network Use.** You may also store or install a copy of the SOFTWARE PRODUCT on a storage device, such as a network server, used only to install or run the SOFTWARE PRODUCT on your other computers over an internal network; however, you must acquire and dedicate a license for each separate computer on which the SOFTWARE PRODUCT is installed or run from the storage device. A license for the SOFTWARE PRODUCT may not be shared or used concurrently on different computers.

   c. **License Pak.** If you have acquired this EULA in a Microsoft License Pak, you may make the number of additional copies of the computer software portion of the SOFTWARE PRODUCT authorized on the printed copy of this EULA, and you may use each copy in the manner specified above. You are also entitled to make a corresponding number of secondary copies for portable computer use as specified above.

   d. **Sample Code.** Solely with respect to portions, if any, of the SOFTWARE PRODUCT that are identified within the SOFTWARE PRODUCT as sample code (the "SAMPLE CODE"):

      i. **Use and Modification.** Microsoft grants you the right to use and modify the source code version of the SAMPLE CODE, *provided* you comply with subsection (d)(iii) below. You may not distribute the SAMPLE CODE, or any modified version of the SAMPLE CODE, in source code form.

      ii. **Redistributable Files.** Provided you comply with subsection (d)(iii) below, Microsoft grants you a nonexclusive, royalty-free right to reproduce and distribute the object code version of the SAMPLE CODE and of any modified SAMPLE CODE, other than SAMPLE CODE, or any modified version thereof, designated as not redistributable in the Readme file that forms a part of the SOFTWARE PRODUCT (the "Non-Redistributable Sample Code"). All SAMPLE CODE other than the Non-Redistributable Sample Code is collectively referred to as the "REDISTRIBUTABLES."

      iii. **Redistribution Requirements.** If you redistribute the REDISTRIBUTABLES, you agree to: (i) distribute the REDISTRIBUTABLES in object code form only in conjunction with and as a part of your software application product; (ii) not use Microsoft's name, logo, or trademarks to market your software application product; (iii) include a valid copyright notice on your software application product; (iv) indemnify, hold harmless, and defend Microsoft from and against any claims or lawsuits, including attorney's fees, that arise or result from the use or distribution of your software application product; and (v) not permit further distribution of the REDISTRIBUTABLES by your end user. Contact Microsoft for the applicable royalties due and other licensing terms for all other uses and/or distribution of the REDISTRIBUTABLES.

2. **DESCRIPTION OF OTHER RIGHTS AND LIMITATIONS.**

   - **Limitations on Reverse Engineering, Decompilation, and Disassembly.** You may not reverse engineer, decompile, or disassemble the SOFTWARE PRODUCT, except and only to the extent that such activity is expressly permitted by applicable law notwithstanding this limitation.

   - **Separation of Components.** The SOFTWARE PRODUCT is licensed as a single product. Its component parts may not be separated for use on more than one computer.

   - **Rental.** You may not rent, lease, or lend the SOFTWARE PRODUCT.

- **Support Services.** Microsoft may, but is not obligated to, provide you with support services related to the SOFTWARE PRODUCT ("Support Services"). Use of Support Services is governed by the Microsoft policies and programs described in the user manual, in "online" documentation, and/or in other Microsoft-provided materials. Any supplemental software code provided to you as part of the Support Services shall be considered part of the SOFTWARE PRODUCT and subject to the terms and conditions of this EULA. With respect to technical information you provide to Microsoft as part of the Support Services, Microsoft may use such information for its business purposes, including for product support and development. Microsoft will not utilize such technical information in a form that personally identifies you.

- **Software Transfer.** You may permanently transfer all of your rights under this EULA, provided you retain no copies, you transfer all of the SOFTWARE PRODUCT (including all component parts, the media and printed materials, any upgrades, this EULA, and, if applicable, the Certificate of Authenticity), **and** the recipient agrees to the terms of this EULA.

- **Termination.** Without prejudice to any other rights, Microsoft may terminate this EULA if you fail to comply with the terms and conditions of this EULA. In such event, you must destroy all copies of the SOFTWARE PRODUCT and all of its component parts.

3. **COPYRIGHT.** All title and copyrights in and to the SOFTWARE PRODUCT (including but not limited to any images, photographs, animations, video, audio, music, text, SAMPLE CODE, REDISTRIBUTABLES, and "applets" incorporated into the SOFTWARE PRODUCT) and any copies of the SOFTWARE PRODUCT are owned by Microsoft or its suppliers. The SOFT-WARE PRODUCT is protected by copyright laws and international treaty provisions. Therefore, you must treat the SOFTWARE PRODUCT like any other copyrighted material **except** that you may install the SOFTWARE PRODUCT on a single computer provided you keep the original solely for backup or archival purposes. You may not copy the printed materials accompanying the SOFTWARE PRODUCT.

4. **U.S. GOVERNMENT RESTRICTED RIGHTS.** The SOFTWARE PRODUCT and documentation are provided with RESTRICTED RIGHTS. Use, duplication, or disclosure by the Government is subject to restrictions as set forth in subparagraph (c)(1)(ii) of the Rights in Technical Data and Computer Software clause at DFARS 252.227-7013 or subparagraphs (c)(1) and (2) of the Commercial Computer Software—Restricted Rights at 48 CFR 52.227-19, as applicable. Manufacturer is Microsoft Corporation/One Microsoft Way/Redmond, WA 98052-6399.

5. **EXPORT RESTRICTIONS.** You agree that you will not export or re-export the SOFTWARE PRODUCT, any part thereof, or any process or service that is the direct product of the SOFTWARE PRODUCT (the foregoing collectively referred to as the "Restricted Components"), to any country, person, entity, or end user subject to U.S. export restrictions. You specifically agree not to export or re-export any of the Restricted Components (i) to any country to which the U.S. has embargoed or restricted the export of goods or services, which currently include, but are not necessarily limited to, Cuba, Iran, Iraq, Libya, North Korea, Sudan, and Syria, or to any national of any such country, wherever located, who intends to transmit or transport the Restricted Components back to such country; (ii) to any end user who you know or have reason to know will utilize the Restricted Components in the design, development, or production of nuclear, chemical, or biological weapons; or (iii) to any end user who has been prohibited from participating in U.S. export transactions by any federal agency of the U.S. government. You warrant and represent that neither the BXA nor any other U.S. federal agency has suspended, revoked, or denied your export privileges.

DISCLAIMER OF WARRANTY

NO WARRANTIES OR CONDITIONS. MICROSOFT EXPRESSLY DISCLAIMS ANY WARRANTY OR CONDITION FOR THE SOFTWARE PRODUCT. THE SOFTWARE PRODUCT AND ANY RELATED DOCUMENTATION ARE PROVIDED "AS IS" WITHOUT WARRANTY OR CONDITION OF ANY KIND, EITHER EXPRESS OR IMPLIED, INCLUDING, WITHOUT LIMITA-TION, THE IMPLIED WARRANTIES OF MERCHANTABILITY, FITNESS FOR A PARTICULAR PURPOSE, OR NONINFRINGEMENT. THE ENTIRE RISK ARISING OUT OF USE OR PERFORMANCE OF THE SOFTWARE PRODUCT REMAINS WITH YOU.

LIMITATION OF LIABILITY. TO THE MAXIMUM EXTENT PERMITTED BY APPLICABLE LAW, IN NO EVENT SHALL MICROSOFT OR ITS SUPPLIERS BE LIABLE FOR ANY SPECIAL, INCIDENTAL, INDIRECT, OR CONSEQUENTIAL DAM-AGES WHATSOEVER (INCLUDING, WITHOUT LIMITATION, DAMAGES FOR LOSS OF BUSINESS PROFITS, BUSINESS INTERRUPTION, LOSS OF BUSINESS INFORMATION, OR ANY OTHER PECUNIARY LOSS) ARISING OUT OF THE USE OF OR INABILITY TO USE THE SOFTWARE PRODUCT OR THE PROVISION OF OR FAILURE TO PROVIDE SUPPORT SERVICES, EVEN IF MICROSOFT HAS BEEN ADVISED OF THE POSSIBILITY OF SUCH DAMAGES. IN ANY CASE, MICROSOFT'S ENTIRE LIABILITY UNDER ANY PROVISION OF THIS EULA SHALL BE LIMITED TO THE GREATER OF THE AMOUNT ACTUALLY PAID BY YOU FOR THE SOFTWARE PRODUCT OR US$5.00; PROVIDED, HOWEVER, IF YOU HAVE ENTERED INTO A MICROSOFT SUPPORT SERVICES AGREEMENT, MICROSOFT'S ENTIRE LIABILITY REGARDING SUPPORT SERVICES SHALL BE GOVERNED BY THE TERMS OF THAT AGREEMENT. BECAUSE SOME STATES AND JURISDICTIONS DO NOT ALLOW THE EXCLUSION OR LIMITATION OF LIABILITY, THE ABOVE LIMITATION MAY NOT APPLY TO YOU.

MISCELLANEOUS

This EULA is governed by the laws of the State of Washington USA, except and only to the extent that applicable law mandates govern-ing law of a different jurisdiction.

Should you have any questions concerning this EULA, or if you desire to contact Microsoft for any reason, please contact the Microsoft subsidiary serving your country, or write: Microsoft Sales Information Center/One Microsoft Way/Redmond, WA 98052-6399.

System Requirements

The sample applications and source code on the book companion CD-ROM require the following hardware and software:

- Computers capable of running Microsoft Windows 2000 Server or Professional, Microsoft Windows XP Professional, or Microsoft Windows .NET Server

- Windows 2000 Server or Professional, Windows XP Professional, or Windows .NET Server

- Microsoft Internet Explorer 5.01 or later

- Microsoft Data Access Components (MDAC) 2.7

- Microsoft Visual Studio .NET (some sample applications only require the Microsoft .NET Framework)

- 20 MB free disk space for the files from this CD

Specific sample applications may not require all of the components listed below. In those cases, the specific requirements are listed in the chapter about that application. For example, the Web Service File Transfer utility does not include the source code. Therefore, Visual Studio .NET is not required on each computer running this utility. However, the .NET Framework Redistributable and Microsoft Data Access Components 2.7 are required. These components can be downloaded at no charge from the following locations:

- The.NET Framework Redistributable. This is available at: *http://msdn.microsoft.com/downloads*

- Microsoft Data Access Components 2.7. This is available at: *http://www.microsoft.com/data*